MY REMARKABLE JOURN

The Autobiography of Britain's First Mu

MY REMARKABLE JOURNEY

*The Autobiography
of Britain's First Muslim MP*

Mohammad Sarwar

with

Bob Wylie

BIRLINN

First published in 2016 by
Birlinn Limited
West Newington House
10 Newington Road
Edinburgh
EH9 1QS

www.birlinn.co.uk

ISBN: 978 1 78027 316 7

British Library Cataloguing-in-Publication Data
A catalogue record for this book is available from the British
Library

Set in Sabon at Birlinn

Printed and bound by
Gutenberg Press Ltd, Malta

Contents

Plates

With Perveen on the day of our marriage, 19 July 1976.

With my political mentor, Jimmy Dunnachie MP, in 1993.

Perveen and I in 1996 after victory in the re-run ballot against Mike Watson MP.

Campaigning in the May 1997 General Election.

With my SNP opponent in 1997, Nicola Sturgeon, at the count in Glasgow.

A victory salute on winning the seat in 1997.

My media team for my appointment as Governor of Punjab – Bob Wylie, Anas Sarwar and Akmal Khan.

Standing for the national anthem at the oath ceremony for the Governorship of Punjab on 5 August 2013.

My state address after appointment as Governor.

At home with my family shortly after appointment as Governor.

The flood refugee camp in the village of Akbarabad in September 2010.

With the children of a primary school in Charsadda redeveloped by the Ucare Foundation after the floods of 2010.

Outside the Houses of Parliament on a visit to the UK in March 2015.

My first speech at a PTI conference with Imran Khan after resigning as Governor in January 2015.

On the campaign trail in the local government elections in Pakistan in October 2015.

Foreword

Rt Hon. John Bercow MP, Speaker of the House of Commons

This is a truly remarkable story about an outstanding individual. Yet despite being immensely and inevitably personal, it also constitutes a wider narrative about our changing world. There are so many aspects to it which are astonishing and which involve considerable cultural challenges. These relate to Mohammad Sarwar's early life and the transition from rural Pakistan to urban Scotland; his extraordinary achievements as a businessman and entrepreneur; his improbable arrival as a local and then national political figure as Britain's first Muslim MP, and then finally as an astounding postscript, his departure from Westminster followed by his arrival as the Governor of Punjab. Any one of these elements could be the basis for an autobiography. The combination of them is compelling.

Mohammad's account of his Westminster tenure is described as 'warts and all', and certainly meets that designation. Some of what he writes about the means by which the House of Commons then operated is not, in truth, especially flattering to the institution in which I have the honour of being the Speaker, but other aspects, especially his dynamic interventions on behalf of his constituents, are the very essence of what makes our Parliament the pearl that it can be.

While this book may, naturally, be of most interest to the Muslim community, I do hope that it secures the widest possible readership. Very few people have led lives like Mohammad Sarwar and can therefore offer insights like he can. We would all benefit from an understanding of them.

Preface

I suppose everyone who writes his or her autobiography is asked the same question, 'Why did you decide to write it?' My answer is that I wanted to put my life on record. There are legions of others, mostly from politics and the media, who have given their view of what has happened in my life. Now it's my turn to set the record straight.

Like any other autobiographical author, I think that my life story is worth telling; there is some self-confidence involved in the decision. I put my life on record so that others, who may be interested, can know what has happened when, where and how. One more important reason is that as a Pakistani I have lived happily as part of an ethnic minority in a country not of my birth for a long time. I started from a modest background, became a successful businessman, was elected as the first Muslim to become a member of the House of Commons, and then became the Governor of Punjab.

Over the years, many of those who hail from the same background have told me that my life has been a source of inspiration for them. I feel a little embarrassed to mention this, as it may be interpreted as immodest, but that is not my intention. I am convinced that my life story may inspire others to believe that it is possible to succeed in life and make great achievements with resilience, courage and determination. In my case, success did not come because of hard work alone. It has been the result of a measure of luck and always having staunch faith that God was on my side.

There is an account of modern history in these pages because I have been lucky enough to get the chance to walk in history's footsteps. I think, for example, having been in the packed House of Commons to witness the late Robin Cook's speech of resignation from Tony Blair's Cabinet, in protest against going to war in Iraq, was to share a moment of history. Being the first person to take the oath of allegiance on the Holy Quran, in the House of Commons, is another footstep of history. Once that was done, it could never be repeated.

Unlike a conventional linear autobiography, which starts with the early years of life and then proceeds in a chronological order, I have selected themes to form the basis of my chapters. With this approach, events are not exactly bound by where they fit in time in my own personal history. For example, Chapter 1 concerns the events of 2004 in my constituency, in Glasgow, Scotland, when I had been an MP for seven years. It tells the story of the dreadful murder of a young white boy, Kriss Donald, by a group of five Pakistani gangsters, three of whom fled to Pakistan after the killing. In many ways, bringing the murderers to justice was one of the most difficult challenges of my life – politically and emotionally. No wonder that my autobiography opens with it.

Chapter 2 deals with the Partition of the Indian Subcontinent in 1947. I have honestly tried to highlight the almost indescribable horror of what happened then, which in the case of my family caused the death of three of its dearest members; two of its oldest and the third its youngest at the time. The underlying idea here is to highlight the struggle endured, and the commitment and dedication of ordinary Muslims to Pakistan, that now seem to be missing in many young Pakistanis I meet. They do not seem to know of the sacrifices made to build Pakistan, and many do not seem to realise why they should take pride in that.

Chapter 3 describes my early years in Pakistan and Chapter 4 relates how my wholesale business was built in the UK; how it was booming and how, at one point, it all literally went up in flames. I offer that example to illustrate the point that my life seems to follow a pattern defined by three steps forward, two steps back. In the same chapter, I have detailed how my multi-million pound Cash and Carry business came to be, and, hopefully with a touch of humour, how I became the 'Prince of Eggs' and the 'King of Tetley Tea Bags'.

To some not concerned with politics inside the Labour Party in Glasgow in the 1990s, Chapters 5, 6, 7 and 8 may seem a little mundane. However, from my point of view, there is a little bit of social history here – the Labour Party then was not what it is now – and also this is the first time my own view of all those events which shaped my political career is being put on record. Additionally, Chapter 8 is significant not just because it tells my own story of being hounded by the dreadful *News of the World* but also because it was a precursor of what was to come – lies, cheque-book journalism and the abdication of moral decency in the tabloid press.

Chapter 9 is dominated by the struggle for the future of Glasgow's shipyards. It remains one of my proudest achievements to have stood shoulder to shoulder with working-class men like Jamie Webster. In the end we won. This chapter is, in essence, a salute to their struggle.

Chapter 10 deals with the events of the 9/11 Wars – Afghanistan and Iraq. The anger, the desperation, and on some occasions, the desolation of the time are reflected here. It is no real consolation that the warnings I gave on the floor of the House of Commons then have been proven right.

Chapter 11 comments on the intractable issues concerning Israel and Kashmir. It outlines my personal views on the flames of future struggle in these lands.

In Chapter 12, on the events of 7/7 in London in 2005, and other reflections on terrorism, I have tried to explain why editorials about violence being inherent to Islam are wrong; why those who seem to think that terrorism started in the modern era with 9/11 are misguided. Pakistan did not decide to attack Afghanistan and Iraq; George Bush, Dick Cheney, Donald Rumsfeld and Tony Blair did. However, that is not to say that wanton acts of terror like the slaughter of the school students in the Army School in Peshawar, in December 2014, can ever be justified.

This book was almost ready to go to print in the winter of 2012. Then, slowly at first, but gathering pace through 2013, events led to my being appointed as the Governor of Punjab in August that year. Given the opportunity I could not forsake the chance to return to my beloved Pakistan, to give something back to the land of my birth, irrespective of conflicting emotions because it meant leaving family and Scotland behind. I will be eternally grateful to the way that my family, especially my wife, Perveen, supported me in that decision. On 5 August 2013, when I took the oath as Governor, my heart was filled with boundless optimism. I felt then that the Government of Pakistan had an unbreakable commitment to change things, to make life better for those who suffer unending, grinding poverty in our country.

Experience has proved the outcome to be different, and after 18 months as Governor I reached the conclusion that it would be easier to fight for the transformation of Pakistan and all its ills outside the walls of Governor House rather than continue to hold a mere title within them. So I resigned. That incredible journey is covered in detail in Chapter 15.

I would like now to make a special mention of those who encouraged and assisted me in the writing of this book. The first acknowledgement is to my family. They are the treasure of my life. My wife, Perveen, has been the rock on which the achievements of the family have been built. That was also the case in the challenge of writing this book. In the same ways, my daughter, Faiza, and sons, Athif, Anas and Asim, have given steadfast support and constant encouragement.

The second acknowledgement is to Bob Wylie, the former BBC journalist. For years, as it has turned out, he has been my constant co-worker in the research, writing and editing of this book. At the start of this venture he told me that, from his experience, writing a book required a certain amount of literary ability, but the most important qualities for such a challenge would prove to be determination and stamina. He was right. His intellectual ability and his commitment to the project have been totally inspiring. Without our unbreakable common efforts, we would not have seen this through.

The same must be said of two others. Bob's lifelong friend, Peter McGinley, has been a tireless sub-editor in the production of the first manuscript. For this, I offer him my everlasting thanks. Then there is my own lifelong friend, Mian Sanaullah, who for a major part of his life was one of Pakistan's finest diplomats. He arrived relatively late in the life of the book project, but his contribution to further editing of the manuscript and indefatigable commitment has been invaluable. By the winter of 2014, I could see the 'winning post' of the completion of the book. Without doubt Sana's efforts have played a great part in helping me to cross the finishing line. I owe him an enormous debt of gratitude.

In Chapters 13 and 14 I have described my charity work in Pakistan. At this stage it seems right to let you know that I intend to donate every penny that I earn in royalties from my renowned publisher, Birlinn, to my charity, the Ucare Foundation. Hence every book sold will assist Ucare's work, in hospitals, schools and in initiating other projects in Pakistan.

Mohammad Sarwar, Lahore, October 2015

Acknowledgements

It is the normal custom to acknowledge those who have assisted in the production of a written work in this section. I would like to do that, but I also want to thank those who, in their own way, have been a positive influence for the stories that are contained in this book. However, I should start with my thanks for the assistance given to me by my publishers Birlinn, and in particular to Hugh Andrew and Tom Johnstone there. Roger Smith also did sterling work on the final proofing and index. Alan Taylor, once of the *Herald* and the editor of the *Scottish Review of Books*, is owed my thanks for reading the final drafts of the book. My personal assistant, Sumiya Siddique, who has made countless print-outs of countless chapters and never wavered in her commitment to the project, also deserves my thanks. In Glasgow, the advice of my sister, Dr Aroona Sarwar, was invaluable. My solicitor, Peter Duff, also gave welcome advice at crucial times in this adventure.

So, if I am to follow the chronology of the stories in the book in these acknowledgements, then in the horror of the story of young Kriss Donald, the steadfastness of many of my friends in Pakistan's police and intelligence services merits mention. In this respect, special thanks are due to Shaukat Javed, Irfan Mahmood Khan, Tariq Pervez and Mohammad Yaqub

In the affairs of politics, and the Labour Party, Lesley Quinn deserves special mention, not least because she read and advised on some of the most contentious chapters here. There is a long list of others, including the late Bashir Ahmed, John Bercow, Adil Bhatti, Gordon Brown, Margaret Curran, George Galloway, Sajjad Karim, Imran Khand, Khalid Mahmood, Shahid Malik, David Martin, Michael Martin, Jack McConnell, Mohammad Amin Mirza, the late Stuart Petrie, Hanif Rajah, Maqbool Hussain Rasul and Sohan Singh. History dictated that my legal eagles played a part in these affairs also – Michael S. Jones, Gordon Jackson and Chris Kelly.

When it comes to my charity work, in particular my thanks are to Syed Sajad Haider. He was the Director of the Pakistan International Foundation, my first charity foundation, and worked tremendously hard to strengthen my charity work in the Health sector in Pakistan.

We have been friends for more than 40 years, and for much of that time he has been a tireless supporter of my work. I also have to register my appreciation of the work done by Mohammad Rajak and the Ucare Foundation team. The dedication of the staff at Rajana and Chichawatni hospitals and the public school in Pir Mahal should be put on record in this regard, as should the assistance given by ex-Director General Mohammad Yaqub and his Pakistan Rangers.

When my time at Governor House in Lahore is given due consideration, I must thank Mazhar ul Hassan, Asher Khan, Tariq Mahmood Pasha and Mashood Shoorish. For the Clean Water Campaign there are many due my thanks, but special mentions have to go to Omer Jillani, Farah Majid, Masood Khan of Pak Oasis, Rabia Zia and her team, and Saad Kazi, who made the Clean Water film with Bob Wylie. It would be wrong not to record something of those days of Governor House and how happy I felt when I was there, so thanks are due to the staff who made that journey such a pleasure. And thanks to all the women's groups who came to Governor House to join hands with Perveen to try to make a difference to the lives of so many people blighted by disadvantage. In these matters I have to express my gratitude to Nawaz Sharif, Shahbaz Sharif and Choudhry Nisar Ali Khan, who allowed me the privilege of becoming Governor by supporting my appointment.

Of course, all of my personal achievements which are heralded in the book could never have been achieved without the love and support of my family. So in these acknowledgements, once again I want to put on record the deep gratitude I owe to my wife Perveen, my sons Athif, Asim and Anas, my daughter Faiza and son-in-law Shahzad, and my daughters-in-law, Henna, Furheen and Shaz. My brother Mohammad Ramzan and his family are also due my thanks, as are my dear sisters, Shamin, Nasreen and Aroona.

There are many more who deserve mention regarding the support and help they have given me. So, I would like to accord my thanks to the following:

Yassir Abbas, Sheikh Afzal, Athif Ahmad and Shabana, Irshad Ahmad, Rana Atiq Ahmad, Sarfraz Ahmad, Sheikh Manzoor Ahmad, Sufi Ali Ahmad, Sabir Ali, Ashraf Anjum, Mian Ashraf, Mohammad Aslam, Sani Baig, Khurshid Bokhari, Asghar Choudhry, Aziz

Choudhry, Sheikh Abdul Ghani, Faisal Jamil Goshi, Andy Hakeen, Mohammad Hanif, Sufi Iltaf Hussain, Umar Ishaq, Nasir Jaffrey, Shah Jamal, Mohammad Afzal Jigar, Fakhar Iqbal, Shaukat Kasuri, Dr Shafi Kausar, Dr Mahmood Khan, Manzoor Khan, Shahzad Ahmad Khan, Khurshid Khokhar, the late Dr O.P. Madhok, Amjad Malik, Arshad Moghul, Naeem Muneer, Mian Nadeem, Faiz Rasul, Hafid Sajjad, Mohammad Tufail Shaheen, Choudhry Saleem, Aslam Sheikh, Javed Saqlain, Shabir Sheikh, Tahir Inam Sheikh, Tufail Hussain Shah, Gurmeet Singh, Sati Singh and Saleem Tahir.

Dedication

To my father and mother, my family, and the people of
Glasgow and Pakistan.

The Kriss Donald Story 1

'Justice has been done. Thank you. It is over.'
Angela Donald, outside the High Court in Edinburgh,
November 2006.

After seven years as a Member of Parliament, 15 March 2004, dawned for me pretty much like any other Monday. I always aimed to make my way to the House of Commons, in London, by mid-afternoon at the latest. For many Mondays, of course, there had to be a red-eye flight to make an early morning meeting in the Parliament.

But on that Monday I had meetings all morning in the constituency and headed to the airport for the three-fifteen flight. I didn't know then that events were about to unfold in the heart of my constituency which ultimately would prove to be my greatest test as an MP, and without doubt, my greatest heartbreak. About the time of take-off, a 15-year-old boy, Kriss Donald, was being abducted by a gang of five Asian men in Kenmure Street in the mainly Asian district of Pollokshields, in the heart of my constituency, on Glasgow's south side. Some eight hours later he would be dead. Brutally murdered.

A long two and a half years after this, in November 2006, at the High Court in Edinburgh, the last three men responsible for the murder stood in the dock awaiting sentence. The trial judge, Lord Uist, told them:

> You have all been convicted by the jury of the racially aggravated abduction and murder of Kriss Donald, a wholly innocent 15-year-old boy. This murder consisted of the premeditated cold-blooded execution of your victim by stabbing him 13 times and setting him alight with petrol while he was still alive. It truly was an abomination.

Lord Uist called the ringleader, Imran Shahid: 'a thug and a bully with a sadistic nature, not fit to be free in a civilised society.'

On that day, the final roll-call added up to a victory for humanity. Imran Shahid, 29, also known as Baldy, was sentenced to life with a minimum term of 25 years. He'll be 54 before he can even be considered for parole. I believe he will never be released unless there is a remarkable change in his behaviour and character. Zeeshan Shahid, 28, also known as Crazy, was sentenced to life with a minimum term of 23 years. He'll be 51 before any review of his case. And Faisal Mustaq, 27, also known as Becks, was sentenced to life with a minimum term of 22 years. He'll be 50 before parole can even be a possibility. All three were convicted of the racially aggravated murder, assault, and abduction of a 15-year-old boy – the first convictions in a case of racially aggravated murder in Scotland's history.

Two years before, in November 2004, Daanish Zahid, 20, who was a cousin of the two Shahid brothers, had been convicted in similar terms, and sentenced to life with a minimum term of 17 years. The fifth accomplice, Zahid Mohammed, gave evidence for the Crown Office, and got the lesser sentence of five and a half years for assault and abduction. He had not taken part in the final execution.

So it's 15 March 2004. It seems it was around three in the afternoon. The streets in Pollokshields in Glasgow were quiet at that time. Kriss and his friend Jamie Wallace were walking down Kenmure Street to get to McCulloch Street where Kriss lived. They were going to Kriss's house to play computer games on the Xbox. In evidence, given at both trials, Jamie Wallace says they were suddenly set upon by an Asian man who came from behind them. Jamie Wallace fought back and then the man attacked Kriss as a silver Mercedes screamed to a halt beside them. Another four Asians jumped out of the Mercedes to join the fray.

Jamie said in court that he was powerless to stop them. He had fought back, so the smaller and weaker Kriss became the target. The assailants bundled Kriss into the back of the car and drove off at high speed down Kenmure Street. The court heard that as Kriss was bundled into the car he yelled: 'I'm only fifteen, what have I done . . .' It was all over in thirty or forty seconds. Unimaginable horror then beckoned – alas, it was only a matter of time.

Jamie Wallace knew the gang leader was Imran Shahid, and ran to his grandmother's house nearby to phone the police. Shahid was notorious for abduction and terrorising the community. He was a violent body-builder, who by the time of Kriss Donald's murder had been jailed twice for serious assault. In 1995 Imran Shahid – known as Baldy in the community due to his close-cropped hair – was jailed for a baseball bat assault on a young man, Paschael Farren, which left his victim with brain damage. Shahid was sentenced then to four and a half years for serious assault.

Then in February 2003 Baldy was again jailed for serious assault, this time for a road-rage attack on a female social worker in Albert Drive in Pollokshields. He punched and kicked the woman and then tried to drive over her with his car. He got a 30-month sentence for that. Now, a matter of five or six months after his release from jail for that crime, Imran Shahid had Kriss Donald in the footwell of a stolen car, taunting him with a knife and threatening to kill him.

Even to this day, despite weeks of evidence in two trials, it isn't certain if the gang had a definite plan about what they were going to do with any victim they got hold of. It's known that the five had met that morning in a flat in Herriet Street in Pollokshields, owned by one of the gang. They met to make a plan to take reprisals for an attack on Imran Shahid which had occurred the previous night outside a Glasgow nightclub. Imran Shahid had recognised some of those who had attacked him with bottles on the Sunday night as white youths from Pollokshields.

In his evidence, Zahid Mohammed said they collected a hammer, a screwdriver and a knife from the flat and put them in a blue plastic bag. He said that Imran Shahid told them all that they were going to cut someone's eyes out in revenge. So it was that the gang went cruising the streets of Pollokshields, in broad daylight, looking for a victim – a white victim – and Kriss Donald was in the wrong place at the wrong time. What is still not known is whether the five left the flat with a conviction that murder was going to be done that day.

One thing is certain – the gang had previously used abduction to terrorise their victims. Before this, on another occasion, when the gang were out for a reprisal it's said they abducted another man, who got on the wrong side of Baldy, and had taken the victim to a flat in Pollokshields. There, they cut off his thumb and put it in a glass of milk and forced the man to drink the milk. The case collapsed in court because the victim couldn't identify his assailants. It's said he had been told if he did, his head would be chopped off the next time – not just a finger.

Once they kidnapped the son of a Glasgow City councillor. He made no complaint to the police when the matter was settled. All of this was part of a reign of terror propagated by Baldy and his cohorts to make sure people knew you could not cross them without the most serious of consequences. They were untouchable at the time – no-one, not even an elected councillor, would give evidence in court against them. So the terror continued.

Of course I reflected on this as the reign of terror developed, not least because I wondered how these hoodlums from an Islamic background could depart so far from the tenets of Islam in their desperate deeds. I had never seen them at the Central Mosque in Glasgow, but I knew that their parents would be the same generation as me and, like me, would have come from Pakistan. So what happened to their sons that they would commit such barbarities? Many people have asked me the same question time and again: 'What has happened to us that those men could have killed that poor Kriss Donald? Not only killed him, but in the way that they did?' Of course I have said many times that it was despicable, but to answer the question 'Why?' other explanations are needed. There may be some clues in immigrant culture.

Immigrants when they come to a new country often suffer by being persecuted for being outsiders, and so it is that many strive to be the best in their own field, somehow as a answer to the accusations of being inferior from their often less than welcoming hosts. My own business history reflects that necessity to be better or best, to go beyond normal achievements. So it may have been the case with the Shahids and their gang. They decided in their campaign of terror, which culminated in the murder of Kriss Donald, that they would be the 'best' gangsters. In that case being the worst, the most capable of atrocity. So, as they promoted their own brand of extortion, intimidation and terror, they began to think of themselves as untouchables. They were the toughest gangsters and they began to think they could get away with anything. They thought they could get away with murder. Literally.

Now let's return to the terrible events of that day. The gang had Kriss in the back of the car, but they knew they could not hide him in Pollokshields for fear of the abduction being seen there, and the police being alerted by Jamie Wallace or others. So they drove to the East End of the city to speak to one of their gangland associates about using his flat. It hasn't been revealed before but it seems Baldy and his associates had drugland ties to the East End which, in part, explains why in the end the boy's body was found there. But when asked to provide a hiding place, the East End hoodlum said no.

Then one of the gang got lucky – Zahid Mohammed. He was on a tagging order for a previous conviction and had to be indoors by five o'clock, so the gang drove next to the Hamilton area and dropped him off.

Incredibly, Dundee, 75 miles away, was their next port of call, to seek another venue for the lessons they were going to teach Kriss. In Dundee there was no hideaway either, and it seems that from that point onwards matters began to get fatally out of hand.

In December 2004, at the first trial involving Zahid Mohammed and Daanish Zahid, it emerged that on the way back from Dundee the gang stopped at a petrol station just outside the city. There, Daanish Zahid bought an emergency petrol can and filled it. He told the court that he was forced to do this by Imran Shahid. He could have alerted the garage attendant to what was going on. He didn't.

If you come off the M74 coming into Glasgow for the East End of the city, then drive along London Road before you come to Celtic Football Club's stadium, you reach the Celtic Supporters' Social Club on the left-hand side of the road. There's a pathway on the right-hand side of the club which takes you down to the banks of the River Clyde. The path is sufficiently robust to be able to take cars. It seems this location was known to Baldy and his gang because they had used its isolation to take East End prostitutes there for drink, drugs and sex sessions.

There are many, many things which haunt me about Kriss Donald's murder. I have often asked myself if Imran Shahid could have been stopped before his Mafia methods culminated in murder. But one abiding horror, and it is here with me now as I write, is the contemplation of poor Kriss's last hours of life. By the time the gang approached the Celtic Supporters' Club in their stolen Mercedes, some seven or eight hours after his abduction, the fifteen-year-old must have been engulfed in sheer terror, alone and abandoned. Sheer engulfing terror. During all this time, and over 200 miles on public roads, passing others going about their everyday lives, the boy was trapped on the floor of the car, hour after hour, all the time terrified, not knowing where he was being taken, why they had chosen him for this horror, or when it would end. Unspeakable.

According to evidence given in the first trial, the gang turned left at the Celtic Supporters' Club on London Road and drove down the pathway to the parkland on the banks of the Clyde. They threw Kriss out of the car, and while two of them held him Imran Shahid stabbed the boy 13 times in a ferocious frenzy. They poured petrol over him, set him alight while he was still alive, and then drove off. Police photos, which I saw later, show that the the boy crawled fifteen yards down the embankment from the spot where he was stabbed before he died. It is awful to contemplate that he may have been trying to douse the flames.

Of course at the time I knew nothing of this horror. It was a day later, Tuesday 16 March, when the news began to emerge. BBC Scotland's crime correspondent, Bob Wylie, had the exclusive on the early evening *Reporting Scotland* news programme that day – a body found behind the Celtic Supporters' Social Club, in the city's East End, was that of a fifteen-year-old boy who had been abducted in Pollokshields the day before. After the news programme Wylie phoned me on my mobile to tell me. He said: 'Sarwar, the boy who was abducted yesterday in the middle of Pollokshields in broad daylight is dead. According to the cops he was taken by five Asian men. The boy's been stabbed and then set on fire whilst still alive. It all happened behind the Celtic Supporters club in the East End, off London Road. He's a fifteen-year-old white boy, Kriss Donald. Sarwar, Jesus Christ, the balloon could go up!'

I'd known Bob Wylie from the Labour Party and then in the early 1990s when he worked as a freelance journalist, and then for *Scotland on Sunday* as their Glasgow news reporter. He'd never given me a tip off that proved to be wrong. So I knew this was serious. I was in the House of Commons at the time of the phone call so immediately I

6

made my way to the Chief Whip's office to seek out the pairing whip, Tommy McAvoy, the MP for Rutherglen. I told him what I knew of the situation – a white fifteen-year-old boy abducted and then stabbed, set on fire whilst still alive and murdered. By five Asian men.

'There could be big trouble on the south side of Glasgow – a big backlash. I need to be in the community,' I told him. I said I had to get home immediately to try and make sure I did everything I could to have the local community react responsibly, even in the face of the provocation I felt was sure to come. Tommy McAvoy was an MP from Glasgow, so he knew how dangerous the situation was. There wasn't a problem securing agreement to let me go. Within half an hour of receiving the phone call I was on my way to Heathrow airport. On the way in the taxi I phoned the Govan HQ of Strath-clyde Police and spoke to a senior officer there. I think it was Chief Superintendent Eddie McCusker, who at that stage was in charge of the investigation. He told me that the boy who had been abducted on Monday, in Pollokshields, had been murdered and his body had been found in the East End.

The police had issued two media releases that day, both around three o'clock in the afternoon. One confirmed the abduction of a teenage male on the south side of Glasgow the previous day, and another confirmed that in the early hours of Tuesday morning the body of a young male had been found in Glasgow's East End near the Celtic Supporters' Social Club in London Road. Two and two had not been put together in the releases, but McCusker said he knew that the story was out as the media office had been taking a large amount of calls, especially following reports on the BBC. He also told me that although things were at an early stage, he was optimistic that the police already had a series of good leads on who the likely culprits were.

In my years as MP there had been a few flashpoints in the constit-uency connected to what might be described as racial tensions. There had been quite serious trouble at the local comprehensive school, Shawlands Academy, with a number of clashes between Asian and white youth outside the school and media stories about race violence. But that was school students, and eventually things all returned to normal.

More seriously, in the September before Kriss's murder, there had been tit-for-tat fire-bombings of shops and cars in Pollokshields, and Asian and white clashes in the area. This was an escalation of gang problems in the area and almost certainly involved Asian gangsters, not school students. The clashes had started with an attack on a young Asian man when he was on his way to prayers at the local mosque by a group of baseball bat-wielding white youths. However even at this point things had never got out of hand. Tensions in Glasgow never reached the scale of the riots of Bradford, Burnley or Birmingham. In no small measure this was due to the good relations between the local Asian community leaders and the local white community. In most circumstances reason had prevailed and things had calmed down.

But the problem was that tensions were always there, if below the surface. So what allowed these gang tensions to continue simmering? One of the problems was that, although there was no shortage of complaints in the Asian community about gang culture, including the identification of Baldy and his gang, no-one would come forward and make complaints to the police, due to the pervasive fear of reprisal which I have already mentioned. This time though, it was different. It was Asian on white violence, and it was a terrible, terrible murder. The significance of that was that this was an attack by part of the ethnic minority community on the much larger and more potentially powerful white majority. I had a meeting at my home when I got back to Glasgow with my friends and constituency workers, many of whom got the news of what had happened for the first time from me. There was a universal dread that if things were not handled properly there could be flashpoint race riots in the area.

The media coverage the next day confirmed my worst fears – almost without exception the press played the race card. The headlines were all of a similar tone: 'Race theory as boy of 15 murdered'; 'Racial war scare after murder of kidnapped boy'. On top of all of this there were growing rumours, confirmed by the police, of the possibility of a fascist right-wing British National Party march through Pollokshields the coming weekend. But to give BBC Scotland their due, on day two their approach was more measured than others in the media. That was a relief, because the BBC can be important for setting the tone on big stories, not least due to the scale and reach of its radio and television operations. On a live broadcast on *Reporting Scotland*, from Pollokshields, on the Wednesday evening, Bob Wylie was asked by the presenter if race tensions were going to boil over in Pollokshields. He answered that there were tensions no doubt, but that it should be noted that the police hotline Crimestoppers had had its highest ever volume of calls with locals from all sides of the community giving information about who might be responsible for the killing. There was a unity of condemnation, with a universal desire to see the killers caught, he suggested.

But then on Friday at the end of this torrid week came what, in my view, could be described as the turning-point. Kriss Donald's mother Angela stepped forward. She and her family issued a media statement, which more than anything else was responsible for cutting across the sort of race tensions which could have carried us to a catastrophe. What she said deserves to be quoted in full:

> I would ask the nation for help in tracing those responsible for the murder of my son Kriss. Five men full of hate, and it doesn't matter what colour these men are, murdered my son. However I would ask the public not to target the Asian community because of his death.

That made the headlines in all the papers on the Friday morning, four days after the murder.

With the passing of time it is possible, as I say, to identify her act of courage as possibly a tipping-point in the history of these events. In my view, without Angela Donald's public statement, there may have been race riots on the south side of Glasgow. One important direct result of her intervention was that the number of calls to the police identifying Baldy and his gang as the guilty parties grew higher and higher. Angela Donald, throughout this monumental test of human endurance for her, which would last for just over two and a half years from the time of her son's death to the final convictions of those responsible, displayed a courage and human dignity that was truly awe-inspiring. In fact, whenever I had reached a stumbling-block in my pursuit of those who killed her son, it was her inspiration that made me press on again with more vigour than before.

After her statement became public on the Friday morning I went to the spontaneous shrine that had been set up on the railings of the bowling green in Kenmure Street where Kriss had been taken. I placed a basket of flowers there. Others were doing the same. There had been huge outpourings of grief at Bellahouston Academy, among Kriss's school friends, when the news broke there earlier in the week. But days later, at the shrine there was also a tangible fear of what might happen next.

I had become totally convinced that I had to devote myself full time to do whatever I could to bring the killers to justice. This was personal and, frankly, political as well. It was personal because the Donald family were my constituents, but political as well because of my fears of the ramifications of the whole affair for race relations in Scotland, and beyond, if the killers were seen to escape justice.

I went to see Angela Donald to offer my condolences and thank her for what she had done. She was obviously deeply upset. I tried to give her an assurance that I would do everything in my power to make sure the killers were caught. I knew, of course, that this would not bring her son back, but thought it might give the family some sort of closure if the guilty ones were caught and sent to jail for a long time. At that time I had no idea how difficult this would be, and how the issue would come to consume a huge amount of my waking hours for the next two and a half years.

As had been rumoured, the British National Party came to Glasgow in the early hours of the following Sunday morning to try to stir up race hatred and exploit the tense situation for their own ends. Their poisonous leaflets raged about 'escalating anti-white racism in Pollokshields'. But thanks in no small part to Angela Donald and her family, the BNP visit to Glasgow, with their leader Nick Griffin at their head, produced no thunder of marching jackboots. Instead it passed with a whimper as the racist crew came, saw, and quietly slipped back out of town. They came in the dark and left in the dark, and most people never knew anything about it.

Mind you, that would not stop them using the Kriss Donald case in their propaganda at every opportunity throughout the UK whenever they had the chance. And it has to be recognised that there was a potential audience for their message in a section of the white community in Pollokshields. One resident of Kenmure Street told the *Herald* newspaper: 'I'd rather have Nick Griffin of the BNP looking after my interests than Mohammad Sarwar. White people are a minority here. Sarwar is supposed to be the MP for the whole community but he only helps one section.' However Angela Donald's statement and the wide publicity it got meant that this sort of racism never had any substantial echo.

Of course linked to the stand taken by Angela Donald was the level-headed response of both sides of the community. There were a lot of meetings and talks which were dominated by debate about what should be done next. All were driven by a desire not to make things worse by any rash course of action. An example was the decision to go ahead on the following weekend with Pollokshields Clean-Up Day. Once a year, in conjunction with the City Council's Land Services, the community councils and other community groups held a clean-up day where everyone went out on the streets to clean up the area. After a lot of consultation we decided to go ahead with it. That was the second weekend after Kriss's death. It went well. It could never have been 'Business as Usual' of course, but it did give a sign that there was still a fairly broad unity of purpose across the community.

One of the fears I had about the killers being brought to justice was that they would abscond to Pakistan to go into hiding. I had a meeting with Detective Superintendent Elliot McKenzie, of Strathclyde Police, who was now in charge of the investigation of the murder. We both agreed that if the killers fled to Pakistan it would make it enormously difficult to bring them back to face justice, as there was no extradition treaty between the UK and Pakistan. On top of that legal difficulty, there was the enormous problem of finding those who might abscond in the vastness of Pakistan with its 200 million population.

A watch was put on Glasgow, Edinburgh and Manchester airports, and details given to the Pakistan High Commission and European consulates about visa applications. But there were strong rumours in the community that the killers had already gone. It wasn't long before the Pakistan immigration authorities had confirmed that this was the case for the three ringleaders – Imran Shahid, his brother Zeeshan and Faisal Mustaq had fled to Pakistan.

I've never been able to work out how they managed that, because they needed visas as they were British passport holders. The most convincing theory is that they went elsewhere in Europe to lie low, and then applied for a Pakistan visa from there. It usually takes five working days to get a visa for Pakistan, so they would have to have travelled elsewhere to wait, before then moving on to Pakistan. There is talk that they went to Amsterdam first and then to Pakistan, but that has never been confirmed. What seems likely, given what subsequently happened, is that their port of entry into Pakistan was Lahore. We know now that the gang leader Imran Shahid stayed at the luxurious Pearl Continental Hotel in Lahore.

However, whilst the flight of the three ringleaders was extremely concerning, there was a consolation – if small – that the other two, Daanish Zahid and Zahid Mohammed, were soon behind bars and charged with the murder. Both blamed the other three for the murder, but also gave graphic accounts to the police about exactly what happened, who was involved, and where they had gone. So the hunt was on for the other three. It was time to make good on my promises to Angela Donald.

So where to start? In this I had what you might call in the circumstances some good fortune. When I became Britain's first Muslim MP, my status across the Muslim world, and obviously in Pakistan, was enormously enhanced. Although I always had good political contacts in Pakistan and had always nurtured them with protocol visits when in the country, my election in Britain transformed that. It meant from then onwards I always had access to Pakistan's political leaders and top government officials. When I visited Pakistan I always exploited that to make contact, offer advice about British politics, and take advice about what was happening in Pakistan. These protocol visits would eventually pay dividends when, seven years after my first election, I was desperately seeking assistance with the Kriss Donald case.

The protocol visits included the then President of Pakistan, Pervez Musharraf, who came to power in the military coup of October 1999. I had first met him late in September 1999, about three weeks before the coup, when he was the chief of army staff. We met in the army HQ in Rawalpindi. At that time he was pleased to meet me to set the record straight on what has become known as the Kargil campaign, which was organised by the Pakistan army when he was in charge. Early in 1999, the Pakistan army had infiltrated thousands of troops across the line of control into Indian-held Kashmir. By the spring they had occupied more than 1,000 square kilometres on the Indian-held side of the line of control, without a shot being fired, and had dug in to a host of fortified positions, high in the mountain areas.

In May the Indian government discovered the seriousness of the Pakistani incursion, and by the end of the month there were armed clashes between the two armies which threatened all-out war. There remain conflicting accounts about how the threat of war was avoided. In the end, after a series of full-scale military engagements, the Pakistan army withdrew. This was seen as a defeat and the whole episode was discredited in Pakistan as a dangerous, unjustifiable, military adventure. To this day the army chiefs, including Musharraf, have never accepted liability.

The meeting with Musharraf was scheduled for thirty minutes but lasted nearer to an hour. After the usual pleasantries were exchanged, most of the meeting was about the Kargil incursion and the fact that the army was being blamed for an adventure. Musharraf was unhappy that the government of the day had not spoken out to defend the army in the light of accusations from the Indian government. At the end of the meeting he shook my hand and said: 'Sarwar Sahib, rest assured we will not let the nation down'. At that time I remember thinking, 'Well, well, well, he's just suggested to me that the army might be coming. That's it. There's going to be a coup.' And a coup there was – about three weeks later, on 12 October 1999.

It was the military coup which occasioned my second meeting with Musharraf. Robin Cook was the British Foreign Secretary at the time. He called me to his office and asked me if I could do anything about going to Pakistan to meet with Musharraf and to see that Nawaz Sharif, the former prime minister who was now in custody, was being treated properly. Earlier Cook had spoken out against the coup, saying that it was not in the interest of the people of Pakistan for the generals to seize power, and that the move by Musharraf was profoundly undemocratic. In his public statement he had also pledged to call for the exclusion of Pakistan from the Commonwealth and for immediate sanctions to be imposed by the United Nations.

As it happens I had already been planning a visit to Pakistan to take up the case of a woman constituent of mine, Shazia Khan, who apparently had been abandoned there by her husband and could not get a passport to return to the UK. I made a few calls and was given the message that I could meet with Musharraf during my visit. So with Cook's blessing I travelled to Islamabad. That would be early in November 1999.

First stop was at the British High Commission to take some advice from the High Commissioner on the political situation in Pakistan after the *coup d'état*. To my surprise most of the meeting was taken up with his complaints about Musharraf refusing to meet him. 'Musharraf is meeting with all the other ambassadors in Islamabad, along with the High Commissioners, but he has no time to fit in a meeting with me,' the High Commissioner told me in his office. I said it looked like I would be meeting Musharraf and would then ask him to give me access to Nawaz Sharif; I assured the High Commissioner that I would intercede on his behalf. Of course I don't mean to make these points to emphasise the importance of my role in all these matters, but to paint a picture of how all these protocols, over a period of years, would eventually bear fruit when I was seeking justice for Kriss Donald and his family.

I met Musharraf at the Prime Minister's house in Islamabad. When I raised the issue of the British High Commissioner being upset at being left out in the cold, Musharraf made the point that he considered Cook rude to have gone to the international media in condemnation of the generals without the courtesy of a phone call to Pakistan to express his concerns. 'Then I could have offered him some explanations of the perilous situation of the country and the paramount need for the army to rescue the situation from dangerous chaos,' he said.

But he then told the military secretary to arrange a meeting with the British High Commissioner as soon as possible. The military secretary countered: 'Sir, aren't we creating a dangerous precedent here, meeting a government which criticises us publicly across the globe before we are finished with meeting our friends?'

Musharraf said to the secretary that he had a point, but added: 'Arrange a meeting, because we are not doing this for the British, we are doing it for Sarwar Sahib.'

Then I requested if he could arrange a meeting for me with Nawaz Sharif. I told him I wanted to make sure that Sharif was being treated properly on humanitarian grounds. Musharraf was reluctant to do this, but when I pressed him he told me he would make arrangements and that his office would be in touch.

Before I left, Musharraf asked me what I thought about the general political situation in Pakistan. I told him that the country needed reform of the police, judicial reforms and a reorganisation of its local government structure. I said that the outside world would not accept martial law as a solution, and that he shouldn't 'blow up democracy'. I suggested that as soon as possible the army should become the referee in a return to elected politics; that the army should not be a player in that game but an arbiter of how the rules of the game would be implemented. Time would tell that those words fell on deaf ears.

The next day I met Sharif. He was clearly surprised to see me. He asked me what was happening in the world and said that he had not seen a newspaper or seen the news for weeks. 'I don't have a clue what is happening – I don't know where my brother is, I don't know where my father is, I don't know where my family is – I was the Prime Minister, my brother was the Chief Minister of Punjab and I don't know what we have done wrong, to deserve this,' he said. He repeated this time after time: 'I don't know what I have done wrong'. It is common for people who are Muslim to approach misfortune in this way, with a questioning of whether the misfortune is a consequence of other misdeeds of their own: 'if God is punishing me, I must have done something wrong'.

I asked him why he had sacked Musharraf as the army chief of staff when Musharraf was abroad. He told me he knew Musharraf was going to take power, so it was an attempt to pre-empt that. I tried to give him some assurances and some comfort that I would maintain a watch on his case. I asked him if he had been subject to any physical violence, but he said he hadn't. Although he was clearly anxious about his detention, he steadfastly maintained his personal composure throughout our exchanges.

What happened then might have done Sharif's cause some good. That evening my meetings with Musharraf and Sharif led the BBC

World Service TV and radio bulletins across the globe. This was, however, really a result of a fortunate coincidence rather than me taking the international media by storm. As I have said already, I had been planning to go to Pakistan to investigate the case of one of my constituents, Shazia Khan. Thus, I was accompanied on this journey to Pakistan by the BBC Scotland correspondent, Bob Wylie, with a camera crew who were interested in reporting the Khan story for BBC *Newsnight Scotland*.

When the whole thing about Musharraf and Sharif developed, the BBC crew went into news mode. Wylie had previously worked for the BBC World Service as a reporter in Budapest, so he knew how the news system at Bush House, the headquarters of the World Service, worked. He took all the necessary shots and interviews with me, did some stand-up pieces-to-camera and then went to the headquarters of Pakistan TV to plead for connections to be made to London. He also had the good fortune that his BBC producer on the trip, Azad Ahmad, had passable Urdu.

So it was that the story was fed from Islamabad to the BBC World Service in London. It made the lead that evening on the World Service. That then set up a media conference the next morning for all of the Pakistani media, who reported at enormous length on the first meeting of anyone with Nawaz Sharif since his arrest following the coup. Without digressing any further, all the publicity around the meeting with Sharif meant that I had kept my part of the bargain with Musharraf. My intervention, combined with some luck, had shown the world that although there had been a military coup, the former Prime Minister was not being mistreated. Thereafter I had easy access to Musharraf to engage in political conversations whenever I visited Pakistan.

That meant that by the time I went to see Musharraf at the President's House in April 2004 to take up Kriss Donald's case, we were on familiar terms. By then I had met Musharraf four or five times. Each time I was in Islamabad I requested a meeting with him to pay my respects, and to exchange information and opinion. The agenda for the meeting concerning Kriss Donald was of that type – it was a general exchange of views, but this time within those parameters I raised the specific issue of the Kriss Donald case.

I told Musharraf that the murder could not only cause irreparable damage between Pakistanis and the indigenous community in Scotland, but also across Britain. I said that it would be catastrophic if two or three of those suspected of the killing could cheat justice by hiding out in Pakistan. In fact I told him bluntly: 'Things are already being said openly in sections of the white community like "Those Paki bastards will never face trial. They're gone forever; those three will never be brought to face justice because the government of Pakistan will give each of them a refuge as one of their own".' I told Musharraf that the British National Party had already tried to exploit the case along these lines.

Musharraf proved to be very supportive. After I had spoken he was quiet for a while as though contemplating the significance of what he had heard. Then he said: 'Sarwar Sahib, this is very serious. Very serious. It is a calamity and one with repercussions for you in Scotland, but also repercussions for us in Islamabad too.' He turned to his military secretary and said: 'Now, whatever help Sarwar Sahib needs on this you make sure you give it to him. Let's start with the Prime Minister. Make sure that Sarwar Sahib gets a meeting with the Prime Minister as soon as possible. He will be able to start balls rolling immediately. This is of great importance.' Then he turned to me and said: 'Look, these people are criminals and we will help you get them back to the UK. But obviously there are procedures and protocols which have to be followed, and the laws of the country which have to be followed.'

So it was that before the end of that day I got a call from the Prime Minister's office, asking if I would be free to come to see him. 'When?' I asked. 'Now!' came the reply from his aide at the other end of the telephone.

On the way to Prime Minister's House, where he had his office, my mood was verging on the euphoric. I thought about how Musharraf was the power in the land, but also how in one day I had got to the Prime Minister who was really the man who could pull strings to make things happen. This impression would, in due course, prove to be wildly over-optimistic, but that is how I felt as we sped along the sweeping boulevards of central Islamabad on the way to the Prime Minister's office.

At the time Shaukat Aziz was the Prime Minister in Musharraf's government. His office was laid out in the same manner as most heavyweight government ministers – the carpets were plush and thick-piled, the desk was the size of a small aircraft carrier and in front of it was an area with ornate armchairs arranged around a small glass-topped coffee table. Shaukat Aziz greeted me warmly and said: 'My friend, I hear you have some problems that are needing some attention from us.'

I sat down on one of the armchairs and laid out the scale of the difficulties in much the same way as I had with Musharraf. When I had finished making the case, he suggested that since this would potentially require a criminal investigation, it would be a matter for the Ministry of Interior, which, akin to our own Home Office, deals with matters of policing and intelligence. He offered to make arrangements for me to meet Kamal Zafar, then the Secretary of the Interior.

The next morning I met Zafar at his office in Islamabad. He too was very receptive to my explanations and my requests for assistance. He told me, towards the end of what was a short and to the point meeting: 'Look, brother Sarwar, this is not a complicated matter. In fact it is rather simple. These men need to be caught and returned to the UK. We will help you on this. I shall make my enquiries and come back to you on this when you have returned to the UK.' I asked him at that point if the lack of an extradition treaty between Pakistan and the UK would not cause us huge difficulties. He said, in so many words, that it would not be a problem because of the nature of the Kriss Donald case. 'No strings attached,' he said.

When I boarded the plane for London the following evening I was happy. But I should have known better; after all I am the one who constantly tells friends and acquaintances that things in Pakistan are not always what they seem to be. I never heard a word from Kamal Zafar for weeks and weeks. So late in May or early June I phoned him. He told me that 'some problems' had emerged, and it would be better to come to Pakistan for another meeting, 'to try and reach an agreement on how these things can be sorted out'.

At home there were also insistent demands being made by Strathclyde Police for potential problems to be sorted out. The trial of the first two who had been indicted for the murder, Daanish Zahid and Zahid Mohammed, was due to start in the coming October. The police were desperate for all five accused to be indicted and go to trial together. Hence they were pleading with me to go back to Pakistan to see if the extradition of the other three, who had fled there, could be agreed. The detective in charge of the case, Elliot McKenzie, asked me to go and 'try again to get all of them in the one court case'. Given that Kamal Zafar had also suggested a meeting, I agreed to go. However, I reminded Elliot McKenzie, who would play a tremendous part in all these proceedings, that even if we got a deal, Pakistan was a big country and finding the ones who had fled would not be easy.

The background to the police anxieties about two trials going ahead related to the botching of a previous murder trial which had racial motives. In November 1998, Surjit Singh Chhokar, who worked as a delivery driver for a Indian carry-out restaurant in Bellshill, in Lanarkshire, was stabbed to death outside his home, in Overtown, in Lanarkshire. The Crown Office indicted three men, Ronald Coulter, his nephew, Andrew Coulter and a third man, David Montgomery, for the Chhokar murder. For reasons known probably only to the Lord Advocate of the day, Lord Hardie, in March 1999, the Crown decided to proceed with the prosecution of only Ronnie Coulter in the first trial. Ronnie Coulter then promptly blamed the other two for the murder. He was found guilty of assault but cleared on the murder charge.

In November 2000, Andrew Coulter and David Montgomery were put in the dock for the Chhokar murder. They blamed Ronnie Coulter for the murder and were acquitted. The case resulted in a public war of words between Lords Hardie and McCluskey, and subsequently, two separate public inquiries, one of which castigated the Crown for bungling the case. This history made it clear why Strathclyde Police were agitated about a repeat of this process if there were two trials in the Kriss Donald case. So, given what Kamal Zafar had said, and the concerns of the police in Glasgow about a split trial in the coming months, off I went once more to Islamabad.

When I had returned from my first visit to Pakistan about these matters I saw the visit as a journey of hope. After the second visit, to try to get something done, that hope had turned to despair. A despair born of what seemed to be insurmountable difficulties on all fronts. In two or three months the ground had shifted disastrously.

First of all, let's take the Secretary for the Interior, Kamal Zafar. His original 'No strings attached' assertion had now turned into its absolute opposite. In the meeting I had with him this time, he raised the issue of the absence of an extradition treaty. He then said that the absence, in itself, was clearly a problem, but one that could be overcome. But only if a deal was done. He then proposed tit-for-tat exchanges of wanted criminals: 'There are two sides to this story. We have people in Pakistan who have been victims of terrible crimes here, perpetrated by criminals who then fled to London. We are powerless to bring them back. So why don't we get round the absence of extradition by an exchange. We give you your criminals and you give us ours. Why should be accept double standards in this? We can't have a situation, surely, where we give you your criminals but you don't give us our criminals.'

I was flabbergasted at the change. For more than a year this would remain Zafar's position for the entire period of negotiations: 'We give you yours, but only if you give us ours.'

There was to be a double blow coming in the shape of decisions set in stone and handed down by the British High Commission. On my first visit, the people there had been equivocal about the possibilities of a one-off extradition of the three accused. I was not that concerned, since my own view was that if Musharraf and the rest were on our side it would matter little what the British High Commission would have to say. Now on their part there was no longer equivocation on the issue – it had been replaced by outright opposition to doing anything about the Kriss Donald case, lest it jeopardise other, grander, plans.

The position adopted by the British High Commissioner in Islamabad was essentially that the Kriss Donald case could not be allowed to rock the boat of British and Pakistani relations, which were at a sensitive stage. The British government was in the process of agreeing an extradition treaty with Pakistan; the UK government had a priority to conclude this, with special reference to the possible extradition of terrorist suspects from Pakistan. There was no doubt that the High Commission had enormous sympathy for the family of Kriss

Donald, and my urgings that something had to be done. Nonetheless, their priorities had been set by the desire to negotiate an agreed extradition treaty between the two countries.

So, an under-secretary at the High Commission told me in a meeting, 'Mr Sarwar, you have to see the bigger picture in all of this. We cannot allow the case of your constituent to complicate much bigger, more significant negotiations.' I told him that securing a deal on the Kriss Donald case would actually be a first practical example of what could be done and could establish the benefit of such relations. The under-secretary retorted in his clipped English accent: 'The bigger picture, Mr Sarwar. The bigger picture, I'm afraid . . .'

What concerned me more than his condescending manner, was that, by this time, I already knew that the High Commission's words were being matched by their deeds. Although there had been an interregnum at a political level about the case, with all this stuff about equal exchange of wanted criminals, I knew via Musharraf and the Prime Minister's office that police enquiries were being progressed by the Pakistani side. I also knew that because the Director General of the Federal Investigation Agency (FIA), Tariq Pervez, an old friend, had raised the issue with me in private. He told me that the FIA had sent the British High Commission requests for details of the suspects and hadn't even received a reply. Then when he pursued this further with the High Commission, he was told in no uncertain terms that there would be 'no further action in this matter meantime'.

A frustrating stalemate beckoned as I returned to Glasgow with only bad news. The Pakistani end was stalled because of the deal they wanted on the exchange of wanted suspects. But even if it were possible to agree on such a deal, it could not happen because the arm of the British government in Pakistan, the British High Commission, wanted nothing to do with anything which was not 'the big picture' of a negotiated extradition treaty between the two countries.

Early in November 2004, this was made even more clear to me at the funeral of Yasser Arafat. There was a military funeral behind closed doors in Cairo, and then Arafat's body was flown from there to Ramallah, in the West Bank, for final burial. At the Cairo event I again met Shaukat Aziz, the Prime Minister of Pakistan, face to face, for a third time. But this time I was in the company of Jack Straw, the British Foreign Secretary. I raised the lack of progress on the case with Aziz, and, in particular, the difficulties about the lack of an extradition treaty and the Pakistani ministry involved now demanding a deal on suspects being exchanged both ways. The Prime Minister's reply was to the effect that the lack of co-operation from the British authorities about requests for details of the suspects who might be hiding out in Pakistan, made progress in apprehending them impossible, treaty or no treaty, deal or no deal.

The intent was clear – co-operation may be forthcoming from the Pakistan side, but all of that was somewhat irrelevant if the possibilities of catching the suspects at large were slim due to the lack of meaningful information about them being passed to the Pakistani authorities. Jack Straw acknowledged what had been said with an 'I see, I see,' and a pledge that he would look into the matter. He told me later that he would make the appropriate enquiries into that element of the case, and at least take steps for briefings to be exchanged. I was encouraged, to some extent, but also disheartened by the fact that all the efforts I had made had failed to make a decisive breakthrough. That being the case, the first trial had proceeded in October 2004 with only two of the accused – Daanish Zahid, 20, and Zahid Mohammed also 20. I was weary.

The fears that these two would get off by blaming the other three who had fled to Pakistan proved to be unfounded. Both the accused lodged special pleadings in defence, naming the three others, but the weight of evidence against them meant that the jury delivered guilty verdicts against both. That was on 18 November 2004, and the jury took only two and a half hours to deliver the guilty verdicts. Effectively Zahid Mohammed gave evidence against all the other four, and Daanish Zahid give evidence against the three who had fled. On the first day of the trial, Zahid Mohammed's plea of not guilty to the murder was accepted, and he was found guilty on the lesser charges of abduction and assault. A month later, on 16 December, Daanish Zahid was jailed for life with a minimum term of 17 years, and Zahid Mohammed was jailed for 5 years. Any consolation that two of the culprits had been brought to justice was wiped out by the horror of the killing made apparent in the trial, and the knowledge that the real ringleaders were still at large. I told the media that: 'We will not leave any stone unturned to bring the other suspects to trial and justice'. But to be honest, by this time, I was beginning to wonder if that would ever come to pass. They were in hiding in Pakistan and it looked as if that was where they might remain.

By the end of January 2005, with an election beckoning in May, I had to take a political decision to put my pursuit of the killers on hold for a period. Of course, in the main, this was a consequence of the pressures of the election period which fall on any politician at election time, but there was another factor. It had come to my knowledge that rumours were circulating, in sections of the community in the Glasgow Central constituency, that I was going to make a grandstanding announcement of the arrest of the suspects in Pakistan in the middle of the election campaign. Fingers were being pointed.

Of course I knew the accusation was not true, but I decided to take time out in case anything that was being done might be interpreted as using the Kriss Donald murder to pitch for votes. The great difficulty in the campaign was that whenever the issue was raised at meetings, or on the streets, I could not offer a full explanation because that might reach the media, which, in turn, could result in the villains in Pakistan finding out that we were after them.

One particular incident typifies the sort of problems I faced from certain sections of the white community. I was canvassing for votes at Bridgeton Cross in the East End of Glasgow. I was in election mode, asking for support, shaking hands and the like. One woman passed by me and yelled: 'I am not shaking hands with you. You have blood on your hands. You helped the real killers of that Kriss Donald leave the country and you are doing nothing to bring them to justice. Nothing. Nothing. They [sic] bastards will never face trial in this country and you know it.'

I was terribly shaken by the fury in her words. In the end, however, I won the seat with an 8,500 majority. I was pleased to see that the BNP's effort, despite the disgraceful smears of their campaign, was a miserable 671 votes. At the count when the result was being announced I did not realise that elsewhere in Britain events were piling up that, in the end, would confound the accusations of the woman at Bridgeton Cross.

In the 2001 election, Khalid Mahmood had joined me as the second MP in the UK parliament from a Muslim background. In 2005 two became four, as we were joined by Shahid Malik, who won Dewsbury, in West Yorkshire, and Sadiq Khan, who won Tooting in London. To celebrate these victories, the Pakistan High Commissioner in London, a renowned intellectual, Maleeha Lodhi, held a celebration dinner in London. That would be towards the end of May 2005. Of course, among the guests was an array of British friends of Pakistan, as well as a large number of dignitaries from Pakistan, including ministers of the government. So it was there that I met the man who would unlock the door through which to bring the killers of Kriss Donald to justice. He was the then Cabinet Minister for the Interior of the Pakistan government, Aftab Sherpaio.

I had known Sherpaio for many years, since he was a long-established family friend. He was a leading light of the Pakistan People's Party in Pakistan when I was the president of the PPP in Scotland. So when he had visits to the UK he always came to see me in Scotland. At the party, I insisted he should come and meet me at the Parliament the next day. I gave him a tour of the Houses of Parliament and took him to lunch in the House of Commons dining room. There I told him, in detail, the Kriss Donald story and how all my efforts to have the last three suspects brought to justice in Scotland had reached an impasse.

'You are knocking on the wrong doors. You should have come to see me before this. I'm in charge,' he said. I told him that, frankly, I had not realised he was in such an important position, but that once the Prime Minister had put me in touch with Kamal Zafar, and assurances were given, I had thought that I was on the right track. 'Besides,' I joked, 'big chiefs like you are difficult to reach in the swamp of the government bureaucracy in Pakistan.' Immediately he gave me his two personal mobile numbers. He said: 'Look, I am the boss of all the affairs of the Interior Ministry. I promise we will not let you down. Come to Pakistan soon and we will get this thing sorted.'

I knew Sherpaio as a man of action, a man of his word, and a man capable of getting things done. So within a matter of days I was again on my way to Islamabad. I travelled there with the new MP, Shahid Malik, who was there to give moral support. When we touched down in Islamabad, I phoned Sherpaio from the airport on one of the mobile numbers he had given to me. True to his word he said: 'Didn't take you long, Sarwar Sahib! Right, tomorrow at my office, 10 o'clock, and all the actors in this drama will be there. We'll knock a few heads together.'

The next morning, at his grand office in the Interior Ministry, Sherpaio did not take 'No' for an answer. Kamal Zafar was there, and immediately started his arguments for an exchange of wanted suspects. Sherpaio was his boss in the ministry and put him in his place in no uncertain terms. He said to Zafar and the civil servants gathered in the office: 'This is not for the British government. I want you to stop going on about exchanges of wanted men. We are doing it for our brother Sarwar Sahib and the Pakistani community in the UK. I don't want any excuses. I want everything to be in place and agreed within one week.'

I remember thinking at that precise moment that all these negotiations would have been completed much earlier if I had made my way to Sherpaio's office in the first place. But that can be the way of things in Pakistan. You have to find the right person with the right key to unlock the door. Obviously, with the President and Prime Minister giving orders on my behalf I thought that all doors would be opened. Not so. Sherpaio was the man with the right key.

There were still significant legal formalities to be overcome in Pakistan, but within three or four weeks a warrant for the arrest of the three suspects had been issued.

With that the hunt was on. One other factor emerged which made capture of the suspects immeasurably more likely, once the politics had been worked out. The chief of police in Lahore, Irfan Mahmood; the director of the Federal Investigation Agency, Tariq Pervez, and the director of the Intelligence Bureau, Shaukat Javed, were all personal friends of mine. The first clues suggested that Imran Shahid was holed up in Lahore. So co-ordination of what happened thereafter was much easier, as all three worked together. However, even then, I thought, 'What happens if we don't get them?' Who would understand the complex difficulties of such a desperate mission?

A matter of weeks after the Sherpaio meeting where he had knocked heads together in Islamabad, the message I had been waiting for, for more than a year, arrived. The mobile rang – it was Shaukat Javed of the IB (equivalent of Britain's MI5): 'We have got the first one. Imran Shahid was arrested today in Lahore.'

It would transpire that this was the result of a joint police operation between Strathclyde Police and their counterparts in Lahore. Strathclyde police officers had provided the police in Lahore with the British mobile phone numbers of those who fled. So it became a waiting game to track the phones and wait for one of them to be used. Eventually Imran Shahid used his, which allowed the Pakistani police to trace him to the relatively upmarket Shadman district of Lahore. Two nights the police lay in wait, but Shahid, aka Baldy, didn't return home. But then on the third night, as he walked up the two flights of stairs to his apartment, the police pounced. The police officer in charge of the raid, Zubair Chattha, told me later what happened when Baldy was arrested.

First of all Shahid denied the murder, and blamed his other two accomplices, his brother, Zeeshan, and friend, Faisal Mustaq, for the crime. Then, when pushed, he said he had been involved, but that Kriss had to be 'taken care of' because he had molested a number of Muslim girls in the area where he lived on the south side of Glasgow. Shahid's final pitch was to offer more than £200,000 to Zubair Chattha as a bribe to allow Shahid to escape. When the police had time to search Imran Shahid's flat, they found that he was running a huge banking swindle from Lahore. They discovered piles of lined account ledgers, carefully marked up with the details of literally hundreds of bank accounts, from all over the UK. The details included names, addresses, passwords, credit cards linked to the accounts, and, crucially, the day of the month that the monthly bank statement statement ended.

For months on end Shahid would transfer sums of money from these credit cards and bank accounts on the day after the card or bank statement end date. This would mean that for weeks at a time, sometimes months, the scam was not identified by the victims. The money was transferred to intermediate bank accounts which were then used for other transactions, seemingly showing that the payments apparently came from legitimate account sources. One swindle he used was hire purchase of expensive limousines using the money from the accounts he had penetrated as down payments. The cars were then sold on for cash by his accomplices to unscrupulous customers.

This was all a continuation from where he had left off in Glasgow, even if the penetration of bank accounts was more sophisticated than his Glasgow operations. In the Lahore flat the police also found false passports and a driving licence with Shahid's ID photo on them. The name on the documents was laughable – Enrique Soprano – adopted from the American gangster series. But Imran Shahid was no Godfather. Real criminal Godfathers allegedly don't give up their accomplices to the police, but that is exactly what Shahid did.

The chief of police in Lahore, Irfan Mahmood, told me the story many months later. We were at a dinner party, in Lahore, and I told him that I knew how the police tracked Imran Shahid but always wondered how they caught the other two – deep in the Punjab – so quickly after Shahid had been arrested in Lahore. Irfan then explained that gangsters in Pakistan, when treated to some police 'hospitality', can last for weeks without divulging information. 'This so-called Godfather of yours didn't last beyond an hour of our generosity before he gave out the names, numbers and locations of the other two. I wish our gangsters were as "tough" as yours,' he told me with an ironic laugh.

The police operation was led by the District Chief of Police, Akhtar Lalika. So it was, that Deputy Superintendent Mohammad Aslam led a posse of the Toba Tek Singh district police officers into a remote village in the Punjab, in pursuit of Zeeshan Shahid and Faisal Mustaq. The two were hiding out in a house, owned by a distant relative, in the village number 348, district Toba Tek Singh. The two of them must have thought that no-one would find them there. But they were wrong.

When the police arrived, the two jumped from a second floor window and tried to make off through the neighbouring farm fields. But they hadn't reckoned with the redoubtable Aslam and his men. They pursued them into the nearby fields and beyond, and, after a struggle, captured both of them. As Aslam declared memorably in a later BBC Scotland *Frontline* documentary about the murder: 'Law is law and they could not stay above the law'. The great irony in all this is that Toba Tek Singh district, in the Punjab, is my home area in

Pakistan. In fact the hoodlums were staying in village 348, which is a mere three miles away from the charity hospital built by my Ucare Foundation at Rajana.

By the late summer of 2005, the three were behind bars in the Central Jail in Rawalpindi. At first, they attempted to prevent their return to Scotland to face trial by taking legal action in the Pakistani courts on the grounds that they would not get a fair trial in Scotland. However, after some six weeks in the jail in Rawalpindi, they suddenly relented and told the Pakistani authorities that they wanted to return to Scotland willingly. The brothers, Imran and Zeeshan Shahid, and Mustaq were transferred from the Pakistan prison system to the custody of the Federal Investigation Agency (FIA) one evening early in October.

I have a vivid memory of TV pictures of the three as they were transferred from jail to the holding cells of the FIA in Rawalpindi, the night before they left Pakistan. They were laughing and joking and posing for the TV cameras as though they hadn't a care in the world. Imran Shahid told BBC Scotland: 'We can't speak now, it isn't safe; but we will speak when we are back in the UK.' In turn the FIA handed them over to the custody of the Strathclyde Police inside Islamabad airport.

Eventually, after months of delays and legal arguments, the three stood trial in the High Court in Edinburgh in October 2006 – two and a half years after they murdered Kriss. Getting them to court to face justice in Scotland is among the proudest achievements of my life and, as I have said already, one of my greatest heartbreaks. When I look back on the time it still seems to me like a miracle. A miracle with heroes like Angela Donald and her family, and Detective Superintendent Elliot McKenzie of Strathclyde Police.

When the first two gang members were convicted and sentenced, in December 2004, Elliot stood outside the High Court in Glasgow and swore that he would not rest until all those responsible for the murder were brought to justice. He was as good as his word. I always thought that Strathclyde Police scored an own goal after the trial by not allowing Elliot to give media interviews, for whatever reason. Instead, the then Assistant Chief Constable for Crime pre-recorded a wooden video statement which just didn't take at all with the media corps. They wanted to speak to the real hero, not one with braid on his cap and lapels, who had never been to Pakistan during the whole operation.

In Pakistan profound thanks were due to the police chiefs Irfan Mahmood, Tariq Pervez and Shaukat Javed. Likewise District Police Chief Akhtar Lalika and Deputy Superintendent Mohammad Aslam, in Toba Tek Singh, and investigations officer Zubair Chattha, and the deputy director of the Federal Intelligence Agency, Shafique Gujjar, in Lahore. On 8 November 2006, after a five-week trial, all three were found guilty of the racially aggravated abduction and murder of Kriss Donald.

Speaking outside the High Court in Edinburgh, that day, his mother Angela said: 'Justice has been done. Thank you. It is over.'

Partition 2

'This mottled dawn,
This night-bitten morning,
No, this is not the morning
We had set out in search of.'
Faiz Ahmed Faiz, Urdu Marxist poet.

'And so in a bewildering frenzy Hindus, Sikhs and Muslims turned on one another.

For the next two months the unparalleled tide of human misery washing across the face of the Punjab would be counted in rows of little red pins on the maps in Government House . . . a caravan almost mind-numbing in dimension, the largest single column of refugees that man's turbulent history had ever produced.'
Larry Collins and Dominique Lapierre, *Freedom at Midnight* (1997).

The India Bill, with its 400 clauses, was passed in the House of Commons in June 1935. It became the rule book for the Partition of the Indian Subcontinent, in the form of the India Act. World War Two intervened, which postponed all the parliamentary intentions set out in the Act for more than a decade. But even in the 1940s, the bell which tolled for the coming of Partition was not heard by many of those who would become victims of what has been described as its 'crescendo of violence'. Millions upon millions – my family among them – had no idea what was about to befall them.

When the Labour Party – which would become my eventual political home in the UK – won the 1945 post-war election with an overwhelming majority, the leader, Clement Attlee, became determined that there would be a wholesale retreat from Empire. It was the mood of the times after the war – better now to build a new

Britain for all, to heal the wounds of war, rather than continue the foolish imperial adventure in faraway places where the British were no longer wanted.

Of course, the British departure from India was not simply the result of a Labour government coming to power. History and revolutions generally require a bit more than a change of governing party. Over a period of decades, the very foundations of the British Empire in India had long been fractured by the mass movement of opposition to British rule. So the departure was a worldly recognition that the movement for independence could not be stopped. In 1945, Archibald Wavell, the former commander-in-chief of the army in India, and by then Viceroy of India, indicated that it was time to go: 'Our present position in India is analogous to that of a military force compelled to withdraw in the face of greatly superior numbers.' In other words, the game was up.

In the aftermath of the War, Wavell was forced to concede an all-India interim government with Nehru as prime minister. The retreat from Empire being marked out by the Labour government, combined with the state of unrest generated by Hindu/Muslim clashes in all the major cities of the Subcontinent, had convinced the British that the Subcontinent was on the verge of being ungovernable.

The opposition to British rule had been led by the All-India Congress Party, which had been formed around the demand for a Indian independence, in the late nineteenth century. Mahatma Gandhi had been the leader of the Congress Party and led the civil disobedience campaigns against the British in the 1920s and 30s. By 1942 the 'Quit India' campaign had Pandit Nehru as the anointed successor to Gandhi. Congress was a Hindu-dominated movement. It is recorded that only 3% of its party members were Muslims. What we now know, with the benefit of hindsight, is that figure probably determined that Partition would be marked by the clash of two great political movements – Congress for the Indian masses and the Muslim League, which would emerge to champion the rights of the Muslims of the Subcontinent.

However today I would argue that the chasm of Partition and all that it brought in human misery was not ultimately the responsibility of the Muslim side of the struggle. Rather it was the insatiable political demands of Congress which determined the outcome. The historian Perry Anderson has written:

> It was not Jinnah [leader of the Muslim League] who injected religion into the vocabulary and imagery of the national movement, it was Gandhi . . . What remained was Gandhi's transformation of Congress from an elite into a mass organisation by saturating its appeal with Hindu imagery.[1]

In my view, Anderson is correct when he suggests that the emergence of the mass movement of the Muslim League was a political reaction to the creation of a mass Congress movement which was unbreakably wedded to Hindu supremacy. So, Indian claims that 'it was the Muslims who broke up the Subcontinent' are disputable according to one's interpretation of history. In fact, the 25-30% of the population who were Muslims had initially organised around political slogans which demanded that their rights, in India, be recognised and that there should be a sharing of power to reflect that. The All-India Muslim League had been formed in 1906. At that time the 'Green Book', declaring its aims, put forward the idea of safeguarding Muslim rights but not the demand for an independent state. The call for an independent state for 100 million Muslims arrived relatively late in the history of the political retreat from Empire.

The idea was first raised by Sir Mohammad Iqbal (1877–1938), the leader of the Muslim League in the 1920s and 30s. At the annual conference of the League, in December 1930, Iqbal declared: 'I would like to see Punjab, North-West Frontier Province (now Khyber Pakhtunkhwa), Sindh and Baluchistan amalgamated into a single state. Self government within the British Empire or without the British Empire, the formation of a consolidated North-West Indian Muslim state appears to me to be the final destiny of the Muslims, at least of North-West India.'

I offer these historical references as a contribution to the lasting debate about who ultimately led the charge to Partition, not least because there seems to be a conventional wisdom that it was the Muslim

1. Perry Anderson, 'Why Partition', *London Review of Books*, vol. 34, no. 14, 19 July 2012.

League. It is interesting to note here that Iqbal's concept of an independent Pakistan from the declaration quoted above was seen as an
entity which would exist either 'within or without' the British Empire.
But even then, Iqbal did not conceive of a completely separate state,
but rather, that an independent Pakistan would be part of a wider
Indian Confederation. In 1930 the new state didn't even have a name.

There is some debate about how the name 'Pakistan' emerged,
but the most consistent explanation credits it to a Muslim student,
Rehmat Ali, who was studying at Cambridge University at the time.
'Pakistan' was the word he had created to take account of a future
Muslim state in the north-western part of the British empire based on
the Muslim Punjabis, Pathans, Kashmiris, Sindhis and the Baluchis.
Different letters or parts of these names were taken to make up the
word 'Pakistan'. The 'i' was added to make the acronym easier to
pronounce.

In Urdu the word '*Pak*' means 'pure', so there was a convenient
coincidence in that 'Pakistan', as a name, was a recognition of the
peoples who would make up the new state but also conveyed the
meaning of 'Pakistan' as the 'Land of the Pure'. It seems Rehmat Ali
coined the term in 1933 and from then it gained some currency.

However if we are looking for an historical breaking point, it
was probably the elections of 1937 which began to put flesh on the
bones of the idea of an independent Pakistan. Before the 1937 provincial elections the Congress leadership had promised they would
form coalition governments in provinces where there were substantial Muslim minorities, but Congress's victories were so overwhelming that after them Nehru declared: 'I am personally convinced that
any kind of pact or coalition between us and the Muslim League will
be highly injurious.'[1]

These sentiments expressed by Nehru were followed by an exhor-
tation from him that the League must abandon its claims for Muslim
rights and 'dissolve itself into Congress if it wished anything"

There is a case to be made that the emergence of this hardline
politics convinced Mohammad Ali Jinnah and the leadership of the
Muslim League that an independent Pakistan, within an Indian Confederation, would no longer be possible. I make these points because

1. Perry Anderson, *London Review of Books, op. cit.*

I have long wanted to set the record straight, from my point of view, about how the great cataclysm of Partition arrived in history. At the Muslim League conference in Lahore, in March 1940, three years after those provincial elections, when the power-sharing pact was renounced, Jinnah said:

> Hindus and the Muslims belong to two different religions, philosophies, social customs and literature . . . It is quite clear that Hindus and Muslims derive their inspiration from different sources of history. They have different epics, different heroes and different episodes . . . To yoke together two such nations under a single state, one as a numerical minority and the other as a majority, must lead to growing discontent and final destruction of any fabric that may be so built up for the government of such a state.[1]

From then on the momentum to create Pakistan became politically unstoppable. The scale of the bloodbath which was to follow in the Partition of the Subcontinent was unforeseen. It was a bloodbath which washed up on the very doorstep of my own family; however, before going into that part of my story I want to draw on the historical record a bit further. Looking back now, it is possible to identify two distinct stages in the Partition; one of which followed the other with incredible haste.

The establishment of the agreement for Partition was announced early in June 1947. Independence Day for Pakistan and India would follow on the 14th and 15th of August. The pillars of the 'One Hundred Year Raj' came tumbling down in a little over ten weeks. Enter Lord Mountbatten and Sir Cyril Radcliffe. Mountbatten – Attlee's man to replace Wavell as the new Viceroy – would get the principle of Partition agreed with sketch maps and broad-brush clauses. The second stage involved the judge, Radcliffe, who would draw up what would become the blood-soaked dividing lines on the map.

Mountbatten arrived in Delhi on 22 March 1947. The growing desperation of events at that time are described by Yasmin Khan in *The Great Partition*:

1. *Ibid.*

By the end of the first week of March . . . quarters of most major cities in Punjab were burning: Lahore, Amritsar, Jullundur, Rawalpindi, Multan and Sialkot all had sections gutted. Gangs roamed the streets, some wearing steel or tin helmets, setting shops and houses on fire, firing weapons and throwing heavy rocks and glass soda bottles.[1]

It didn't take Mountbatten long to draw the conclusion that Partition was unavoidable. There would have to be a Pakistan – one way or another. The two great protagonists, the League and Congress, were irreconcilable. However, if the motto for the building of the British Empire had been: 'Divide and Rule', in Mountbatten's hands, as the Subcontinent slipped from its grasp, it became: 'We Divide – You Rule'; the 'You' referred to here being Congress. There was an historical carve-up to follow of gigantic proportions. As Mountbatten declared: 'Administratively it is the difference between putting up a permanent building and a Nissen hut or a tent. As far as Pakistan is concerned we are putting up a tent.'[2]

It might be noted at this point that when the Attlee government in Britain had announced, in February 1947, that India should have its independence, the date given was 'by June 1948'. Mountbatten was asked at a news conference in June 1947 only days after the hasty Partition announcement: 'Do you foresee any mass transfer of population?'

'Personally I don't see it,'[3] came the reply.

Anderson, in the *London Review of Books*, points the finger of accusation:

If partition was to have any chance of being carried through peacefully or equitably, at least a year – the year that London had originally set as the term of the Raj – of orderly administration and preparation was needed. Its conveyance within six weeks was a sentence of death and devastation to millions . . . Having lit the fuse, Mountbatten handed over the buildings

1. Yasmin Khan, *The Great Partition* (Yale University Press, 2008).
2. Perry Anderson, *London Review of Books*, *op. cit.*
3. Perry Anderson, *London Review of Books*, *op. cit.*

to their new owners hours before they blew up, in what has a good claim to be the most contemptible single act in the annals of Empire.[1]

There had been an established expectation before Independence, not least in the mind of Mountbatten himself, that Muslims who lived beyond where the border was drawn, in India, and Sikhs and Hindus who found themselves to be in what would become Pakistan, would be able to continue to live where they were. Life would go on as it always had. My own family history is living proof of these misconceptions.

My father's brother, Ghulam, went to the UK in 1938. He worked there as a salesman as my father would do after him, selling all manner of things – socks, ties, shirts, nylon stockings among them – from a suitcase. Ghulam was the first in the family to go to Britain. As always it was the result of connections. In my father's family there were three brothers – Abdullah, my father, Ghulam and Shah Mohammad – and one sister, Fatima. She married a member of the extended family who had returned to Pakistan after working for a number of years in Britain. When Fatima's husband then returned to the UK in search of more work, he took Ghulam with him. So began Ghulam's connection with the UK.

When Ghulam returned to undivided India, after working in the UK for many years, there was still no real understanding of what Partition would mean for the future of the Muslims of the Subcontinent. So when Ghulam came back with money from his British adventures, he invested it in buying a bit more land and extending the family house. Right there, in our village of Khairanwala, some miles in the countryside outside the city of Jullundur, in what he must have known was certain to become part of India when the Partition took place. New rooms were built on to the standing brick-built family house in the months after his return.

This simple fact demonstrates the reality that at the time of Partition the masses on both sides of the border may have had some understanding that there was going to be an India and a Pakistan, but they believed that the new borders wouldn't make any differences to

1. Perry Anderson, *London Review of Books*, *op. cit.*

their lives or their villages. Muslims who lived in what would become India, and Hindus and Sikhs who lived in what would become Pakistan, would stay where they were. There is no other explanation as to why Ghulam returned from the UK and sank almost every penny that he had made there in his property, in what was likely to become part of the new India.

Clearly our family believed that Khairanwala would stay the same. After all, although we were the only Muslim landholders in the village, my grandfather was a respected member of the council of village elders. My grandmother was also highly respected in the village, and the poorer Hindus would often come to see her and touch her feet as a mark of great respect when they were seeking advice or charity. Why would we fear for the future in these circumstances?

This reality also explains why our extended family was among the last to leave their home and take flight to Pakistan. Almost all their life savings had been invested in the permanency of the 'new house', so it was very difficult to reach a realisation that they would have to give it all up; that they would have to abandon what they had achieved in a run for their lives, that they would have to look back on the house where almost all they had was invested, wondering if this was a last goodbye to the house, the land-holdings and the money that had been spent. Their flight was part of a movement of millions. The biggest in history.

In total, independence for India and Pakistan produced a cross-migration of at least 12 million people. Some estimates put it at 18 million. That's like the population of the present day London and the South East of the UK moving elsewhere. Some 7 to 9 million moved from what became India to what was to become Pakistan. Those numbers were greater than those going the other way, although the Pakistan to India movement still embraced more than 5 million people.

The scale of the initial movement was incredible. In the first three months after Independence, 8 million people crossed the border to or from Pakistan. That works out at a movement of more than 100,000 souls, every day, for three months. It was in Punjab that the greatest spectacle of Partition was played out. More than 5 million of those who moved to Pakistan, moved from the east (India) to the west (Pakistan) inside what had been Punjab, which now split in two. Convoys of 40,000 people, some 20 miles long, fled from India on foot to Pakistan, many of them bringing only what they stood in.

This was ethnic cleansing on a scale of millions. The new Pakistan and new India would wash up on history's shores in waves of blood. The 'crescendo of violence' reached its peak in the months directly after the Partition of 14th and15th August 1947.

In her book on the Partition, Yasmin Khan makes the point that it was the 'phenomenal extent of the killing which distinguishes it as an event'. In case what Britain bequeathed a tortured India and Pakistan is overlooked, her acid words are worthy of note:

> Children watched as their parents were dismembered or burned alive, women were brutally raped and had their breasts and genitals mutilated and the entire populations of villages were summarily executed. Eye-witnesses in Punjab reported the putrid stench of corpses and the crimson blood-stains on walls, station concourses and roads . . . Broken bodies lay along roadsides and on train platforms, while charred wood and rubble were all that remained of large quarters of Amritsar and Lahore. The two cities were de facto war zones; barbed wire had to be coiled along the length of station platforms in Lahore to keep people apart, looted objects lay abandoned in deserted streets, vultures perched on walls . . . large suburban areas of bustling jewellers, bakeries and bookshops were now reduced to voluminous debris which took years to be bulldozed away.[1]

The numbers who perished are, to this day, disputed. To my family, and so many others, the extent of killing and dying was never clear, but the fear and the suffering they lived through would leave their souls scarred forever. A million deaths perhaps may seem too many with the benefit of hindsight; two hundred thousand dead, often quoted, seems far too few. The truth definitely lies much nearer that million figure than the latter. However, if there is some uncertainty about numbers there is none about the horror that engulfed those involved; there's no doubting the 'enormity of anguish and

1. Yasmin Khan, *The Great Partition* (Yale University Press, 2008).

suffering beyond imagining and beyond the human spirit's capacity to endure'.

The major problem was this – the killing had started and it couldn't be stopped. Each fresh killing on one side gave impetus to another blood-letting revenge. This tit-for-tat killing on both sides was of epic proportions – this wasn't an eye for an eye, it was tens of thousands of eyes for tens of thousand of eyes. There was no law across huge swathes of the entire continent. Families and generations were being wiped out in the violence. The hearts and the minds of the people across the Subcontinent had been partitioned, not just the territory.

The savagery knew no bounds. In *Freedom at Midnight*, the authors note that Captain R. E. Atkins, as he makes his way through the Punjab, found that in Lahore: 'The gutters . . . were running with blood. The beautiful Paris of the Orient was a vista of desolation and destruction. Whole streets of Hindu homes were ablaze while Muslim police and troops stood by watching.' When Atkins travelled on to Amritsar he reported that the Muslim sections of the city 'were nothing but heaps of bricks and debris, twisting curls of smoke drifting above them into the sky . . . the pungent aroma of decomposing corpses permeating the ruins.'

According to my father, at the time of the coming of Independence there had not yet been attacks and killings of Muslims in Khairanwala and the surrounding villages, even though there was a large Hindu-Sikh majority in those villages. But elsewhere in the area, it seemed to be an established trend that where there was a majority of Hindus and Sikhs in a village, it became a near certainty that they would attack the minority to force them out; terrifying them so much that they would flee, leaving land, home and possessions behind, which would then fall into the hands of the attackers. There was tit-for-tat killing on the Muslim side as well.

The panic first spread in Khairanwala because of the trickle of people passing through the village, making their way towards the border. They came with stories of killings and atrocities, of burnings, and terror behind them. There had been a long history of such 'communal violence' in the Subcontinent, but this was of a different order. This was horror on the move, and it had come to villages near to my family. That first trickle of flight to what would become Pakistan, in a matter of weeks, became a flood; hundreds on the move became thousands, and then hundreds of thousands.

At the time the first prophets of doom arrived the attitude taken by the Muslims in our village had been: 'Look at them! Are they crazy? Why would you want to leave your village, your land and your house? It won't happen to us. It won't happen here.' But, as the movement of people grew and grew, the possibility of having to flee was being debated in every Muslim household. Every family was still hoping for the best, but plans were being hatched to prepare for the worst.

Then came the news of the killings in nearby villages to Khairanwala. Folk who had shared milk from their cows with each other had turned on one another. My family had delayed and delayed and refused to go. Now they were being forced to consider the unthinkable – they would *have* to go. In my opinion, in the slaughter that took place at Partition it was the Muslims who suffered by far the most at the hands of Hindu and Sikh mobs. But undoubtedly a spiral of revenge violence – as I have already mentioned – developed on the Muslim side as well. This, certainly, is what happened in Saleempur where my family eventually settled. At the time of Partition there were about ten families of Hindus in the village. Every family – men, women and children – was eventually put to the sword in revenge killings, in response to rumours arriving of the slaughter of innocent Muslims elsewhere.

In the villages in Pakistan in those days, as is still the case, extended families lived together in keeping with the traditions of kinship to share the burdens of life, including buying or building a house and keeping a smallholding. My father, Abdullah, his parents, Omar and Alladin, his brothers Ghulam and Shah Mohammad, all lived together with their families. My mother's parents and other extended family lived in nearby villages within a ten-mile radius. This was, and remained, a network of support. I make this point because, when they finally succumbed to the dictates of Partition and had to make the trek, there were generations of the same families all caught up in this caravan of despair.

The last straw came in the shape of the leader of the village elders in Khairanwala. He was a Sikh. He told my uncle Ghulam and my father that there were armies of Sikh militants coming down the valley slaughtering every Muslim in their path. 'I can no longer guarantee your safety here. If you don't go you too will be slaughtered,' he told them. That same evening, after these warnings, my mother's brother, Ali, arrived at the house around midnight. He told them that huge numbers of Muslims in nearby villages had been murdered by marauding gangs of Sikhs. The most dire of his tidings was that among those who had been killed were family members – in-laws of his. So they left. They locked the doors and took the keys because, even then, there was still a faint feeling, a faint hope that after all the trouble had died down, maybe they would return.

Their first objective was to reach a place of safety and then wait for the arrival of the British army to guarantee a safe passage to the border. There had been transit camps set up to deal with the movement of people across the borderlands. The nearest of these camps to our village was less than five miles from Khairanwala and so it became the family's first stopping place. In spite of all the warnings and all the deliberations, the final departure was done in haste and wide-eyed panic.

It was dead of night. They didn't have time to take much and so left behind most of their prized possessions. The women, however, took their jewellery, concealed in their clothing. They left in search of the transit camp. My father and mother were put in charge of the two oxen and their bullock cart. They had no idea, at that point, that their journey beyond the newly established border between India and Pakistan would become a terrible march on foot of almost 150 miles.

The most precious item they took with them turned out to be a feather quilt. My grandmother Alladin had saved money – between 9,000 and 10,000 rupees in cash – and sewed this into the quilt, along with our land registration certificates for our holdings in Khairanwala. This is an indication of how relatively well off the family was. In those days 10,000 rupees was a considerable amount of money. This would prove to be the most precious quilt the family had ever owned. Before they set off, Alladin gave the quilt to my father. She didn't want to shoulder the responsibility of looking after it so she gave it to her favourite son.

The right to have a land concession in the new Pakistan, combined with judicious spending of the 'quilt' money is what allowed the family to gain their first land holdings when they reached their chosen destination in Pakistan. In fact, it is true to say that, had it not been for this piece of foresight from my grandmother, the entire history of the family could have been different – no land holdings in Pakistan, no money for my uncle Ghulam to travel again to the UK, and in the last resort, no Cash and Carry empire, and no Muslim Member of Parliament for Glasgow Govan.

The other life-saving move the family made concerned what they did with the money they had in the bank. Ghulam was advised to transfer the money held in the bank, in what was to become India, to an account in Karachi. They chose Karachi because that was where the head office of the local bank they were using was located. Further, among the uncertainties of the establishing of final borders, there was no doubt that Karachi would be within the new Pakistani state. It was a long time before the thousands of rupees wired to Karachi could be redeemed, but in due course they were. That part-funded my uncle Ghulam's return trip to Britain and further land purchases in Pakistan. The wire transfer had been made just in time – a matter of a day or two before they had to flee.

That night when the group reached the first transit camp, my grandmother, Alladin, made a confession. She told my father that she had left a large stash of gold coins buried in a metal box in the garden. Without letting anyone else into the secret, my father decided to return to the house to retrieve the money. When he reached there all that was left was the hole in the garden where the deposit box once had been. It seems that the family's loyal Hindu servant knew too many family secrets. The jewel of the family's life – the newly extended house – had already been ransacked and wrecked; the doors were all gone as well as the windows. In a matter of hours the house had been reduced to near ruin, in the riots and pillaging following their flight. All that remained now of their pride and aspirations of the past was a brick skeleton testifying to scale of disaster that had befallen them.

Father had returned alive to the camp but, alas, none the richer for what was undoubtedly a courageous, if desperate and foolhardy, expedition. That reality helped them reach another turning point. All the illusions that one day when all the divisions and differences had dissipated, there could be a return, had now gone. There was nothing to stay for, all was lost. They had to strike out for a new life in the new Pakistan.

There was another makeshift camp a further five miles away at a place called Meharpur, where they had been told there was greater security from attack among the greater numbers of people camped there. So after only one night in the transit camp, they headed to the bigger camp at Meharpur.

They would stay there for about a month, in the vain hope that the British Army or the Punjab Boundary Force would arrive one day to guarantee them safe passage to the border, wherever that was. My whole family and our neighbours had been transformed overnight into refugees. They needed to know that where they were going was better and safer than where they'd been, and that they could get there alive. They were desperate. They were driven by hope and fear. Many of them had never travelled beyond the village, ever.

It might be noted that in the early days after Partition there was nothing for the congregations of people in these so-called refugee camps other than a certain safety in numbers. There were no UN tents, no food or water rations, no international charities to give succour to the legions of the desperate. As time passed and the gravity of the crisis became irrefutable, the two new states began to make organised provision in state-run refugee camps.

However the gathering at Meharpur was not one of these state-sponsored camps, rather it had emerged as an unofficial refugee camp, a stopping place. The family found shelter there where they could. In these circumstances where there was nothing to eat, the women would stay with the children at night and the men of the family would go on foraging raids in gangs around the area to find food – to steal something from somewhere. They would steal fruit and vegetables from the fields; it was the time of the harvest. It wasn't their food, but if the farmers were Muslims they would have already fled before them. Food was stolen to survive. It was dangerous; if they got caught, they could be killed.

There were other gangs, Sikhs and Hindus, marauders, roaming the countryside killing innocent Muslims. One of our relatives was killed in an ambush in one of these attacks. For simple farmers and country people, these were the panic-stricken, seemingly never-ending, worst days of their lives. Eventually the realisation dawned that there was not going to be some sort of official safe passage to the border. At that time my father and his brother, Ghulam, had a further discussion about what was to be done. They decided the family group should split. The decision was taken so that there would be a increased likelihood that some of them would make it through, rather than all perishing together in some unforeseen calamity of violence.

My father, Abdullah, and mother, Rashida would lead one group and head for the border, with the oxen and cart providing respite from walking for the elderly and infirm in the group, including my grandfather, Omar. The other group was led by Ghulam. They would trek the 20 miles or so to the nearby city of Jullundur, and from there take the train to Amritsar and on to Lahore. (Jullundur is the name used during the British Raj for the nearest city to our village, Khairanwala. So I will use that spelling in this chapter. However for the purposes of identification it should be noted that the spelling, post-Partition, in India, became Jalandhar.)

My father's other brother, Shah Mohammad, had passed away before the horrors of Partition. His wife, Fatima Bibi, originally came from the Toba Tek Singh area, and so there were family relations there. The plan was agreed that both groups, taking different routes, would make for Fatima Bibi's village, Chak 331 GB/Saleempur, as it was known in what would be Pakistan. God willing, they could all be re-united there. Saleempur lay around 20 miles south of the town of Toba Tek Singh, in the district area of the same name. Toba Tek Singh was south west of Faisalabad, which in turn was west of Lahore. To-day if you took the Route 1 from Lahore to Saleempur it would be a journey of around 160 miles.

So the group, with Ghulam at its head, made their plans for heading to Toba Tek Singh in the far west. Ghulam's wife, Azmat Bibi, was in that group as were Fatima Bibi, the wife of Shah Mohammad, her two sons and my grandmother, Alladin. My father was especially close to his mother. He adored her, so, when the time came to part, there were tears and my grandmother wailed with the anguish of it all. He didn't know it then, but this was the last time Abdullah would see Alladin alive. She died on the road to Jullundur. The story in the family is that it was all too much for her and she collapsed and could not be saved. With the calamity of what was happening it seems that the parting with her favourite son became the 'final straw'. It was too much for her to endure.

The way we lost my grandmother remained a source of great personal pain for the family. Especially for Ghulam, until the day he died, as it was he who carried the sorrow of being there when my grandmother passed away. He had a great struggle to get Alladin buried properly, not least because the group weren't carrying spades with them for digging a grave. So Ghulam carried my grandmother's body on his shoulders for miles until he was able to find a spade to dig a grave. The grave wasn't marked, so where she was laid to rest has never been established.

It was commonplace for the bodies of those who had collapsed from exhaustion to be left where they fell, because of the pressure to keep moving in the human caravan heading for the border. Thankfully, that indignity was avoided for us. Despite such tribulations, Ghulam's group never gave up hope. Eventually they made it to a point where they could cover almost all of their journey by train to Toba Tek Singh, and then the last stretch to Saleempur, where there was solace and shelter with Fatima Bibi's relations. Their endurance had held. They had made it to Pakistan.

The group headed by Abdullah and Rashida had the same aim, but their route would be much different. They were going on foot with oxen and cart. Their first objective was the border crossing at Wagah, west of Amritsar on the road to Lahore. After what seemed like an eternity, they reached the main road beyond Amritsar. They were a mere few among the tens of thousands in the huge kafila heading west. It had taken weeks to reach here. Sometimes when there was forewarning of Sikh attacks they would stop during the day and advance more safely under cover of darkness. On other occasions they had to double back on their route, as news reached them that the road ahead was blocked by disturbances and killings.

My father used to talk vividly about the heat, the dust, the flies and the stench of rotting corpses. The flies came in black plagues.

Dust storms were frequent in the plains of the Punjab at that time of year, so, depending on their frequency, the convoys of refugees could resemble an army of ghosts blasted white in the wind and dust – shuffling forward, day after day, without respite. Collins and Lapierre describe the road from Amritsar to the border, then Lahore as a vision from hell:

> The forty-five miles from Amritsar to Lahore, along which so many passed, became a long open graveyard . . . Captain Atkins would always sprinkle a handkerchief with after-shave lotion and tie it around his face to temper the terrible smell. He remembered 'Every yard of the the way there was a body, some butchered, some dead of cholera. The vultures had become so bloated by their feasts they could no longer fly, and the wild dogs so demanding in their taste they ate only the livers of the corpses littering the road.[1]

The last part of the family expedition to Wagah was to become a living proof of the adage 'so near but yet so far'. Between the fields where they had stopped, only a matter of miles from the actual border post, was a no-man's land which had been turned into a war zone. Tales were being told of Sikh warriors appearing from nowhere and attacking the unwary in that territory of terror. I had always wondered if my father's tales of men having their heads lopped off by Sikhs wielding kirpans were apocryphal. Then one day I turned one of the pages of *Freedom at Midnight*:

> Lieutenant G.D. Lal would never forget an old Muslim in a column that he was escorting tugging towards Pakistan the only possession he had saved from his homestead, a goat. A dozen miles from the frontier of his new home, the old man's goat began a panicked dash toward a stand of sugar cane. The old man followed in frantic pursuit. Suddenly, like a vengeful wraith, a Sikh arose from the sugar cane, beheaded the old man and ran off with his goat.[2]

1. L. Collins and D. Lapierre, *Freedom at Midnight* (1982).
2. Collins and Lapierre, *op. cit.*

Such cruel realities meant that they were stuck where they were, for days on end. There would never be a way back; now it seemed there might not be a way forward. Salvation appeared in the form of a detachment of the Punjab Boundary Force, which arrived to guarantee their convoy an escort to the border. At last, they had made it to Wagah. And here, for the first time in an age, some good news. Repatriation officials at the border were explaining to the new arrivals that there were land concessions being made in district Faisalabad – here was the possibility of land to replace what had been lost in Khairanwala.

There and then my father and mother decided to head to Faisalabad. Of course they had made the pledge with Ghulam to try and reach district Toba Tek Singh, but this was the possibility of land which could not be neglected. In any case they had no way of knowing whether Ghulam and his group had survived or perished. The demands of the time meant that such an opportunity could never be squandered. Everyone was living on the verge of desperation. At this point no one in this company knew about the tragedy of my grandmother's passing, for example. They had to take decisions for their own well-being – nothing else. Thus far, they had come about 70 miles from the village to get to the border. The city of Faisalabad was still some 150 miles away, but within its district there was the promise of a new beginning for all. They travelled on.

Bashira, who would have become my eldest sister, was only around two years old at the time; she was being carried in the group which included my grandfather, Omar; they trudged wearily, desperately, towards Faisalabad. By now they were a solitary band. The mass movement of refugees had vanished. Still, though perilously few in number, they made it. When they reached the camp outside Faisalabad they were immediately able to make a compensation claim for a landholding. They were told that land was available at a village, 109 GB Roda, as it was called, east of the city of Faisalabad. It had been agreed by both governments that those who had owned land in India, and had to migrate to Pakistan, could get equivalent land holdings there provided they had certificates of land ownership. And similar arrangements were in place for those forced to travel, in the opposite direction, from Pakistan to India.

Accordingly, my father was able to negotiate for 18 acres of land at Roda which represented what the family had owned at Khairan-wala. There were three divisions of 6 acres – one for my father, one for my uncle Ghulam and one for Fatima's family. Our family had the property deeds to prove what they owned and were there in person to make their claim. Unfortunately they didn't get similar compensation for Alladin's considerable landholdings because the family did not have the proper property deeds to establish ownership. We always regretted that we didn't get our full entitlement in Roda. Still, they were all alive and thanked God for that. They knew they were a lot better off than many millions of others, and while it had been the worst of times, they had survived the journey. That said, if it were possible, greater heartaches were lying in wait.

A matter of a week or so after the family occupied the small mud-brick farmhouse in the village of Roda, little Bashira was consumed by a raging fever and died. It has never been established what was the cause of my sister's death other than a severe febrile condition, of some sort, which came on very suddenly. In the circumstances in Roda there was no doctor available to treat her, no hospital to which she could be admitted as an emergency. It might have been cholera, given the journey the family had been forced to take and the conditions they had to endure on the road and in the camps. The other likely condition, given her symptoms of severe fever, is meningitis, which was a scourge of the very young in those days.

My mother and father never talked about it much. All we know is that Bashira never settled at Roda. For days she asked my parents when she would see her grandmother, Alladin, and told them she wanted to go home. Then the fever came. It might be that Bashira might never have grown up to be a healthy child, that there was something wrong with her which, until that point, had not been detected. However, there's no doubt that, no matter what condition afflicted her, her chances of survival were immeasurably reduced by the horrors of Partition suffered by my family.

So, too, for Omar, my grandfather. Not long after Bashira died he had what we think was a stroke which left him lingering on the edge of death for months. My mother looked after him all that time; he had to be fed and washed as the resultant paralysis had left him bedridden. Then one night he passed away in his sleep. The only consolation, if there could be one, amid this Himalaya of sadness, was that Omar had the proper family funeral that could not be granted to Alladin. It had been the worst of times indeed.

Some weeks later my father made it to Saleempur. He had travelled there more in hope than expectation. When he was reunited with his brother and other members of the family there was an unprecedented, uncontrollable outburst of sheer joy. Tears flowed, first with celebratory happiness, and then when the story of Alladin's passing was told, followed by the news of the deaths of little Bashira and Omar, reported by my father, the shrieks of joy were replaced by the wailings of the broken-hearted.

So here, in my own family's story, was the experience of Partition, shared by millions on both sides of the new border; uncontrollable joy for those who survived the horrors, but unbearable sadness that the oldest and youngest in the family had fallen victim to those historic events. There was joy and sadness to follow when all those in Saleempur returned with my father to unite with the rest of the family in Roda. It had been a remarkable journey.

My father and Ghulam then made a plan that Ghulam would return to the UK. The idea was that Ghulam would go first to the UK to prepare the way for the rest of the family to go there at a later stage. Ghulam's wife, Azmat Bibi, did not want him to go to the UK. So the two brothers went to Karachi on the pretence of getting the money that was in a bank there; the money sent from Kharianwala before Partition. However, when they got there, Ghulam bought his ticket in Karachi for the journey to UK. Then, when the two brothers managed to get the rupees from the bank in Karachi, Ghulam started to prevaricate – he argued that perhaps they could use the windfall for a better life in Pakistan. My father told him it was too late for such considerations. The die was cast. The ship ticket had been purchased. A new chapter in the family history was about to open up.

The Early Years in Punjab 3

'There, behind barbed wire, on one side, lay India, and behind more barbed wire, on the other side, lay Pakistan. In between on a bit of earth which had no name lay Toba Tek Singh.'

Saadat Hasan Manto, *Mottled Dawn* (Penguin Books India, 1997).

I was born in Roda on 18 August 1952 into the searing summer heat of the Punjab. The kind of heat when it seems the Fahrenheit thermometer is about to run off the scales – 110°F (45°C) was common. Maybe that was a warning that hot times, or getting into 'hot water', would be with me for the rest of my life. I have never really been able to get used to the heat of summer in the Punjab. All the more so since my years in temperate Scotland have made my body clock accustomed to the days of endless rain and cold.

My earliest memories are of how central my mother's work was to the life of the family. This was dictated by the necessities of life in the village. If there is no electricity and no refrigerator, then the perishable staples of life – milk, yogurt and bread – have to be provided day by day. I can remember waking up, before sunrise, with the village in a misty grey light when the only noise was the sound of the crickets. Every day as I rubbed sleep from my eyes there was the vision of my mother who had risen from her bed long before me, working in the corner of the room making butter or yogurt from the cow's milk for breakfast time. She would be with one of my sisters pulling ropes to make the wooden paddle in the pot whisk the milk into butter or yoghurt. Breakfast was a chapati or a paratha with yogurt or maybe some curry from the previous night's meal. Mornings where there were boiled eggs or omelette were a treat. There was never lunch in my life then – only breakfast and the evening meal.

When the yoghurt-making was done mother took the buffaloes out of their enclosure in the other part of the house, fed them and put them out to the fields. Vegetables, fruit and cotton were picked by the women. My mother used to spin the cotton to make it into thread on an old wooden, foot-powered spinning wheel. The men would do the heavier work in the fields – ploughing, irrigating the fields daily and harvesting the crops when they were ready. Every day life had the same rhythm. These details may not be of interest to everyone but they are a record of what life was like there, as a contrast to what it would become much later in Glasgow.

My other recollection of those times is of my mother continually telling me to apply myself in school; that education was the key to a better life was her watchword. Even before I was school age she intoned daily: 'You must go to school and learn your lessons. You'll be clever. You'll go to the university and one day you'll be a doctor. You'll never have to work in the fields.'

Funnily enough my father did the same thing with my sister, Aroona, when she was in the UK. If you asked her she would tell you that my father insisted on the importance of studying because he believed that his not being able to read and write had been a huge handicap when he arrived in Britain. When he was young he didn't apply himself to his own education; he believed his future would be working on the farm, so who needed books and reading and writing? In fact he was working in the fields long before the end of his primary schooling, which he never finished.

My mother's insistence that I should become a doctor was a life-time mantra. Over the years it was given even greater emphasis, if that was possible, by two accidents. When I was about eight I broke my leg playing in the village. That would be in 1960. In those days there was no doctor or hospital in the area; instead there would be a healer in each village – usually a woman – who people would go to when they were injured and she would fix them up. The healer put my leg in two wooden splints. The bone didn't set and it was agony. It had to be reset at a later stage, in hospital, and caused me great discomfort for a very long time. In fact, the pain went on and on for months. That was the way things were; you just had to make do.

Then, while I was at High School, I dislocated my shoulder. I had been on holiday at my aunt's village, which was quite a long train journey from home. On my return journey I missed my train connection and had to walk about seven miles to my village. I got caught in torrential rains, fell going down an embankment and dislocated my right shoulder. It was dark when I got home, so I had a night in agony. In the morning I could hardly move. No-one in the village could help, so a few of my friends put me on a bed in the back of an oxen cart and we set off to a neighbouring village where we knew there was a healer. She couldn't put the shoulder back in place. I passed out with the pain. Still with oxen and cart, we went to the nearest town, Pir Mahal. No luck there, either.

Eventually we had to get a bus to another larger town. There we found a healer. My friends held me down while the healer put one foot on my chest and gave my right arm an enormous yank, which sorted the dislocation! I can still remember the huge relief from being in excruciating pain for the best part of a whole day. These rather mundane examples show how primitive life was in the villages of Pakistan when I was young. Perhaps they explain why my mother longed for me to become a doctor to serve the people of district Toba Tek Singh.

I never fulfilled my mother's cherished dream. It was my sister, Aroona, who did that. She's a doctor now, a General Practitioner in Glasgow. My own contribution to health care in my home area has been my charity work to build a new hospital at Rajana, and redeveloping another at Chichawatni. Nowadays, if you dislocate your shoulder in my home area you don't need to travel for hours in an oxen and cart, then get on a bus to find a healer somewhere! So maybe I partly fulfilled my mother's dreams.

1957 was a big year for the family. We left our holdings in Roda for yet another new beginning. I was five years old. By then, the family had been in Pakistan for ten years. My father's brother, Ghulam, never really settled in Roda and wanted all the family to relocate to Saleempur. That was where he had originally settled after Partition, and he had always liked the area.

So Ghulam made a deal with my father. He bought 30 acres of land in Saleempur. He gave the title for 6 acres to my father, Abdullah, so that he would have the same size of holding there as he had in Roda; that was on the understanding, at the time, that Abdullah would manage the remaining 24 acres on Ghulam's behalf. These were the deals of rural life in Pakistan in those times. Village 331GB/

Saleempur, as we knew it, was about four or five miles outside the nearest town, Pir Mahal, and some 20 miles south of the district capital, Toba Tek Singh. It was deep in the heart of rural Punjab. This style of identification by numbers, village 331GB, was a legacy from the days of the British Army's Ordnance mapping, seemingly designed to erase indigenous culture and establish the dominance of the Raj.

Although Ghulam had enough money to buy the land in Saleempur, our family were still a long way from being well off. Even in the new place our living conditions remained very basic. We had owned a brick house before Partition, in what became India. In Saleempur our home was a flat-roofed mud house, and we had to walk some distance to get to our land holdings. The house had two bedrooms and one sitting room. The livestock were kept in an enclosure attached to the house. There was no electricity, no water and no sanitation.

One of the big bonuses for me of life in our new place, in Saleempur, was that the primary school was actually in the village. Before, in our old place in Roda, it was a two-mile trek to primary school – a long way for me and my schoolmates when we were only five years old. When I left primary school my Middle School was in village 333GB. So once again I was walking two miles or more to the school house every morning, and two miles back. In Middle School there were classrooms but we were still sitting on the floor in class. There were no desks, no chairs, not even school benches. We were taught sitting on mats spread out on the floor. It's funny how you never forget some things – the teacher wielded his lathi stick liberally whenever he deemed it necessary to impress upon the class that if you were not paying attention there could be fearsome consequences. 'Yes Master! No Master!' was the order of the day.

In primary school the lessons were taught in Urdu. In Middle and High School the teaching was in Urdu and English. As the time approached for me to go to High School I can still remember the thrill of contemplating having a school desk to sit at for the first time in my life. By then, when I was eleven years old, I had a basic knowledge of English which meant that by the time I went to Government College in Faisalabad at 17, my English was good enough to become a second language for education purposes.

53

A year after the move to Saleempur my father left to work in the UK. It was 1958. I wouldn't see him again in the flesh for nine years. In 1967, he came back for about a year or so, before returning again to work in the UK. When he left I was six years old, and I cried for days because I never left his side when I was at home. I missed him so badly at first. He just told me that he was going to England with uncle Ghulam because he could earn much more money there and send it home to us so we could have a better life in Pakistan; it was always England he spoke of, not Scotland, or UK, just England.

I still have very clear recollections about my father's journey in 1958. He took a local train from the village to Shorkot, the nearest town of any size, and from there another train to faraway Karachi. That train journey was more than 500 miles. Then he boarded ship in Karachi for the 28-day journey to London. There were no telephones so we waited for weeks for news. Eventually, word came by telegram that father had made it to Glasgow.

My father told me a long time ago that he was haunted by his leaving us, and wondered if I, in particular, would understand how much he loved me and whether I would think that he had abandoned me. The truth is that, at first, the very fact that I did understand how much he loved me, made it more difficult to take. When I was young he had convinced me about how much he cared for me, so his departure raised the question: 'How could he leave me if he loved me so much?' However, as I grew older, especially when I could see the fruits of his sacrifice, and what it meant for our lives at home, doubts were replaced by admiration. Although I missed him still, the second question became: 'How could he have the strength to make such a personal sacrifice just for us?'

I have a huge respect for my father. Sadly he passed away in April 2013, but he is in my thoughts daily and I will never forget what he did for the family. I also have a huge respect for my mother for the way in which she accepted all the burdens of running the family home in his absence. All of us, my sisters, my brother and I, owe everything about where we are in life now, to them.

We had some sort of village connection in Glasgow, and so my father went there after he reached London. At first he lived with another family – they gave him a room, or more likely a bed in a room, and fed him and looked after him, free of charge, until he found his bearings. Kinship meant that newcomers were always offered this type of help. People looked after each other then – I don't suppose you would get that sort of generosity now.

His first job was selling clothes and other items from a suitcase, door to door. He had very little choice. He couldn't speak much English, far less write it. So, in those days, if you were from Pakistan, illiterate and couldn't speak much English, the best thing to do was to make a business connection with one of the Pakistani warehouses in Glasgow; it was simple, there you could do business in Punjabi.

My father would go to the warehouse and negotiate for goods – jumpers, shirts, ties and socks and household things. He would fill the case and then go to some of the more outlying districts of the city which did not have good local shops, and sell his wares to make a daily profit on what he had paid for them. At the warehouse they would give him some advice about prices so he had an idea what he had to charge to make a return. Over time, part of that profit was then paid to cancel the standing debts. He had to remember everything in his head as he could not read or write. I always remember that it was his mental arithmetic that astonished me when I first reached the UK.

The huge housing estates on the outskirts of Glasgow, like Pollok, Castlemilk, Drumchapel and Easterhouse, had been built as 'homes fit for heroes' after World War Two. They were miles from Glasgow's city centre and had few shops, so my father started hawking his goods in these peripheral housing areas, 'schemes' as they were known. After a while he branched out and made the working-class housing schemes in Port Glasgow, Greenock and Gourock his target, because there wasn't much competition there from other door-to-door traders. These towns were, after all, more than twenty miles from Glasgow. In those days some of the ferry connections to the islands in the Firth of Clyde departed from Gourock. This gave my father the idea of going to Rothesay on Bute – one of the biggest islands off the Clyde coast. He became a regular traveller there – first, by train to the coast, and then to Rothesay by ferry. He'd get the last boat back to Gourock or Wemyss Bay and then the train to Glasgow. It can be said without contradiction that the beginning of what became my £200 million a year Cash and Carry empire had its origins in trading out of a suitcase in Rothesay!

In time we had 20 acres in the Saleempur area, but our family also managed my uncle Ghulam's holding which had grown to around 75 acres. Everyone thought that this was our land, so – when I came of age – I had the status in the village of being a landowner with 95 acres! I also had a certain social standing, because I was good in school and could read and write; most of the villagers couldn't. People would come to me to read their letters for them, and in most cases, to make the necessary replies on their behalf. That involved giving advice about what the reply should be, so, by the time I was a teenager, my opinion on a host of issues was respected throughout the village. I started the letter-writing when I was as young as eight years old, and as I grew older that skill became all the more significant for my reputation.

In those days there were no telephones and any urgent business would be done by telegram. A telegram usually meant bad news. The villagers would come to me at our house carrying the telegram and I would read it to them. Of course it would sometimes be good news – somebody got a new job, there was to be a marriage or a child born – but they always came with some trepidation. One time I remember a woman in the village arrived in a terrible state of anxiety. Clutching her telegram she told me she was sure it would contain bad tidings. 'Not at all,' I told her 'you've just become a grandmother!' 'There's a telegram, we have to go and see Sarwar' became an everyday phrase in the village.

All this, the land-holding, the letters and my father's absence, were influential in my becoming the 'Headman' or 'Chief', of the village by the time I was in my mid-teens. It is strange to think of this now, because I must have been one of the youngest 'elders' in Pakistan. In the earliest days we had sharecroppers on our land. There was little money in circulation then, so everything was done through barter. The landholding was split among tenant farmers and they had to give fifty per cent of what they harvested to us, as the way of paying rent for the land. At harvest time they came to the house, the crops were weighed and we were given half. We sold the excess we had at the market.

Over the years, the sharecropping system changed as the money economy developed, and cash replaced barter. There was a transitional stage when the rent was paid partly in crops and partly in rupees. In time, everything was paid in rupees. We rented the land at the rate of 2000 rupees per acre, per year. So, for a 10-acre smallholding we would be paid 20,000 rupees each year – half at 6 months, the balance at 12 months. The land was not all in the same place – there would be 10 acres here, 5 acres there, and each parcel was let to a family. As I recall the total family landholding – our land and Ghulam's holdings – produced an annual income of almost 200,000 rupees. Costs of production were shared with each farmer, but the size of the landholding we had managed to purchase still made us one of the better-off families in the village.

The ownership of land was the key to status in the village. The poor were defined by the fact that they did not own any land. When I was young I considered the caste system – which developed originally when land was the only measure of wealth – as part of the natural order of things. Now I see it entirely differently. The rigid caste system, and the enormous difficulty of breaking out of caste, has condemned countless millions to lives of poverty for generation after generation. Caste still determines the life chances of the poor from birth.

Since the lower castes had no land, they had to find other ways of making a living, so they became artisans supplying services of one type or another. For example, there were travelling barbers who would do haircuts and shaving, and provide that service for everyone in the village. In sharecropping times they would be paid by the village twice a year with a certain amount of the crops. That's just one example; there were others who provided other services like welding pots and pans or, in later times, fixing machinery or tractors. In our village there was even a makeshift laundry service provided by the 'dobis' as they were known. They would come and collect the family clothes and take them to the nearby canal and wash and dry them. They would then heat their irons on hot coals and iron the clothes, which would then be brought back to us. All those people, who were landless peasants, were tradesmen known as 'kummees' – the lower classes – those who had no land on which to make a living.

57

Among their number were the '*mashkees*' – the water men who came to the village with huge leather sacks on their backs filled with water. They would come and fill the large mud pots in the house from the nozzle on the leather bag. They would go back to the water course, return, and serve the next house and so on. In the villages which were designed by the British, there was more order. Each of them had a central square, in the middle of which was a well. So in those villages the water-men frequently used water drawn from those wells to serve the villagers. Like the barbers, in the early times they would be paid in wheat, until the economy went over to cash. The delivery of water is still done in villages without running water today, but now the supply comes in big tanks pulled by oxen or a tractor.

Today, this work is still carried out by landless workers. The poor who were servants, working at other people's homes as cooks or cleaners, would be paid in wheat, and some cash maybe once a month. I accepted the system when I was young, but I always tried to look after people. Even later when I was earning £40 a week in Glasgow, I still tried to save and send some money back to the village, so our family relations could give money to the poor. The whole thing about charity in my life came, not only from my faith, but also from my mother. When anyone came to our house to ask for help, I never once saw her refuse a request. The poor would come to ask for money to pay for a daughter to be married, or to pay off the debt collectors or a thousand other things, and and she never let them down. Sometimes she made loans; other times she just gave the desperate ones the money. I wouldn't like this to appear immodest but I think I have managed, in a different way, to carry on the same traditions. Certainly my present charity work had its beginnings in my mother's philanthropy in the village.

When I lived in Glasgow, our family home had every possible facility you would ever need. Sometimes when I go to the bathroom and turn on a tap it takes me back to the way life was in my days in the village. The latter has always made me appreciate the former. I am always telling my children that they don't know how lucky they are. And sometimes it makes me a little angry, because I don't think they appreciate how easy their lives have been and how much they have. Because of my life experience, from time to time when I turn on the tap and the hot water gushes, I have a smile to myself. I appreciate that, because I still remember the way life was for my family in my early years.

It is important to acknowledge that we in the West are the privileged of the Earth. There are billions of people – according to *The Economist*, 70 million of them in Pakistan alone – who have no access to clean drinking water. During my time as Governor of Punjab I created a clean water project for schools in Punjab by installing water filtration plants. It was not on a huge scale, but in the schools and residential homes where water plants were installed it made a huge difference to the health of the children involved. In one orphanage the incidence of chronic diarrhoea among the children dropped by almost 50% in the first month! Humanity has the technology to send a space probe to Mars, 150 million miles away, yet people die because they don't have medicines; because they don't have doctors. This global inequality is an eternal shame on us all.

When I look back on the history of my family it becomes clear that there have been a series of turning points which have been crucial in determining our future. Of these, Partition was probably the greatest of all. The move from Roda to Saleempur was also vital, because the new lands there made us relatively well off for the first time. The third great turning point was the departure of my father to work in the UK. That meant a considerably increased income for the family in Pakistan as a result of the money he sent back, but, as I have said, it also meant a huge sacrifice for my father. It also inspired a certain lifetime resilience in those he left behind. After dealing with my father's departure, it seemed that the family became capable of shouldering any burden.

In the context of turning points, 1974 emerges as another significant year for my family. By then my younger brother, Ramzan, was approaching his sixteenth birthday, and so he was reaching the cut-off point for being allowed into the UK as one of my father's dependents. My mother begged my father to take Ramzan to the UK. In the end my mother, brother and younger sister, Aroona, all went – leaving me with my younger sister, Nasreen, to run all the family affairs in Pakistan. By then we were both over 18 and so no longer qualified to go to the UK as dependent children. As had been the case before, when my father left for the UK, any resentments I might have felt did not endure. In a matter of weeks I realised that, at 21 years old, I was truly in charge of the family business and was now highly respected in the village in my own right.

The next two years became a proving ground. I had to take all the business decisions about the running of the landholdings. For nearly 100 acres of land rented to tenants, that was a considerable responsibility. It included managing the income and expenditure and securing proper margins which actually allowed us to invest in expanded landholdings later on. Many years later, this experience of decision-making would prove to be crucial, when I was faced with huge turning points in my own business life in Scotland. The two years of challenge in Saleempur produced a personal dividend of self-confidence for me without which I would never have achieved what I did in business and politics later in life.

I have recorded here what I consider to be the great turning points in my family history, some of which also proved to be highly significant for me. Another series of events which had a huge influence on my later career took place a year before my mother, Ramzan and Aroona left for Glasgow. In 1972 I became a political activist and strike-leader. In this instance, history forced this on me – it was never the case that I was looking for trouble. Rather it came looking for me. Nonetheless, the challenges I endured prepared me for those which would confront me in the years to come. I suppose, like so many, I had first become political, with a small 'p', in 1968, when I was in High School. That was during the national movement against the Ayub Khan military dictatorship. We were organised through the students' union. On days of protest we would go to the town and have sit-down demonstrations to block the roads, yelling slogans like 'Ayub Khan out'. It all started with Zulfikar Ali Bhutto opposing Khan's dictatorship. In 1965 there was the war between Pakistan and India over Kashmir. Eventually Ayub Khan and Shastri, the Indian prime minister, went to Tashkent in Uzbekistan to negotiate a ceasefire in the war. The agreement, pressed upon both protagonists by Moscow and Washington, became known as the Tashkent Declaration. It turned out to be Ayub Khan's political death-certificate.

From that time on, Bhutto accused Ayub Khan of selling out Pakistan's interests in the deal. That became the inspiration for the movement against Khan which, early in 1969, brought him down. Khan had been in power since 1958 as the nation's first military dictator, and had been responsible for providing the USA with secret military bases, from which they launched covert actions against the USSR including, in May 1960, Gary Powers' spy-flight in a U-2 plane which was shot down in Soviet airspace. That, and India's closer relationship with Moscow at that time, meant that the Russians were always going to favour Shastri and not Ayub Khan.

The anti-Khan campaign was my first taste of politics. That developed further when Zulkifar Ali Bhutto formed the Pakistan People's Party (PPP). That would be the first time I had any coherent thoughts about politics as a collection of ideas which added up to a political philosophy. Bhutto was seen as a radical socialist who was for the poor and against the rich. He campaigned about poverty and inequality, and that made him an enormously popular figure with the masses. Here was someone who wanted things to be different. Here was a champion for the dispossessed. Suddenly it appeared that there was a chance of a new Pakistan.

But if the Ayub Khan campaign leading to the coming of the PPP was my political baptism, it was, perhaps ironically, a local campaign against a PPP-controlled administration in Punjab province which gave me my real coming of age in politics.

In mid-1972 the National Irrigation Department suddenly cut the irrigation waters to the countryside by half. The distribution system ran from the rivers and central reservoirs through irrigation canals, and then branch channels from the canals took the water to local areas. Our belief was that it wasn't a cut to save money, but a diversion of the waters away from our area to another where the better-off had paid big bribes to make this happen. Half the water meant half the land was not irrigated, which, in turn, meant a halving of the crops which could be produced. It also meant we couldn't grow wheat any longer because that needs so much water; the same for animal feed. There were around 40 villages in our irrigation catchment area; around 60,000 people living on the land were directly affected. Overnight, the farmers were faced with a looming disaster.

We organised big protests at the government offices in the local town, Pir Mahal, but to no avail. The local officials told us they couldn't do anything. So then we organised a big public meeting of all the villages and all the farmers to discuss our strategy. The time had come to fight. This was not like a trade-union dispute over wages and conditions in a Western economy, rather it was a life and death struggle. Rather than being slowly starved to death we decided we would be better off fighting to the finish – 'Better dead than only half alive' – became the slogan of the hour.

We gave the government in Punjab one month's notice; if they did not restore the water supply at the original level to our lands we would shut it off and not take *any* water to our lands. We declared we would then stop paying their water taxes in retaliation. Shutting off the water supply to our lands carried the threat of flooding elsewhere in the system, since we were not draining off our supply. No taxes and floods. These were the two bullets in our guns of protest, although we offered not to take this action at all if the waters were restored to their original levels. The National Irrigation Department planned to bribe some of the farmers not to join the protest by supplying them with the normal amounts of water and starving the rest out who wouldn't do the deal. I heard about this tactic from some of the farmers in our area who had been approached, so we called another big meeting for the day before the planned shut-off.

Everyone in the meeting had to come to the front and take an oath on the Quran. It was along the lines of 'We will support the protest, we will shut off the water tomorrow, and we swear we will not be bought off. We swear on the Quran!' Everyone there took the oath. We decided that the following morning, at six o'clock, all the farmers would join the protest – every single water course from the canal would be shut off: 'Better dead than only half alive' for sure. After the pipes were blocked we planned to march on the government offices in Pir Mahal in protest.

After this the police started to make arrests of the leadership of the movement. In the first sweep they arrested hundreds of farmers, including the General Secretary and President of the Farmer's Association, which was then banned under the existing emergency laws. A few days later, we had a meeting where we decided on a new tactic. It was based on the civil disobedience idea of peaceful protest – *Satyagraha* – that had been part of the struggle to throw the British out of the Subcontinent. One day after another, thousands of farmers would go to local government headquarters and police offices and make a sit-down protest. We had struck a deal with the police chiefs that we would have peaceful demonstrations, and then 50 farmers would come forward each day to be arrested – 'Fill the Jails' was the slogan.

After a week or two of this, the jails in Toba Tek Singh and Faisalabad were full to bursting point. To be fair, at first the police were sympathetic to the farmers. However, that didn't last long. Once it was realised that our tactics had filled the jails, the police changed their strategy and became viciously brutal. One day the 50 protesters who were volunteering to be jailed were arrested but not put in prison. Instead they were held in the central courtyard of the police headquarters during the day. Then that night there was a co-ordinated attack. All those in the courtyard were severely beaten by a huge contingent of police. Heads were cracked and bones broken everywhere. It was a terror tactic to stop the sit-down strikes and break the protest movement, but it didn't succeed.

I emerged as the eventual leader of the whole campaign. I was forceful and outspoken and I quickly became prominent in the movement. I had spoken at one of the early protest rallies, where I gave a fiery speech in which I drew on the teachings of Islam. The Imam Hussain was the Prophet's grandson and is one of the great martyrs of Islam. He symbolises the struggle against tyranny for the oppressed. His tomb today is in Karbala, in southern Iraq. It was there in the desert that Hussain's forces stood against the ruler and tyrant of Syria, Yazid. Imam Hussain refused to pay allegiance to Yazid, whom he claimed was departing from the ways of the Prophet and Islam. Days before the final battle in which Hussain was martyred, the enemy forces blocked the river waters flowing to Hussain and his men as a tactic to weaken them before battle.

I drew on this story in my speech to the farmers. I said: 'Today we are fighting the modern-day Yazids, who, like those of old, are depriving the righteous of water. Like the Prophet's grandson we shall not pay allegiance to our Yazids, we shall never submit to their tyranny. Better dead than only half alive!' Well, it was like I had detonated a human explosion. They loved it. I had touched their souls and there were rolling roars of approval. I was acclaimed as the Acting General Secretary of the Association – which was re-named the Society to Defend the Rights of Farmers to avoid the emergency laws which had banned the Farmers' Association.

As a result, the police identified me as a target, and for weeks I was forced to go on the run. I never slept in the same house for consecutive nights. On one of our biggest demonstrations, a phalanx of armed policemen tried to break through our ranks to get to me to arrest me as the leader. But the human barrier of hundreds of farmers blocking their path saved the day, despite the beatings they had to suffer.

Day by day the protest movement was growing, with more and more farmers blocking their channels and not taking in the irrigation waters. What has to be understood is that the farmers saw this as being all or nothing. They understood that their future was at stake; they knew they were confronting a probable catastrophe and so they knew they had nothing to lose. After a few weeks the protests spread widely across the Punjab, as almost every famers' association in Punjab joined our struggle.

Eventually the government agreed to send the Irrigation Minister to meet us. We insisted that the meeting be held in Pir Mahal in front of the the main town buildings. More than 5,000 farmers turned up. I demanded that the waters be restored to the previous level and I warned the Minister that we would never give up the struggle until our demands were met. I said that we would continue our campaign unless the government agreed, in writing, that they would restore the waters. I raged against the injustice of it all, the police brutality and beatings: 'This, all from the Pakistan People's Party government of the Punjab province – the same PPP who told the world that it was on the side of the poor and the workers and against all the privileges of the rich and powerful.' Then I yelled at the top of my voice: 'Well, we are poor, and we are workers, but the PPP of the Punjab is not on our side! And we will not forget this!'

It was a very emotional speech and, to be honest, I think that the Irrigation Minister was surprised by the strength of feeling in the crowd and what he had heard and seen about what was going on.

Before the rally started we had paraded about three dozen farmers who had received the most severe beatings. After it we insisted he should come with us to the hospital to see those who were even more severely injured: 'Look, this is how the Government is dealing with peaceful protests,' we told him. After that the Irrigation Minister invited us to a meeting the next day at his offices in Lahore.

At the meeting in Lahore we told him that we had taken legal advice and found out that, by law, the Government had to give six months' notice to farmers about any reduction in water supplies, and that during that time there had to be consultation. The law also stated that after consultation the maximum adjustment, at any one time, was ten per cent. So they didn't have the authority, even after consultation, to do more than a ten per cent cut. And here we had been faced with a fifty per cent cut for which there had been no consultation.

The minister proposed that there should be an independent arbitration, and that, if we agreed to this, those in jail could be released and meantime, until its findings were known, the irrigation waters would be restored to their previous level. There was a senior retired chief engineer who had been with the Irrigation Department for many years who was well-respected locally; we agreed to his conducting the arbitration.

The findings were published two weeks later. The irrigation waters would be restored permanently to their previous level! In return, for nothing, the farmers would clear the irrigation canal from the silt build up. There would be no charges made against the President and General Secretary of the Association, nor the others who had been thrown in jail. They would be released immediately.

It was a tumultuous victory. There were tears of joy on our side. The lesson I learned from this struggle stayed with me for the rest of my life – 'Never, never, give up the fight!'

Later in the year, what would turn out to be beginning of another life-changing event for me took place. My uncle Ghulam, his wife and his daughter, Perveen, came to visit Pakistan from Lossiemouth in Scotland. I met them all when they landed at Faisalabad Airport. Perveen and her parents stayed in Saleempur for about three months. I was still going to College and staying there during the week, but we saw each other at weekends. I think it was my mother who first raised the possibility with my uncle of Perveen and I getting married. Later on, when my mother arrived in Scotland, she and my father went to Lossiemouth, met my uncle and his family, and the marriage was arranged. At this point Perveen's father told her that marrying me would probably mean that she would have to leave Scotland to return to Pakistan to live there with me, because I did not have rights to emigrate to the UK. To my eternal gratitude she told her father that this made no difference, because she was sure that she wanted to marry me.

Exactly when we would be married was still in doubt, because of the obstacles to my emigration to the UK. Then possibilities took a dramatic turn. Late in 1974, the Labour Government changed the immigration laws. For the first time, this allowed women whose spouse or fiancé was still living in Commonwealth countries to bring them to the UK. This meant that, as Perveen's fiancé, I could leave Pakistan and go to the UK to marry her and settle there.

Perveen was my cousin and cousins marrying is not the usual practice in Britain. In Pakistan, however, in the rural areas in particular, due to the isolation of life in the villages and the poverty which forces family and extended family to come together to share living costs, it is still commonplace for cousins to marry. The security given by the kinship of the extended family and tribe affects social relations. It is still a tradition in the countryside for whole families to live together and common for cousins to marry.

My journey to the UK was from Faisalabad by plane to Karachi, then Karachi to London, then London to Glasgow. When I boarded in Faisalabad it was the first time I had been in an aeroplane. It was strange and not a little discomfiting. A friend of mine told me I should travel from Pakistan in national dress so I travelled in my *shalwar kameez* – the long shirt with the baggy trousers. My two nieces, Ruksana and Sameena, met me at the airport. They had been brought up in Lossiemouth and had never been in Pakistan – so they thought I had travelled to the UK in my pyjamas! When I phoned Perveen the next day, she asked me why I had come from Pakistan in my pyjamas, because the nieces had been embarrassed at the airport!

We got married on 19 July 1976. I had left Pakistan two months before that in May. Ghulam had been in Scotland a long time by then, and was almost half-Scottish; they were the only Pakistani family in Lossiemouth. The wedding ceremony was first an Islamic service, and then we went to the local Church of Scotland to get married by its minister, the Reverend Forbes Watt, in a second service. That is what Ghulam wanted, so that was the way it was done. Ghulam arranged it all.

Mind you, the events of the wedding day may have given Ghulam second thoughts. The minibus in which my wedding party were driving to Lossiemouth conked out half way there. It seems somebody thought it was an amusing trick to put sugar in our petrol tank. We arrived two hours late which meant that we managed to reach the Church of Scotland service with only minutes to spare before the minister gave up and closed the church!

When Perveen came to stay with my family in our tenement flat in Glasgow – in Cottar Street, Maryhill – my life got better, but before that I must admit I had a rough time. I had become depressed. I had expected so much and I was now achieving so little. From a life of freedom, open air and listening to the birds singing in the sunshine, here I was in dark and dank Glasgow, where it seemed to rain constantly; everything was a struggle, with the odds stacked against us. The only thing I was making was more and more debts. I kept wondering, day after day, how I had chosen this path. How could all this lead to a better life than what I had at home in Pakistan? It was all so difficult and demoralising.

From Corner Shop to a Cash and Carry Empire 4

'Anyone we were selling eggs to, we said, "Right, here's the cheese as well!"'

Mohammad Sarwar, February 2013

'We were taking big leaps forward in the business, armed only with a hope, a prayer and an electronic calculator.'

Mohammad Sarwar, February 2013

There's a religious principle in Islam about Heaven and Hell; it is part of our beliefs. If someone's good deeds in life are greater than their sins, they will get entry to Paradise. If the balance is the other way, then entry to Paradise is denied and they go to Hell. There is a proverbial story about a man arriving at the gates of Heaven. The angels tell him that his good deeds in life are matched exactly by his sins, so, in this situation, he can choose whether to go to Heaven or Hell. The angels take him to Heaven, where it is very quiet and people are sitting reading the Quran and praying. Hardly a word is spoken. Then the angels take the man to have a look at Hell. The Devil meets him at the gates and takes him for a short tour. There, where the sinners are, it looks like a gigantic party with dancing, drinking, smoking, gambling and debauchery of all sorts. The man is tempted and decides Hell looks better.

So he goes back to see the angels and tells them he is going to Hell. When he gets there, the Devil prepares to throw him into the burning inferno below. 'What happened to the everlasting party, the drinking, the gambling and the women?' the man asks. The Devil replies: 'Ah well, what I showed you was just a showpiece. You didn't expect me to tell you what it was really like. In life nobody ever tells you what it is really like, do they?'

The old story certainly rang true for those who had been to Britain and came back to Pakistan to see their family – 'Nobody told us what it was really like'. Everyone who came back from Britain said it was 'a land flowing with milk and honey', that 'there was money growing on trees', and if you worked hard you couldn't fail to get rich. Of course, in retrospect I realise that this is the emigrant's universal tale; no one ever wants to admit that they have uprooted their lives and gone off in search of betterment only to have to admit to their families that life is as difficult, if not worse, in their new country. This way the myths of 'money growing on trees' and 'streets paved with gold' are perpetuated and the next generation packs its bags to follow suit.

That included me, so in 1976 my plan was simple. I would go to the UK, work long enough to amass a small fortune, and then return to Pakistan a rich man. I soon found the words of the old story to be brutally real. What I had been told about the UK, like the man seduced by the debauchery of Hell, turned out to be untrue – nobody had told me what it was really like. My first months in Glasgow were among the toughest of my life. I worked as hard as I ever had, and was nearly penniless.

My brother Ramzan had gone to the UK long before me, and had a shop in the city's Maryhill district – in partnership with a distant cousin, Mohammad Ashraf. My first start was in the shop as a shelf-packer. It soon became clear that there were not enough takings for three wages, and I had to try to make a living some other way. I decided to try the markets. There were no massive shopping malls in those days, but most towns in Central Scotland had significant street markets two or three days a week. They were hugely popular, as people, especially the less well-off, went there looking to buy all manner of goods at bargain prices.

I bought an old van for around £200 and went to the big Pakistani-owned warehouses, like Sher Brothers and Zaman Brothers, to start the business on credit; much like my father had done before me. I bought a stall which I had to erect on whatever pitch I had negotiated with the market-owners and then at the end of the day's trade I dismantled it and packed up the van ready to move on to the next pitch the following day. I negotiated stalls for the sale of cheap clothes – anoraks, jackets, knitwear, shirts and trousers – in Edinburgh, Coatbridge, Airdrie, Paisley and Largs, and for months

I traded there trying to make enough money for myself and Perveen to make ends meet.

However, instead of making a living I was actually running up debts. It was very dispiriting. I was living on the edge of depression. One day Perveen's father came to my market stall in Airdrie. He told me he knew that the business wasn't making any money, and offered to buy me a clothes shop he knew was for sale, and said he would pay me to run it for him. I was tempted, but I knew that if I agreed that would only be the beginning; I would be in his debt forever. Even though I was in financial trouble, I couldn't swallow enough of my pride to allow me to accept his offer. I was wavering but, although in desperate straits, refused his proposal.

I can still remember the day I decided that I had to give up the stall business. It was heartbreaking. I was on the pitch in Largs. At the start of the day I had to lay out £10.00 for petrol. By 12 o'clock I had not made a single penny, and along comes the market boss to collect his rent for the pitch, which was £5.00. So by one o'clock I was £15.00 out of pocket and hadn't made a single sale. I didn't make a sale for the rest of the day and, near to tears, I decided there and then, 'No more'. That was after about six months – all had come to nothing; in fact I had debts of about £300.

On that very day I learned a secret. I asked the stallholders near my pitch how they could they make ends meet running a market stall, because I had failed. I told them that despite my best efforts I couldn't make a profit. Two of the characters in the market then told me, 'Mohammad, the secret is to run the stall *and* claim social security. That's the way to make ends meet and more. That's what you should do.'

I can't say that in my desperate financial state this did not have a certain appeal. But there and then I decided against it, I thought that apart from it being illegal, claiming benefits would become like an addiction which I could never shake off. I had to find another way. Maybe if I had taken that route then and subsequently been found out and prosecuted as a benefits cheat, the stain on my character it represented would have barred the gate to my becoming an MP some 20 years later!

By this time my brother's business – the store he ran with his partner Ashraf – was also in a parlous state. His debts weren't in the hundreds, but the thousands. However, you might say, with the benefit of hindsight, this cloud would turn out to have a silver lining. Ramzan was totally fed up and wanted to get out of the shop. I felt that somehow Perveen and I could make a better go of the business. We decided to take a chance – frankly, based only on a hunch that the business had potential that wasn't being realised. Perveen had saved some money from her time in Lossiemouth – £2,500 – so we used that to buy the shop and the stock from Ramzan and Ashraf.

I went to the bank and told them I was putting all the money we had into the shop, because I thought it had great potential. The bank – the United Bank Ltd – matched our £2,500. It was all a huge challenge; the shop was in a terrible state, and there were big debts owed to the suppliers – we owed money to the bread-man, we owed money to the milkman, we owed money to the rolls-man, and we owed money to the eggs-man. It seemed we owed money to everyone. When the debts were added up the total owed was about £6,000 – including to the bigger Cash and Carry places.

I told all the creditors the same story – that I was the new owner and thereby not liable for the previous owners' debts. The stock in the shop was worth £2,000 and the debts £6,000. But the creditors spoke with one voice: 'This is what you guys do. You change the ownership to the brother and think you can get rid of the debts that way.' I insisted I was not liable for the debts, but told them that, if they would allow me time, then I would pay the debts anyway. Some agreed on a payback over a year, and some of the bigger creditors, who were owed larger amounts, settled for a two-year pay-off. It was a very risky leap of faith. Not least because the the creditors didn't know we had a plague of rats which were, at that point, literally eating the shop's profits.

The shop was at 925 Maryhill Road, in the north of Glasgow, which was a redevelopment area. As each of the old tenements was demolished, the rats migrated to the next one and, in due course, the plague reached the doors of the shop at 925. Left to their own devices, what the rats could consume overnight was little short of in-credible. Night after night they wreaked terrible destruction – bread, milk, biscuits and chocolate were all set upon to satisfy their appar-ently everlasting hunger. They were even capable of eating into juice cartons and getting the plastic tops off lemonade bottles – presumably so they could have a drink to wash down the chocolate biscuits!

Now we had rats in Pakistan, of course, but the Glasgow breed were much more difficult to exterminate. We tried everything – poison, more poison, strong enough to kill a horse, and then traps. Then we got two cats which, believe it or not, were killed by the rats. I had left Saleempur, in Pakistan, and now I was involved in a life or death struggle, in Glasgow, with rats as big, if not bigger than, cats. About three weeks after I took over I was standing in the shop regretting the decision to take it on. An older man came into the shop. He said that I was looking pretty glum and asked me what was wrong. I told him we had a never-ending problem with rats which we could not conquer and that, frankly, it was on the verge of driving me out of business given that the takings hardly matched the amount of stock that the rats were destroying ever night.

He said: 'I'm Peter. I'll help you beat the rats.' Peter suggested that all round the walls of the shop we should move the shelves forward about two feet. Then we would build a wall in the space created, seal it at the top also, and so create a brick wall, all round the inside of the shop, that the rats could not penetrate. I asked Peter how many days I would have to close the shop to get the work done. 'None,' he said, 'I'll do it at night after you close at six.'

That day we went to a builders' merchants and bought bricks, sand and cement. It cost me around £200, as far as I can remember. Peter set to work after the shop closed at six. It took him a week to complete the brick wall sealing the inside of the shop. I think I paid him £100. It was the best £300 in total that I have ever spent in my life. Peter, the Pied Piper of Maryhill, banished the rats and saved my business. After that he became a family friend, and for many years I employed Peter as the handyman of the business.

Very soon after the rats had gone, the shop started to make money. Perveen and I were staying with my father and mother, and my brother and sister, at 10 Cottar Street, in Maryhill. For months I couldn't see anything other than dark, dank tenements and rain. Now, suddenly, it was if the clouds had lifted and life had possibilities in Glasgow, after all. That was an important lesson for us; where Ramzan and Ashraf had failed, Perveen and I had succeeded. We had beaten the rats. My brother went off to work as a bus conductor. But our victory against the rats, and their insatiable appetites, would prove to be a turning point which, much later, would lead to great business success.

With the shop making profits I started paying all the creditors weekly, in some cases £10.00 a week and others much more. I figured that if I owed someone money and was paying them every week, they must realise that my intentions were serious; I was buying supplies in cash and also paying something to the previous balance. In little more than a year I had paid off all the debts. All of this was extremely good for my reputation – 'You can trust Sarwar. He will pay you,' seemed to become the general point of view. This was indicated by the fact that after six months the suppliers had started giving me goods on credit, which took some pressure off the business.

This perception that I was trustworthy was all the more important, because there had been a number of bigger Asian merchants whose behaviour had tarnished the Asian community's reputation. Around this time a number of the bigger merchants had relentlessly extended their credit limits at the bank and then, once the new higher limit had been reached, absconded to India or Pakistan, leaving all their creditors high and dry. In some cases the limits had been reached by a huge cash withdrawal from the bank, before departure to the Subcontinent the following day. In other cases there was no flight to India or Pakistan; instead debts were written off by the debtors declaring bankruptcy.

With all these stories swirling round the town, it was important to have established a record for payment and trustworthiness. So in our first year business was good. We had solved the rats problem, all the debts had been paid off, and there was enough in the bank to invest in some improvements. At this time things were looking up, although I might mention that as well as real rats there were, from time to time, some human rats to deal with – racist rats.

They were the ones who delivered the occasional venomous asides, usually attached, one way or another, to the epithet: 'Paki bastard . . .'. But it seldom got beyond gratuitous insults. I remember one day a group of louts started abusing me when I was unloading the van for the shop. Then an older gent, who was passing, came up to me and said: 'Just ignore them son, I'm really sorry. But I'm glad you didn't respond to them because one day, with all your hard work, you will be a success in this country, and when that happens they will still be nothing more than a crowd of thugs.' The words of the elderly Glaswegian had a big effect on me. Somehow they suddenly convinced me that I should not let things get on top of me – that I shouldn't let things get me down. Soldier on, always keep going, never give up. Beating the rats and racism actually gave us faith in our future. It was simple but true.

Then, about six months later, a letter dropped through the letterbox. It was a notice from Glasgow City Council that the shop was on the list for demolition, by the Council, under new clearance plans. I knew that the Maryhill district was one of Glasgow's areas for clearance of tenements and redevelopment, which was a longstanding policy, but the notice could not have arrived at a worst time for our morale. Perveen and I were near to tears, asking ourselves 'Is everything we have done until now going to be lost?' Looking back, I think this pattern of events became typical of the way my life developed. Every time things were going well, suddenly a bombshell of one type or another would land, testing all my ability to go on and never give up. It was to happen time and again throughout my life.

After this demolition bombshell I went to the City Council Estates Department, the next morning, with my head swimming and a knot in my stomach. I pleaded with the young man at the window in the council offices. I told him, 'If you want to demolish my shop, then no problem, but please give me another shop somewhere to replace it; this is all I have in the world. Please, please, you must help me.'

I suppose I was lucky that day on two counts. Firstly, the young Council guy I saw in the Estates Department was friendly and sympathetic. Secondly, because Maryhill was a redevelopment area, many established businesses had already moved out. The redevelopment of an area meant that people were moved to other parts, and so there was a huge fall in the numbers of customers using the local shops. That meant that there was a supply of empty shop properties which could be leased at reasonable rents for the medium term.

So the council official said he would show me three or four other shop units the next day, and I would be able to choose one if I was interested and we could agree a reasonable rent. I chose a shop unit at 279 Maryhill Road; it was still an old shop, it was in a mess, but I liked the location. It was a relatively low rent and also some distance from the rats! I put in an offer and I got it. That wasn't the end of our troubles, though, because we had no money to fit out the new shop, which was much bigger than the previous one.

Again fortune smiled on us. Perveen's relations in Lossiemouth were long-established in the grocery business there, and had just completed the renovation of one of their shops at around the same time as we took the new lease on this shop at 279 Maryhill Road. I pleaded with them to give me all their old shelves and old stands. They told me that they were only fit for the rubbish tip, but I persuaded them to let me have them if I could organise bringing them from Lossiemouth to Glasgow. When they agreed I did just that. Looking back on this, it is difficult not to smile. Not many people know that the £200 million empire of United Wholesale Ltd had its beginnings in old shelving and stands from Lossiemouth, that were saved from the scrapheap. At that time Perveen's brother was also kind enough to give me a loan of £2,000 for the business. We used that money to renovate the shop, and when the renovation was complete, all we had to do was get the stock to sell. This time, though, there was not a great problem, because as I have mentioned, we could get credit to buy stock because of the way I had paid off all the old shop's debts.

It needs to be understood that in these circumstances credit did not mean a huge loan. It meant that the small suppliers, like the bread-man, the milkman and the paper-man would give me advance credit for a month, at the end of which, the balance had to be paid. I also paid for other major supplies from the Cash and Carry warehouses by cheque. This dictated that I had to be extremely vigilant with the cash flow of the business, to make sure there was no chance of cheques bouncing. Fortunately I made the right calculations at the time, but like many business decisions, this was partly by design and partly by luck.

I established the routine that I always bought major stocks from the big Cash and Carrys by cheque on a Wednesday night. I knew that this meant the suppliers would not bank the cheque until the Thursday, which would probably not be presented at our bank until the following Monday. This meant that I had shop sales for Thursday, Friday, Saturday and Sunday, and I could put the money in the bank first thing on Monday to guarantee there were always funds to meet the outstanding cheques. So I ran the new business on a financial tightrope – always buying large purchases by cheque on a Wednesday so I had time to sell the goods before I had to pay for them. I can still remember the first weekend's trading at the new shop. We took more than £3,000 which was much more than we had done in a week in the old place. Monday morning we opened at nine o'clock and then at eleven o'clock I went to the bank to lodge the £3,000 in cash to cover the purchases from the previous Wednesday. If I had decided to stock up on a Tuesday I would have been been sunk, because, at one time or another, the cheques could have been presented by Friday before the takings were in the bank to cover them. So the decision to buy goods on a Wednesday night proved right for the business cycle.

At first this seemed like a vicious circle; in time, though, I realised that the Wednesday purchases, combined with the month's credit on milk, eggs and bread was giving me a vital financial breathing space where I could use credit to finance new lines of business for the shop. At the end of each month the bill for the milkman and the bread-man was £2,000. That was met by sales from other stock – so, in effect, I was making the money go round to establish a free loan of £2,000 every month. That was a lot of money in the late 1970s and I used it to bring more and more product lines into the shop – a business principle I adopted from that time onwards.

The move to 279 Maryhill Road would prove to be a one of the turning points in my business history. In a matter of months the shop's turnover was £6,000 a week. On those takings, the amount of credit I was advanced had increased, because there was always cash in the circle to pay the balance, and more credit meant more to invest to make the business grow. This wasn't robbing Peter to pay Paul; it was using Peter's money to pay Paul and Paul's money to pay Andrew and Andrew's money to pay Peter. Money was making the world go round in my shop.

Just about then, the main business for supplying eggs to small grocers' shops in the west of Scotland went bust. In business these things sometimes happen out of the blue. Everyone in the trade was astonished. I needed a supplier immediately. I went to a Pakistani cash and carry in Paisley Road West on Glasgow's south side – Sadiq Brothers. I felt that there was an opportunity to sell eggs cheaper than the Sadiq Brothers' offer, but meantime I had to accept and buy from them. I had no alternative.

Some time later I went to Noble Cash and Carry, who were big on eggs. They had a long established business and a good reputation for being reasonable and reliable in business dealings. I asked Mr Noble what was the price for 10 cases – the amount I sold in the shop each week. It was higher than what I'd been paying beforehand. Each case contains 20 dozen eggs. I had been shopping around the egg wholesalers and I knew that small shop-owners like me would be struggling to find an egg supplier at a decent price. So I asked Noble to give me a price for 100 cases. He told me that if I bought 100 cases it would be a pound cheaper per case – so on 10 cases the price was £10.00 per case and on 100 cases the price was £9.00 a case. I decided to take the risk and go for it. We struck a deal. I would take 100 cases a week and pay cash up front. He agreed that I could take the cases in a lot of 40 cases followed by two lots of 30. That meant that I was, in effect, using his Cash and Carry as my warehouse; it also reduced loading time as I loaded up at Noble's and then went straight out in search of customers, directly from his warehouse. I had a good idea where to start, because those days at the Cash and Carry warehouses, all the Asians used to chat to each other while they were waiting in line to pay. So everyone knew where everyone else's shops were.

It was hard work, as the van had to be loaded, and then at each customer's shop the eggs had to be taken out of the van and carried into the back of their shop. This was a significant business development. Perveen and I still had the Maryhill shop, but, in effect, I was moving into wholesaling eggs. This would have a huge impact on the business, but again chance played its part because the opportunity only opened up because the previous egg-man went bust.

I had a hunch there would be a market if I made the price attractive. So my price per case was £9.50, which was 50p cheaper than the cheapest Cash and Carry to pick them up. I was delivering to the shop, so that meant the shopkeeper didn't have to waste time going to the Cash and Carry. At £9.50, they were saving 50p a case, and I was making 50p. On 100 cases I would make £50.00 a week. I took my first 40 cases and paid Noble £360 cash. I dropped 10 cases at the shop and then started on my rounds. At that price they went like wildfire. I knew I was on to something. Within weeks I was up to 200 cases. That was making me £100 a week.

The deal was simple; I deliver, so the customer does not need to go to the Cash and Carry for eggs; I give them a case at 50p cheaper than the Cash and Carry so they buy from me. Eggs were very bulky to transport in the big boxes used by the suppliers, so most shop-owners were making at least two trips to get supplies. The first trip was for eggs and then a second trip to get the other supplies – groceries, toiletries, soft drinks, confectionary etc – for their shops. When I came along offering to sell them eggs, not only were my prices lower than the Cash and Carry but the delivery directly to the door of their shops undoubtedly cut the number of trips they had to make to the Cash and Carry for their supplies. As news of the direct supply of eggs spread the customers multiplied.

The average wage in the UK in 1980 was £6,000 a year or £120 a week. So now I was making £100 a week just on eggs, as well as what I was making in the shop at no. 279. When I was at 100 cases I collected from Noble, but when I went to 200 cases a week I said to him: 'Well, now I am a good customer what is the possibility of you delivering the eggs to me in the same way, broken down into lots?' To my surprise he agreed. I was learning that good customers can dictate terms to a certain extent.

There were 24,000 eggs in one hundred cases. So when we reached 200 cases we were selling 48,000 eggs a week. I was chuffed at the way whole business had just mushroomed – Sarwar, the Prince of Eggs.

When I left Pakistan I didn't really have a clue about business. Sure, I was capable of running the farm and its tenants, and doing some buying and selling of goods produced on the farm, but this, now, was cut-throat competition where every 50p was a prisoner. There were three main egg suppliers at that time in the west of Scotland: Noble, Thompson P.E.E.G. in the west end of Glasgow, and

William MacNiece in Airdrie, outside Glasgow. Slowly I began to realise that once I had established a certain economy of scale in eggs, I could play the prices to get a cheaper deal – sometimes it was the Airdrie people I went to, other times it was Noble. Most of the time I stayed with Noble, but the others' prices sometimes forced him to negotiate a better price for me. I would say to him, 'Look, this week Thompson P.E.E.G are selling a case for £8.90' and he would match the price. Sometimes suppliers would phone in the middle of the week saying they needed to get rid of 100 cases. Even if I didn't need them, I would buy them at rock-bottom price and try and move them on at the £9.50 price. I was learning, as the so-called Prince of Eggs, that buyers can exercise a real power in the marketplace, once their business is of a certain scale, and that 'price is King'. Sell-by-date was also critical for the suppliers. Once their eggs were within a week of their sell-by-dates, the big dealers become keen to shift the stock at bargain prices. I could do deals on cut-throat prices because I knew that my direct delivery system meant I could shift large amounts of sell-by-date stock within a day at rock-bottom prices, which made my offer very attractive to shop-owners.

I say 'I was learning', because that was the process – learning as the business developed. And, of course, learning by my mistakes, of which there were more than a few. My markets were the Asian grocers in Glasgow, then Paisley, then Airdrie and Coatbridge and beyond. I was running the eggs business and Perveen was running the shop.

Although the egg business was hard work, it was proving to be so lucrative that I was able to take on an assistant to help with the deliveries. One day we were delivering to a shop in Possil, in Glasgow, which is one of the city's poorest districts. Normally we both unloaded the van, but in Possil one stood and watched over the eggs, and the other did the deliveries to the back of the customer's shop. However this day, at one stage, the assistant abandoned his post and came into the shop. In a flash, a case of 20 dozen eggs disappeared. When I realised this had happened, I remonstrated with the assistant in the street. A passerby inquired what was the problem and I told him how a box of 20 dozen eggs had vanished into thin air. 'Look son,' he replied with a wink, 'this is Possil. Some folk in these parts can steal the sugar out of your cup of tea.'

At one stage, with the egg business flourishing, we decided to go into partnership with a friend, Saleem Dar, as by now we had too many customers for me to handle on my own. Some months into the partnership he said to me, 'Look, we are just selling eggs, what about cheese as well?' We went to see Gilmour, the main cheese wholesaler in Glasgow, and offered him our usual deal based on the egg experience. 'The more we buy, the lower the asking price.' We started our offer at 100 boxes of cheese.

'Gentlemen there is a lot of cheese in 100 boxes, so how are you going to pay for it?' he asked.

'Cash,' I replied.

He responded: 'You know this cheese goes off in a week, and then you can't sell it?'

'We know that,' I told him.

'How can you sell 100 boxes in a week? That's a huge amount!' he said, because he didn't believe we could shift them all. Eventually we agreed a price. We calculated that if we could sell 100 boxes of cheese every week we would make £1.00 a box.

We sold 100 boxes in the first week. It was good-quality Galloway cheese and the marketing was simple. We traded on the egg customers – anyone we were selling eggs to we said, 'Right, here's cheese as well.' Almost all of them said OK to the cheese pitch, and so in one week profits rose by another £100. We offered the exact same deal as the eggs – we were selling at less than the Cash and Carry price and delivering to the doorstep. No one else was doing cheese. The prices were set by the wholesalers and you had to buy there. Then we came along and made our offer at 50p cheaper. The customer's margins were increasing and so were ours.

After that we applied the same logic to margarine and cooking fat. So in the end we were selling four things at a lower price than the Cash and Carry. This was all because of the deals we could negotiate for the amounts we were buying. The money was rolling in. But as I had to use my own shop for storage, there were problems. All these boxes of eggs, cheese, margarine and cooking fat, were causing a lot of to-ing and fro-ing in the shop and the customers were getting irritated. The shop started to suffer – people could not put up with it always being so busy. I told Saleem that the size of the business now dictated that we had to look for other premises which we would use as a mini-warehouse.

There was an important factor in the argument I put to Saleem about where I wanted to buy the larger premises. My brother, Ramzan, and I had become house owners. We had saved £1,500, which was enough for a deposit to buy a flat at 41 Keir Street, in Pollokshields, on the south side of the city, where a large percentage of Glasgow's Asian population lived. The flat at Keir Street had four bedrooms, so both families could move there. We borrowed the balance of £5,000 from Glasgow City Council, who gave loans to prospective home-buyers in those days. It was a family milestone. I still look upon it as the first great achievement in our business history – the fact that we had made enough money to buy a quality property.

Saleem told me that a friend of his had a shop at Anniesland Cross, in the west end of the city, which we could rent for £30 a week. I didn't know it then, but this would prove to be a parting of the ways for our partnership. I said that Anniesland Cross was too far away from our shop in Maryhill, and also too far away from Pollokshields, where the majority of the Asian community in Glasgow lived, who could be potentially new customers. I argued that I had found a much better place at 317 Maxwell Road, in Pollokshields. I told him it was bigger and had a cellar which could be used to store dairy products, like cheese, butter and margarine, in cool conditions. He wasn't convinced. The argument went on for more than a month. His view was that 317 Maxwell Road was £100 a week rent, or £5,000 a year, so we were risking all we had made in the last year of the partnership. He said, 'Look, we have worked hard and made £5,000 clear in one year. Clear after everything is paid for. Now we will have to spend all the £5,000 to renovate this place at Maxwell Road, and then on top it will be £100 a week rent – that's £5,000. We will be left with no profit. Nothing. We will not make money but lose all we have. You want to spend every penny we've made on this gamble in Maxwell Road.'

I said to him that we needed to invest to make more money, and argued that the location in Maxwell Road would increase our trade. I told him that since almost all the Asian shopkeepers, from all over Glasgow, lived in Pollokshields we would increase our passing trade substantially because they would come and buy from Maxwell Road, every morning, on their way to their shops. So not only would Maxwell Road be a distribution centre for us, but also a point of sale for passing trade. 'That won't happen with Anniesland Cross,' I insisted.

He said that he was not prepared to take the risk with the money he had worked so hard to make. So we struck a deal. I bought him out by giving him half the profit – £2,500. I became the sole owner of the Maxwell Road business. We had Perveen and my brother, Ramzan, who was off the buses now, at the Maryhill Road shop, and I was in charge of Maxwell Road and the distribution business. It was all a calculated risk, although to be honest, after the deal was done, I was praying that my hunches would be proved right. I had doubts as well, with not just the cost of the rent but additional costs we had to take on for business rates, electricity and the like. When I think of that now, I was taking a gamble. Any competent accountant would probably have told me that Saleem Dar was right.

When Maxwell Road was opened, we had people coming to buy their own stock almost immediately. My gut feelings proved to be correct. The merchants who lived in Pollokshields were coming to us, at a time which suited them, so they then knew that the stock for their own shop was secured. This meant the worry of waiting for deliveries to their shop was taken out of their business. Many shopkeepers who were not former customers started to buy from Maxwell Road. They didn't know where Maryhill was – but when we opened in Pollokshields, they saw our sign, and in they came. They were soon queuing up for boxes of cheese, margarine, cases of eggs and much more. They knew we were cheaper.

In three months the average sales doubled. We had taken a big step forward. We decided to go into the cigarette market, buying cigarettes in bulk and selling direct from the Maxwell Road shop. This move would prove to be what nowadays they call 'a tipping point'. It was inspired by two factors. First of all the success of Maxwell Road was giving us a bigger cash flow which, as ever, meant we could use the money to increase the number of lines of products we could sell. The second reason was my ambition to become a Cash and Carry owner myself, and adding cigarettes to the lines we supplied was another step in that direction.

I had had that vision of the business for a long time. In those days, when I went to the Cash and Carry warehouses I noticed that most of the customers were Asian. As I have already mentioned, I also had the feeling that, quite a lot of the time, they were treated disrespectfully. It wasn't overtly racist, but there was an unwarranted impoliteness and abruptness. I knew that if I had a Cash and Carry I would treat my customers with civility, decency and a smile, and they would come running. So the cigarette lines made it possible to buy more and more different goods to sell from our shop; more product lines meant more customers, and that brought the dream of my own Cash and Carry that little bit closer.

We built a strong-room for cigarettes and opened for business. It is strange but even now – more than thirty years later – I can remember my credit limits. For Gallaghers it was £2,000 a month and for W.D. and H.O Wills it was £1,000. The cigarettes flew off the shelves. United Wholesale is still dealing with Gallaghers and Wills to this day. Now the credit limits are £6 million with Gallaghers, and £5 million with Wills. Mind you, the secret remains the same – buy on credit and sell for cash to make the money go round. After a year or so the credit limits, for each company, were increased to something like £10,000 a month. That meant that the cash flow coming into the business was increased by £20,000 a month, which could be used to finance more lines of business. The cash flows from the cigarettes, for example, allowed us to diversify into new lines of confectionery – Mars, Cadbury and Rowntree Macintosh.

When we were selling cigarettes at Maxwell Road we were lucky if we made a half of a per cent margin, but the important thing for the business was that it created a cash bonanza. I bought the cigarettes on the first of the month and had to pay by the tenth of the next month. That gave me five weeks to use the money coming in, in cash, from the cigarettes. And if I paid by cheque for the cigarettes it wasn't usually presented to my bank until the fifteenth – so I was using *their* money for six weeks. If you borrow from the bank to finance new lines of business it costs you money in interest on the loans, even if you are lucky enough to get one; using the cigarette money didn't cost us anything. Of course in those days the pernicious effects of cigarette smoking, and its link to lung cancer, were not as clearly identified as such a malignant plague on society. But then, as now, we took the view that if there was customer demand for a product we would cater for it. The same thing happened later with our stocking additional confectionery, toiletries and other products to meet customer demand.

At this stage we still had the shop in Maryhill, but no longer used it for storage and warehousing. Everything was concentrated in Pollokshields. I was doing the same – delivering everywhere – Ramzan, who had joined us, was in the shop in Maryhill, and we had someone working at 317 when I went on the deliveries. I had six route maps, Monday to Saturday, a different area for each day. Two days in Glasgow, one north, one south; then Paisley – start in Paisley Road West and then all the way to Paisley. Then another day, the Airdrie and Coatbridge side, and so on. Every customer knew what day I would arrive and when. The delivering was hard work, and, as a result of all the carrying and walking involved, I was fit as a fiddle. By this time I was probably shifting upwards of 500 cases of eggs a week.

We now had sufficient trade to miss out the middle man – the Cash and Carrys – and go straight to the wholesale supplier. In this case it was Bruce Barr Ltd, in Northern Ireland, who became the main supplier of eggs. We had a really good business deal – he knew I was a good payer and that I had a reliable and growing customer base. So let's say I heard that the egg price at the Cash and Carry warehouses, in Glasgow, had gone up. I'd phone Bruce in Belfast – 'How many cases you got spare?' He might say 300, and I'd say I'll take the lot, because he's selling to me at the old price. So that's 300 cases at £9.50 a case, but when they are delivered I am going to sell them at the new price of, say, £10.75. He knows he's selling at the old price, but he also knows he's getting cash in hand for clearing his stock.

The key to the business was knowing the going prices for everything we were running with. That was the name of the game, and still is. If you are not aware of price movements, then it is only a matter of time before you are in trouble. Imagine you have bought 500 cases of eggs, at say £15 a case, and the market price drops to £13 a case. Unless you are on the ball and watching the prices like a hawk, on just one consignment of eggs you can lose £1,000. That's enough to sink a small business if it takes you beyond the credit limit set by the bank. So when the prices drop you have to move hell and high water to shift the stock. The contrary also applies; if you know the prices are going up, you buy as much as you can at the old price and sell at the new price to increase your margins.

When I reflect on this now I can recall the agonising over the split with Saleem Dar and taking on 317 Maxwell Road. At the time of the move, the turnover of all our dairy products was between £8,000 and £9,000 a week. After a year, with the new trade in cigarettes and confectionary, at 317, the turnover zoomed to £35,000 to £40,000 a week. When that was maintained month after month, it became clear that with £40,000 a week coming in, we had to begin to look for bigger premises because the demand was outstripping our ability to supply. We had so much produce coming in and going out, including the sweets and the cigarettes, that we were almost overwhelmed.

We started to look around for bigger premises. It was 1979/80 when we took the lease on 317 Maxwell Road. The soft drinks company, Barr's Irn Bru, had a distribution depot only just round the corner from 317. It came up for sale early in 1981. 317 had about 1,000 square feet on the ground floor and a cellar of 500 square feet – so there was 1,500 square feet of floorspace. The Barr's place was 12,000 square feet which was set in an acre of land. The booming success of the move to Maxwell Drive had filled us with the confidence to be audacious and go for it. We bought the Barrs' place for £150,000, which was a big turning point on the road to creating a real large-scale Cash and Carry. The move took us into what was new business territory, although we had actually only moved a hundred yards down the road. Everyone knew where the new premises were. They were right there before their eyes. So the move didn't cost us any loss of customers and we gained many more, because the bigger premises meant we could stock more and more lines. 'Come to United Wholesale – Everything You Need Is Here', might have been our branding tag-line.

We took risks, but we were making money, and each time we made a move we were sure it was going to be manageable within our cash flow. But that is not to say that each time it was not a gamble.

Our cash flow determined how we could expand the business – how we could use credit to our advantage, how much we had in the bank, how much the bank would lend us. If you move from 1,000 square feet to 12,000 square feet you have to find the money for the purchase of the new place; it has to be done up and renovated, new shelving and displays and machines need to be bought; then there's money needed for the car park and ten times more stock to fill the new space. That's a big outlay, and if you don't do the sums correctly and the cash flow doesn't come in, or you fail to pay Gallaghers for the cigarettes one month, they simply withdraw the line and you can be sunk. This was all pressure. If we had lost that element of the cash flow because one month we couldn't pay them, there would have been the equivalent of a motorway pile-up in the business as one failure in the cash-flow chain would lead to others. It's not an exaggeration to say that, at certain critical junctures, the whole house could have come tumbling down. We were taking big leaps forward in the business, armed only with a hope, a prayer and an electronic calculator.

The history of the business is built around two or three big calculated risks. And it might be said that whatever boldness we demonstrated, and risks we took, would not have been taken by other businesses of the same size. However we had two important advantages: we had a huge market in the Asian grocers, and the bank was supportive. Looking back, the move from Maxwell Road to the Barr's Irn Bru site was a crucial one in the history of United Wholesale, because of the scale of the change. The fact that the business was now known by this new name gave an indication of the direction we were moving in. We were going from one property to another almost ten times the size. At the time of the move from 317 to the Barr's place we had a turnover of around £40,000 a week. It would have been easy to say at that time, 'Let's take it easy for a year or two take stock and steady the ship for a while.' But I knew I wasn't going to do that. I was still chasing the dream of becoming a major Cash and Carry owner. I knew, even when we moved into the Barr's site, that 12,000 square feet wasn't enough. I knew I wasn't going to stop there. That's not to say that I didn't recognise that it was time for a period of consolidation. I knew the creation of new lines of business at the Barr's place would create a bigger business platform for the next move, but the plan was to do that step by step, to avoid reckless, over-ambitious expansion.

The move to Barr's allowed us to expand what we were doing in cigarettes, and to introduce new lines in soft drinks, confectionary and crisps. Before that time we could not sell crisps because they were too bulky and we did not have the space, but now, suddenly, with the Barr's 12,000 square feet, we had room to grow. This included toiletries like soap and toothpaste. So the plan was to go for crisps, confectionery, soft drinks and toiletries, added to the usual staples of eggs, cheese and the other dairy products. We had a much bigger range of products, so I figured we would attract more customers and generate more sales from them. We also knew that existing customers would buy more from us if there were more lines on offer. I was confident we could treble the turnover of the business and reach the magic figure of more than £100,000 per week.

With the introduction of toilet rolls and kitchen towels as sale items, this proved to be the case. Customers who came to us for other goods bought these new lines in great quantity, because it was convenient for them – one-stop shopping. We worked on the basis of offering deals on this or that product according to what was moving on the stock and what wasn't. We didn't look for huge profits on this or that product specifically – we believed in keeping prices low to generate turnover to produce cash flow and profits. That was our marketing strategy – people came to the warehouse because they knew there were lines and lines of goods and that there was always the prospect of a low price offer somewhere in the ranges of goods on offer. On some occasions we would run 'loss leaders' on some goods – buy at £10.00 and sell at £9.90 – just to generate trade. We calculated that the losses on such deals would be more than compensated for by whatever else the customer would buy when in the store. It was simple. If we didn't offer some bargains to tempt them to come to the shop we wouldn't get their custom for other products. We discounted, let's say, kitchen towels and toilet rolls for a period, and while they came to buy those lines they also decided to buy cigarettes, soft drinks, and crisps while they were there.

When I think of all this now, at that time of building the business, the idea that, one day, I would become a British MP meeting the President of Pakistan and then returning to the UK to brief the British Prime Minister, Tony Blair, on the details of my meetings in Pakistan, could never have been among the wildest of my wildest dreams. If you had come to the new warehouse which we bought from the Barr's people, and told me that my business career in Glasgow would eventually lead to my meeting with Presidents and Prime Ministers of Pakistan, the leaders of the Muslim world and taking first-hand reports of these meetings directly to Prime Minister Tony Blair, I would have escorted you off the premises, advising that you needed to seek medical attention.

After the Barr's purchase there was the Kerrygold saga. I had suppliers from Ireland bringing the butter over in pre-packed boxes. Sometime late in 1982, in the UK, there was the changeover from the use of pounds and ounces – imperial measurement – to the metric equivalents, kilograms and grams. To explain further, let's take the traditional pound of butter. It was replaced by the equivalent metric measurement of 500g. But 500g is actually 1 pound 2 ounces, so the price for a pre-packed box went up quite sharply, by around twenty per cent if my memory serves me correctly. The company which was supplying the eggs offered me Kerrygold butter packed in the older 1 pound measurements – Ireland had not gone metric at that stage. I ordered 100 cases as a trial, and the customers were keen to buy it because it meant they could offer that butter at a much reduced cost compared to the new metric packs. The 100 cases were sold in two days. So I bought large quantities of 1 pound Kerrygold stock, and to my surprise the sale of butter rocketed. In a couple of weeks I was selling 1,000 boxes a week, at £2,000 a week profit, from the suppliers of the 1 pound butter packs at the old prices.

In the early 1980s that was a lot of money. The butter bonanza lasted for months, and made us good money which was useful for investing to build the business later. However, one day representatives of Trading Standards in Glasgow City Council arrived, and told me it was illegal to sell Kerrygold butter in pound packets. I told them I thought that there would be a period of grace to allow manufacturers and wholesalers to dispose of the 1 pound stock. They told me they could confiscate all the Kerrygold butter in the warehouse but instead gave me a final warning to stop selling the 1 pound packets, which I did.

Then in 1983 there was another piece of good fortune, that made an enormous short-term difference to the business. The Northern Ireland suppliers who were providing us with butter, eggs and other dairy products used to send an agent once or twice a month to our warehouse in Glasgow. They came to take orders for the following month. One day the agent was looking at our stock and she said to me, 'Your prices for cases of Tetley tea bags are high.' Now what I did not know at the time was that Nambarrie and Punjana tea bags were by far the most popular brands in Northern Ireland, and had a dominant market share. Tetley – the most popular brand in the UK – was running a marketing campaign with low prices on their cases of tea bags in Northern Ireland in an attempt to capture a better share of that market. They were prepared to make these low-price offers there, even if it meant that, in the short term, they were selling at cut-throat prices. They were taking risks to get a stronger foothold in the market in Northern Ireland in a 'tea bag war' with Nambarrie and Punjana.

A case of Tetley tea bags contained two dozen boxes, with 100 tea bags in each of them. In Glasgow we were selling a case, wholesale, for £19.80. 'How much do you sell a case of Tetley for in Northern Ireland?' I asked. The agent said that the price was £15.80. Right away I offered a straightforward business deal. 'I'll give you £1.00 profit for every case you can deliver to my warehouse.' She agreed the deal there and then and suggested she would send 100 cases of tea bags with the next delivery of eggs. We dropped our wholesale price for tea bags from £19.80 a case to £18.80. The 100 cases went in two days. The next week she sent me 200 cases and they went in two days. The word was out – United Wholesale was the place to get Tetley tea bags. The third week we went up to 500 cases and they shifted in three or four days. The more we bought, the more we sold, and soon we were touching 1,000 cases a week. This went on for about three or four months before anyone noticed. By then the big Cash and Carrys in Glasgow, like Booker and Castle, were feeling the pinch and were complaining to Tetley that they could not sell any of their tea bags. Nor could anyone else. In Glasgow, Sarwar, the Prince of Eggs, had become the King of Tetley Tea Bags!

Around this time I was told that the Tetley bosses in England were originally delighted with the success of their marketing campaign in Northern Ireland. Little did they know that it was based on their product being bought there but sold in Scotland. While we were enjoying the tea bag bonanza, representatives of Tetley arrived on our doorstep. They didn't know I had a supplier from Northern Ireland who was buying tea bags from Tetley, at the prices offered for Northern Ireland, and then transporting them to me, for similar prices, in Glasgow, along with my butter, margarine and eggs.

'Where are you getting these Tetley tea bags from? Why don't you buy from us?' they demanded to know.

'That's my business, but I am buying them cheaper elsewhere than the prices you offer,' I told them.

Then they accused me of running a racket in stolen tea bags. 'Call the police,' I said. 'All of this is entirely legitimate and I have the bona fide receipts to prove it. I'm paying by cheque.'

At this point they did not seem to understand that the difference in wholesale prices that they were offering to Northern Ireland could create a micro-market in nearby Scotland. It had not occurred to them that the difference in the price offer for Northern Ireland and Scotland could be exploited if transport costs were already being paid for the transport of other goods. Put it this way: their thinking was that they could offer the lower prices in Northern Ireland because the costs of transporting the tea bags from Northern Ireland to Scotland would cancel any potential price advantage. However, if, like me, the buyer was already buying in bulk from Bruce Barr in Northern Ireland, it was just a case of loading up the tea bags along with the dairy products in the same lorry, and a tea-bag bonanza beckoned. That was the advantage that made the deal. The Tetley people left the warehouse in a very disgruntled mood, muttering about scams.

However, a matter of months after that, Tetley put the pieces of the Tetley tea-bag jigsaw together. They realised that the differences in wholesale price between Northern Ireland and Glasgow had created a market differential which I was exploiting. At first they introduced conditions that wholesalers in Northern Ireland would only get supplies at the lower prices if there was no sell-on back to the UK. But market forces eventually dictated that Tetley had to abandon their marketing campaign and equalise their prices for tea bags in Northern Ireland and the UK. There was no other way of controlling their product distribution.

By then I think United Wholesale had made around £40,000 exploiting two sets of market prices for the same product. Of course to make such profits then, on tea bags, was a significant success for the business. The Tetley experience also greatly increased our total turnover, because we gained a host of new customers, who originally came to us for the tea bags, and stayed to buy much more. Tetley never did break the dominance of Nambarrie and Punjana in the Northern Ireland market.

At that time all my energies were devoted to the business, to the point of total preoccupation. Politics? Not for me – I'm going to be Britain's biggest and best Cash and Carry owner. At the start of 1984 the optimism I had for fulfilling that ambition knew practically no limits. It would turn out to be misplaced. I was forgetting that the history of my life often had three steps forward followed by one or two steps back – the exhilaration of success was quite often followed by the misery of crisis.

So it turned out in 1984, when another bombshell dropped. I was at home sleeping in our flat at Keir Street, in Pollokshields, when the phone rang. It was about one o'clock in the morning. It was Strathclyde Police. They told me that the warehouse in Maxwell Drive was on fire. I rushed there to see the flames leaping into the night sky. I told the fire brigade officer in charge that the strongroom with the cigarettes was at the front of the building near the entrance, and pleaded with him to try and concentrate the fire brigade's efforts on saving that part of the building. All we could do was pray. I knew that we had insurance for the cigarettes of about £300,000, but that the stock was worth double that. The explanation for that amount of stock was simple. It was coming to the end of the financial year, and there was a Government Budget in the offing, so in anticipation of wholesale prices going up we had stocked up at old prices – as we always did when a Budget approached. Unfortunately, the prudence we demonstrated in stocking up at the old prices hadn't been replicated by altering the extent of the insurance cover for the increased stock. That would turn out to be a costly oversight.

I was devastated on two counts. Firstly, before my eyes my livelihood was going up in flames; and secondly, I thought my reputation would be ruined, with fingers being pointed. In those days it wasn't unknown for a business that was in trouble to be rescued by the insurance payments after a fire. In those days in Glasgow there wasn't a shortage of accusations flying around about torchings, fires and fraud. Of course it wasn't just the Asian businesses which were accused of this – there had been many occasions in Glasgow business history where companies owned by Jewish businessmen, Irish businessmen, Scottish businessmen and others, had fires on their premises which, dare I say it, apparently paid off all their debts through insurance claims. We were not in that position. The business was going well and we didn't have any debts. Also, as just explained, we were under-insured for the stock and buildings because we were taking risks – so when that was considered there would be no gain for us in an insurance pay-off. In fact it was almost a total disaster.

My argument in the face of the accusations being cast in my direction was that if the fire was some sort of 'insurance job', as they were referred to, in those days, then it would have been at least prudent to be properly insured. The other certainty, in all of this, was that if the cigarettes were gone so was the business. I remember how I felt when I went back to the flat after the fire. I told Perveen that we would know in the morning whether the business had survived. We would find out then whether the cigarettes had been saved. She was her usual calm self. She looked at me and in a quiet voice said, 'What will be will be. There's no point in damaging your health now over something you can't change. We can't change the fact that there has been a fire.' She has been the true strength in my life as we built the business, and of course well beyond that. Always, in the darkest hours, she had this inner confidence that we would be alright, that God would look after us. She has probably been braver than me at the times of great crisis.

There's one story, famous in the family, which illustrates this. When we had 317 Maxwell Road I would carry the takings from a Friday, Saturday and Sunday back to the flat each evening, so that on a Monday morning I would go directly to the bank with them.

Someone from the Maxwell Road shop would come to collect me at the flat. Quite often there could be £20,000 in cash in my brief-case, from the three days' takings. One Monday, when I came out of the flat in Keir Street, four men with knuckle-dusters were wait-ing for me. They were after the money. One of my rogue employ-ees had betrayed me by telling them that on a Monday morning I would leave the flat to go to the bank with the weekend's takings. The thugs started beating me ferociously. I couldn't really defend myself as I was hanging onto the briefcase with the cash in it for dear life. They rained blow after blow on me, but as I was falling I managed to fall on top of the briefcase, whereupon they started kicking me viciously. There was uproar. I was screaming; there was blood everywhere. Perveen heard my shouts and ran out of the flats brandishing an old table leg from a broken piece of furniture and started beating the men. As they ran off, she took off in pur-suit of one of them. She chased after him through the local streets for more than five hundred yards. The robber must have thought 'Enough!' and stopped to take her on. He tried to punch her and she knocked him out with the chair leg. She stood over him until the police arrived and arrested him. She told me later that she was in such a frenzy because she thought they had killed me. In court the judge told her she was a very brave woman. You can see that, with such courage at my side, whenever there was a crisis in my life, there were always two of us ready to take it on. So it was with the fire.

The morning after the blaze we both went to the site. We had to be escorted into what remained of the building by fire officers and police officers to inspect the damage because of the dangerous state of the place. The first piece of blackened joy was the strong-room. It had survived and so had roughly half a million pounds worth of ciga-rettes, although we lost £100,000 worth of cigarettes which had been on display outside the strong-room. Therefore we still had a chance. In the strong-room we opened the safe and there were cheques for tens of thousands of pounds there and also about £20,000 in cash. If I had known there was going to be a fire, would all that have been left to chance, to the risk of it being consumed by the fire? I don't think so. You might say that 1984 nearly saw all our dreams go up in smoke. That's why there was no official police investigation of the blaze. They saw the cheques and the money with their own eyes when we opened the safe.

The insurance investigation into the fire found that it had probably been caused, perhaps ironically given that the cigarette trade had helped to build the business, by a cigarette-butt smouldering and catching fire. At that time we had a contractor in the warehouse who was renovating the floors at the back of the store and building new shelving areas.

The disaster meant we returned to our business roots – eggs, cheese, and margarine, operating out of 317 Maxwell Road. The cigarettes saved us, because, like before, they guaranteed a cash flow. A friend of mine, Andy Hakeen, had a well established credit line with cigarettes – so I was also able to buy cigarettes from him, on credit, which kept the cash flow going. Sufi Ali Ahmed gave the bank a guarantee of £100,000 on my behalf, an act which helped to sustain the business that I will never forget. People were generous and, in fact, it was the help offered from friends, and the saving of the cigarettes, which kept the business alive.

This difficult period for the business lasted for about six to nine months as the Maxwell Road building, damaged in the fire, had to be demolished, and there were ongoing disputes with the insurers about the amount they would pay out because we had been underinsured. In the end I think we got about £350,000 from the insurers, which would hardly have covered the stock losses. In addition to that, we had to pay for the demolition of the damaged building and the building of the new premises from our own resources.

In all this time the bank had given us great support, mainly because the business had been so successful and they always got what they were owed on time. So when one of their clients with a warehouse went bust, they opened negotiations with us about taking it over. It was 73 Wallace Street, in the Tradeston district of Glasgow, south of the river. The bank was able to offer it to us with a substantial loan to pay for the purchase. We decided to go for it. This came at the right time for us because, by then, we had received the insurance payments which meant we could purchase the stock for the new premises, and carry out some renovations to make everything right for a Cash and Carry business while still having something to spare to have Maxwell Road rebuilt.

We were lucky because our customers at Maxwell Road, before it burned down, remained loyal and came to Wallace Street when we developed the same lines of business. Wallace Street was about the same size as the old Irn Bru site, 12,000 square feet, so we knew how to work the space. Also our suppliers had been loyal in the time of the crisis, continuing to supply us and giving us time to pay. We had established a trust and confidence that we could be relied upon to pay our bills. This was always important to me. Wallace Street was opened late in 1984, about six months after the fire.

One of the other things that allowed us to overcome this crisis was that we had always been careful with our personal spending as the business developed. When the catastrophe of the fire engulfed us, we were still living in the flat in Keir Street which we had bought, with my brother, as I have said, for £6,500. So when the fire disaster struck we were not hit with a simultaneous crisis of personal outgoings. Frankly we didn't have too many responsibilities at that level – we didn't have heavy mortgages for big houses to pay, we didn't drive big expensive cars and we didn't go on flash foreign holidays. I was always cautious on the level of personal obligations I was prepared to undertake. I made sure that I did not over-commit myself.

What I have learned in life is that when the going is tough, it is best just to keep your head down and don't take on the rumour-mongers directly. The majority of people are fair-minded; they know the difference between right and wrong. I have learned that if you know you are right, the time will come when you can confound your accusers. This has been a law of my life. If you are not guilty of the charges made against you, in the end, you'll be proved right. What is the point of trying to argue about things in the short term – that only fuels the fire. Those who steal money from the taxman or make this or that false claim, in the main, don't succeed in the fullness of time.

The Wallace Street project was boom-time from day one. We had about 1,500 customers registered on the books, and we simply sent out flyers with some cut-price offers saying we were opening at Wallace Street. It had the desired effect – they came in droves. Once again, on the same basis – they knew we had a lot of product lines so there could be one-stop shopping; they knew we were cheaper than most, and they knew they would get credit if they were registered with us.

It took us about a year and half to rebuild Maxwell Road. The new building was 20,000 square feet, so this was another step on the journey to a real full-size Cash and Carry. We knew that this was a proper Cash and Carry, even though we needed double that floorspace to be up with the really big boys. In August 1986, the new place opened for business. That meant that by the end of 1986 we had two Cash and Carrys on the south side of Glasgow, at Wallace Street and Maxwell Road, and both were doing well, taking us towards the eventual goal of an annual £40 million turnover. By then we recognised that having two big warehouses, in roughly the same area of Glasgow, meant that, to some extent, they were competing for customers against each other. So we began our quest to find a site north of the river for a new Cash and Carry which would establish a new customer base.

The Teacher's whisky bond warehouse, in Springburn, on the north side of the river, came on the market. Taking it over was a very ambitious project to contemplate. It was a twelve-acre site. In 1988 we bought it for £1.8 million. The whole site was 400,000 square feet. Our plan was to use part of the building for a warehouse, and then to sublet the rest. We built the Cash and Carry there at around 65,000 square feet, and sold the rest of the building for £750,000 to a big British carpet and furniture concern. After about one year, Springburn was proving to be a big success. We decided then that it would make sense to rationalise the business. We had waited to see what would happen with Springburn, and what impact such a large undertaking would have on the rest of the business. Our aim had always been to have two major outlets – one on the north side of the city and one on the south to maximise customer retention and, importantly, to reduce operating costs. We decided to close Wallace Street to allow us to concentrate on Maxwell Road and Springburn. Our business model remained the same – to make reduced offers regularly, develop 'one stop' shopping as far as possible, and offer generous credit terms.

In the early 1990s business was good; we had overcome difficult times; we had been lucky; we now had one facility which was large enough to have genuine Cash and Carry status. At that point, my plan was to build more enterprises across Scotland and then to develop in England. Politics intervened in those ambitions. I stood as a Glasgow City Council candidate in 1988 and was narrowly defeated. I won the same council seat in 1992. I believe that if I had not become involved in politics, United Wholesale would have been in the top ten wholesale chains in the UK, and I would have been pretty high up in the likes of the *Sunday Times* Top 500 Rich List. But the decision to go into politics meant that I went on a different path, away from big business. That move had huge implications for United Wholesale, because my political involvement meant that I could not devote my energies to the business one hundred per cent. When I was elected as an MP in 1997 my brother Ramzan effectively started running the business on his own on a day-to-day basis because I was consumed totally by politics by that stage. I could not have done that without him. But eventually this provoked an irreconcilable conflict with my brother, which led to a split. This after we had been together in business for more than 20 years. Ramzan took the business in Springburn, and I got Maxwell Road.

The weekly magazine *The Grocer* reported on 8 December 2001 under the headline 'Not United Anymore':

> Labour MP Mohammad Sarwar's United Wholesale Grocer's business in Glasgow is being split into two independent companies. The Springburn operation, owned and run by Mohammad Ramzan, will retain the trading name of United Wholesale Grocers and concentrate on food, drink and non-food. The Pollokshields business, owned by Sarwar, will trade as United Wholesale (Scotland) and focus on its grocery offer, including a new frozen food facility. It will be run by Sarwar's son, Athif. The new structure will be implemented on January 1.

That is a very matter of fact statement but it conceals the heartbreak and weariness that was consequent upon the split. My brother and I have long since settled our differences and our relationship is courteous and respectful. Still, it cannot be denied that the bond we had through building the business together, was broken then and cannot be restored. I remember when the split eventually took place the total business, north and south, had a turnover of around £100 million – a remarkable achievement since the early days of the shop in 279 Maryhill Road. The Springburn depot had around £60 million annual turnover and Maxwell Road some £40 million.

The split wasn't amicable and Ramzan fired the first shots in a 'Cash and Carry war' by opening his second warehouse at Polmadie, on the south side of Glasgow, which was about five minutes' drive from Maxwell Road. That was in 2004. My response was to open my own second warehouse on the north side of the city, at Queenslie, which was competition for his depot at Springburn. That took much longer to set up than Ramzan's opening, but by 2007 United Wholesale Scotland had its second warehouse. The competition had been cut-throat with, as they say, no quarter asked or given. Now, what seemed *then* like a fight to the finish, seems so different now. Instead of a winner and loser emerging from the business struggle, we have produced two winners. Both businesses have not only survived, but prospered. The combined annual turnover for United Wholesale Grocers and United Wholesale Scotland is now more than £400 million.

My business life has given me some cause to reflect. The media often used the 'millionaire' tag when describing me – 'The millionaire Labour MP Mohammad Sarwar . . .' was a commonly used phrase. I can honestly say that while I recognise that the family business has made me wealthy, I have never striven to become a millionaire. In fact I don't even know, at this point, if I am a millionaire. The business is worth millions, but I genuinely don't know the extent of my own worth. However, I have learned the importance of being in business and what that can mean for wealth creation.

There is an important difference between a life in business and a professional life and it is this: you can work for an employer for many years but it is unlikely you will ever become really wealthy; there are exceptions to the rule, but, on average, the truth holds – most employed people can put savings away year on year but they will never be rich. It is true to say that had I come from Pakistan and worked as an employee in some concern I could never have reached 'millionaire' status. Only becoming a major entrepreneur created that possibility. On occasion, business people have the opportunity to make enough money in a special year that might set them up for life. That is an important difference. While others can save enough for a nice house and a nice car and so on, they will never be truly financially independent.

If you have five good years in business you can have an income which potentially can make you a millionaire for life. The corollary also follows. It is this: in business you can make enough to make you rich in a way that employees of a company are unlikely ever to be, but the dizzying heights of business success also mean that in certain circumstances you might lose almost everything.

I speak from experience. Disputes with the banks involving the withdrawal of loans, unforeseen problems with the tax authorities, disruption of supplies from wholesalers or sudden international crises, are among many other things that can leave you suddenly staring into the abyss of business catastrophe. From the outside commentators may look at our business history and see it as one of constant steady progress to the heights of our present achievements. Not so. There is no yellow-brick road to be walked to success. Rather it is a story of periods of growth and development interrupted by setbacks, difficulties and the prospects of calamity. The fire at our Maxwell Road warehouse is only one example of triumph being haunted by sudden imminent disaster.

Nonetheless we have always been able to survive, to overcome times of trouble and move on to greater prosperity. Today the business is flourishing. We have multi-million-pound expansion plans for our Maxwell Road and Queenslie Cash and Carrys; we have a restaurant chain, an hotel, and a new children's adventure centre in Perth; so the prospects are good. I also believe that God has looked over us and been good to us. That's the only possible explanation for our being able to overcome desperate and uncertain times.

If God is good to you, you have a duty to give something back. In life I have never forgotten that it is a duty to help the poor and those less privileged than yourself. My charity and aid work is one way I pay my dues to God for the bountiful generosity He has shown me and my family. Those values have shaped my business life and my political philosophy.

Into Politics 5

'You are free; you are free to go to your temples, you are free
to go to your mosques or to any other place or worship in this
State of Pakistan. You may belong to any religion or caste or
creed – that has nothing to do with the business of the State
. . . We are starting in the days where there is no discrimination, no distinction between one community and another, no
discrimination between one caste or creed and another.'

> Mohammad Ali Jinnah, Address to the Constituent
> Assembly of Pakistan, 11 August 1947.

'Islam is our faith; Democracy is our policy; Socialism our
economy.'

> Zulfikar Ali Bhutto, at the founding of the Pakistan
> People's Party, Pakistan 1967.

It was the early evening of the 3rd of April,1979 when the official
party approached the jail cell of Zulfikar Ali Bhutto, the prime minister of Pakistan. He was being held in Rawalpindi Jail. In reality,
theirs was a funeral march, for they were on their way to notify Bhutto of his coming execution. In the party were the Jail Superintendent,
Yar Mohammad, his assistant, Ghulam Rasool, the prison doctor,
Sagheer Shah, a magistrate, Bashir Ahmad Khan, and an army Commander, Lieutenant Colonel Rafi ud Din.

The official record states that Bhutto was lying on his mattress on
the floor when the party entered his cell at 6.05 pm. The Jail Superintendent, Yar Mohammad, then stepped forward and took a typed
sheet of paper from a large envelope and read out the following:

According to the 18th March 1978 order of the Lahore High
Court, you, Mr Zulfikar Ali Bhutto, are to be hanged for the
murder of Nawab Mohammad Ahmad Khan. Your appeal in

the Supreme Court was rejected on 6th February 1979 and the review petition was turned down on 24th March 1979. The president of Pakistan has decided not to interfere in this matter. So it has been decided to hang you.

A little over seven hours later, Zulfikar Ali Bhutto was taken to the gallows in the courtyard of Rawalpindi Jail. The record shows that at precisely 2.04 am on 4 April, 1979, the executioner pulled the lever to open the trapdoor below the gallows and Bhutto was hanged.

I have researched Bhutto's final hours one more time because he had an enormous effect on my life. In the early 1970s it was Zulfikar Ali Bhutto and his Pakistan People's Party (PPP) which first drew me into socialist politics in Pakistan. Bhutto formed the PPP with the declaration: 'Islam is our faith; Democracy is our policy; and Socialism our economy.' These words have been central to my own personal politics for much of my life.

From the time of my youth there had been two great influences on my life: the founder of Pakistan, Mohammad Ali Jinnah, and our national poet, Dr Allama Mohammad Iqbal. Bhutto arrived as a third influence which would shape my politics for a long time. There is no mystery about this. In Britain you will hear politicians speak of being inspired by Winston Churchill, Aneurin Bevan, Michael Foot or whoever. In the same way Zulfikar Ali Bhutto was my political inspiration. Although history has not dealt too kindly with him, for me he always represented the struggle against injustice, the struggle of the poor against the vested interests of the rich and the struggle for a better Pakistan – all ideals which inspired me when I was young.

However, there is also a direct line between Bhutto and my becoming Britain's first Muslim MP. Why? Because in 1979, some three years after I had emigrated from Pakistan to Scotland, it was the prospect of Bhutto being hanged, on trumped-up charges by the murderous junta of General Zia ul Haq, that propelled me into active politics in my newly adopted homeland.

In January 1977, Bhutto and the Pakistan People's Party (PPP) won a resounding victory in the national elections. They won 155 of the 200 seats in parliament. But the Opposition, under the banner of the Pakistan National Alliance, refused to accept the result, accusing the PPP of ballot-rigging. Now, there was no widespread ballot-rigging, as millions voted entirely legitimately. However, the Opposition had some grounds for complaint. There were a few constituencies where their candidates were effectively barred from standing because it was decided that they had failed to file their nomination papers as candidates on time. In some cases this involved prospective candidates being arrested and held until the nomination deadline had passed. This had effectively prevented them standing, and electoral areas included where the Prime Minister and Chief Ministers were candidates and were being challenged by the Opposition.

In another 20 constituencies there were also justified complaints of ballot-rigging. All of this was enough to provoke months of nationwide street protests which plunged Pakistan into chaos. That eventually became the justification for the military coup led by General Zia ul Haq, even though Bhutto had agreed with the Opposition to declare the first election null and void and hold a new General Election. Zia ul Haq later organised the judicial murder of Bhutto.

Late in 1976, in what must surely have been the greatest political miscalculation of his life, Bhutto had made Zia ul Haq the Chief of Army Staffs. Some seven months later, in July 1977, General Zia returned the compliment by staging his coup and throwing Bhutto in jail. Worse was to follow. By October that year Bhutto was on trial for conspiracy to murder a political opponent, Ahmed Raza Kasuri, and for the actual murder of Kasuri's father, Nawab Mohammad Ahmad Khan. This allegedly took place in an ambush organised by state security forces. Key to the indictment was the charge that it was Bhutto who sanctioned the secret police attack on Kasuri and his family.

The former United States Attorney General, Ramsey Clark, attended the trial. He was quoted as saying it was not a trial for murder but the overt murder of a trial. He wrote later:

> The prosecution's case was based entirely on several witnesses who were detained until they confessed, who changed and expanded their confessions and testimony with each reiteration, who contradicted themselves and each other, who . . . were

relating what others said, whose testimony led to four different theories of what happened, absolutely uncorroborated by
an eyewitness, direct evidence, or physical evidence.[1]

In March 1978, Bhutto was found guilty and sentenced to death.
Almost a year later, in February 1979, his appeal to the Supreme
Court of Pakistan was lost by four votes to three. The guilty verdict
and the death sentence were upheld. When Bhutto was framed on
these bogus charges and found guilty, there had been a huge international protest movement. The loss of the appeal against the death
sentence took the campaign to an entirely new level.

The Save Bhutto Committee was organised from Stanhope Mews,
in central London, where the sons of Zulfikar Ali Bhutto, Murtaza
and Shahnawaz, lived. In the year following the trial, they had concentrated their protests on the scale of the miscarriage of justice that
the trial and verdict represented. One of the most successful compo-
nents of that campaign was the organisation of a two-day conference
in London – the Convention of International Jurists.

This involved legal authorities from all over the globe considering the charges against Bhutto, the trial, the verdict and the sentence. On every count they found that the conviction was unsafe and
should be quashed. This was reported in the international media on
a huge scale. Yet all this was to no avail when, in February 1979,
the appeal against the trial and verdict was lost. This took the Save
Bhutto Committee's work onto a much more political path. It also
developed a much greater urgency and scope, since what had been a
campaign against a miscarriage of justice, and contravention of human rights, became a matter of life or death.

Fatima Bhutto, the grand-daughter of Zulfikar Ali Bhutto, and
the daughter of Murtaza Bhutto, has captured this in her book,
Songs of Blood and Sword. In the section where she is talking of the
Save Bhutto campaign she writes about how the movement changed
in 1979:

> The campaign had grown exponentially. The Save Bhutto Com-
> mittee was holding large rallies across the United Kingdom and

1. Fatima Bhutto, *Songs of Blood and Sword*, Jonathan Cape, 2010.

galvanising Pakistani communities in cities across the world – in Sweden, in France, in the Gulf States, and in Canada and the United States. Stories of the international protests against Zia's junta were carried across to Pakistan on the BBC overseas service, bringing news to a country whose own press had been brutally silenced. 'Deep inside, despite everything,' recalls Tariq Ali, 'there was a feeling that they couldn't do it – they couldn't kill Zulfikar Ali Bhutto – that something would stop it from happening. I think initially, Murtaza and Shahnawaz felt that too. He was the most popular leader. There'd be mass uprisings, people would storm the prisons . . .'[1]

My part in that campaign was to help organise the work of the Save Bhutto Committee in Glasgow. Until this point, I had devoted my every waking hour to my business. Now, for the first time since moving to Scotland, I was involved in active politics. The aim of the campaign was to get leading figures in public life in Scotland to support the movement for the repeal of the death sentence facing Bhutto and the quashing of the charges.

This brought the Glasgow Save Bhutto Committee into direct contact with church leaders, union leaders and MPs. There were trades union resolutions passed, letters from MPs, motions in the House of Commons, and special protest meetings held all over the UK, all demanding clemency for Bhutto, in a campaign which lasted for months. The then Labour Prime Minister, Jim Callaghan, appealed for mercy for Bhutto at a number of these special rallies. In the end it was all to no effect. Nothing could shift Zia's brutal determination to assassinate Bhutto using the cover of the courts in Pakistan.

So in the early hours of 4 April 1979, Bhutto was hanged. He was not even allowed the human dignity of seeing his family before he died. At the time we could hardly believe it. We did not think that Zia would go through with it. We believed that his cruel ambitions would be chastened by the uproar on the streets of Pakistan. Perhaps we, in the UK, underestimated what had happened there.

We had also had some warnings about the ruthlessness of military dictators who would 'decapitate' radical mass movements through

1. Fatima Bhutto, *op. cit.*

the execution of key leaders. The history of Latin America is littered with such assassinations, usually taking place with the assistance and connivance of the government of the USA or their agents. For example, only six years before the death of Zulfikar Ali Bhutto, the elected President of Chile, Salvador Allende, was murdered by the military junta of General Augusto Pinochet when it seized power. Looking back at the recent history of the time we should not have been surprised when Zia had Bhutto hanged to prevent the possibility of his political resurrection at a later stage.

Fatima Bhutto records the views of the leaders of the Save Bhutto Committee in London at the time in *Songs of Blood and Sword*:

> What we didn't take into account was how badly Zia had brutalised the population. Public floggings, stonings and humiliating displays of torture were being carried out in Pakistan. There had never been such an overt display of the state's capacity to commit violence towards its own people before. There couldn't be a mass uprising to save the country's first Prime Minister, people were too frightened.[1]

The death of Zulfikar Ali Bhutto brought the Save Bhutto Committee's work to a crossroads. Many, like me, thought the campaign should be maintained but transformed into an appeal for the restoration of democracy in Pakistan against the brutalities of the Zia regime, exploiting all the channels used in the Bhutto campaign. Murtaza and Shahnawaz Bhutto and most of the London leadership thought differently. They argued that words of reason had not prevailed, and so it was time for armed struggle. They then went off on an adventure in Afghanistan to build a guerrilla struggle against the Zia dictatorship. That campaign failed utterly and came to nothing, but the divergence in tactics at the time of Zulfikar Ali Bhutto's death split the original movement. It was infantile leftism; Pakistan in 1979 wasn't Cuba in 1959.

The Glasgow Save Bhutto Committee decided to maintain the campaign against Zia for the restoration of democracy in Pakistan by using all the contacts we had made in all walks of life in Scotland.

1. Fatima Bhutto, *op. cit.*

In reality what became the Council for Human Rights in Pakistan was made up of the leading figures who had played significant roles in the Save Bhutto Committee before it. It was a genuine response from all of the Pakistani community in Scotland to what happened to Zulfikar Ali Bhutto, his murder and the continuation of the brutal dictatorship of Zia ul Haq. Its main focus, like the Save Bhutto campaign before it, was the Labour movement in Scotland, and in particular, the Labour Party. Thus, all the work of the campaign drew me closer and closer to the Labour movement.

As a result of her father's death, Benazir Bhutto went into exile in London. In Pakistan she had to flee for her life from Zia ul Haq and his henchmen. I didn't know Benazir then, and was still mostly preoccupied with business not politics. Some years later I found out that she was staying in the Barbican development in London and I wrote her a letter expressing my huge sadness about what had happened to her father, her family and to her, inviting her to come to visit Glasgow at any time. I think that was in 1985. Some time later she phoned me to thank me for my condolences and we agreed to meet. I visited her at her apartment at the Barbican, which proved to be the start of an enduring friendship.

I am not sure why she made that first entreaty, because at this stage I wasn't prominent in Scottish politics. Of course, I did have substantial business interests then, so perhaps she considered me to be a useful point of contact in Scotland. Not long after our initial introduction, the newly established Pakistan People's Party (Scotland) invited Benazir to come and address a public meeting in Glasgow. It was held in Govan Town Hall and was a huge success. The roars of 'Pakistan Zindabad!' – Long Live Pakistan – rang out, with more than 1,000 people in the hall. It may be that this occasion cemented our friendship, since it established beyond question that there was an organisation capable of mobilising the Pakistani community in Glasgow. Benazir was quite emotional after the meeting. She said 'Sarwar, at some stages in the meeting it was just like being home. Wonderful.' We were friends for more than 20 years after that, and whenever she came to Scotland she would visit my family and frequently stayed at my home.

One thing that has always stayed with me about Benazir was her astuteness, and the clarity of the way she expressed herself.

Discussions with her were, without fail, an illuminating experience. In this respect her book, published posthumously, *Reconciliation – Islam, Democracy and the West*, is testimony to that. Consider the erudition in these words:

> The stakes could not have been higher. Pakistan under military dictatorship had become the epicentre of an international terrorist movement that had two primary aims. First, the extremists' aim to reconstitute the concept of the Caliphate, a political state encompassing the great Ummah populations of the world, uniting the Middle East, the Persian Gulf states, South Asia, Central Asia, East Asia and parts of Africa.
>
> And second, the militants' aim to provoke a clash of civilisations between the West and an interpretation of Islam that rejects pluralism and modernity. The goal – the great hope of the militants – is a collision, an explosion between the values of the West and what the extremists claim to be the values of Islam . . . And as the Muslim world – where sectarianism is rampant – simmers internally, extremists have manipulated Islamic dogma to justify and rationalise a so-called jihad against the West. The attacks on September 11, 2001, heralded the vanguard of the Caliphate-inspired dream of bloody confrontation, the Crusades in reverse.[1]

In some ways the events of what has become known as the Arab Spring may have altered this view of history, but as an analysis of Islamic extremism it is concise and pertinent.

The other characteristic of Benazir's which always comes to mind when I think about her is her great personal courage. She was the epitome of fearlessness; a fact which ultimately contributed to her assassination in Rawalpindi on 27 December 2007. Two months before Benazir was to return to Pakistan for the last time in October 2007 – when three million people turned out to greet her in Karachi – she came to Scotland on a visit. We had a meeting with Des Browne, then Defence Secretary in the Labour Government, at the Crowne Plaza

1. Benazir Bhutto, *Reconciliation: Islam, Democracy and the West*, Simon and Schuster, 2008.

Hotel in Glasgow. There is a little part of that introduction which sheds some light on Benazir's insistence on correct details. I introduced her to Des Browne, saying we had been friends for 20 years. She looked at me and said: 'No, Sarwar, 22 years actually.'

After the Des Browne meeting, she and I, with a number of senior PPP leaders, went to lunch at the Duck Bay Marina on Loch Lomond. During the lunch she told me of her plans for government – she was confident that there would have to be an election to restore democracy, and she was confident that she would lead the PPP to victory. She asked me to consider taking a prominent post in Pakistan.

She said she had to have people beside her who would tell her the truth, because she believed that many simply told her what they thought she wanted to hear. She suggested that my experience, as a prominent MP in the Westminster parliament, combined with my talent in business, would be invaluable for Pakistan. She said, of course, that I would have to first become an elected politician in Pakistan as a member of the National Assembly or Senate, but then following that a Minister's position in the Punjab or even the post of Foreign Secretary would not be beyond my reach. I had then been a member of the House of Commons for a decade. I told her I was deeply honoured by the offer, but said that I thought I could better serve the people of Pakistan by continuing my work as an MP in the United Kingdom.

We then discussed the general situation in Pakistan. Benazir was absolutely convinced that the election in Pakistan would be rigged in favour of the party supported by Pervez Musharraf of the Pakistan Muslim League (Q). She asked me to put together a small team of British MPs who could act as impartial election observers. I agreed to do that, and said I would come to Pakistan to make arrangements before the election.

She was also deeply concerned about the rise of Islamic fundamentalism. I said then that she had to make her own security her number one priority; that Pakistan was now a changed place. She said that she thought the military in Pakistan were exaggerating the danger to her life so that she would not return. 'They are trying to scare me and I won't be scared,' she said. Then she added, 'No Muslim will kill their own sister.' Alas, she was tragically wrong about that.

The news of her assassination was totally shattering. Disbelief then gave way later to overpowering sadness. I think she had learned many lessons from her previous time in power, and her death remains a great loss for the country. At the time of her assassination I was actually in Lahore making provisional arrangements for the election monitoring. I remember that shortly after the assassination, the British High Commissioner in Islamabad phoned me to tell me to stay in my hotel, as there were riots on the streets in protest at Benazir's murder. He described her murder as a tragedy for Pakistan.

As I have explained, it was Benazir's father's murder and the campaign to prevent it that drew me towards the Labour Party in the UK. But there was more than that. The Party's values of fighting against poverty and inequality, and for education for all and its general commitment to social justice, reflected my own values. Then I was still totally committed to my business, which consumed most of my energies, but, after the Zulfikar Ali Bhutto and the PPP campaigns, it seemed logical for me to join the Labour Party. I think it was 1981 when I first applied.

Thereby hangs a tale, because applying to join the Labour Party in those days was not the same as actually joining. Inside the Party there was a fierce war being waged between the left and right for its future, with Tony Benn the figurehead of the left. My local party, in the Glasgow Pollok constituency, was controlled by the Marxist Militant Tendency. They were extreme left Trotskyites who, years later, would be expelled from the Party. But in those times, the Militants in Pollok were planning to mount a challenge to take the Labour Party parliamentary candidate's position. They held most of the office bearers' posts, including the powerful Constituency Secretary position. They exploited those positions to vet all those who wanted to join the Party, so they could maintain their dominance in preparation for taking the prospective parliamentary candidate's position.

A bit of explanation of the structure or Labour politics in those days is probably necessary. Everything was based on the set-up for national and local elections. The bottom of that tier was the local areas, or wards, which were the units for election to Glasgow City Council. Each ward in Glasgow elected a councillor to the Council. A number of wards taken together made up the parliamentary constituency for the election of an MP to the Westminster Parliament. Labour's organisation mirrored that. Local branches were made up usually of a number of ward areas put together. The local branches then sent delegates to the 'Constituency Labour Party' – the body which selected the candidate to stand for MP. It usually met once a month and was the main decision-making body. In my own case Pollokshields/Shawlands was my local branch, which was one of the subdivisions of Pollok Constituency Labour Party.

David Dick was the leader of the Militants in Pollok. He had a passing resemblance to Lenin with his goatee beard and sharp eyes. He and his wife Margaret were prominent in the Pollok Constituency Labour Party but, along with their other Militant 'comrades', they also controlled the local Labour Party branch in Pollokshields/Shawlands on Glasgow's south side. They laid down the rule that in order to join the Party you had to be a member of a trade union. That blocked my membership for more than a year, because as a self-employed businessman I wasn't eligible to become a member of a union! Eventually, though, these obstacles were overcome when I took out a subscription for a weekly copy of the red banner *Militant* newspaper. That and some careful words in the right places from my friend of those days, Adil Bhatti, meant I eventually got my first Labour Party card in 1982.

By that time my business interests were expanding in a big way, and my brother, Ramzan, and I had the two large Cash and Carry businesses described in the previous chapter, one in the Kingston area in Glasgow and one in Maxwell Road in Pollokshields. So I did not have time for what could seem like endless local Labour Party meetings. However I was elected as a delegate from the Pollokshields/Shawlands branch to the Pollok Constituency Labour Party (CLP) Committee and played a part there. The CLP meeting was where all the major decisions about Labour Party business – resolutions to Conference, the selection of councillors and, most importantly, parliamentary candidates – were voted on. That's why the Militants controlled the membership applications so closely.

In the end their campaign to capture the Labour parliamentary nomination for Pollok foundered. At the selection meeting there was a split vote between the Trotskyite Militants and the other leftists.

A middle of the road Labour councillor, Jimmy Dunnachie, won the nomination. I worked hard for him in the 1987 General Election, particularly in campaigning for a Labour vote among the Pakistani community in the Pollokshields area. This was the start of a long-term friendship with Jimmy – who was something of an old right-wing war horse – a friendship which would prove to be crucial in later years.

Early in 1988 Mrs Thatcher was still in power, and about to use Scotland as a trial run for the Poll Tax – a new system of local taxation which favoured the well-off at the expense of the poor. It seems a long time ago now. P.W. Botha was still in power in South Africa, Nelson Mandela was still in jail and *A Fish Called Wanda* was about to hit the cinema screens. My priority in life was still the same – building my Cash and Carry businesses. At this stage, the two United Wholesale warehouses had an annual turnover of almost £50 million.

By then I was finding time for a local commitment to Labour Party politics. Unlike many in those days, I wasn't a committed activist, but my face was well enough known in the local Labour Party to be elected to the all Glasgow City Labour Party as well. So, in time, I began to take part in the affairs of the Party at a Glasgow City level, as well as my local Constituency Party. The District Council elections were due in May 1988. There were two tiers of local government in Scotland then; the district councils, in this case Glasgow, and the regional councils, for the west of Scotland, Strathclyde. The 1988 elections were for Glasgow District Council.

The procedure for the selection of prospective Labour candidates was organised through what was known as the Panel system. A committee of elected Labour Party members, councillors and officials ran the Panel. You had to appear before them and be interviewed to establish whether you could be approved as an acceptable Labour candidate, and your name would then be added to the Panel of possible Labour candidates.

I think that it was at a local Pollokshields and Shawlands ward meeting, in December 1987, that a trade union member in the ward approached me and suggested that I should try to get accepted for the Panel of candidates, as 'there would be no harm done'. I remember him saying, 'Just go for the Panel, and if you don't want to stand, don't stand, but at least you will have the choice if you are on the Panel of candidates.'

The interviews were held in the Glasgow City Chambers, the headquarters of the Council, in George Square in the city centre. To be honest, despite putting my name forward, I wasn't going to bother turning up for the interview. I had decided it wasn't for me. I mentioned this in a phone call to one of my Party comrades and he insisted that I must go for interview. So, on what was the last evening for acceptance as a candidate, I presented myself in one of the committee rooms at the top of the imposing marble staircase in the Chambers.

I don't remember much about the interview; there were questions about why I joined the Labour Party and when, why did I want to be a Labour councillor, and what contribution had I made to the Party since joining. There were more questions about the local Labour Party and the local area. I was also asked whether I would pledge to vote in the Council with the Labour Whip. Not saying 'Yes' to that question would have ended my fledgling political career!

After about twenty minutes I was asked to take a seat in the corridor. To my astonishment, a few minutes later I was called back to the interview room and told I had been accepted on the Panel of approved Labour Party candidates. This was a crucial first step in my involvement in elected politics, but of course I did not know that at the time. Nor did I know where all of this would lead.

The next significant step was taken about a month later at a meeting of the local Labour Party branch in Pollokshields. To put it bluntly nobody wanted to stand as the Labour candidate in the East Pollokshields/Maxwell Park ward. The seat had been held for decades by the Tory Party, with a rock-solid 700-vote majority. In local government elections that was deemed to be unbeatable. So the comrades – as we called ourselves in those days! – asked me to stand.

'What the hell,' I thought, 'might as well give it a go.' At the back of my mind was the idea that if we could get votes out of the Asian community in the ward area, we could reduce the majority to a more respectable three or four hundred. I only had a small team to help deliver leaflets and knock on doors, so the electoral journey was more in hope than expectation. There were two elements to our strategy

– if that isn't too grand a description of a plan for a local ward election. First of all we set out to target what might be called the 'Asian vote' in the Pollokshields area. That part of the plan was simple and two-fold – first to encourage all those who had never bothered to vote to change their mind and vote; then to persuade them to vote Labour. The more we knocked on doors, the more we realised that there was a huge number who didn't vote and who were very open to persuasion to vote Labour.

Obviously, since I was Asian there was an immediate identification with me being from the same community, but we also talked on the doorstep about schools, the issues in the local area and the need for a local community centre. Simple stuff, but I have always spoken to people honestly and on their terms and it seemed to work. We could feel we were having an effect.

However, what became very clear even at that early stage in campaigning was that there would be language difficulties in mobilising the Asian vote for Labour. English was obviously a second language for most of the older members of the Asian community in Pollokshields, and even when people could speak English, many could not write it. We had to make special efforts on voting day to make sure potential voters could be helped in the voting booths by their sons or daughters who could interpret the voting paper. We also made huge efforts to make sure voters knew that 'Sarwar' was the fourth down on the voting paper. These difficulties would surface later in a far more crucial manner when I challenged Mike Watson MP for the Labour nomination in the Govan parliamentary seat.

As well as the 'Asian vote', we also decided to target a section of the vote that could be won back to Labour. In the large detached houses of the ward, in Maxwell Park in particular, which were some of the richest parts of Glasgow, we believed that the Tory vote was rock-solid. So spending a lot of time there trying to find Labour votes would be pointless. However there were other parts of the ward where good-quality sandstone tenements were home to young married couples, many of whom came from working class families, but were now young professionals; teachers, social workers or working in local government. The 'Teacher vote' was the shorthand we used for them.

In 1987 Margaret Thatcher had won a third landslide victory for the Tories in the UK. What became termed 'Thatcherism' – her policies of attacking the poor, the unions and the welfare state to make the rich richer – was running rampant. In those days the Scottish Nationalists were pushing the idea that the way to defend Scotland against the privations of Thatcher was to vote for the Scottish National Party (SNP). As I have mentioned, the sitting councillor in East Pollokshields/Maxwell Park was a Tory. So we knocked on doors and argued that this local ward election was about taking on Thatcher's Tories and that 'getting the Tory out' could only be done by voting Labour. In other words we attempted to turn a local ward election into a protest agains the hated Thatcher. We ran with that day after day – 'Want to get rid of the Tory? Vote Labour, Vote Sarwar' – nothing more complicated than that.

In those days the votes for elections in Glasgow were counted at the Kelvin Hall, in the west end of the city. It turned out to be a close-run thing. There was sweat on the Tory candidate's brow and on mine as the bundles of counted votes for Labour and Tory grew – one total matching the other. After two counts the Tory candidate was declared the victor by 70 votes. I had entered the contest with very little hope of winning, yet I can still remember how disappointed and dejected I was when I realised I was beaten.

I made a personal vow then in the Kelvin Hall that next time it would be different. Although I was beaten, the battle in East Pollokshields/Maxwell Park had changed my reputation in Labour Party circles in Glasgow. I had made my mark and the activists realised that. Sure, I had been defeated, but it was being said that I had nearly achieved the impossible. And despite the result, I had thoroughly enjoyed the whole thing. I would be back for more.

So, in 1992, when the City Council elections beckoned once more, I was keen to stand as a Labour candidate again. But there was a dilemma. By this time I was recognised as a Labour Party stalwart and was being encouraged by many comrades to throw my hat into the ring for selection as a candidate in a safer seat than East Pollokshields/Maxwell Park, which despite my performance was still regarded as marginal. Along came my friend George Galloway, the MP for Hillhead, whose trenchant advice shook my convictions about standing in the East Pollokshields/Maxwell Park Ward. He told me, 'Sarwar, losing once is bad, but losing twice means that you'll have little future in Labour politics in Glasgow. A two-time loser will be branded that forever. If you have long-term political ambitions you have to go for a safe seat. You can trade on your reputation now and fight for selection in a winnable ward.'

That blunt advice gave me food for thought. But some days later I went back to George and told him that I was convinced I could win the Pollokshields seat and that it would be great for my political standing if I could take it after the Tories had held it for generations.

So I went for selection as the Labour Party candidate in East Pollokshields/Maxwell Park and was successful. But those brave words to George Galloway and my selection all came before the 1992 General Election. It was won by the Conservatives, led by John Major, who had become Prime Minister after the forced resignation of Margaret Thatcher. The 1992 defeat was seen as a disaster for the Labour leader, Neil Kinnock, because it took place against the backdrop of a deep economic recession and was seen by most political commentators as the election which Labour lost, rather than the Tories won. I thought that was unjust. Kinnock had led a commanding campaign and I never agreed with the tabloids nicknaming him as the 'Welsh Windbag'. I felt it was, in part, a slur on him simply because of his nationality.

Labour had started the battle well ahead in the polls, and among Labour activists there was a huge expectation of victory. That explained the utter desolation and demoralisation in Labour's ranks when the results were known in April 1992. So it was that a month later I was standing in the Council elections in Glasgow, in a Tory seat, when nationally they were riding on the crest of a huge political wave.

The demoralisation in the Labour Party went from top to bottom, and included our constituency. I remember clearly one of the activists in my ward apologising when telling me he wasn't going to work for the Party in the Council elections and saying: 'Sorry, Sarwar, but how the hell do you think you can win a Tory seat in these circumstances? I am not going to waste my time. You can do so if you want, but not me.'

When all was said and done, we were left with a team of maybe ten activists who wanted to work in the campaign. This taught me one of the most important lessons of my political life – a committed ten is worth fifty or more who are only partially committed to the cause. I had my team. We all worked together and proved that the commitment of key handfuls of individuals is crucial.

Also, for us, 1992 – including Major's victory – was not 1988. I had developed a much greater base of political support in the intervening years. Firstly, there had been the Poll Tax campaign. The Militant Tendency, who, as I have already noted, were prominent in Pollok, led the anti-Poll Tax movement, so our constituency had a higher profile in that battle than many others. I took part in the campaign because I was convinced the Poll Tax was iniquitous and would seriously damage the lives of ordinary families who would have to pay *more*, proportionately, for local services, as the rich paid *less*. That gave me a greater grass-roots profile than might have been the case otherwise.

Here it is reasonable to note that Tommy Sheridan, the Militant Tendency leader, who led the Poll Tax campaign, played a magnificent role in this movement. He was at the time a member of the Pollok Constituency Labour Party. He was a marvellous political street fighter and inspiring speaker, as were many others associated with that extreme left organisation. I had great misgivings when the Labour Party decided to expel all the Militants in the late 1980s, because they were judged to be a 'party within a party'. It removed a radical edge from the Labour Party at the time, although there was no disputing the fact that the Militant Tendency had political views well beyond the parliamentary road to socialism, and were undoubtedly functioning as a totally independent organisation within the Labour Party. So they had to go.

I was sorry to see Tommy Sheridan expelled, because he was a young fighter at that time who brought a real commitment to socialism within the Labour Party. He was later elected as a Member of the Scottish Parliament (MSP) which was probably his finest hour. What came after, with accusations of his being mired in a sex scandal by the *News of the World* newspaper, and his eventual conviction for perjury severely damaged his political career.

To return to 1992, however. In that campaign we applied the same general strategy as in 1988. We knew there was a large base of support in the Asian community. We used the same approach – make sure you vote and, when you do, vote Labour. We also targeted parts of the area where we believed the appeal of 'Vote Labour to get the Tory out' would be even greater than before. The second time around there were no sweating brows at the count for East Pollokshields/ Maxwell Park ward; after about an hour I knew we had won.

In the end my team had secured a 400-vote majority for Labour. We had ended a 30-year dominance of the local Tory Party in the ward; in four years turning a 700-vote majority for the Tories into a majority of 400 for Labour. Labour had lost council seats all over Scotland. I recall when Donald Dewar MP was asked on a TV panel why Labour was losing seats all over the country, he replied, 'There has been a Labour gain over the Tories, in Pollokshields, in Glasgow! Mohammad Sarwar has won it.'

I remember being on the stage at the count when the result was announced. This was me, Mohammad Sarwar, who had only been involved in Labour Party politics for little more than a decade, now an elected councillor in the biggest council in Scotland. Not a bad achievement for a boy from the Punjab, whose English could have been much better – even at that time. The triumph would change my life utterly.

The Battle for Govan 6

'I think it was a fair result. It has been a very difficult 18 months in Govan, but the contest was run by the rules of the Labour Party.'

Donna Mackinnon, Govan Constituency Labour Party Secretary, *Glasgow Herald*, 11 January 1996.

'I think some of the demands made on Sarwar are calculated to ensure he doesn't survive. I also can't get rid of this feeling that for some he is a Paki too big for his boots, and doesn't know his place, and that ain't Westminster which is still a gentleman's club. A white gentleman's club.'

Jimmy Reid, *Glasgow Herald*, 6 May 1996.

I was elected as a Labour councillor in May of 1992. By the time of the summer break in July I knew I had a big decision to make about my future. The demands of my Council position and politics were competing with the demands of the business. I was a councillor for a ward area with more than 20,000 people. I was also the chief executive of a Cash and Carry empire with a turnover of £100 million every year. Something would have to give. It wasn't long before I decided to make politics my priority, and although I was still involved in the business, my brother Ramzan took over the day-to-day running of business affairs.

Two factors were important for me. I was beginning to be consumed by politics, and enjoyed the change from fifteen years of relentlessly building the wholesale business. More importantly, however, politics presented me with the opportunity to serve, to help people, to put something back into the community. Although I always wanted to be a successful entrepreneur, I also knew I did not just want to spend my life making money and being preoccupied with that. I have always thought of the meaning of life as being much more than the amount of money you have in the bank.

The more I became involved, just as in business, the same old personal imperatives started to assert themselves. I was absorbed in my work as a councillor, but soon I dreamed of going further, to fulfil greater ambitions. The more I was able to deal with the challenges of Council politics, the greater my aspirations became. My goal, going beyond local politics, was to become Scotland's first Asian, and Britain's first Muslim, MP. I recognised that this was a long-term aim, not something that was part of my immediate future in politics.

In the summer of 1993, the Tory government, which had been in power for a very long fourteen years by then, announced a review of all Scotland's parliamentary constituencies. It was widely acknowledged that one of the aims of that Boundary Commission Review was to reduce the number of Labour MPs that Scotland sent to the House of Commons. Within that general objective, reducing the delegation of Labour MPs sent from Glasgow to the House of Commons was recognised as a particular priority. Enter Jimmy Dunnachie, the MP for the Pollok constituency in Glasgow, who had become one of my prominent supporters some years after I had joined the Party. He was actually responsible for concentrating my mind on going for a parliamentary nomination as a Labour candidate sooner than I had ever contemplated.

I don't recall precisely when he approached me, but it was a long time before any of the initial results of the Boundary Commission's deliberations were known. I think it was after a Labour Party meeting, when Jimmy and I went to the social club of the local junior football team, Pollok Juniors, one of Jimmy's favourite haunts. He told me he was going to retire before the next General Election, and that I should consider throwing my hat into the ring as a contender to become the Labour candidate in his seat when he stood down. I remember that I said right away that the time might not be right for me, that I wasn't well enough known, and that there could be a backlash against me because I was Pakistani. He said: 'No, Sarwar, you have a good base of political support in your area and in the Constituency Party, and you can do it. Waiting for the time to be right sometimes means the right time never comes.'

I told him I needed time to consider. But I also asked, pointedly: 'Jimmy, are you sincere? You're not saying this to me and then you'll speak to six others about standing?' This was exactly what happened most of the time in Scottish Labour politics, when an MP was ready to retire. Jimmy insisted that he was serious, that he would rather see his seat passed on to me than to any of the sitting MPs on the south side of Glasgow. 'You've got the votes to win it, your votes and my votes. You can stop any of the others,' he argued emphatically.

In those days, George Galloway was one of Glasgow's big political figures. In 1987 he had become the MP for the Hillhead constituency by defeating Roy Jenkins, a one-time Labour Chancellor, who had defected to the Social Democratic Party. George had been a prominent leader of the left in the Labour Party for a long time, an international standard-bearer for the Palestinian cause and, related to that, other Muslim causes, like that in Kashmir. So, as my involvement in Labour politics in Glasgow developed, it was inevitable that we would link arms during the struggles within the Party. In these matters, though, he was far more experienced than me, and in fact became a valued advisor. When Jimmy Dunnachie made his proposal, the first person I discussed it with was George Galloway. I remember him saying encouragingly, 'Sarwar, this has potentially earth-shattering possibilities for you, my brother.'

Some weeks later I went to see Jimmy and told him I would stand. We struck a firm pact there and then. He gave me his word that he would tell Labour officialdom that he was not going to retire from the House of Commons, which would provoke the certainty of a contest for candidates for the new seats post the Boundary Commission findings. This was enormously significant, because his announcement meant that there would be eleven MPs fighting to win a nomination for the reduced number of ten constituencies. This created a political atmosphere that there was a certainty of candidates' contests. Had Jimmy announced his retirement, the MPs would have been reduced to 10 and there would have been enormous pressure, particularly from the trades unions, to ensure that there should be no challenges – the 10 remaining MPs should share out the 10 new constituencies, thus avoiding the possibility of political bloodshed in the city. Jimmy's indication that he would stand meant there was general acceptance that there would be contests and that, in turn, meant that I could not be accused of splitting the Party by standing.

Jimmy told me he had enough of the life of travelling to London every week, but wanted to depart while being at least, in part, responsible for influencing who his successor would be. He was determined it would not be Mike Watson or Ian Davidson. They were respectively MPs for Glasgow Central and Glasgow Govan at that time. Jimmy, being on the largely working-class right of the Party, had a huge contempt for the middle-class left. He told me that his own preference would be to see Ian Davidson out of the picture. Davidson had the knack of, almost always, inspiring personal loathing wherever his footsteps fell. Jimmy liked to joke that Davidson was a real force for unity in the Party because everywhere Davidson went, he was universally disliked! Jimmy saw Davidson as an interloper in Glasgow Labour politics. Davidson came from the Borders in Scotland and had become the Labour MP for Govan in 1992.

It was the winter of 1993 when the first review of the Boundary Commission was published. It covered all Scottish parliamentary constituencies but for Glasgow there were two headline-makers in the Commission report. The first was confirmation that the number of parliamentary constituencies in Glasgow was to be reduced from 11 to 10. This proved that the pact I had made with Jimmy Dunnachie had been crucial.

The second headline was that the Glasgow Central constituency was to be carved up among the remaining ten seats. So for me, the next question was: 'Where is Pollokshields on the new electoral map?' The answer was, in the newly defined Glasgow Govan constituency, which had bits of the old Central constituency, combined with areas taken from the old Pollok, Cathcart and Govan seats. It looked as if, for me, it would be a case of challenging for the Govan seat. This remained uncertain because the first report of the Commission was set only in the form of recommendations. The Labour Party, and the sitting MPs, still had the right to lodge an appeal against the Commission findings.

When the Boundary Commission proposals were published, political tensions were running high among the MPs in Glasgow who were confronted with a fight for their political lives. On 12 November 1993, the *Glasgow Herald* reported: 'Gloves off as MPs look at which seat should go'. This described a meeting of the MPs to discuss the Party's response to the draft Boundary Commission findings. By this time Mike Watson had fought what seemed to be a successful internal campaign in the Party for the rejection of the Commission findings, on the grounds of retaining his Glasgow Central seat as a standing constituency. His stance on rejection was supported at the Party meeting, which then put the Provan seat of Jimmy Wray, MP in the East End of the city, in danger of break-up.

The opening lines of the *Herald* article told the tale:

James Wray, ex-amateur boxer and Labour MP, has warned his fellow MPs that they should prepare for the political equivalent of a bare knuckle contest if his Provan seat is axed next week by an appeal to the Boundary Commission . . . He said: 'Let's face it, in this situation, it's dog eat dog and I'll take on anybody in any constituency that borders mine.'

In the days that followed, George Galloway proved his near unrivalled ability, in those days, to ride the rough seas of internal Labour politics. He worked tirelessly for days on my behalf. Eventually he and Jimmy Wray reached the conclusion that if there were to be a dog-fight it should on the south side of the city. That agreement was vital to any deal getting done. The phone calls were made and the vote was fixed as far as that was possible among the sitting MPs. Essentially Galloway convinced the others to out-manoeuvre Watson and Davidson.

So it was that at a meeting of MPs and party officials on 22 November, the previous decision taken to oppose the axing of the Glasgow Central seat was rescinded. The MPs and Labour officials decided to accept the Boundary Commission recommendations that the number of parliamentary constituencies in Glasgow would be reduced from 11 to 10. They also agreed that the recommendations for the boundaries of the 10 new constituencies would not be challenged. This meant that Glasgow Central would be abolished and its breakup shared out among other seats. My own Pollokshields ward would go into a new Glasgow Govan seat, and that determined where I would run for the Labour nomination, against Mike Watson as it turned out.

Not long after this, the two MPs, Mike Watson and Ian Davidson, came to visit me in my office in the United Wholesale warehouse, which at that time was in West Street, in the Tradeston area of Glasgow. Their manner was brusque and they meant business. Davidson was confrontational, reminiscent of the famous Godfather movie, along the lines of, 'Sarwar, we are here to make you an offer you cannot refuse.' Watson said that I would need to stand down from selection for the Govan seat, because he was going to stand for it. I think it was Davidson who then added: 'You'd better not stand . . . it is in your own interest not to stand. Why would you stand when you are going to get slaughtered?'

I said to them: 'It's a democracy. If I lose I will support you; if you win, what is the problem? If I am going to get slaughtered, surely there's no problem to you if I stand?'

Looking back now, I suppose the die was cast then. They both stormed out of the office.

I have always considered the visit of Watson and Davidson to the warehouse to insist that I should not stand for Labour candidate as a great paradox. In Glasgow politics, both were considered as leading figures on the left of the party. The organising committee of the Left in those times was called the Labour Co-ordinating Committee, or LCC as it was known. Watson was, for many years, the secretary of the LCC in Scotland.

One of the LCC's great political programmes to transform the Labour Party was to introduce the right of Constituency Labour Parties to de-select their MP. Put simply, at the time of an approaching General Election, the local Constituency Labour Party would have the right to vote on who the Labour candidate in the coming election would be. The grand plan was for the left to transform the politics and programme of the Parliamentary Labour Party by deselecting right-wing MPs and replacing them with a new breed of left-wing socialists. That policy was one of the great bastions of the left, yet, when Watson was faced with a possible democratic challenge from me, what was his response? He retreated from his principles and adopted a version of the divine right of kings inside Labour's ranks – 'You cannot deselect me, I am the sitting Labour MP.'

But there was another huge paradox that developed in the battle for Govan concerning the programme and politics of the left. The key activists who fought against me for the constituency nomination were leading lights on the left, and members of the Labour Co-ordinating Committee. Things are different now, but in those days different Party groups campaigned for their own political policies within the Party. One of the policies that the Labour Co-ordinating Committee promoted was positive discrimination for black people within the structures of the Party. They supported the setting up of special Black Sections within the Party to advance that. They were also in favour of positive discrimination for black people in the process of the selection of Labour candidates where, on occasion, they supported the idea of all-black shortlists for some candidate selections. The key activists in the Watson camp were all members of the LCC. So all their campaigning for positive discrimination for black people in the Party was discarded when it came to opposing me as a candidate for Labour.

Worse than that, their reaction when confronted with a challenge from me was to play the race card. It was played cleverly, but nonetheless the race card it was. The whispering campaign directed against me, as a consistent mantra, wasn't around the crudely racist slogan 'We don't want a Paki here.' Rather, it was much more subtle and blamed the so-called backwardness and racism of the average working-class voter. So the political line of my opponents was the oft-repeated warnings that 'We don't think the voters are ready to vote for a Pakistani; we don't think they will accept a Muslim becoming their MP; will members of the Orange Order vote for a Pakistani?' It was a war of attrition by insinuation.

The second element in their propaganda was that Labour now had a chance to win power in the next General Election, probably in 1997, and that every single seat could count in securing a Labour majority in what at that time we thought would be the closest fought of elections. Every potential Labour seat was vital to the greater cause of securing a Labour government. Their argument then ran that in putting me forward as a candidate when the Glaswegian working-class were not ready to vote for a Pakistani and Muslim, we were not only endangering the Glasgow Govan seat for Labour but, in turn, that potential defeat meant the possibility of a Labour government was also endangered. Every seat lost placed a Labour majority in jeopardy.

It soon became clear to me that the Watson camp had established their 'party lines' in the campaign against me, and had a certain unity of approach concerning how to argue against my selection, how to play the race card effectively, and how to develop their opposition effectively and consistently.

I got what I consider to be concrete proof of my perceptions from the late Jimmy Reid, the one-time leader of the shipyard workers in Glasgow, and recognised working-class hero. He was a member of the Labour Party in our ward by then, earning his living as a journalist. He phoned me one day as the campaign for the Labour nomination was gathering pace, and asked me to stop by his house sometime for a cup of tea.

Jimmy told me that Watson and Davidson had visited him earlier asking for his support. They had reiterated the exact same arguments about Glasgow not being ready for a Pakistani MP and that putting me forward as a candidate in effect might jeopardise the coming of a Labour government if I lost. Jimmy told me that his inclination had been to vote for Watson, as he seemed to be much more to the left than me, but that from that day on he had become a Sarwar supporter.

Our camp took the opposition head on. We had the big advantage of being able to argue that my victory in the Council seat was evidence that people would vote for me, but we also accused the Watson camp of being underhand in their accusations. We used the argument that they were guilty of saying one thing and doing another – they seemed in favour of party democracy, but now were opposing the right of members to vote on who should be the Party candidate at the next election. Secondly, we said that they had been supporters of ethnic minority rights in the Party, but were now saying a Pakistani couldn't win.

The 1994 Scottish Conference of the Labour Party provided stark evidence of how bitter the struggle for Govan would eventually turn out to be. At that Conference I was standing for election to the most powerful body of the Labour Party in Scotland – the Scottish Executive Committee. It was elected each year at the annual conference. Watson and his cronies from the Labour Co-ordinating

Committee, including Ian Davidson MP and Mike Connarty MP, spared no efforts in trying to block me. They approached delegation after delegation, and asked them to vote for alternative candidates of the left rather than a 'right-winger' like me.

In the end I got lucky and was chosen to speak on an Employment motion. I spoke about Govan shipyard. I said that the Labour Party must stand shoulder to shoulder with the workers at Govan shipyard and that the coming Labour government must do everything in its power to defend the future of the jobs at the yard. That was met with great applause. I was still speaking when the bell went to signify my time was up. I managed to get a bit of extra time by joking that it was justified, since the newspapers that day had reported that the grandmother of leader Tony Blair came from Govan. I still think that being chosen to speak might have tipped the balance in the Conference in my favour. When the results of the election were announced I had sufficient votes to be elected on to the Scottish Executive Committee – a not insignificant achievement in the light of the controversies to come.

Back in Glasgow, the new focus of all the efforts, made by both camps, was on securing enough delegates' support to determine which side would win control of what would become the new Govan Constituency Labour Party. That new CLP would be made up of delegates from the new ward areas, along with delegates from the unions and other Labour Party affiliated bodies that had been defined as part of the new Govan seat.

The Constituency Party would be the body which would control the selection process of the Labour candidate, hence the dogfight by the factions in the Party to win control of it. There were three factions at that time – the Sarwar camp, the Watson camp, and the Women's Caucus who were a group supporting the selection of a woman candidate, in this case Margaret Curran. In the end the Women's Caucus double-crossed us. We had a pact with them that we would vote for Johann Lamont for the chair if they supported our candidate for the Secretary's position. Johann Lamont – who would become the leader of the Labour Party in Scotland many years later – was elected, but when it came to the secretary's position they voted for the Watson camp nomination, Donna Mackinnon. This would prove to be a serious setback for our campaign. Mackinnon then systematically exploited her position to promote Watson's candidature and restrict as many of my supporters from voting in the selection battle as was politically possible.

Mackinnon was a veteran of National Union of Students (NUS) politics in Glasgow. Over a number of years she had been the organiser of several key campaigns to secure the election of Labour student candidates to key positions in student politics. Some who know her from those days say she never put herself up front as a candidate, but instead her political ambitions were satisfied by working for others and basking in the reflected glory of their victories. So she arrived as the perfect foil for Watson – all the limelight was for him while she plotted in the shadows. There's no doubt in my mind that she was recruited by the Watson camp to become the chief organiser of the campaign to save him. Before she enlisted for that battle, I believe she was working at the NUS headquarters in London.

She seemingly arrived out of the blue, and wasn't prominent in the local Party before the Annual General Meeting of the new Constituency Labour Party. Then, suddenly, she had enough votes to be elected as the CLP Secretary. It was a remarkable transformation – from relative political obscurity in London to holding the highly influential Secretary's position in the Pollok constituency. I don't know how she managed to make ends meet at the time, but she gave every appearance of working full-time for the Watson camp. And she spared no effort in doing that. With Donna Mackinnon, it seems, every battle became personal. Whenever our paths crossed it looked to me as though her eyes were burning with hatred for me, because I was standing in the path of the man who had become the object of her latest political devotion.

The first stage of Mackinnon's strategy to defeat my campaign was to restrict the number of Party members who were eligible to vote in the selection battle by blocking their membership of the Labour Party. This included any excuse she could find, from late payment of subs, to lost membership applications, and moving addresses out of the constituency; you name it, she found an excuse. As far as Donna Mackinnon was concerned, if you were not a certainty to vote for Watson in the selection battle, the Labour Party was 'full up'. Mackinnon's ability to conduct this campaign of exclusion was based on her authority as the Constituency Secretary. This underlined what a serious setback it had been for us to lose control of the Constituency Labour Party at the AGM. Her aim was to gather the maximum number of nominations for Watson. If these reached two-thirds of all nominations, there would be no selection vote, but despite all their machinations the Watson camp failed to secure the magic number.

The one win for us, in 1995, came in the new City Council elections in May. In my Council seat the Labour majority more than doubled to 911. We had transformed the seat to a safe Labour certainty – no mean achievement. This also provided us with a useful antidote to the whispered campaign that the voters in Glasgow weren't ready to vote for a Pakistani. The scale of the victory meant that it was difficult to deny that a bulk of the white electorate in the ward had voted Labour and voted for Sarwar! Otherwise such a majority would never have been attainable.

At the end of the year, as the selection meeting for the Labour candidate approached, we were confident we would win. In fact, it would be accurate to say that when we counted up all the possibles for us, we thought we had a victory margin of between fifty and a hundred votes. We had not reckoned with Donna Mackinnon's last desperate throw of her political dice – challenging the postal votes.

The process of submitting a postal vote was quite complicated. It involved a set of signatures which had to match if the final ballot paper was to be counted in the selection contest. When the member applied for a postal ballot, they had to sign an application form – let's call that form A. They were then sent a ballot paper. It was sent with an identification form which also had to be signed – let's call that form B. This was to confirm that the person who had applied for the postal ballot on form A was the same as the person who submitted the ballot paper with the authorisation signed on form B.

The ballot paper was completed and put in a sealed envelope. The sealed ballot paper and the authorisation form B were then put together in a second envelope and sent to Party headquarters. The first stage of counting the postal ballot papers was for the Party scrutineers – there were six in all, each pair representing one of the three final candidates – to accept the ballot paper if it was agreed the signatures on form A and form B matched. The final candidates were me, Mike Watson and Margaret Curran, who later became an MP and member of Ed Miliband's Shadow Cabinet.

The count was held in the City Halls in the centre of Glasgow on the afternoon of 14 December 1995. Donna Mackinnon was Watson's chief scrutineer. As she would see it, her finest hour in this 18-month political battle was about to arrive. Based on her knowledge of the rules, she knew that if she challenged any postal vote being approved it had to be set aside for further consideration. The rules did not operate on a majority decision of the six scrutineers being binding; a veto of one scrutineer was enough for the ballot paper to be set aside as disputed. Mackinnon also knew that the final adjudication of the inclusion or exclusion of a ballot paper did not rest with the scrutineers but would then pass to the Labour Party official in charge of the ballot. In this case that was Lesley Quinn, the Assistant General Secretary of the Labour Party in Scotland at that time.

As the process of deciding on the eligibility of the postal votes started, Mackinnon's motives were to exclude as many of my supporters as possible. It wouldn't be hard to identify the Asian voters, most of whom were with me, but due to the months she had spent poring over membership lists, she also knew who were likely to be my voters beyond the block of Asian voters who were likely to support me. Their number was double that of the Asian votes.

Mackinnon set to work. There were hundreds of postal votes to consider. When they had been scrutinized, 180 ballots were contested; Mackinnon had blocked 140 of them. Her pile of vetoes was more than three times bigger than all the rest put together. If, for example, Mrs Ali had signed like that on form B, but as Khadija Ali in the first application, that was enough for Mackinnon, this Boadicea of Party democracy, to raise an objection and have the ballot paper disputed and possibly made void.

One party member who supported me, Ella Chesney, had signed her application for a postal vote as Isabella Chesney. She had signed the ballot paper form as Ella Chesney. Donna Mackinnon vetoed the vote on the grounds that the signatures didn't match. My understanding is she also vetoed votes where the signatures matched by complaining that the handwriting was different. Before the actual count could begin, there had to be an adjudication of what votes in the 180 disputed ballots could count and what votes couldn't. Now the matters were in the hands of the Party officials, especially Lesley Quinn. She was in an impossible position. I was sure that she thought that Mackinnon's actions were reprehensible, but she also had to acknowledge that they were within the rules as they stood then. At the end of several hours' argument, the count eventually went ahead with 52 votes declared ineligible – most of them my supporters.

The result of the first ballot could not have been any worse for the Labour officials, because even with 52 ballots excluded, the result was on a knife-edge. Watson polled 237 votes, I polled 236, and Margaret Curran 18. 17 of her voters had noted second preferences, and when these were shared out for the final count, Watson had 245 votes and I had 245 votes – a dead heat. The rules dictated that in the event of a dead heat there had to be a count back to the result of the first ballot – so Watson would be declared winner, on the result of the first ballot by one vote.

When the result became known there was pandemonium in the hall. The candidates had not been present at the count, but when Gordon Archer, who was the chief of my scrutineers in the hall, told me what had happened I was outraged. I didn't have much time, as it was clear that Lesley Quinn was being urged by the other officials to announce the result to the waiting media as soon as possible; they were now crowding on the stairs leading to the hall.

I approached Lesley Quinn and demanded that she should postpone the announcement of the result until there had been an opportunity to seek further adjudication on the 52 ballot papers which had been ruled out. I recall that I put three distinct arguments to her about the disputed ballots. Firstly, I argued that the 52 excluded papers should be reconsidered by the scrutineers, and where there was a majority of them in favour of a particular ballot being included, then it should be counted. I told her that if she did this I would accept the result. I argued that in effect she was allowing one scrutineer, Donna Mackinnon, to rig the election. I asked: 'If there are six appeal judges on the bench and five decide on a not guilty verdict but one says guilty, is it the guilty verdict which stands?'

Then I made a second offer that if the disputed ballots were sent to any handwriting expert I would accept their adjudication on which signatures matched and which didn't, and after that, the result of any ballot with some of the rejected votes included. Finally, I said that if the announcement of the vote was postponed and an independent inquiry made on the voting, I would accept its findings.

Lesley Quinn was clearly shaken by the position she found herself in. I felt that she was sympathetic to my cries of injustice. She conceded that she would seek the advice of the General Secretary of the Party on what should be done, given the circumstances. After she had phoned London she came back and told me: 'They say a contest is a contest. The rules have been followed and Watson wins by the rules.'

I was devastated, but burning with anger at the blatant manipulation of the vote by Donna Mackinnon. I have always felt that Lesley Quinn was put in an impossible position, not least because it is questionable that she was given the responsibility of running the count in what was recognised as a highly controversial contest. It remains my view that Jack McConnell, who was then the General Secretary of the Party in Scotland, should have administered the count. He avoided doing that by defining the selection meeting as a 'local' matter.

Lesley Quinn did what she could to have the result reconsidered, but when London said it should stand she had no alternative but to proceed. When the result was announced to the media there were gasps of disbelief. Robbie Dunwoodie, the Scottish political correspondent of the *Herald* wrote: 'The big clue was the look on the face of the Central MP Mike Watson – glazed, haggard, and unsettled. And he was the winner.' [1]

When Watson spoke to the journalists at the City Halls he said that he wished the result had been more decisive, but the result had been determined by the rules and it was time now to move on. One of his supporters told the *Herald*, 'All it takes is one vote.' I told the media that I would be appealing to the National Executive Committee of the Labour Party, because the election process had been totally flawed and that an injustice had been done which would have to be righted. To be honest, however, I wasn't at my most coherent, as I could hardly control my rage.

1. *Glasgow Herald*, 15 December 1995.

Jack McConnell, who would become an MSP and Scotland's First Minister at the Scottish Parliament in Holyrood, gave the result his stamp of approval. Since June 2010 he's been Lord McConnell of Glenscorrodale. As I have already noted, he wasn't at the count in the City Halls, but, seeming to echo the views of the Watson camp, he told the *Herald*:

> The selection has been a long and time-consuming process which shows that the Scottish Labour Party takes the electorate in Govan seriously. This result finalises the democratic choice of the members of the Govan Labour Party. Everyone in the Party should now accept the result and rally behind Mike Watson to ensure a Labour victory in Govan at the next General Election and the ending of 16 years of Tory rule.[1]

When I read that the next morning I was very angry – 'finalises the democratic choice of the members of the Govan Labour Party', when 52 of their number had not had their votes counted! I phoned McConnell and told him that there needed to be a re-ballot, and that the vote had been a travesty of justice. A few weeks later he phoned me and asked for a meeting. He told me that it was time to move on and, more or less, read me a sermon about the importance of Party unity.

I told him that I was a Party loyalist and didn't want to damage its reputation, but that I was not prepared to walk away from an injustice on this scale. I told him that if nothing was done about the injustice it would damage the reputation of the Party and could cost Tony Blair dearly. I said that hundreds of thousands of Asian votes could be lost because there was a growing perception in the Asian community across the UK that the vote had been fixed in favour of a white man to stop a Muslim getting to Parliament. He replied that there would be other options available for my political future – there would be the Scottish parliament on the horizon, where I would be guaranteed to win a seat. I warned him that if the Party didn't support a re-run, our differences would end up in court. He seemed surprised by the vehemence of my warnings. Sharp though

1. *Glasgow Herald*, 15 December 1995.

our exchanges were then, we have long since put our differences aside and have even joked about our clashes from those days. In any case, in due course, McConnell actually became a supporter of my case for a re-run of the ballot.

Enter Donald Dewar, who was then Shadow Secretary of State for Scotland and the leader of the Labour Party in Scotland. We met on a Labour demonstration in Glasgow, where he urged me to accept the decision for the sake of the unity of the Party. He then walked off to another part of the demonstration, but as he left he said, 'Leave it with me. I'll come back to you.'

I thought, that's the last I've heard from him, but, true to his word, I got a phone call from him a few days later. For once there was none of his usual 'uhms' and 'ahs'. He came straight out with the offer of a deal. 'Mohammad,' he said, 'I've been speaking to senior people in the Party. If you accept the result and stand down, we guarantee you'll get a seat in the Lords. You'll be number one on the list of Party nominations when the next Honours list is negotiated. It can be delivered.'

I told him again that I couldn't accept the injustice of the vote, that one of the reasons I had joined the Labour Party was to fight injustice and now it was confronting me personally inside my own Party. I also alerted him to the fact that if this wrong was not seen to be righted that might give the wrong signal to the Asian community across Britain about the Party's commitment to racial equality. I said that would cost the Party votes at the next General Election. I told him everyone in the Asian community across Britain knew what had gone on. He said that he was disappointed that I couldn't accept what he thought to be a very reasonable offer to resolve the dispute.

By that time our campaign for a re-run was well established. We had decided to make a tactical shift to what might be called a twin-track strategy. Within the Party, we argued consistently for an independent inquiry to establish what had gone on at the vote. Our political demand was along these lines: 'Look, there is an ongoing controversy about this in the Party. Our side says it was all a fix and the other side says the rules were followed and the decision has been taken. Why not have an inquiry to establish once and for all who is right?'

That proved to be tactically critical in the first stage of our campaign. Who could argue against clearing the whole thing up once and for all by enlisting the assistance of an independent adjudicator? Even those who were not on our side had difficulty mustering arguments against an inquiry. Why not get the facts out in the open, in order to resolve the ongoing dispute? We also reckoned that to demand a re-run inside the Party from the start would have allowed senior Party officials to hide behind the rules and argue that they couldn't risk opening the Party up to legal action by Mike Watson.

Not long after the original vote in the City Halls I had a meeting with Tom Sawyer, then General Secretary of the Labour Party. The line of argument about an inquiry, to get things out in the open once and for all, seemed to appeal to him. He was desperate to get the furore closed down, and by the end of the discussion, it was clear that the call for an independent inquiry allowed him some room for manoeuvre. I knew that the National Executive Committee (NEC) had been deluged with thousands of letters of protest from Party members from all over the UK, complaining about how the vote had been conducted. An independent inquiry allowed him to be seen to be doing something about the protests, without coming down on one side or the other.

While the internal campaign for an independent inquiry seemed to be proving persuasive there was no doubt that one single factor, above all else, was forcing Party officialdom to recognise that they could not simply wait it out hoping that the steam would run out of our protests. That single factor was the late Jimmy Reid. He was working as a columnist for the *Sun* by this time, although it was his former connections with the *Herald* newspaper which allowed the controversy to explode on to the front pages and letters pages of the *Herald*, Glasgow's only broadsheet newspaper. He wrote a series of articles on the controversy, arguing that 'a serious miscarriage of justice has to be righted'. The more he wrote, the more he provoked the Watson camp into replying in the pages of the newspaper; the more it was guaranteed that the controversy grew and grew.

It isn't possible to quote the thousands of words exchanged. They had the effect of creating an inferno of political controversy – which became an uncontrollable blaze. Jimmy Reid's first column was published before Christmas 1995. In it, he made the point that racism is deep-rooted in society, and asked the question whether the machinations of the Govan count reflected that. Watson's camp replied, through Archie Graham, Watson's campaign manager. He wrote:

> Jimmy Reid concludes by stating that part of his reaction to the selection in Govan was one of shame. I, too, felt a deep sense of shame – shamed by those, both Asian and white, who chose to play the race card in order to have the result overturned . . . Jimmy Reid, however unwittingly, has simply added fuel to the fire.[1]

This was a harbinger of the way the battle would unfold in the pages of the press. Remember, there was no Internet in those days. The Graham letter was published in the *Herald* letters' page but it provided material for a news article on the lines of 'War in Govan'. The Watson camp didn't seem to realise that if 'fuel was being added to the fire' it was their camp which kept the blaze burning.

Each time they attacked Jimmy, he replied with interest – as on 6 January 1996:

End the Shame of Govan

> It is about time the Labour Party admitted the ballot was a fiasco. The leadership has no alternative but to organise a new ballot under the auspices of an outside organisation. Labour is doing great damage to itself in Govan . . . things have turned nasty . . . we have got a Donnybrook, dirty tricks abound, and the suspicion is growing that race was a factor.

Days later, another 1,000-word article concluded, 'A serious miscarriage of justice has to be righted. It will be better for my Party if it righted this wrong itself. But one way or another it will be righted.'[2]

By mid-January Jimmy's words were beginning to look prophetic. Party officials in London had by then decided to bring in an independent agency, Unity Security Balloting Services (USBS) to look

1. *Glasgow Herald*, 28 December 1995.
2. *Glasgow Herald*, 11 January 1996.

at the ballot and the final 52 rejected ballot papers. USBS helped organise ballots in the unions and the wider Labour movement. They were required to report to the NEC of the Party before its meeting at the end of February 1996.

The central conclusion drawn by USBS was that the whole ballot had been conducted on the basis of a flawed membership list, which had been drawn up by the Party secretary, the Watson loyalist, Donna Mackinnon. Their report stated:

> This list used in the constituency was headed Computing for Labour and was not drawn from the national membership system. It had been prepared by the Constituency Secretary and it is our opinion that no reference was made to the national membership system to check membership details. The list was given to the Scottish Officer as a true record of membership, without any record or report, of how it had been compiled or verified with national records.

Accordingly USBS then went on to find that 18 people who had actually voted were not entitled to vote:

> Altogether according to the records at Head Office 11 members participating in the ballot were in arrears, 5 did not meet the 12 months membership criteria, 1 had resigned, and 1 had lapsed membership.

On the excluded ballot papers USBS found that:

> There must be reasonable doubt that the ballot papers excluded from the count, on the grounds that the signatures on the two forms didn't match, should actually have been excluded.[1]

The USBS final recommendation was that, given the narrowness of the margin of victory, the result should not stand.

According to the late Robin Cook MP, some time shortly after

1. *Glasgow Herald*, 6 May 1996.

the USBS report was published, Watson made what would be a fatal political mistake. Cook was Labour's Shadow Foreign Secretary in those days and a powerful figure on Labour's NEC. Cook told me one night in the House of Commons, years after the actual events, that Watson went to see him and asked for his support. Watson told Cook, 'Let's close this thing down, otherwise it will go on forever. Note the report and put a motion to the NEC to endorse me as the candidate. Be done with it.'

Cook told me he asked Watson, 'What is the problem with a second ballot?' To which Watson replied, 'Sarwar will win, that's the problem with a second ballot.'

From that point on in the battle for Govan, Cook became a powerful advocate of a second ballot. However, despite the USBS recommendations, there were months of delay as one Party inquiry was ordered and then another. Early in May 1996, Jimmy Reid fired his final written volley about the whole process, in an article in the *Herald*. In effect he accused the Party of dubious motives in all the delays:

> I believe their objective now is to delay a re-run and hope that a General Election will intervene. There will then be no time for a re-run. The NEC will then be urged to impose a candidate, any candidate, as long as it isn't Sarwar.

He then finished with a blunt assertion that if everything that had occurred was reduced to its essence there was racism afoot:

> I think some of the demands made on Sarwar are calculated to ensure he doesn't survive. I also can't get rid of this feeling that for some he is a Paki too big for his boots, and doesn't know his place, and that ain't Westminster which is still a gentleman's club. A white gentleman's club.[1]

Who knows whether Jimmy Reid's last rage against the injustice of the first ballot had any effect on the final decision of the NEC? I believe his reference to delaying tactics may have been critical in casting all the delays in a new light. It seems Robin Cook used that and more

1. *Glasgow Herald*, 6 May 1996.

at the May National Executive Committee meeting when he moved a motion in favour of a re-run of the ballot. It was carried by a margin of 2 to 1, with 23 and 24 June agreed as the likely voting dates.

Two days before the poll, the Watson camp went to the Court of Session, in Edinburgh, in a last-ditch attempt to block it. The grounds for Watson's legal action were that the new list of voters, which had been established by Scottish Party officials, and approved by Labour's NEC, allegedly had 25 members on it who were ineligible. The irony of this complaint was compounded by the fact that throughout the re-run battle Watson's camp had said that my threats to go to court proved I was nothing but a careerist, who had no loyalty to the Party. The difference being that I only threatened to go to court, while Watson actually raised a legal action against the Party in reality. He lost his case.

The re-run vote was held at the Labour headquarters in Glasgow at Keir Hardie House. Voters had to bring their membership card and passports as evidence of identity and were checked off on a list before being given the ballot paper. They voted in a booth. Few postal votes were allowed. The result was announced at five o'clock in the evening on 24 June 1996. It turned out to be a complete and utter vindication of our campaign for a re-run on the grounds that the previous poll had been rigged. I polled 279 votes, Watson 197. Watson's previous 'victory' by one vote, on a count-back, had been transformed into an 82-vote majority for my candidacy.

I told a news conference arranged inside Keir Hardie House that I was proud to have been selected as the Labour candidate for Govan, and that I would represent all the different communities of Govan regardless of 'race, culture or religion'. I was astonished to be asked by one of the pack of journalists if I would be 'a Muslim MP or a Labour MP.' I asked the reporter if he would pose the same type of question to a prospective Labour candidate from any other religious background. Would the question be raised: Will you be a Catholic MP, a Jewish MP or a Labour MP? I then told him that, if I won the election, I would be a Labour MP, who happened to be a Muslim.

I remember that after the news conference was finished I had a moment's reflection. It concerned the former Labour leader John Smith. He had become Party leader after Labour lost the 1992 General Election. At the 1993 Labour Conference, Smith put his leadership on the line by supporting a conference motion to change the Party's selection of parliamentary candidates to a one-member one-vote system, thereby ending the union block vote in the selection of Labour candidates. Smith had lost the Conference vote on OMOV, as it was known, the previous year. But he stuck to his guns and pushed for the change. Unfortunately Smith died suddenly of a heart attack in 1994. I think he was one of the finest Prime Ministers the UK never had. I owe him a debt, and thought about that after the news conference was over. If it had not been for the change to one-member one-vote finally clinched by John Smith, I would never have had a chance to win the Govan selection and then become the first Muslim to win election to the House of Commons.

Shortly after the selection in Govan, George Galloway, then a Glasgow MP, gave an interview to the *Herald* where he spoke out about the scale of apparent 'dirty tricks' which had been played against me in the battle for the Labour nomination. He asked how it had come to pass that so many Government and other public agencies seemed to have an unremitting number of inquiries about the running of my Cash and Carry business in what seemed a concerted fashion – all of which came to nothing. George made the point in the interview that these included raids by Customs and Excise, by Trading Standards and a series of investigations by Glasgow City Council. All of which seemed to be known in advance by the media. As were the legal instructions to Strathclyde Police from senior officials in the Procurator Fiscal's department for further inquiries into this or that spurious allegation. 'Sarwar – new probe' seemed to be an almost daily headline. Not a single public explanation was offered by any spokesperson for any of these agencies about why this host of inquiries had come to be, and why all had come to nothing.

In conjunction with what undoubtedly had the look of an organised conspiracy against me, of some degree, there then came the emergence of this shady character, Mohan Singh. Here's what Audrey Gillan of *Scotland on Sunday* subsequently reported about her investigation at the time:

> Then, two weeks before the election, a mystery man called Mohan Singh appeared in Glasgow. He claimed to be working for

the *News of the World* and was grubbing around for sleazy
information on Sarwar. There was no evidence whatever that
such information existed but Singh was offering large sums of
money for a useful bit of malicious invention. I was intrigued.
I obtained Singh's mobile phone number and called him, pre-
tending to be Lynn, a woman who had 'knowledge' of Sarwar.
In the course of our conversation, Singh offered me £250,000
to reveal potentially damaging information about Sarwar. He
also promised 'Lynn' relocation and a new life 'away from
Glasgow'.[1]

At the time Audrey Gillan thought that Singh may have had connections with Indian intelligence whose interests would be served
by discrediting and even thwarting the election of a pro-Pakistan
Muslim to the British Parliament. If they were not Singh's backers,
the question still remains who was? That question has never had an
answer. I will tell this story in more detail in Chapter 8.

1. *London Review of Books*, 22 January 1998.

The Haq Family and 'Honour' Killings

7

'On 30th June 1995, Nazia was coerced into marriage with her father's 40-year-old nephew, Mohammad Iqbal. She was still 13-years-old, which makes the match illegal under both Pakistani and Islamic law. Rifat had been married the day before. In the months that followed both of the girls tried to kill themselves.'

Audrey Gillan, *London Review of Books*, 22 January 1998.

'It is a tragedy, a horror, a crime against humanity. The details of the murders – of the women beheaded, burned to death, stoned to death, stabbed, electrocuted, strangled and buried alive for the "honour" of their families – are as barbaric as they are shameful. Many women's groups in the Middle East and South-west Asia suspect the victims are at least four times the United Nations' latest world figure of around 5,000 deaths a year.'

Robert Fisk, *Independent*, 7 September 2010.

My selection and approval as the Labour candidate for Govan in July 1996 marked the first critical victory in the march to Westminster. However, rather than continue with that part of my story, I'd like to look back at an earlier episode. I am referring here to the abduction, and then forced marriage, in Pakistan, of the Haq sisters, Rifat and Nazia, carried out by their father Abdul Haq. Early in 1996, I'd gone to Pakistan and helped to free them from their terrible plight there. I should tell the story of those events at this point, because the aftermath of the rescue of the Haq sisters and their mother is indispensable to an understanding of what developed during, and after, the 1997 General Election. What became known as the Haq controversy shaped future events.

It was around September 1995 that I first became aware of what would give rise to that controversy. A social worker from Glasgow

City Council had approached me and asked if I knew anything about the three Haq sisters, Rifat, Nazia and Somera, or their whereabouts. She told me that they had gone to Pakistan during the summer holidays of 1995, but had not returned to school after the holidays were finished. I thought immediately that something might be wrong, as it was unusual for a whole family to go to Pakistan and not return – especially since Rifat, the older sister of Nazia and Somera, was at university in Glasgow. I told the social worker that I would make some enquiries. I did so but couldn't find any leads.

Then, at the beginning of 1996 a journalist from the *Scotland on Sunday* newspaper, Audrey Gillan, who was working in the newspaper's Glasgow office, came to me with the story. [1] Audrey had spoken to Nadeem, the brother of the girls, who had told her everything. In June 1995, the family, including the three girls and their mother, Fatima, had gone to Pakistan for a holiday. When they landed at Multan airport, in the south of Punjab, they were kidnapped by their father, Abdul Haq, step-brother Zulfikar Haq and a number of their father's relatives. Two weeks later the father forced Rifat and Nazia to marry cousins in his extended family.

Rifat, who was 20, was forced to marry her cousin, Khalid Mahmood, a 27-year-old, previously unknown to her. That was on 29 June 1995. This was shocking enough, but the day after Rifat's forced marriage, her younger sister Nazia, a child of 13 years, was coerced into marrying another cousin, Mohammad Iqbal, who was reportedly 40 years old. This was illegal under Pakistani and Islamic law. In order for Nazia's marriage to be completed, the father lied to the authorities about her age. He had told all those concerned that Nazia was 16. He would repeat this lie when eventually confronted by Audrey Gillan and Shelley Jofre from BBC Scotland's *Frontline* team.

When Audrey Gillan came to see me she had just returned from Pakistan. She had been to the village where Rifat was now staying with Mahmood. She had met Mahmood, who told her that his wife was happy. She had also tracked down the father, Abdul Haq, to a village, Jahania, outside the city of Multan. She said the mother

1. Audrey Gillan has already been referred to in the previous chapter regarding the role she played in exposing the Indian agent, Mohan Singh.

and youngest daughter, Somera, were living under virtual house arrest imposed by Abdul Haq. She told me that the father had said he had rights in Pakistan to marry his daughters to whom he liked, and when he liked. Audrey showed me a copy of Nazia's birth certificate which proved Nazia was only 13!

Audrey Gillan asked me if I could do anything to help. I told her that I was extremely sympathetic to the plight of the girls and that I would consult with the community leaders and come back to her. I consulted with half a dozen leading members of the Pakistani community in Glasgow. Every one of them advised against my becoming involved, because it could damage my reputation, especially with the conservative element in the community. Then I discussed the issue with my wife, Perveen. She said that if it was true that the girls had been forced into marriage against their will, and one was only a girl of 13, then something would have to be done – and I would have to do it.

So I decided that this injustice could not remain unchallenged, and if the girls were being held against their will then I would go to Pakistan to bring them home. This would be highly controversial – only partly because Abdul Haq had told everyone that Nazia was 16 – as it could be interpreted as interfering in the personal affairs of the family and challenging the father's rights as head of the family. I did not realise then that the repercussions for me would turn out to be so serious. In effect, the controversy that was ignited in the community over the Haq girls would become a focal point for all those who were my political enemies. It united Peter Paton, who became a champion of the father, Abdul Haq, with Jamil Abbasi who also opposed what I did, along with Badar Islam. He would later tell the High Court in Edinburgh that one of his reasons for standing against me in the 1997 General Election was the Haq controversy, which had divided the Asian community in Glasgow.

Peter Paton's alliance with Abdul Haq was no surprise. He had been a sworn enemy of mine for years after I laughed him out of my office, when he asked me to get the Asian community to support him as the Independent Conservative candidate in a local election. I told him he needed his head examined, as I was in the Labour Party. Badar Islam became an enemy when I confronted him in public about money he owed my business – the £10,000 I had given him as a business loan which he had not repaid. When I bumped into him at the Ambala Restaurant, in Pollokshields, I called him a crook and a liar and he never forgave me for that. Abbasi became the third member of the gang of three when the Haq controversy developed. All three stood against me in the election in 1997. So what would develop much later in the *News of the World* 'bribe' scandal involving Islam, did not emerge by coincidence. This was a continuation of a plot which had its genesis in the Haq family events and my rescue journey to Pakistan.

It turned out that I had a distant cousin in Jahania, where Abdul Haq was living. I phoned the relative and he confirmed everything that Audrey Gillan had told me, although he also warned me that Haq was an important member of the local community and that taking him on in his local area would not be easy. This was a difficult decision, but the sense of injustice made my mind up for me, and I contacted Audrey Gillan to tell her that I would help.

It was useful that I was able to consult an extended family member in Jahania. It was also critical that my best friend in Pakistan, Irfan Mahmood Khan, was the Deputy Chief of Police for the Punjab province. I had known him for more than 20 years and we were close friends. I had first got to know him in 1973 when he was posted to my home area of Toba Tek Singh, as the Assistant Superintendent of Police. My distant cousin knew the exact whereabouts of the girls in Jahania, the place they were being held. When Irfan became involved, he was able to get the necessary legal warrants to remove the sisters and their mother to a place of safety. They were taken to a relative's home in the city of Burewala, east of the city of Multan, where they were put under police protection.

On 26 March 1996, Audrey Gillan and Shelley Jofre of BBC Scotland, a television crew and I, flew from Glasgow to Lahore. It was mid-morning when we arrived. Irfan Mahmood met us at the airport. When we went to his offices in Lahore, we learned that Abdul Haq had been in the High Court in Lahore that very morning. He had applied for an injunction to prevent the girls leaving the country. In court Haq had alleged that I had kidnapped his daughters and should not be allowed to take them out of Pakistan. Then, to increase the likelihood of obtaining a court order, Haq's lawyers told the court that since Nazia and Somera were 'both under 16', Haq had parental rights to secure their return to his custody. So for this court action the two youngest were 'under 16', but when Nazia was married she was 'over 16'. For any court injunction to take effect it had to be served on me and the girls personally; we were now involved in a race against time to get them out of the country, before any legal injunction could be implemented, if it were granted after the judge had time to deliberate.

Before our departure from Scotland, there had been some publicity in the Scottish press about my journey to Pakistan to help the Haq girls. Abdul Haq would have found out about that and when the mother and three girls had been taken into police custody in Pakistan, he would have realised that my intention was to take all four back to Glasgow, if that was their wish. We had intended to rest in Lahore overnight and then depart for Burewala the following morning. However, given the urgency of the situation, we left Lahore in the afternoon, with an armed police escort, heading south for Burewala. Even with the police escort it took about five hours to get there, so it was late at night, and dark, when we arrived.

The girls and the mother were still petrified. They were convinced that the father and his relatives knew of their whereabouts and so could come to get them at any minute. Burewala was about 60 miles east of Jahania, but even with this distance separating them from Abdul Haq, they didn't feel safe. I tried to reassure them that there was nothing to worry about now, but, given their state of anxiety, we thought it would be better to move on to another place of safety. We decided to move everybody to my family farm, in another part of the Punjab. It was around 75 miles away. There would be little chance of Haq finding them there. It took more than four hours to get there because of the state of the roads. Once again we had a police escort, and continued police protection at the farmhouse. It was five in the morning when we reached the farm.

The next day Audrey, Shelley and I left the family at the farmhouse and went back to Jahania to confront Abdul Haq. Shelley Jofre marched into the house and demanded to speak to Abdul Haq. He told her: 'In this country a father has the right to marry his daughters.

I have done it the right way. The law of 16 years is a British law, not a Pakistani law.' She demanded to know why he could think that marrying his 13-year-old daughter to a man who was 40 years old was the right thing to do. Haq said that Nazia's husband, Mohammad Iqbal, was 28, not 40, and that Nazia was 16, not 13. We had him on camera for *Frontline Scotland* saying that. As I have already noted, this contradicted what was said in court when Haq was pleading for an injunction. He also said that the girls had not been forced into marriage, and if they were saying that they were lying.

When I got back to my farm things were more relaxed, and the girls were more prepared to talk about their ordeal. They told me a number of stories about what had happened – which became more horrific the more they spoke. Rifat told me that, at one stage early in their abduction, the father took her mother and her youngest sister, Somera, to the local graveyard in Jahania. He then told the mother that if she did not obey his orders and accept the marriages he had chosen for Rifat and Nazia, this was where she would finish up.

Then they explained how they had been beaten and drugged, and locked up for days on end, to force them into submitting to the forced marriages. Nazia said that on the day of her marriage she was asked to sign a set of papers and refused. Her mother was then brought into the room and a gun put to the mother's head. Nazia was told if she didn't sign the papers her mother would be shot dead. Probably the most harrowing aspect of Nazia's story came out when she told Shelley Jofre how her 40-year-old husband tied her up and forced her to have sexual relations with him.

To this day Abdul Haq's motivations in all of this remain obscure. It may be that he wanted to maintain his position as the head of the extended family by providing brides for two of his male relatives. He would probably have been rewarded financially by the families of the two men involved. On the other hand, equally for financial gain, perhaps Haq had arranged the marriages of his daughters so that at a later stage their husbands would have a legitimate reason to be allowed to join their respective wives in the UK. The question has never been answered.

Whatever doubts I may have had about whether what I was doing was the right thing in these circumstances, vanished forever after that late evening discussion with the two Haq sisters. It convinced me beyond all doubt that I had to get the family out of Pakistan. However, serious difficulties remained. Abdul Haq had confiscated everyone's passports and plane tickets. Travel visas and passports for the UK could only be obtained at the British High Commission, either in Islamabad or in Karachi. Our farmhouse was in the district of Toba Tek Singh. Karachi was more than 600 miles to the south; we decided to go there since we figured that the legal agents of Abdul Haq would assume that we would depart from Islamabad – only 300 miles from Toba Tek Singh – and if granted an injunction they would go there to try to serve it.

The British Consul General in Karachi was exceptionally helpful. He even opened the High Commission on a Sunday morning to help deal with our difficulties. The girls were all UK citizens, all born in the UK, so the issue of passports for them did not provide a major problem. After a two hours' wait, the Consul returned with three brand new passports for Rifat, Nazia and Somera. Their mother, Fatima, was a different case. She was still a Pakistani citizen. We knew a travel document, issued on her behalf by the British High Commission, might not be accepted by the Pakistani authorities.

Later, at Karachi airport, our initial misgivings proved to be true. The police at border control, in the airport, would not allow Fatima to travel. They said that she was a Pakistani passport holder, and as a result couldn't travel on a British travel warrant. The whole escape plan was then put in jeopardy, as the girls declared that they would not leave Pakistan without their mother. Frantic phone calls were made, and the intervention of my friend, Tariq Pervez, Director General of the Federal Investigation Agency, eventually negotiated a safe passage for Fatima. He saved the day. However, given all the obstacles that had to be overcome, it was only when we were all sitting in the Pakistan International Airlines' departure lounge that I felt comfortable enough to think we had done it. I was interviewed there for the BBC *Frontline Scotland* film. I recall saying: 'It has been a hectic five days; in this time I've spoken to countless numbers of people to make this happen. I'm glad it's all over.'

It wasn't all over. In fact, it was just beginning. The events provoked a political war in the Pakistani community in Glasgow. It was a war which would start then, and last well beyond the General Election in 1997. Audrey Gillan's exclusive story was the front page splash in *Scotland on Sunday* on 31 March, the day of our return. A few days later a 'community' meeting was held in the local Pollokshields Development Association Hall. It condemned my actions in Pakistan and called for a boycott of my Cash and Carry warehouses, because I had brought disgrace to the local Muslim community. A media release giving more detail was then given out in the name of the 'Pakistani Media Relations Committee'.

A week or so after that I watched Shelley Jofre's *Frontline* film. I thought that the horrific detail in it would seriously undermine the case being put forward by my critics. It didn't. It seemed a pattern was being established that critics of my actions were going to be given generous coverage in the local media every time they spoke out against me. The journalist corps in Glasgow had been desperate to interview me all the time I had been in Pakistan with the Haq girls, and had given generous coverage to 'blow by blow' accounts of how the story was unfolding. At the time their reports were replete with headlines about 'mercy mission', 'ordeal family' and 'kidnap four'. Now the hacks became equally keen to give coverage to any spurious allegation raised against the very same 'mercy mission'. That included frequent accusations about my motives, which suggested I may have only become involved in the rescue because it would bring positive publicity to my continuing political campaign to secure the Labour Party candidate's nomination for Govan. It seemed their Stage 1: 'Sarwar the Hero' was now being followed by their Stage 2: 'Sarwar the Villain?'.

Mike Watson, my opponent for the Govan nomination, didn't miss the opportunity to jump on the bandwagon. This so-called champion of women's rights was quite prepared to avoid the substance of the case – the gross persecution of two young women in a Pakistani family, including the truly dreadful ordeal of a 13-year-old – in order to join the chorus of conservative critics in the local community. Watson made cheap references to 'acts of derring-do in Pakistan', and dismissed my actions there as an adventure and 'a political stunt'.

The Haq sisters, Rifat and Nazia, remained resolute and spoke out on a number of occasions, about what had happened, saying that before my intervention, there had been times while they were in Pakistan when they were in fear of their lives; that there were also times when they had each contemplated suicide. This was important in countering the critics, but there remained a drip-drip of criticism which lasted for months. Each article published in the newspapers seemed to have the effect of reigniting the controversy.

Then, in December 1996, Abdul Haq returned from Pakistan and held a media conference. A report in the *Herald* from 9 December 1996 actually notes that the press briefing 'was organised by Mr Peter Paton, the Independent Labour prospective parliamentary candidate for Govan, and Mr Jamil Abbasi, the Independent Conservative PPC for the same seat.' At the briefing Abdul Haq said that I had broken his family, and that all the allegations made by his daughters were lies. It was Paton who did most of the talking. He opened the briefing by explaining that Haq had returned to the UK to clear his own name and would be suing me for defamation.

According to the *Herald* article Paton then added:

> Mr Haq is here to speak for himself because he feels his human rights have been trampled all over by unscrupulous people who have hijacked the story for their own political gain. He is taking this action because his personal reputation and integrity have been damaged by Councillor Sarwar's involvement in a private family matter.[1]

Given the facts that had already been established in the BBC documentary, I expected that Paton and his crew would be dismissed by the media as deranged. Instead they were treated as if their point of view needed to be heard, as though they had legitimate complaints to make. Paton, Abbasi and Islam were fully aware of, and seemingly untroubled by, the fact that the women and children in Abdul Haq's family had been abducted, beaten, held against their will; and the youngest daughter, aged only 13, had been forced by her father into a grotesque marriage to a middle-aged man, who had repeatedly abused her.

Their interpretation of all this horror as merely 'a private family matter' was totally bizarre. These were the people who would stand

1. *Glasgow Herald*, 9 December 1996.

for public office, in a modern twentieth-century democracy, a little over a year later. When questioned by their voters about this business what did they say? That for the sake of multiculturalism it is necessary to accept that a father can traffic his 13-year-old daughter to have her raped by a 40-year-old man? Their assertion that Haq's personal integrity and reputation had been damaged was laughable. When Paton was asked about Nazia he replied: 'Mr Haq has said that the youngest daughter was fifteen and a half at the time and the marriage was solemnised in Pakistan and it was accepted in Pakistan.'

I have quoted at length from the relevant *Herald* article because otherwise it would be difficult to believe what was said. It requires a special state of mind to interpret what had taken place at the hands of Abdul Haq as *his* human rights being 'trampled all over'.

Rifat went on the record to say: 'We are standing by what we said at first. We were taken against our will and forced into marriages. He [Abdul Haq] got people to beat me. I was forced to stay [in Pakistan] because if I left the country he kept it in my mind that my mum and sister were still there and he would harm them. He has got such a cheek to come back after all this and say we are lying. I don't think we would even be here today if it wasn't for Mr Sarwar.'

Nazia was also quoted. She said: 'He [her father] forced me into a marriage against my will and he beat me up as well, quite a lot of times.'[1]

This didn't deter Haq, Paton and Abbasi. That day they announced that Haq and his son Zulfikar were suing me for £1 million. Two weeks later there was another press conference organised by Paton. At that briefing Paton announced, on behalf of Haq and his son, that the defamation claim had been doubled to £2 million because I was continuing to 'defame their name'.

Late in January 1997, the Alice in Wonderland saga had a setback. Mrs Fatima Haq was successful in gaining a court order banning Abdul Haq from visiting the family home in Glasgow's West End, and from having any access to his daughters. This legal ruling vindicated my decision to help the women of the Haq family. It was also an important political decision as, in the context of the coming General Election, it was proof for all Govan voters to see that

1. *Glasgow Herald*, 9 December 1996.

Haq and his co-conspirators were lying. Eventually, in July 1997, the defamation action came to court. It was dismissed by Sheriff David Converey, almost with a wave of his hand. Of course, by this time the gang of three – Paton, Abbasi and Badar Islam – had trapped me in a *News of the World* bribe scandal. Nonetheless it was the Haq affair that first brought them to act in concert against me.

People often ask me if, confronted with a similar situation to the Haq sisters, would I do the same again. My answer without any hesitation is an emphatic 'Yes'. That is partly based on what I learned about the problem of forced marriage, as a result of my championing the Haq cause. I became the focal point for literally dozens of forced-marriage cases from all over the UK. Young women – some already trapped in a forced marriage and others about to be trapped in one – contacted me and asked for help. I tried to help in every case. I was more successful in some than others.

In those days I learned about the scale of the problem from my own personal experience. Nowadays there are official statistics to prove the point that forced marriage remains an enduring social problem, particularly among families from a Pakistani background living in the UK. In 2012 the Prime Minister, David Cameron, announced that forced marriage was to become a criminal offence in the UK. This was intimated, in Parliament, largely in response to the sort of pressure exerted by women's groups – especially Asian women's groups – across the country. It is now a reality.

The *Guardian*, as far back as June 2012, noted that in 2011 the Government's Forced Marriages Unit (FMU) dealt with almost 1,500 cases. The figures for 2012 were similar, 1,485, and for 2013, 1,302. According to the FMU figures, each year about half of all the UK cases involved families who came from Pakistan.[1] These figures are, of course, only the tip of the iceberg.

From my own caseload I remember one young graduate vividly. We'll call her Khadija for the sake of confidentiality. She had graduated with Honours in English Literature and History. One day her parents came to me and told me that she had run away and that they thought she was staying in a Women's Refuge run by Glasgow City Council. I told them I would help. I made the necessary inquiries with

1. www.gov.uk, Home Office Forced Marriage Unit Statistics.

the Social Work Department and completed all the formalities to allow me to go and see the girl.

When I met Khadija she told me her side of the story. A month earlier her parents had taken her on a holiday to Pakistan, to the father's village, outside Lahore. They introduced her to a man who was a farm worker and did not speak English. Then, to her horror, her father told her he had selected the man – her cousin – to be her husband. When the family returned home to Scotland a huge dispute developed. Khadija told her parents that if they had wanted her to marry a farm worker who didn't speak English, they shouldn't have sent her to university and bought her a car; they should have taught her Punjabi.

She told me that her father said that she was humiliating the family, as he had already given his word to his nephew's family that Khadija would be his wife. The father had threatened that he would kill himself by jumping off the Erskine Bridge, outside of Glasgow, to avoid the shame it would all bring on the family. She said that her mother told her that her father was suicidal and that the girl would be responsible for her father's death if she didn't agree to marry her cousin. It was all too much for Khadija and she left home. When Khadija was telling me her story she concluded by saying: 'These people aren't my parents. They're blackmailers.'

Unfortunately stories like Khadija's are not unusual. It is mind-boggling to think that the mindset of the parents was such that they could conceive of this proposal. Khadija, a 25-year-old university graduate, was to spend the rest of her life in a dirt-poor village in Pakistan, with a man who couldn't speak English. And all because her father had decided that this was to be. What the story demonstrates is that, despite the fact that the parents had lived for two decades, in a modern city, Glasgow, and despite the fact that their daughter was a distinguished university graduate in English and History, the dead hand of centuries of backward tradition still weighed so heavily on them that they themselves could not escape forcing Khadija into a marriage within their extended family in Pakistan. This also illustrates the way that forced marriage has permeated the culture of the more socially backward sections of Pakistani society.

All this is done in the name of Islam, although there is no writing in the Quran which, in any way, justifies such intolerable conduct.

As I have said, my own marriage was an arranged marriage, based on the mutual consent of both partners. I respect that tradition. As the Haq story, and thousands upon thousands like it, shows, forced marriage is a disgraceful tyranny. A disgraceful tyranny which seems to be everlasting.

In the end Khadija was fortunate. After I'd had a number of meetings with her parents, they realised that if they wanted their daughter back they couldn't carry out the forced marriage. They backed down. Khadija returned home and, a year or so later, married a husband of her choice, with the approval of her parents. As I say Khadija was lucky.

Uzma Naurin wasn't. In 2008, she married a former constituent of mine, Saif Rehman, at a ceremony in Glasgow. They had met earlier, at another Pakistani wedding in England. They had wed without the approval of Uzma's parents. Three years later, in June 2011, Saif, who was 31, and ran a mobile phone business in Glasgow, hosted another marriage celebration in Glasgow. This was an attempt to encourage reconciliation with Uzma's parents. The signs were positive because her father, Muzaffar Hussain, attended the ceremony, travelling from his home in the USA. This second wedding banquet was also to mark the start of the couple's new life together, in the United States. Uzma lived in New York, so much of the first three years of marriage had been spent apart. Now Saif had obtained his green card to allow him to work in the USA, and a lifetime together there beckoned.

Uzma had been married once before. Then, she had accepted the arrangements made for her by her parents. They live in Jersey City, in New Jersey, USA, where the father is a taxi driver. It seems that Uzma's first husband committed suicide in tragic circumstances. Sometime after that, her father told her that he had made arrangements for Uzma to marry her dead husband's brother. The brother was much younger than Uzma. She refused and, in the ensuing family dispute, she split from her parents and went to live in New York.

In the autumn of 2011, Uzma's hopes of a lasting reconciliation with her family were raised further. She and Saif had gone to Pakistan, to the Gujrat area of the Punjab, to attend Saif's brother's marriage. Uzma's father also travelled to Pakistan to attend the wedding.

That was his second gesture of seeming approval, coming a matter of months after his attendance at the Glasgow commemoration ceremony. Uzma's mother hadn't spoken to her since Uzma had left the family home, but the couple hoped that if there could be a resolution of the dispute with the father, then, in time, the mother would come round. With the father attending the Rehman family wedding in Pakistan, there was hope that things seemed to be turning out for the better, after all.

After the wedding the father returned to his own village in Pakistan, to his house there. The next day he was admitted with chest pain to a local hospital, in the town of Kharian. Uzma and Saif rushed to see him and stayed in the hospital with him. It seems that sometime the following day the father insisted that the couple should use his driver, Adil Ahmed, and his car, to go on a shopping trip to the nearby city of Gujrat. They would never get the chance to wear the new clothes they bought or give out the presents for relatives.

On the return journey from Gujrat, the party had reached the outskirts of the town of Lalamusa, when the driver received a call on his mobile phone. It was around 5.30pm in the evening. Ahmed left the car and it was immediately ambushed by a gang of four gunmen. They pulled Saif out of the car and shot him dead. Then they abducted Uzma and drove off in their 4x4 jeep. This much is known because Saif's sister, Fauzia, along with her baby, was with the couple on the shopping trip. She witnessed all that happened. The gunmen were only after Saif and Uzma. Fauzia, Saif's sister, was spared. Uzma was driven into the countryside and murdered. Her body was found in bushes at the roadside four or five hours after the ambush.

Shortly after this time, the father, Muzaffar Hussain, discharged himself from hospital. Extraordinarily, given the traditions of Islam, he made no attempt to claim his daughter's body. It appears that he showed no concern over his daughter's death, didn't wait for her funeral, but instead drove hundreds of miles to the port city of Karachi, and took the first flight back to the USA.

The Pakistani police have reports that show the mobile phone logs for the driver's phone prove that the father, Hussain, was in contact with the driver several times on the return journey from Gujrat. The last call Adil Ahmed received from Hussain was shortly *after* the ambush and Uzma's abduction took place. Ahmed has been arrested and charged with conspiracy to murder and the police in Pakistan have named the father, Muzaffar Hussain, as a prime suspect also. He has been interviewed by the police in the USA, although it's unlikely that any attempts to secure his extradition from there to Pakistan will succeed. Hussain has denied any complicity in the murders of his son-in-law and daughter. The Pakistan police believe that the murders have all the hallmarks of an 'honour killing'. They have now joined the long list of such killings in Pakistan where, too often, those responsible escape justice.

The statistics on so-called 'honour killing' in Pakistan are horrifying in every sense of the word. For example, in what is a typical report of recent years, in 2011, the Human Rights Commission of Pakistan (HRCP) noted:

> According to media monitoring, and field reports from HRCP volunteers, at least 943 women were killed in the name of honour, of which 93 were minors. The purported reasons given for this were illicit relations in 595 cases and the demand to marry of their own choice in 219 cases. The murderers were mostly brothers and husbands; in 180 cases the murderer being a brother and in 226 cases being the husband of the victim.[1]

A long time ago I knew about what was going on – perhaps not the actual scale of what was happening as is clear now – and decided that this book would give me the opportunity to collect some of the facts and speak out about this appalling stain on the reputation of the country of my birth. Then, in 2011, by coincidence, I came across the Aurat Foundation. Its researchers were holding a conference in an Islamabad hotel where I had gone for a business meeting. The Aurat Foundation had just published its research report on 'honour killings' in Pakistan. That allowed me to get authoritative sources for my assignment.

The Aurat pilot study, by Maliha Zia, on 'Honour Killings in Pakistan and Compliance with the Law' notes:

1. HRCP Annual Report, 2011.

A total of 557 women were killed in the name of 'honour' in Pakistan in 2010, whereas 604 women were killed in 2009, and 475 killed in 2008 . . . These crimes have brought our country into disrepute and there is evidence that our failure to contain and address this issue has resulted in a spill over of 'honour' killings to a number of foreign countries, primarily through Pakistani immigrant communities.[1]

It is now a matter of record that, in recent years, this tidal wave of bloodshed has been been brought about, by among other things, women wandering outside the home too often, choosing to marry someone other than the husband who had been chosen for them, and being a victim of abduction. We now know more about 'honour killings' in Pakistan than we did at the time of the Haq family controversy. What is clear from these findings is that if, in 1996, the Haq sisters had remained in Pakistan and then subsequently revolted against their forced marriages, they could have become victims of an 'honour killing' to restore the 'honour' of the husband, and father, they had 'shamed'.

Maliha Zia, in her study, states further:

Once a woman has behaved in a manner that has shamed a man and his honour, he has to restore his honour in any manner whatsoever . . . It is with him the community sides and not the 'bad' woman. In order to restore his 'lost honour' the man must return the shameful act with one of equal intensity in a very public manner. In honour-bound societies female chastity represents the family's 'symbolic capital'. To protect it, the offending woman must be killed rather than divorced or excommunicated . . . Killing her removes the offensive act, redeems family honour, and resurrects its prestige . . . In this way the man regains his honour.[2]

1. Maliha Zia, 'Honour Killings in Pakistan', Aurat Foundation, November 2011.
2. Maliha Zia, 'Honour Killings in Pakistan', Aurat Foundation, November 2011.

In her invaluable report Zia argued that the concept of 'honour killings' is linked to the tribal custom of honour, and in the circumstance of a 'shaming', how honour is restored in the community, rather than it being a consequence of this or that interpretation of Islam, and the writings of the Prophet in the Quran. Many other academics argue that there is nothing in the Quran which justifies 'honour killings'.

They insist that the Quran, on the contrary, notes that the most basic right is the right to life:

> For that cause We decreed for the Children of Israel that who-soever killeth a human being for other than manslaughter or corruption in the earth, it shall be as if he killed all mankind, and whoso saveth the life of one, it shall be as if he had saved the life of all mankind. (Quran 5:32.)

It is interesting that Benazir Bhutto, in her writings on Islam and democracy, in *Reconciliation – Islam, Democracy and the West* adopts a similar line of argument. She says that the original sayings of the Prophet, from the seventh century, are among the most enlightened views of humanity ever produced, with particular reference to the equality of the sexes and the sanctity of life.

For example, Islam recognised the right to the inheritance of property for women, in the time of the Prophet, 1600 years ago – long before Western democracy granted women these rights. However, subsequently the enlightenment of the Quran was overtaken by the interpretations of reactionary jurists who re-imported codes and customs from the tribe, and over time they became mistakenly understood as concepts of Islam. Thus there is, in certain circumstances, a false justification of 'honour killings' as drawn from Islam, when they reflect not the Quran but a version of the social norms of the tribe. These revisions then subjected the precepts of Islam to further degeneration. As an example of this Bhutto notes in *Reconciliation*:

> In some Islamic countries, such as Saudi Arabia, women are not allowed to go outside without a male guardian, but this prohibition is not Quranic. It came from later Muslim

jurists. This is another example of Muslim jurists prescribing activities or restrictions based on their interpretations of the Quran, which are influenced by the society and culture in which they live, and not shared by other jurists. Thus, even though the Quran does not put such a restriction of movement on women, some jurists have added these restrictions due to the context in which they were living.[1]

We should be clear, what is being said here is that, through the centuries to the present day, often what is done in the name of Islam is not Islamic. The obscurantist justification of the oppression and persecution of women in Muslim societies is not a valid interpretation of Islam, but rather a departure from the original enlightenment of the words of the Prophet.

The huge scale of 'honour killing' is now, without doubt, an established fact. In 2010 Robert Fisk, of the *Independent* newspaper, published a report on 'honour killings' following a ten-month investigation. Then he put the global figure of 'The crime wave that shames the world'[2] at 20,000 murders every year. Fisk identified Pakistan as among the worst countries in the world for this savagery. The others on his list of dishonour and shame include India, Turkey, Iraq, Kurdish Iraq, Jordan, the Palestinian territories, Lebanon, Syria and the tribal lands of Afghanistan and Iran.

In 2004 the Pakistan government passed the Criminal Law (Amendment) Act. It amended the Pakistan Penal Code and the Criminal Procedure Code to define *karo kiri* ('honour killings') as murder with penal punishments. Historically, judicial practice in relation to 'honour killings' in Pakistan has been affected by what was Section 300(1) of the Pakistan Penal Code. This allowed the court to make dispensations for those guilty of 'honour' crimes. It read: 'Culpable homicide is not murder if the offender, whilst deprived of the power of self control by grave and sudden provocation, causes the death of the person who gave the provocation.'

1. Benazir Bhutto, *Reconciliation: Islam, Democracy and the West*, Simon and Schuster, 2008.
2. Robert Fisk, *Independent*, 7 September 2010.

That provision has remained as the legal precedent in the administration of the law in Pakistan, even although it was deleted in the 1990 Qisas and Diyat law. That law allowed other dispensations for those guilty of 'honour' crimes. Those guilty could have reduced sentences if compensation were paid to, and accepted by, the family who were victims of a crime.

Despite the new codes of the 2004 Act, these two legal principles – the respective roles of 'provocation' and 'payment of compensation' – have continued to set precedents in the Pakistan courts for 'honour killing' in a high proportion of the cases. Indeed, since 2004, the numbers of 'honour killings' has increased markedly, as the figures of the Human Rights Commission of Pakistan now show. That fact dismays all those who are campaigning in Pakistan against this abomination.

The Aurat Foundation, and the Maliha Zia report, are critical of the loopholes in the 2004 Act, which are seriously limiting its effectiveness. Zia notes 13 separate loopholes which need to be closed by amendment to the Act, if it is to have real effect. However, although Zia offers these criticisms, she also acknowledges that the 2004 Act has promoted positive changes, having 'the effect of bringing to light a growing social intolerance of honour killings.'

In correspondence she wrote:

I think the main change that has come about is the social mindset. People are speaking openly about 'honour killings', whereas previously it was a taboo subject. Criticisms are made about the practice. Islamic clerics have spoken out against it. There was enough social pressure to actually pass a law on it . . . We find when we discuss 'honour killings' now, there is so much more knowledge and support on this issue. Even the Sindh police itself led a United Nations project on 'honour killings' in which the police attitudes, investigation techniques etc were examined and then training conducted on how to investigate and handle 'honour killings' cases.

I have always spoken out against forced marriages and the horror of honour killings, but it might be fair to say that I was not completely aware of the scale of the problem. I am setting the record straight now, not least because I believe that forced marriage is the start of a continuum which leads ultimately to 'honour killing'. The demands raised here by the Aurat Foundation need to be made law in Pakistan and then implemented, if the continuing terror of 'honour killing' is to become a thing of the past and the real honour of our country restored.

The 1997 Election and the *News of the World* Sting 8

'You saw Badar as he twisted and turned and wormed and weaselled in the witness box for nearly a week. Nobody who watched that performance could believe that Badar is not a seriously bad man.'

Michael S. Jones, defence counsel for Mohammad Sarwar, at the High Court in Edinburgh, 23 March 1999.

'So to a crucial extent, Badar was the key to the case. The mountainous Badar, who spent a week in the witness box, came across as the kind of man you would shake hands with and count your fingers afterwards.'

Bruce McKain, *Glasgow Herald*, 26 March 1999.

I was approved as the Labour candidate for Govan in July 1996. The election was called in March 1997 and by that time I think I had knocked on the doors of at least half of the households in the constituency. I needed to do that to counter the media campaign which had surrounded the selection battle. My campaign team and I worked day and night to meet the ordinary voters and convince them that I was their man.

There were three major concerns about my candidacy. Firstly, that I was Asian and a Muslim and would only serve my own people; secondly, that I was a businessman and would spend my time serving the interests of my business, rather than the interests of the people of my constituency; and finally, that this constituency was a working-class constituency and what did a millionaire know about the lives of ordinary people. I worked on the doorsteps tirelessly to convince all of the voters that these concerns were ill-founded. It was a hard and a long campaign.

The ability to patiently explain the case in politics is crucial. So I would tell them when accused of being an 'out of touch' millionaire that I knew all about poverty from life in my village in Pakistan; that I went to a primary school where we were taught while sitting on a sandy floor because there were no school benches; that in my young life there was no such thing as 'lunch'. I also argued that I now had a track record as a Labour councillor, and that in my five years on Glasgow City Council I had never abandoned the ordinary people of the city; that I had proved time and again that I was on their side.

Nicola Sturgeon of the SNP emerged as my main challenger for the seat. She was not then the Nicola of today, and in fact, had she been the confident, sharp politician with a smile that she is now, then the fight for Govan would undoubtedly have been much closer. She was new to street politics and, if I may say, in those days she was the epitome of the Scottish term 'nippy sweetie' – which means she was a bit sharp and dismissive. She was talented, of course, but she was also serious to the point of being dour, and lacking in warmth; lacking in what might be called 'the common touch' – the ability to speak to people on their own terms. In those days that was a failing of hers. In politics you have to be able to speak to people face to face, to make an impression. I have always been fairly good at that, since I learned the importance of communicating directly with people in the struggles during my student days in Pakistan.

The SNP put a lot of effort and resources into the battle for the seat, as they believed that they could exploit the unfavourable coverage of the selection battle and profit from the clear divisions within the Govan Labour Party after the defeat of Mike Watson. So my first task was to try to unite the Party, and build bridges over the great divisions, for a common battle against the SNP. I went to the chief Watson supporters and told them we had to fight for the seat together to ensure that a Labour government would be elected at the next election. Some were prepared to 'bury the hatchet', others not.

The election was held on 1 May 1997, and during the day I felt that the tide was moving decisively in my favour. I had always been confident that we could deliver the Labour vote, but on the day of the vote itself, the momentum was clear. The British National Party fascists had put up a candidate which meant the rest of the candidates for Govan refused to share the platform with them. So when the announcement was made that Labour had taken the seat, I was not on the platform but standing in the body of the hall.

I remember thinking two things when I heard the result. British colonialism had lasted for centuries. And the 'Jewel in the Crown' had been the Indian Subcontinent. But never throughout this history had a Muslim voice been heard in the House of Commons. I was the first Muslim to be elected to the British Parliament – in such terms this was a momentous breakthrough. Secondly, all along it had been in my head that this is the Mother of Parliaments, which had ruled an Empire stretching over half the world, a Parliament which had been responsible for the creation of my own motherland, Pakistan. It was truly a great feeling that now I, a son of Pakistan, had made my mark on history.

This elation was, even then, tinged with fear. I felt that I had made myself a greater target than ever before for the forces of reaction who, now more than ever, would be out to get me. For my thirteen years in Parliament, that fear never left me. Never a day passed without my wondering if it would emerge that somehow, somewhere I had been trapped; that a plot to destroy me had been successful. That burden of fear only lifted from my shoulders on the day I left Parliament in 2010. This might seem strange. It is how I felt.

I have learned that defeating the British establishment is more dangerous than being defeated by them. They never forget. On 17 May 1997, only days after the General Election a phone call came from a journalist. I was on my way to Gordon Archer's wedding, which was being held in Rothesay, on the Isle of Bute, off the west coast of Scotland. We were just about to join the M8 motorway when the phone rang. It was a *News of the World* reporter, who told me that they were going to run a story the next day under the headline: 'Sleaze bombshell – Labour MP in bribe scandal.'[1]

He told me that he had information that confirmed I had bribed an election rival, Badar Islam, with £5,000. I took the call on my mobile phone, the line was bad and I lost contact. The reporter phoned back and I could not hear him properly. He repeated the bribery allegations again. I told him I still could not hear him properly and that

1. *News of the World*, 17 May 1997.

the 'bribe', as he had called it, was a loan. From that moment on I was thinking: 'Trapped. I've been trapped.' In fact I turned to Perveen and said: 'The bastards have trapped me.'

It has always been a suspicion of mine that there were hidden hands behind all this. As already mentioned, there was concrete evidence, before the election, of the Indian agent, Mohan Singh, cruising the constituency offering new identities and £250,000 for anyone with 'dirt on Sarwar'. He told my friend Sohan Singh that he wanted to frame me. According to Sohan he said: 'If we can't get some women to say they slept with Sarwar, can't you find me two prostitutes and we will pay them to say that.' As always my friend Sohan stood shoulder to shoulder with me and told Singh where to go. Mohan Singh approached another friend of mine, Andy Hakeen, to offer the same bribe. Hakeen told me: 'Singh wasn't interested in anything to do with business, only sex. For instance, if you had been in saunas or with prostitutes.'

On 20 April 1997, Audrey Gillan wrote an article for the newspaper *Scotland on Sunday* about this. It carried the headline: '£250,000 to Smear Sarwar'. The next day the *Glasgow Herald* ran an article with the headline 'Claim of Campaign to Smear Sarwar'. It declared: 'A London-based Indian is claimed to be offering up to £250,000 for sexual scandal implicating Mr Sarwar, who is a prominent Glasgow councillor and millionaire businessman.'[1]

My opponents in the locality didn't have such money to scatter around, but in a way were capable of inflicting more damage. The stand I made in bringing the Haq sisters back to Scotland after they had been abducted by their father in Pakistan, when each of them had been driven into a forced marriage, divided the Pakistani community in Glasgow, and my enemies in the gang of three – Badar Islam, Jamil Abbasi and Peter Paton – sought to exploit those divisions to thwart my political ambitions. In the election the three, Islam, Abbasi and Paton, scarcely mustered 1,000 votes, but that meagre total didn't reflect the scale of rumour and innuendo they broadcast to the police and the media about my campaign. We now know that the most dangerous of the three was Badar Islam, because he was the most debt-ridden and most desperate.

1. *Glasgow Herald*, 21 April 1997.

At one point in the election campaign there had been clashes between my supporters and the small crew working for Islam, who were verbally abusing our Labour Party people. Then, one night, our election campaign headquarters was vandalised. Some windows were broken and it was spray-painted. I found out that those involved in the vandalism had been supporters of Badar. I phoned Badar Islam's election agent, Tariq Malik, and told him it all had to stop; that although we had our differences things should not be allowed to get out of hand and we should respect each other and have our supporters do the same.

He immediately asked for a meeting between himself, Badar Islam and me. Eventually I made the mistake of agreeing to a meeting to get the matter over and done with. Sometime during the election the three of us met at Glasgow Airport to 'smoke the pipe of peace'. That is all that there was to it. I didn't suspect then that it was a trap. I was naive to consent to the meeting. It allowed Badar Islam and Tariq Malik to make allegations later that the business of the meeting involved me promising to pay Badar Islam a bribe, after the election, if he eased off on his campaign.

That naivety was bad enough but I compounded the misjudgement a million times more, after the election. Islam and Malik came calling again. Badar Islam was in a terrible state and told me his house was about to be repossessed by a debt recovery agency, that he had big debts to money lenders who were after him, and that he was about to be evicted for non-payment of his mortgage. He told me that his son was ill in hospital, and due to be discharged, but if the house were to be lost Islam would not be able to provide a home for the boy.

I have spoken about my consistent aim in life to do my duty to look after the poor and the those less fortunate than me. In what I think would be the greatest misjudgement of my entire life I agreed to give Badar Islam a £5,000 loan to help him out. Now, as I have already mentioned, Badar Islam still owed me £10,000 for goods he received from my Cash and Carry when he was setting up his hotel business in Paisley. It is a fair question to ask why I would be prepared to be duped for a second time by giving him a second lot of money.

Firstly, there is the obligation, within our community, to help those in difficult circumstances. So I felt it was my duty to help. I also had the experience, in the past, where Badar had borrowed from me and did not clear his debts. So, this time, unlike the previous occasion, I told Badar and Malik that I wanted someone to guarantee the loan, so that if he didn't pay it back I could redeem the money. They got a backer, a former employee of Islam, Mumtaz Hussain, who was a good customer of our United Wholesale Cash and Carry and agreed to stand as a guarantor for Badar Islam.

The plot was hatched. Badar Islam had realised that there was money to 'dish the dirt on Sarwar' from the coffers of the *News of the World*, so he had set up the whole scam through his contact with the newspaper. He would be paid much more than £5,000 for this by the *News of the World*. What was established at my trial is that he was paid £45,000 for the story, as well as an additional £500 per week, for who knows how long, supposedly to pay for the hire of security guards to look after him. It turns out that some of the security guards seem to have been unnecessarily attractive, young, blonde women! This £45,000 was only the amount of money that was traced by our lawyers after a legal battle with the *News of the World* to get access to their accounts. It was generally believed in the community that the actual sums paid to Islam were much greater than what appeared in the 'official' accounts.

Islam confessed at my trial that, after I had given him the money, he immediately went to meet a reporter from the *News of the World*, in a Glasgow hotel, and showed him the money. He told the reporter: 'You wanted the evidence. You have got the evidence.'[1] Tariq Malik, who accompanied Islam to the meeting with the reporter, told the trial that the *News of the World* reporter exclaimed: 'That's it we have got him now.'[2] That's how the 'Sleaze bombshell – MP in bribe scandal' story was put together.

Of course we know now, after the phone-hacking inquiry that brought down the *News of the World*, and totally discredited the Murdoch empire, that such practices were actually the 'house style' of the *News of the World* and other Murdoch tabloids. The seri-

1. *Glasgow Herald*, 26 March 1999.
2. *Glasgow Herald*, 16 February 1999.

ous point here, in my case, is what happened was an act of deliberate conspiracy to subvert the democratic process by usurping the
rights of voters to elect an MP of their choosing. So much of what
happened to me was a harbinger of what, fifteen years later, would
bring about the downfall of the the *News of the World*, including the
Queen of Sleaze, herself, Rebekah Brooks.

In these desperate days there were a number of people whose help
kept me from giving it all up. The first, of course, was Perveen my
wife. She was unswerving about why we had to see this all through.
Within my own political community Hanif Raja and Imran Khand
were stalwarts who had faith in me which banished all doubts. Both
have stood by my side during my entire political life. Then there was
the late Harry Conroy. Harry worked as my PR-consultant in those
days. He was a tower of strength. On the Saturday night when I
knew about the story going to appear, I told him what had happened;
that the so-called bribe they were going to expose was actually a
loan, but that the *News of the World* would make it look as bad as
they possibly could. On the Sunday morning we both went to see my
election agent, Margaret Curran. We went through the newspaper
article, line by line, to say 'That is a lie, this is a lie.' She was furious
and remonstrated with me: 'Why, oh why, could you have been so
stupid?' When Harry and I returned to my house, there was a huge
media scrum waiting on the doorstep. It seemed to me at the time
that every journalist in Scotland was there. There was sheer pandemonium. I made a short statement, saying that the *News of the
World* allegations were not true. I had been summoned to see the
chief whip, Nick Brown MP, at his residence in Downing Street, so I
had to dash for the airport to take a flight to London.

I met with Nick Brown, then the Party's Chief Whip, and Party
officials, in London on the Sunday afternoon. I told him that I had
committed a grave error of judgement in giving Badar Islam the money, but that it was a loan and not a bribe as the *News of the World*
was alleging. I explained to Brown how Badar Islam had told me that
he was in desperate financial trouble and that, true to my principles,
I had agreed to help him out. Nick Brown was sympathetic – in fact
he would testify to these discussions taking place when he was in the
witness box at my trial. However he did say that what mattered was

how the whole thing looked and what the newspapers and media would turn it into: that was the problem.

I told Nick Brown that Harry Conroy was organising a media conference at an hotel near Glasgow airport for my return so we could set the record straight. Brown, and his officials, went into panic mode and warned against that. They told me to cancel the news conference, as it was better to call for a police investigation; that way I could say that I couldn't comment further as I didn't want to compromise any official investigation and also wouldn't be exposed to more pressure from the media. We agreed a media statement on these lines – calling for a police investigation – at the meeting. It was published from the Chief Whip's office but with a quote from me welcoming a police inquiry. I phoned Harry before I left London to tell him to call off the media conference. He was furious. He told me he believed that I had taken the wrong advice.

The next day I started proceedings to sue the *News of the World*. The legal advice following that move was to make no further comment on the allegations. That was founded on the understanding that we did not wish to give the story 'oxygen' to keep it going by commenting on the case in public, but also a caution about giving anything away about my line of defence. It was argued that defeating the 'bung' accusation early on would only produce more outlandish smears. I realise why that advice was given at the time, but long after the trial, Harry reminded me: 'Sarwar, if you had taken my advice in the first place about having the news conference we might have killed the story stone dead and never finished up in court.' There remain two sides to that particular debate; it is a matter of judgement as to whether Harry or the solicitors were right.

Then events took a strange turn – out of the blue Tariq Malik came to my house. I think his conscience troubled him. He told me that the *News of the World* account was wrong, that he had been in London for a week or more staying in an expensive hotel, that all sorts of money had changed hands between the *News of the World* and Badar Islam, and that he had been pressured to back Badar Islam's story about the money but had refused. He said that what had been written in the paper was false, that his words had been twisted and that he wanted to swear an affidavit to the effect that the newspaper's report was inaccurate and that 'Mr Sarwar had done nothing wrong.'

The significance of this was not lost on me since, at the same time, it offered corroboration of my story and undermined that of the *News of the World* and Badar Islam. I arranged for Tariq Malik to make the declaration at my solicitor's office the next day. That he did so would become important evidence at my trial. After Malik had signed the declaration we made it public through Harry Conroy and my lawyers. We decided that Malik's statement was so significant that it was worthwhile to break the media embargo. There was wide coverage of Malik's rebuttal.

In the week that followed the article, the Parliamentary Labour Party suspended me indefinitely under the rules of 'bringing the party into disrepute'. The organisation committee of the National Executive Committee (NEC) also reported that week that I had undertaken actions detrimental to the Labour Party and should be suspended. In due course, towards the end of the month, I was thrown out of the PLP indefinitely; the NEC endorsed that suspension, and closed down Govan Labour Party.

It seemed to me that the Party establishment were, in effect, signalling to all and sundry that I was guilty as charged. To say I was sorely aggrieved about the way I had been treated is an understatement. I still believe that the *News of the World* chiefs were determined, at first, to stop me being elected. When this didn't work they worked to arrange my downfall, once I was elected, because of what my victory represented as a challenge to the international politics they espoused for the Middle East, for Palestine, Kashmir etc. I would be a voice against their right-wing extremism, their support for Israel, American imperialism, and their anti-Muslim racist propaganda. No efforts would be spared in their campaign to get me, and so they had got what they wanted.

The months that followed were among the most miserable of my life. I was in a weak position and agreed with the Whips Office that it would be better for all concerned if I did not appear at the House of Commons. This is another decision which, with hindsight, I should have questioned, but that is what happened at the time. However, after a period of months when my spirits were very low, my anger began to grow. By November this took me to the point of jettisoning the 'gentleman's agreement' about my non-appearance at the Commons. I began to negotiate with the Whips Office about my maiden speech.

I argued that, irrespective of the allegations made against me by the *News of the World*, I was still an elected member with a duty to represent my constituents. I also made the point that the police investigation had been going on for months and, as yet, there had been no charges made whatsoever. So, I requested a date for making a return to the Commons to give my maiden speech. Then I offered what might have been taken as a veiled threat. 'You wouldn't want me to go to the media and say I was being gagged by the Parliamentary Labour Party, would you?' A few days later I received notice that I could make my maiden speech on 5 December.

This turn of events and what followed would prove to me that the powers that be were lined up against me; this time in the shape of the Lord Advocate of Scotland – the highest law officer in the country – Lord Hardie. Not long after the news of my impending maiden speech became public, I received notice from Strathclyde Police that they wanted to interview me on 5 December on the charges I would face, the very day that had been agreed for my maiden speech.

My solicitor, Chris Kelly, spoke to the police and offered alternative dates or alternative times on the same day. He was told by one of the officers involved that they had been instructed by Lord Hardie that if I did not make myself available for police interview on that day I would be arrested. The officer said that Hardie told him: 'Tell Mr Sarwar that if he doesn't appear at this time he will be arrested.' I thought of making the speech and then they could arrest me at the House of Commons, so what? My solicitor advised me against such a head-on confrontation. 'They're out for your blood so don't make it easier for them,' he told me. So, instead of going to the House of Commons to make my first speech there, I presented myself for interview at Partick Police station, in the west end of Glasgow, on the morning of 5 December 1997. I wasn't surprised that charges were going to be made. I had been forewarned. I was surprised at Hardie's vindictiveness and remain so to this day.

James Freeman was then the crime correspondent with the *Glasgow Herald*. He had a fine reputation as a reporter who could get to the bottom of any story. His sources within Strathclyde Police were known to be impeccable. Harry Conroy, who'd been a journalist at the *Daily Record* for many years before launching his PR business, knew Freeman well. One day, some weeks before I was charged, Harry came to my office at the Cash and Carry. He told me: 'Sarwar, there's good and bad news. I've just had a chat with Jim Freeman at the *Herald*. He's been briefed by a very senior source at the top of Strathclyde Police – well above the level of the current investigation. The bad news is that they're going to charge you with electoral fraud, bribery and perverting the course of justice.' Then he continued: 'The good news is that the source has told Freeman that they don't have the evidence to make the charges stack up in court, you'll be acquitted.' Good old Harry – forewarned was forearmed. I recall that a journalist friend of mine once told me they used to joke that if Harry, God rest his soul, met the Virgin Mary, and took her for a glass of wine, she would have eventually told him her most sacred secrets.

What happened to me on 5 December 1997 at the hands of Strathclyde Police will stay with me forever. By that time I was already nursing grievances about the conduct of their officers. I was a Member of Parliament facing serious allegations. In the seven months since I had called for a police inquiry there had been regular leaks to the media, from the police, that they had completed their investigations, on this or that matter, and had enough evidence to charge me. Yet, in all this time, I had not even had a preliminary interview to state my case or even a meeting to tell me what the procedures would be. I believed that if I'd been a white MP things would have been handled quite differently. In fact, I believed that the *News of the World* were now running the agenda against me and had enormous influence on the course of events, including the Crown Office and the police. It seemed to me that the police were prepared to go to any lengths to make sure they'd get some evidence that would stick. The events of 5 December confirmed in my mind that that there was also racism at work in all of this.

There would be no discussion of my side of the story. When I entered Partick Police Station the officer in charge of the investigation, I think he was of Superintendent rank, a Mr McConnell, took me to a room and read out the charges. They concerned offences against the Representation of the People Act for allegedly encouraging voters in the constituency to make false registrations, and allegedly under-recording election expenses. In addition, there were two charges of perverting the course of justice by allegedly bribing Badar Islam, an election rival, to make a false affidavit to clear me on the false electoral registrations by blaming others, and allegedly conspiring with another, Mumtaz Hussain, to say the alleged bribe was actually a loan.

When McConnell read out the charges I was actually relaxed because there and then, I realised, that there was nothing to answer. I asked him: 'Is this really the best you can do after more than seven months of police investigation? I'm telling you right now I'll be cleared of these charges. There's no evidence to back this up. You don't have a leg to stand on.' I told him that the whole thing was at best a joke and at worst an attempted set-up. He wasn't pleased.

He said that I had to go now to the Sheriff Court to be formally charged. He asked for my watch and my wallet and then said that I had to remove my tie and give it to him. I asked him why he wanted my tie and he replied: 'I want it in case, under pressure, you decide to hang yourself.' I told him that he wasn't talking to someone who was a coward but a man of courage; that the charges were garbage and nonsense, so why on earth would I want to contemplate suicide? I continued: 'I'll be cleared of this one day and you'll regret what you are doing. You should more careful with your language and shouldn't treat people like this.' His reply to the other officers in the charge room, at that point, was: 'Right, handcuff him.'

At that point my blood was boiling, but that changed a bit when I realised that the officer who was cuffing me was really reluctant to be obeying the orders of his boss. He was clearly uncomfortable. I remember that he actually said that I shouldn't worry, that I'd be fine because all this would come to nothing. This raised my spirits, because here was an ordinary police officer quite clearly disapproving of the way I was being treated.

It was around ten in the morning. They took me in a police van to the Sheriff Court in Glasgow where I was down to appear to be charged at the afternoon sitting at two o'clock. They locked me up in the cells below the court until it was time. I remember thinking about my suspicions of racism. I sat in the stinking cell and asked myself, 'Would they have treated a white MP like this?'. However, those feelings were partly dispelled by the way in which the security officers were sympathetic to my plight and frequently asked me if I needed anything. It may be that orders for my arrest and indictment had been issued from on high, but the ordinary rank and file seemed to think it was all wrong.

I was duly arraigned before the judge in the afternoon sitting, when the charges were read out. I pleaded not guilty and was re-leased on bail. That was 5 December 1997 – seven months after the *News of the World*'s first allegations were printed. It seems scarcely believable now but it would take more than a year – until 26 January 1999 – before I stood in the dock again to face these charges, this time at the High Court in Edinburgh.

I must make a qualification here at this point. In all my time as an MP I have found the officers of Strathclyde Police enormously helpful and dedicated to their jobs – not least those I worked very closely with in the Kriss Donald investigation. My differences remain with those who were in charge of the investigation against me in the period following the infamous *News of the World* story.

1998 was one of the worst years of my life, as the purgatory of waiting to go to court dragged on and on. It had seemed to me that any agreements struck between the powers that be in the La-bour Party and me, regarding my staying away from Parliament, had been made null and void by the length of time the police inquiries were taking, and Hardie's intervention to humiliate me and block my maiden speech. So I told the Whips' Office that I wanted to return to my duties as an MP, which included making my maiden speech. Permission to do so was granted just before the Christmas recess in 1997. The date given was 14 January 1998 in a debate on regional development.

The time for the speech duly arrived. It would be at precisely two minutes past seven on the evening of Wednesday 14 January. As the time for me to be called by the Speaker, Michael Martin, came closer, the difficulty of my situation began to bear down on me. It was a challenge for me to make my speech in the House of Commons – as any maiden speech is for any new member – but I was speaking as a new member facing charges of bribery, corruption and perverting the course of justice. I had decided to make the content of the speech as straightforward as possible about the constituency, and this helped my delivery. My nerve held.

I started in the name of Allah to match my taking the Member's oath by swearing on the Quran – both of which made history in the House of Commons, irrespective of the shadow of the criminal charges hanging over me:

I start in the name of Allah, who is the most beneficent and the most merciful. I have taken the opportunity to prefix my maiden speech in the traditional Muslim custom by starting in the name of God. This, I believe, is a testament to the fact that Britain is now a multicultural and multi-religious society, of which we are all members.

I begin by paying tribute to the late Jimmy Dunnachie, the former Member of Parliament for Glasgow, Pollok, which includes a substantial part of my new constituency. Jimmy Dunnachie tragically passed away at the beginning of September 1997. He was a popular and well-respected Member of Parliament and will be sadly missed in Glasgow.

I am extremely grateful to the people of Govan for the privilege and honour that they have conferred on me by electing me as their Member of Parliament. They have subsequently stood by me through some difficult times. Govan is a rainbow state, representing Christians, Muslims, Hindus, Jews, Sikhs, Chinese and Africans who include professionals, academics, the self-employed, employees and employers. Some would say that the political spectrum in Govan is perhaps too awash with colour. We have right-wingers, old lefties, Blairites, liberals, communists, Militants, nationalists, and even the odd Tory can be seen early on a Sunday morning.

The early beginnings of Govan were as a centre of Christianity. During the mid-1800s, Govan grew to become a burgh, and by the end of the century had developed into one of the world's industrial powerhouses. Between the war years, heavy engineering industries and the Clydeside shipyards continued to employ thousands of men and women. However, after the Second World War the decline of shipbuilding and the consequent reduction in heavy engineering took their toll, and the economy of greater Govan went into decline.

For that reason, my constituents were disappointed by the recent decision of the Secretary of State for Defence not to site the royal yacht *Britannia* on the River Clyde, which is its natural home. I hope that the future of shipbuilding on the Clyde and the problems faced by Kvaerner Shipbuilding at Govan Cross will be addressed satisfactorily by our Government.

It is interesting to note that, even in its darkest days, Govan produced and nurtured people of the highest calibre. Bruce Millan, a successful politician who represented the people of Govan with dedication and diligence, became the Secretary of State for Scotland during the late 1970s, and later became the second European Commissioner.

Alex Ferguson, the manager of Manchester United, is one of the greatest football managers in the world. He is leading British football in Europe and we wish him and Manchester United every success. Who in the Labour Movement could ever forget the world's first work-in, orchestrated by Jimmy Airlie and Jimmy Reid, whose speech inspired the shipyard workers on the Clyde to stand up for their right to work? Those individuals are well known, but the real heroes are the people of Govan, who have faced the challenges of a steady decline with dignity and passion. Those are the people whom I am proud to represent.

The people of Govan and Glasgow were delighted by the recent decision of the Millennium Commission and the Glasgow Development Agency to award a grant of more than £50 million towards Scotland's first national science park in my constituency. A further £19 million for the park still requires final approval from the European Commission in Brussels, but I am confident that approval will be granted and that the development can be concluded before the millennium.

I hope that you, Mr Deputy Speaker, and Honourable Members will take the opportunity to visit the centre when it is up and running. The national science park is a perfect example of the role that development agencies can play in attracting inward investment. Development agencies, in conjunction with local government and the private sector in Scotland, have played an extremely important role in tackling economic and social decay.

In Glasgow, for example, Scottish Enterprise and the Glasgow Development Agency, in partnership with Glasgow City Council, Strathclyde Regional Council and Govan Initiative Ltd., have been successful in tackling the economic and social problems that the city experiences. The regeneration of the Merchant City, the development of the Scottish Exhibition Centre, the Burrell Gallery, the Royal Concert Hall and the Kelvin Hall all demonstrate the huge difference that development agencies have made in Glasgow, so much so that Glasgow is seen as a prime example of urban regeneration, and only last week was described by *The Big Issue* as the coolest city in Britain. That is why I believe that the Bill is an important element in the process of democratic renewal and local empowerment.

I believe that the success of our Government will be measured simply by the real actions that we initiate to combat poverty. My constituents look to the Government to deliver practical, real-life solutions. Unemployment in Govan, which stands at 14 per cent, is still far too high. Until last May, too many people had no hope of employment. Too many of our young people are involved in drug misuse and too many leave school without the right skills. Many people are still forced to live in intolerable housing conditions, while many pensioners must still make a choice between heating and food – especially during the cold winter months.

One development that has increased the level of poverty is low pay. The introduction of a national minimum wage is vital if we are to ensure that that level of poverty does not continue. Other countries, not least the United States, have shown that a reasonably set minimum wage helps to improve economic performance and productivity.

My constituents are also expecting significant progress in housing. The Scottish people rely more on public sector housing than those in the rest of Britain. More resources should be made available for building and, in particular, for renovating houses. Renovation is important, as merely concentrating on building further housing will shift attention away from areas such as Govan, where demand for housing can be met adequately only by regenerating and renovating the existing stock.

Education is another area which is of great concern to the people of Govan. The schools in Govan do a tremendous job under severe financial pressures, but they need further support from the Government. The July Budget, which gave £2.3 billion for school repairs and raising literacy and numeracy standards, was greatly welcomed in my constituency.

An issue that has come to concern me increasingly over the years, and one which I hear about repeatedly from the Muslim community in Britain is the growth of Islamaphobia. The Runnymede Trust's report 'Islamaphobia, a challenge for us all' is an excellent insight into that prejudice, and I trust that my Right Hon. Friend, the Home Secretary, will take on board the recommendations made in that report. I should like to draw the attention of Honourable Members, and of the Government, to the poor representation of ethnic minorities – including the total exclusion of Muslims – in the House of Lords. I trust that our Government will change that unacceptable situation.

I look forward to making my own contribution by working fully with the Labour Government and by realising our vision of a new Britain where power and resources are in the hands of the many and not the few. [1]

The reaction to the speech fell within the rules of House of Commons protocol. The three speakers in a debate who follow a maiden speech, are bound to make reference back to it, which they did. The first up on his feet was the Tory MP for Bury St Edmunds, David

1. *Hansard*, 14 January 1998.

Ruffney, who said: 'I acknowledge the speeches made so far – particularly that of the Hon. Member for Glasgow, Govan, which I am sure Hon. Members found very interesting.' The next to rise was the Labour Member for Huddersfield, Barry Sheerman. He was slightly more complimentary. Then the member for Faversham and Mid Kent, Andrew Rowe, rose. He was a Tory, but one with a record of being anti-Thatcherite. He had a reputation of being off the old block of the 'One Nation' Tories, and, for example, at the height of Thatcher's union-busting went on record to say that the trades unions 'were an indispensable part of a free society.' In other words, Andrew Rowe was probably to the left of much of New Labour!

That night he opened his remarks by saying: 'I should, perhaps, begin by noting that it can never be easy to make a maiden speech, and to have done so under the difficulties that the Hon. Member for Glasgow, Govan, is currently enduring is a tremendous additional effort. I learned more about Govan in 10 minutes than I could have imagined. I am sure that the House will feel that, if the difficulties are cleared away, the people of Govan will be represented by someone who is very knowledgeable about their interests.'[1] His words made my spirits soar. At the end of the sitting, on our way out of the chamber, I managed to get close enough to thank him for his support. My recollection is that he said: 'Courage, Mr Sarwar, I admire bloody courage.'

As 1998 worn on I needed more courage to continue to stand my ground and remain resolute, since with every passing day, the pattern of events was confirming that Strathclyde Police were indeed going to extraordinary lengths to provide the Crown with evidence, which would justify continuing proceedings against me. Under Scottish law the police are the investigating authority and provide reports for the Crown, in this case the Lord Advocate's office, which lays out grounds for criminal proceedings, which are then prosecuted by the Crown.

In late January my election agent, Margaret Curran, who organised my election campaign, and was responsible for submitting all my election expenses, was charged, by Strathclyde Police, with offences under the Representation of the People Act. The background to that

1. *Hansard*, 14 January 1998.

provided more evidence of their desperate efforts to get any accusations against me, or my supporters, to stick.

The rules for the submission of election expenses involve the election agent making the appropriate records and then going to a solicitor or Justice of the Peace and swearing *in their presence* that the records are a true account. Margaret Curran signed off our accounts, but on the evening she was due to go to see the Justice of the Peace, in this case a Glasgow City Councillor, Stephen Dornan, her ten-year-old child took ill. Margaret signed off the accounts and had them delivered to Stephen Dornan, who countersigned them and sent them back to Margaret. She then submitted them on time.

It transpired that Strathclyde Police had somehow found out about this minor discrepancy and interviewed Margaret Curran. When asked she admitted she had not actually made a verbal swearing in front of the Justice of the Peace and was then charged under the Representation of the People Act. I can vouch, without fear of contradiction, that in relation to the 1997 General Election, Strathclyde Police did not interview any other election agent in their area with the same line of inquiry, nor did any other police force in the rest of Scotland. Only the 'Get Sarwar' campaign, sponsored by the strange triangle of sections of Strathclyde Police, the *News of the World* and the Crown Office, could have mounted such a ridiculous line of inquiry.

In the end both Margaret Curran and Stephen Dornan had to appear later in the year before a High Court judge to explain what had occurred and to seek admonishment. The charges were then dropped. So this was all a total waste of police time, but part of a deliberate tactic by the police to keep pressure on me, on all aspects of the case, and to keep their investigation in the public eye, through media coverage. This 'drip, drip' approach was also designed to create enough 'noise' to convince the Crown authorities that too many questions had been raised to allow any consideration of dismissing the charges against me. The atmosphere the police wanted to engender was along the lines of 'Something has to be done about Sarwar, there's no smoke without fire.'

The longer the waiting went on for a trial date to be set, the greater the anguish. This wasn't about what might happen in any trial, but instead the day-today anguish brought about by the enduring 'cloud over my head' and the desperate desire to get the whole thing over and done with. In these difficult days a number of MPs loyally stood by me. George Galloway, then MP for Glasgow Kelvin, Michael Martin, who would later become the Speaker, Anne McGuire, MP for Stirling, Rosemary McKenna, MP for Cumbernauld and Kilsyth and Tom Clark, MP for Coatbridge and Airdrie, were stalwarts at my side, among others. In different ways, they kept delivering the same message: 'These are difficult days, but you'll see it through.'

The other factor that sustained me, perhaps surprisingly, given the media coverage, was the level of support in the constituency. I don't recall a single incident where there were public accusations thrown at me, whereas there were countless examples of people coming to my MP's surgery, or even those just passing by, expressing support and suggesting I was being victimised. There seemed to be a widespread sentiment of 'Don't let them get you down, Mohammad'. In this regard one particular incident stands out from the rest.

In January 1999, about a week or so before my trial was due to start, I was outside Cessnock Subway station, in Govan, with Gordon Jackson. He was standing as the Labour candidate in the forthcoming May election for the Scottish Parliament. We were handing out leaflets when a woman came out of the Subway station and approached me. She told me that the previous Sunday she had been praying for me in church, as she believed I was being persecuted because I was Asian and Muslim Then she said: 'It came to my mind, as if it was a message from God, that I should give you a Bible, for you to have throughout the ordeal of your trial. It was as if the Lord was saying to me, "Buy him a Bible and he'll be fine."' Then she told me that she had gone to town earlier that day and bought the Bible, when it occurred to her that she had no idea where to find me to give me it.

'I said another prayer to the Lord, asking Him to help me find you, and I was just thinking about how I could do that when I came out of the subway, and here you are standing in front of me,' she said. There were hints of tears in her eyes when she handed me the Bible. As she left she said: 'My prayers have been answered. I'll be praying for you. You are going to win.' It was a remarkable moment. I kept the Bible in the house, in the bookcase, and any time when I felt down, if the Bible caught my eye, I would remember the woman, and her faith in me, which always gave me renewed strength.

There was to be a follow-up to this wonderful story. I was found not guilty on all charges at the High Court in Edinburgh on Thursday 26 March 1999. On Saturdays it was my custom to hold a surgery for constituents, in the morning at the local Asda supermarket, in the Govan area. On that Saturday morning the Asda manager announced that I was in my usual room at the front of the supermarket if anyone wanted to go to see me. The first person who appeared was the woman who had given me the Bible. She just smiled and said: 'Mr Sarwar, I told you my prayers would be answered.' Then she shook my hand. I was almost lost for words; however I managed to say that her moral support and prayers had been an enormous source of strength for me, in what had been the most difficult of times. Some time later she again came to see me at the surgery in the Asda supermarket. She said she had popped in to say goodbye because she was moving to England. I wished her well and took her address and phone number so I could invite her to come to see me in the House of Commons for lunch or afternoon tea. Unfortunately I mislaid the piece of paper so I hope if she happens to read this book now she'll know how much her gesture meant to me.

The trial was scheduled to start on 25 January 1999. It actually started the next day after a day of legal debate about procedures. The original set of charges stood: that I had committed electoral fraud in colluding with voters to make false registrations, had submitted false election expenses and attempted to pervert the course of justice by bribing an election rival and conspiring to give false evidence to the court regarding that, and creating a cover story of a loan guarantee to conceal the alleged bribe.

The opening days of the trial proved to be a false start for the prosecution. The bungling Advocate Depute, Duncan Menzies QC, led witnesses against me regarding the electoral fraud charges I faced. The Advocate Depute is the law officer in the Scottish legal system who makes the case for the prosecution. The charges, as I have mentioned before, alleged that I had fraudulently induced four voters in the constituency – between January and March 1997 – to tell lies about when they had moved into the area so that they could be registered to vote.

In the campaign for the 1997 election we had indeed made a big push to get electors, who were eligible to vote but were not yet on the voter's roll, to register properly. The mathematics of the first evidence led by the prosecution turned out to be laughable. Questioning an election official, Menzies established that there was concern when there were 279 late voter registrations from Govan. Then he asked the election official, a Mr William Johnson, what happened next. The exchanges turned out to be revealing, as recorded in the *Herald* newspaper at the time:

> Mr Johnson added that he had spoken to a Fraud Squad detective who informed him that the police were under instructions from the Lord Advocate to investigate all the claims in the Govan constituency. Cross-examined by Mr Michael S. Jones QC, for Mr Sarwar, Mr Johnson accepted that the vast majority of the 279 claims that he was able to investigate gave no cause for concern at the end of the day.[1]

There was an alleged flood of potentially false registrations but only four were judged to be substantial enough to justify the pressing of charges. Although that stretches the interpretation of the word 'substantial'.

The Crown's allegation was that I had encouraged each of these voters to give a false date for the time they had moved to a new address within the constituency, so that they could be registered to vote. The Crown's first witness was a woman, Shadia Hussain. She had moved from a flat in Leven Street, where she lived with a friend, to a different address in the same street. In other words, since she had only moved to a house in the street she would have been eligible to vote in the Election anyway. She had given a statement to the police that I had gone to her door with electoral registration forms and told her to say she had moved to her new address in August 1996, instead of November 1996, so that she would be eligible to vote. She told the court that she was no longer sure that it was me who had visited –

1. *Glasgow Herald* 27 January 1999

The day of my marriage to Perveen, 19 July 1976. After an Islamic service we had another ceremony in Lossiemouth. Here we are signing the register with the Reverend Forbes Watt of the Church of Scotland.

With my political mentor, Jimmy Dunnachie MP, in the summer of 1993.

Perveen and I on 24 June 1996 greeting supporters on the steps of the Labour Party headquarters, Keir Hardie House in Glasgow, after victory in the re-run ballot against Mike Watson MP.

Campaigning in the May 1997 General Election.

With my SNP opponent in May 1997, Nicola Sturgeon, at the count in Glasgow.

A victory salute on winning the seat in May 1997.

My media team for my appointment as Governor of Punjab – Bob Wylie, Anas Sarwar and Akmal Khan.

Standing for the National Anthem at the oath ceremony for the Governorship of Punjab on 5 August 2013. To my right is Chief Minister Shahbaz Sharif and to my left is Chief Justice Atta Bandail.

Pledging to fight for a better deal for the children of the Punjab in my state address after appointment as Governor.

At home with the family shortly after my appointment as Governor. Left to right: Asim, Faisa, Anas, me, Perveen and Athif.

The flood refugee camp in the village of Akbarabad outside Charsadda in north west Pakistan, September 2010.

In August 2011, I'm with the children of a primary school in Charsadda which Ucare Foundation redeveloped after it was stricken by the floods.

Outside the Houses of Parliament on a visit to the UK in March 2015.
(Photo by Alex Hewitt)

My first speech at a PTI conference with Imran Khan after resigning as Governo in January 2015.

On the campaign trail in the local government elections in Pakistan in October 2015.

'At that time I thought to myself it was the truth . . . now I am not so sure . . . I may have jumped to the conclusion that it was Mr Sarwar.'[1]

The second Crown witness was Mrs Shamin Ahmad. In an earlier statement she had identified me as having come to her door with electoral registration forms which she completed for herself and her husband. Asked by Duncan Menzies if she had positively identified me previously, she replied 'At the time, yes, but I was wrong at the time.'

The next day Menzies produced his so called 'star witness', Mrs Muntaz Arif, who said she had seen and heard me trying to persuade her friend to make a false electoral registration. The friend, in this case, was Shadia Hussain, who had already told the court that she was no longer sure it was me who had come to her house. Nonetheless Mrs Arif told the court that 'Mr Sarwar told her that if she filled in a form she would be able to vote. It would have to be backdated.'[2]

However under cross-examination from Michael S. Jones, my QC, Mrs Arif had to admit that her husband was pursuing a compensation claim for £20,000 against my company, United Wholesale Grocers Ltd. The claim followed an accident which took place when the husband worked there. A gasp was heard round the courtroom when this was said. Michael S. Jones then suggested to Mrs Arif that because of this she was pursuing a vendetta against me. Menzies had laboured and produced a grandiose zero. Some eight or nine weeks later, towards the end of the trial, Menzies told the jury that he was withdrawing the electoral fraud charges 'for legal reasons'. The 'legal reasons' being that they were a nonsense from day one.

Engaging Michael S. Jones as my QC was probably one of the best decisions I made in the whole legal imbroglio in which I was trapped. Jones has a forensic legal mind and, day after day, he picked the prosecution case apart. He demonstrated the height of these powers when he dealt with Badar Islam's evidence. Here's how the peerless legal correspondent of the *Herald* of those days, Bruce McKain, wrote about Badar and Jones:

Badar was the key to the case. The mountainous Badar, who spent a week in the witness box, came across as the kind of

1. *Glasgow Herald*, 28 January 1999.
2. *Glasgow Herald*, 29 January 1999.

man that you would shake hands with and count your fingers afterwards . . . The failed restauranteur and hotelier had been bankrupted twice in spectacular fashion, leaving debts of £1.5m, a fact which did not seem to have left him particularly shameful or regretful.

An enthusiastic gambler, Badar had also been barred from various casinos in Glasgow, once after allegations of cheating, according to Sarwar's defence team . . . He was being threatened by loan sharks as well as legitimate creditors and when he got paid for his story by the *News of the World*, he made sure the sharks were fed first. The jury heard that Badar had even stooped so low as to pocket the proceeds from a cancer charity event attended by former Pakistani cricket captain Imran Khan. By the end of a merciless grilling Jones had reduced Badar to a quivering wreck.[1]

Michael S. Jones set about his personal demolition of Badar's evidence in a step-by-step fashion. He sought to establish first that Badar had desperate debts and needed money; that he knew there were rumours that the *News of the World* would pay money for stories that would smear me and that Badar was a long-time bankrupt and discredited liar. He achieved that, and more, in his first day of cross-examination of Badar's evidence.

In part of their first exchanges Jones asked Badar about the scale of his personal debts – could they be as much as £50,000? Badar replied: 'I owe maybe more than that. How do I know? It doesn't matter how much I owe. It may be a million. Who knows?'[2] Gasps of astonishment were audible in the court after that admission. In the questioning that followed Jones also forced Badar to admit that he knew there were rumours that there were newspapers willing to pay money for smearing me, and that he had stood against me as an election candidate because I had split the Asian community by interfering in the affairs of the Haq family, when I had gone to Pakistan to rescue the Haq sisters. All things considered, it had been a good day for us in court.

1. *Glasgow Herald*, 26 March 1999.
2. *Glasgow Herald*, 5 February 1999.

By the end of the second day Jones had Badar admitting that he owed my business more than £10,000 in goods given to him on credit when he set up his hotel business in Paisley and that he had acted to get personal vengeance on me for shaming him in public by calling him a bankrupt and liar in front of several others. Jones finished the day with another loaded question to Badar: 'For you the truth is something you can stick to or depart from as it suits you, isn't it?' [1]

Badar was finally reduced to a 'quivering wreck' on the last day of his evidence when he admitted that on top of the £45,000 he was paid by the News of the World, the newspaper also paid him £500 a week for him to arrange his own 'security' for months after the newspaper story. So here was a man who had gained more than £50,000 for selling a story about me. If this planted doubts in the jury's minds about Badar's motivations from day one, the final coup de grace to his evidence was delivered by his former election agent Tariq Malik. He told the court that after Badar had been given the £5,000 loan he said to Malik: 'Sarwar wouldn't trust me. He wouldn't give me more than £5,000 so now I am going to the News of the World people.' [2]

If Badar's evidence had degenerated into a farrago of lies, then what followed had elements of farce about it. Peter Paton came to court and said that I ruled the Asian community with 'an iron fist' and that my rescue of the Haq sisters from Pakistan had been 'a politically motivated stunt'. However Paton reached the height of absurdity when he told the court: 'I believe Sarwar abducted the girls from their father in Pakistan and he is the real kidnapper'. [3]

Rebekah Wade, now Rebekah Brooks, followed Paton's lead into absurdity. She was the acting editor of the News of the World when the 'Sleaze Bombshell' story was published. She told the court that in all her experience as a journalist she had never known two men as frightened as Badar Islam and Tariq Malik when they were being questioned by her reporters at a London hotel. She said that she thought Islam and Malik regarded me as 'some latter day mafioso

1. *Glasgow Herald*, 6 February 1999.
2. *Glasgow Herald*, 13 February 1999.
3. *Glasgow Herald*, 11 February 1999.

kind of person who was going to have them shot for betraying him and the Asian community.'[1]

As I reflect on the court case now I believe that two contrasting testimonies became crucial in influencing the final judgement that was delivered. The first came from my own former election agent, councillor Gordon Archer, who by then had defected to the SNP. He gave evidence to the effect that I had 'cooked the books' by not making a full declaration of election expenses in under-declaring what we had spent on the hire of election rooms during the campaign. I felt he had let me down, not just because he had been a close comrade for years and was a key organiser in the election campaign, but because he had always known that it was common practice for the Labour Party to rent vacant shops as election headquarters, and then to lease them out to local Labour Parties. This allowed more of the local Party funds to be spent on the local campaign. We had been part of that process, like most other constituency parties in Glasgow, and elsewhere, at the time. Archer knew that, without doubt.

At the end of his testimony he was asked if he had ever asked me for money or if he had ever suggested to another Party member that they could make money by selling their story to the *News of the World*. Pressed three times by Michael S. Jones, Archer answered that he had never asked me for money nor suggested to others that he could get money from selling a story about me to the *News of the World*. In fact, he had asked on two occasions for me to give him money to help out with his business problems.

Michael S. Jones then laid the trap. As I recollect, he told Archer that he wanted to ask a hypothetical question. He then asked that if Mr Sarwar had taped your conversations when you raised these issues with him, would you still reply that you had never asked him for money? Archer then said he had become confused by the line of questioning and was nervous, as he had never been a witness in the High Court. He said that indeed he now remembered that he had asked me for money because he desperately needed £5,000 to stop his business going bust, and that he was angry when I refused after all the time we had worked together.

1. *Glasgow Herald*, 20 February 1999.

The trial judge, Lady Cosgrove, was furious. Previously, because of the length of time that Archer was in the witness box, she had granted him permission to give his evidence sitting down. She now told him to stand up. She asked Archer, in strident tones, if he knew it was wrong to tell lies in Court, and that he was now in danger of having committed perjury. So it became clear for every member of the jury to see that one of the Prosecution's key witnesses was damned for lying in court.

The contrasting testimony in our favour came the following week, from Nick Brown MP. He was then the Minister for Agriculture but at the time of the *News of the World* scandal had been Chief Whip. It was Brown that I had gone to see, at his office at 12 Downing Street, on the Sunday the story broke. Brown was dignified and resolute in the witness box. He was asked if at the Downing Street meeting I had told him the £5,000 was a loan and not a bribe. 'Exactly so. Yes he did,' [1] he replied. He went on to say that, in the context of the solidarity within the Asian community, and one member of the community helping another, the loan did not strike him as being that odd or unusual. So a Government minister confirmed to the court that from the very outset I had insisted the money was a loan, and that the practice of making loans within the community was relatively common.

Michael S. Jones told me at the time that he thought the two testimonies could turn out to be a crucial microcosm of the case. Brown was to the point, unshakeable and honest, and confirmed our version of the events. In the eyes of the jury, Archer may have confirmed that a number of the prosecution's witnesses contradicted their own evidence when in the witness box, or alternatively, were in the pay of the *News of the World*; or both. There would still be three weeks to go in the trial after the Brown testimony, but following discussion with Jones I became convinced that we might have reached a turning-point.

Then came an historical legal thunderbolt – the prosecution called my solicitor, Chris Kelly, as a prosecution witness. As far as I have been able to determine, this is the only instance of this happening in the history of Scots law. In other words, the calling of my solicitor was without legal precedent. Kelly was cross-examined about

1. *Glasgow Herald*, 2 March 1999.

the details of the preparation of my case – including confidential exchanges between Kelly and myself which had taken place more than a year before the trial began. Later the Advocate Depute tried to use Kelly's evidence to accuse me of lying. I told him in court in no uncertain terms: 'You think the only trustworthy man in Britain is Badar Islam. Actually he is the biggest liar in Britain. You might trust him but he is the biggest liar.'[1] I had lost my temper. However, part of the reason for my outburst was that I was actually still outraged by the prosecution calling my solicitor to give evidence against me.

Even before I had to go into the witness box, two sets of charges against me had been dropped. As already noted, Menzies, after eight weeks of the trial, told the jury on 8 March that the electoral fraud charges about false registration of voters had been dropped 'for legal reasons'. There was no further explanation offered. Then the next day, Lady Cosgrove ruled that there was no case to answer on the alleged under-declaring of expenses, as the Crown case had no effective corroboration. So with the charges that had been withdrawn and those dismissed by the judge, it came down to whether or not the money I had given Islam was to make him write a false affidavit on my behalf, and whether or not Mumtaz Hussain's emergence as the guarantor for the loan was actually an attempt to cover up.

I can remember when the jury was out to deliberate on its verdict that a number of photographers from the newspapers approached me and asked if they could have a picture in which I was not smiling. One said: 'We need a pic where you look worried in case you don't get a result'. I told him I had slept every night throughout the trial and would be found not guilty. Nonetheless I obliged and produced a pose, with a frown. It was never used. On 25 March 1999 I was cleared on all charges. The jury's deliberations exemplified the weakness of the Crown's case – after 9 weeks, and 39 days of evidence, they decided on 'not guilty' verdicts on the remaining charges in less than three hours.

When I emerged from the court I gave an impromptu media conference from the steps at the side of St Giles Cathedral, which is adjacent to the High Court in Edinburgh. I told the assembled crowd of reporters: 'I have always maintained from the outset that

1. *Glasgow Herald*, 13 March 1999.

the allegations against me were false and I am glad that the jury has found me innocent of all charges brought against me. Today the truth has triumphed and I have been vindicated.'

Some time after my acquittal, my sister Aroona told me how she had gone to see my mother as the trial was coming to a close. It was to prepare my mother for the worst – that I may not get a 'not guilty' result. My mother told her that she would not countenance any discussion. She said: 'Your brother is innocent, so he will be found not guilty.' I thank God that my mother had such faith in me, which was proved to be justified.

I certainly cannot say the same for the denizens of the Scottish media. The newspaper editors said, in the light of re-selection controversy and the accusations which emerged in the court case, that Labour would lose the Govan seat in the coming 1999 elections for the Scottish Parliament; especially given that the SNP candidate was Nicola Sturgeon, who most commentators openly favoured. The general sentiment expressed in different ways was that I may have been found not guilty in court, but the court of the people would reach a different verdict in the coming elections to the Scottish Parliament. They were all wrong. Gordon Jackson won the seat, beating Sturgeon by 1,756 votes.

We began to believe that the impossible was possible about ten days before the poll. We had a big public meeting in Kinning Park, at the old cinema there. About 700 people turned up and the atmosphere was really electric – there was almost a tangible feeling in the meeting that the News of the World and their like had not beaten us in court and they wouldn't beat us in the election on our territory either.

The 'court of the people' also left the newspaper scribes with egg on their collective faces two years later, when it came to my own performance in the General Election of June 2001. My majority more than doubled from 2,914 in 1997 to 6,400 in 2001. By 2005 when I stood in my last General Election as a Labour candidate in Glasgow Central, my majority turned out to be just over 8,500. Perhaps it is just as well that I paid no heed to the doomsayers and accusers who wrote their holier-than-thou editorials in the aftermath of my court victory. The people did have their say and they spoke in my favour in increasing numbers.

I may have acted differently in the face of this barrage of criticism following the court victory if I had my time again. Perhaps I should have been more combative and railed against the media attacks, criticising their collective pusillanimity about the disgraceful excesses of the tabloid press, notably News International, in my trial. It is a fact that almost all the key prosecution witnesses led against me – Archer excepted – were in the pay of the *News of the World*. The most notable being Badar Islam, the key Crown witness, who was paid more than £50,000 for his lies.

I believe that chequebook journalism corrupts the British legal system. I may go so far as to say that anyone paid large amounts of money by a newspaper for their story should be disqualified from being a witness in a criminal trial. It is a self-evident fact that someone like Badar Islam, paid tens of thousands by a tabloid newspaper for a story, is going to stand by their story if it somehow results in legal proceedings. Once the money changes hands, Badar was never going to stand in the dock and say: 'OK, to tell you the truth it was a scam against Sarwar. I did it all for the money, made a plot to get him with News International.'

However, what we know now, is not what we knew then. In 1999, armed with today's revelations and insights, I might not have dropped my legal action against the fixers and liars at the *News of the World*. At that point I took a political decision that it was time to serve my constituents and that I had already lost enough ground, in that regard, due to the charges made against me and the disruption caused by the trial. Today I might well have pursued them, with all my energy, to the ends of the earth.

In May 2012 the same Rebekah Brooks, who gave evidence against me in my trial, her husband, Charlie Brooks, and four of her work colleagues were charged with conspiring to pervert the course of justice. Then, in July 2012, she was also charged with conspiring to intercept communications without lawful authority between October 2000 and August 2006, and later hacking the voicemails of the murdered teenager Milly Dowler.

Andy Coulson, one-time communications director in Prime Minister David Cameron's team, was Brooks' deputy editor at *News of the World*. He succeeded her in that post in 2003 when she became chief executive of News International in the UK. Coulson faced a range of charges similar to those pressed against Brooks. Both Coulson and Brooks issued vehement denials of guilt at the time the charges were made public. They both displayed shock and outrage that they would be accused of such things; these pathetic displays were difficult to watch after the callous destruction of countless lives, at their whim, in their days as editors within the Murdoch empire.

By the time their infamous trial started in October 2013, Brooks was also charged along with a senior *Sun* journalist, John Kay, with bribing public officials. It was alleged that Brooks and Kay paid Bettina Barber, a senior official at the Ministry of Defence, £100,000 between 2004 and 2011 for news stories. Coulson was also charged, along with the former *News of the World* Royal correspondent, Clive Goodman, with paying public officials for information, including servants at Buckingham Palace.

However the roll call of charges went well beyond Brooks and Coulson. Alongside them another eight former journalists at the *News of the World* faced hacking charges, involving more than 600 victims, as well as related conspiracy to pervert the course of justice charges. An additional 14 co-defendants, charged with conspiracy to pervert the course of justice, were directly or indirectly connected to Rebekah Brooks. Three of them – her husband, her former personal assistant, Cheryl Carter, and her ex-chauffeur Paul Edwards, were accused of agreeing to conceal evidence, in July 2011, from detectives investigating the phone-hacking allegations.

I have gone into this detail to lay out the extent of the charges made against all the defendants. It may be worthwhile recalling that in July 2009, when the *News of the World* sought to counter a *Guardian* story about the scope of their phone-hacking practices involving 'thousands' of victims, News International issued a statement declaring:

There is not and never has been evidence that *News of the World* Journalists had accessed anybody's voicemails or instructed anybody to access voicemails or that there was systematic corporate illegality at News International . . . It goes without saying that had the police uncovered such evidence, charges would have been brought against other *News of the World* personnel. Not only have there been no such charges but the police have not considered it necessary to arrest or question any other member of the *News of the World* staff.[1]

After the 33-week trial at the Old Bailey, Brooks was acquitted on all charges, as were all the defendants charged with offences linked to her. Jonathan Laidlaw, Brooks' QC convinced the jury that his client was innocent, and as editor of the *Sun* and *News of the World* knew nothing of what her journalists were up to. The £5-7 million costs for Brooks defence can now be deemed to be money well spent. The *Private Eye* cover at the time of the verdicts carried a front page page picture of Brooks with Andy Coulson. Her voice bubble declared 'I've just got away with Murdoch'. Andy Coulson's QC was not able to get his client acquitted. Coulson was found guilty of phone hacking and related charges and sentenced to 18 months in prison. Two other senior executive editors at *News of the World* were also found guilty – Greg Miskiw, given 6 months and Neville Thurbeck, 6 months.

Although the Metropolitan Police eventually carried out their duty in relation to this monumental scandal, the sins of the leaders of the Met in these matters should not be lost in the acres of newsprint commenting on the Brooks verdict. Their 2006–7 investigation of the initial allegations found that there were only two people to be charged – a journalist and a private detective – for these nefarious and cruel practices. In July 2009, when the *Guardian* newspaper ran its first substantial piece on the new phone hacking allegations the Metropolitan Police still insisted there was no new evidence which would justify a re-opening of the 2006–7 inquiry.

The Met Commissioners held that line for two years before the Milly Dowler accusations came to light. That involved the almost incredible fact that the 14-year-old Milly's mobile phone was being hacked by the *News of the World* while there was an ongoing police investigation of her likely abduction and murder.

1. Nick Davies, *Hack Attack – How the Truth Caught up with Rupert Murdoch*, Faber and Faber, 2014.

After Brooks resigned from News International with a reported £16 million pay-off and the *News of the World* was closed down, the resignations of the Metropolitan Police Commissioner, Sir Paul Stephenson, and Assistant Commissioner, John Yates, followed.

Sue Akers, a Deputy Assistant Commissioner at the Met later told the *Guardian* that there were almost 5,000 victims of phone hacking. That is a long way from the earlier assertions by the Met that there were only one or two individuals involved. This allowed the *News of the World* to protest, for a numbers of years, that only 'one or two rogue reporters' had been responsible for the tapping and entrapment excesses. Some say now that a dangerous collusion had developed between tabloid journalists and the police, to which a blind eye seemed to have been turned for an eternity. Others have used another word. Corruption.

Battling for the People of Glasgow 9

'The Clyde will have the best job security in more than 20 years. We are all very relieved after years of uncertainty, but fortune favours the brave and we've all been bloody brave and determined.'

Jamie Webster, Shop Stewards Convenor, Govan Shipyard, *Scotsman*, 31 January 2003.

'The new aircraft carriers will be about 300 metres long – that's nearly the length of three Hampden football pitches.'

Daily Record, 1 May, 2002.

Life in Parliament was tremendously busy. At that time there were avalanches of mail delivered to the offices in London and Glasgow and hundreds of emails every week. I held two surgeries in the constituency every Friday. There was almost always a queue of people waiting to see me. I suppose that when you begin to develop a reputation as one who always tries to get something done for people then they will come to seek help.

Sometimes, on a Friday, as the surgery queue seemed to be endless, I'd wonder if someone had been touring the constituency in a loudspeaker van belting out the message, 'Go and see Sarwar. He'll help you'. I don't think that any MP in the West of Scotland had more constituency surgeries than me. I had the two Friday surgeries and five on the first Saturday of the month, in five different locations. And, with few exceptions, I attended them in person.

I was equally assiduous in my parliamentary work. I would go to the House of Commons cafe for breakfast every morning, read the newspapers, and then the day's work would start with meetings; committee meetings, visitors, and then in the afternoon attending debates in the Chamber and more meetings. In those days the Parliament used to sit long into the night and often into the small hours of the morning, so it was possible to arrive at the House of Commons at nine in the morning and still be there sixteen hours later. Robin Cook certainly did every parliamentarian a great favour when, as Leader of the House, he amended the hours of the sittings and made it all a bit more like a working day.

There was an additional pressure for me as Britain's first Muslim MP. It meant that there was a huge ethnic minority element to my caseload from all over the UK. Of course I would pass individual cases about grievances of one type or another to the person's own constituency MP, as is the established practice, but nonetheless there continued to be a large element of the work which was what might be called ethnic minority politics. For example, as I have mentioned elsewhere, at one stage a large number of women across the UK who were in forced marriages sought my help, not as their local MP, but as an MP who was a Muslim, whom they believed would be inherently more understanding of their predicament. It was also the case that other MPs whose constituents had problems at home in Pakistan, would refer those cases to me because of my connections there.

There were other issues which developed in a similar way and resulted in an increased workload for my office on issues which were not directly associated with constituency business. For example, at one stage my office became a focal point in the debates about extradition. One extradition agreement in particular became significant in this respect, the treaty between the USA and the UK, and how it impacted on the Gary McKinnon case.

Gary McKinnon was the young Scot who hacked into a host of US government defence and secret intelligence sites, including NASA. He has always said that he did so to search for evidence of defence and intelligence agencies suppressing information about sightings of UFOs, and that he came across sensitive intelligence material purely by chance. In 2002 he was charged by the US authorities on seven counts of hacking, which carried possible sentences of 70 years in jail. So the battle to prevent his extradition to the United States began; it would last for years, one legal challenge following after another. In the end, his extradition was blocked by the Home Secretary, Theresa May, in October 2012, on medical grounds – it had been established that McKinnon suffered from Asperger's syndrome, a form of autism, and was a high suicide risk if extradited.

I supported the campaign because I felt that the extradition treaty between the US and the UK conferred unfair advantages to the US authorities seeking to extradite individuals from the UK to the USA, advantages which were not reciprocated at the UK end of the treaty, when any extradition from the USA was being sought. In November 2008, I was one of the movers of an Early Day Motion in support of Gary McKinnon, and my office became inundated with messages of support, requests for meetings and the like.

My involvement with the McKinnon case led me to a clash with the Whips Office when the general matter of extradition was debated in the House the following year. In July 2009, I got a call from the Deputy Chief Whip, Tommy McAvoy MP, who had done me many favours in the past and was seeking one in return. The following week there was to be a vote on a procedural element of the Extradition Bill, which had been passed some years earlier. Tommy McAvoy could be a bruiser, and he told me that he expected me to be at the House of Commons on the following Tuesday to support the Government. I told him that it was Eid – the celebration at the end of Ramadan – on that Tuesday and that I really should be in the constituency at that time. He roared in reply: 'Don't give me that, Mohammad. Eid for Khalid Mahmood MP, Shahid Malik MP and Sadiq Khan MP is on the Monday. Be there or else.'

I tried to persuade Tommy that it was possible to have Eid on different days in different parts of the country and that in Glasgow Eid was going to be on the following Tuesday. He wasn't for listening so I decided I would make my Eid prayers in the morning at the Central Mosque, in Glasgow, and then leave to be in London by the evening for the Commons vote. Later on the same day, McAvoy met the then Scottish Whip, Frank Roy MP, in the corridors of the Commons. He told Roy with relish how he had brought me to heel about the Extradition vote. Then Frank asked him if he had asked me how I intended to vote. After this I got a phone call from Tommy. 'Mohammad, how do you expect to vote on this Extradition thing on Tuesday?' came the question from the Deputy Chief Whip on my mobile. I told him that I thought the current agreement with the US was not on an equal footing, like for like. He interrupted: 'Don't give me all that crap, how are you going to vote?'

'Against the Government,' I told him.

'Mohammad,' he said, 'I've had some thoughts about all this since we last spoke. It would be unthinkable for me not to spend Christmas in the bosom of my family, and I know that Eid is a similar family celebration in your culture. Forget about coming to vote on Tuesday. Be with your family, by all means.' Such consideration was in his own interest, of course.

My workload also had a considerable international element, which many MPs would not have had, again as a consequence of my 'title' as Britain's 'first Muslim MP'. That meant that any delegation to the parliament from an Islamic country or from an organisation connected to the Muslim community in the UK, or elsewhere, felt that it was their duty to seek me out. This is not a complaint, of course, merely an observation, but it did make an enormous difference to the scale of my workload. It also gave me a significant profile internationally, since the links made with delegations provided me with an understanding of many international issues and, as a result of that knowledge, a certain compulsion to speak out about them.

However, as I reflect on my time as an MP, the biggest challenge I faced was not speaking out on Afghanistan, Iraq, Israel, Kashmir or Lebanon, all issues close to my heart. It was much nearer to home than that – the battle to save the Govan shipyard. The warning sounds about the possible closure of the Kvaerner shipyard there had first come my way in December 1998, in a meeting I had with trade union leaders at the yard. What had been part of the Upper Clyde Shipbuilders had been taken over by the Norwegian concern years before. The owners had been big on promises and small on delivering them.

The convenor of the shop stewards at Govan was Jamie Webster, who would prove to be a stalwart in the coming campaigns to save Govan shipyard, which lasted for the best part of three years. That December he told me that the order-book for ships at Govan was running out and that there was talk of Kvaerner, the owners, pulling out of shipbuilding, not just in Govan, but everywhere in their global business. I had a meeting with a local manager at Kvaerner.

He told me there were some rumours, but nobody knew anything for certain.

All through the early months of 1999, the speculation mounted. Late in January, Jamie Webster came to see me one weekend, and complained about a letter the shop stewards had sent to 30 MPs in the West of Scotland, earlier in the month, asking for their support for Govan shipyard to get a new order for a survey ship contract. Weeks after the letter was sent, only two MPs had replied. I agreed to send out another letter drawing attention to the shop stewards' letter requesting their support.

On 9 February the workers at Govan shipyard were informed that the survey ship contract was going elsewhere. By that time, even after my letter, only 17 of the 30 MPs had responded to the Govan stewards. An article in the tabloid newspaper, the *Daily Record*, of 11 February 1999, was headlined: 'Thirteen Labour MPs accused of snubbing shipyard workers.' They were named in the newspaper, and they were furious. That probably set the seal on what a number of Labour MPs thought of Jamie Webster from that point onwards.

Many believed that, politically, Jamie was a nationalist, a 'sleeping' member of the Scottish National Party, and had raised his complaints in public to embarrass the Labour Party. It became impossible to change this impression that a large number of Labour MPs had, especially since Jamie is someone who does not hesitate to speak his mind, to put it mildly. When I think about him the description 'No Holds Barred' frequently springs to mind. I knew that the accusations that he was an SNP supporter were wrong. In fact, in the coming battles for the yard, he would prove that the only party he was a paid-up member of might be called the Govan Shipyard Workers Party, which had one demand on its manifesto – Save the Yard!

However, these observations need some further clarification, because there were other factors influencing perceptions. The problem was that Scottish Labour MPs thought the fight for Govan was the responsibility of the Glasgow MPs; in turn the Glasgow MPs thought it was really my responsibility as the constituency MP.

In the early months of 1999 I was fighting a battle for my own survival in the courts, facing the stark possibility of seven or eight years in jail. That made me feel really guilty, since it meant that I could not give my full commitment to the fight for the yard because of the legal case. I knew that there were whispers: 'Look at Sarwar, he's stuck in the High Court when he should be fighting for the shipyard workers in his constituency.'

Those dilemmas took an entirely different turn, after the court case ended with my acquittal on all charges. Days later the Kvaerner bosses ended the uncertainty about the yard when they announced, in Oslo, that they were pulling out of all their shipbuilding businesses worldwide, including Govan. That was in the middle of April, by which time I was totally preoccupied with the political battle in Govan to get Gordon Jackson elected in the first elections to the new Scottish Parliament. This meant that the fight for Govan shipbuilding was still taking second place, and the shop stewards in the yard probably resented that.

When I could finally devote my full time energies to the fight, I knew I had some ground to make up to convince the workers of my commitment. When Kvaerner announced that they were getting out of shipbuilding they also made it clear that as far as the Govan yard and Scotstoun yards were concerned, they were willing to sell if a bidder came forward and the price was right. The future of shipbuilding on the Clyde was, yet again, at risk: something like 8,000 jobs were immediately at stake; at Govan around 1,000, Scotstoun 2,000 and ancillary suppliers to the two yards, 5,000.

Tony Blair had bought a number of so-called 'technocrats' into his government to give it an extra weight with the business community. One of them was Lord Gus Macdonald. He had been made Baron Macdonald of Tradeston in October 1998, and shortly thereafter was appointed by Blair as Minister for Business and Industry at the Scottish Office. Macdonald had spent the most significant part of his working life in television journalism, notably as managing director of Scottish Television. However, he had been a one-time shipyard apprentice on the Clyde and had roots in the Labour movement, so he seemed a potentially good ally in the fight. When Kvaerner announced the closure, Macdonald appointed the former union leader, Sir Gavin Laird, to head a task force to find a buyer for the yards. So far so good.

A matter of weeks later there were two pieces of good news to encourage us. The Task Force announced that there were serious discussions with the engineering giant, GEC, about the purchase of the Kvaerner yards; and just about then, the redoubtable John Reid was appointed as the Scottish Secretary of State, in a Tony Blair Cabinet reshuffle. I tended to think that with John Reid it was, as they say in Glasgow, 'His Way or No Way'. However I believe that it was our determination to continue to fight, combined with John Reid's unwavering support, that eventually saw us through. The deadline for mass redundancies and closure was set for 16 July. By early July there was no sign of salvation. No deal, and the clock was ticking.

Then, on 6 July I got a phone call from a member of the media who told me that, later that day, GEC were going to announce that they would be making Kvaerner an offer for Govan which they expected to be accepted. I was euphoric – against all the odds it looked as if we had done it. I tried to reach Jamie Webster and John Reid, but neither of them were available at that time. Later on, I heard that Jamie Webster had been interviewed on the Radio Clyde evening news bulletin, waxing lyrical about how there couldn't be anyone on earth happier than him and how he felt his prayers had been answered.

Eventually I managed to reach Jamie on the phone for a near ecstatic exchange. The workers had arranged to go to the Kvaerner headquarters in London the next day to hand back the redundancy notices that had been served, and I had also arranged meetings for Jamie and the shop stewards at the House of Commons with Scottish Labour MPs, and thereafter a meeting with John Reid. We deliberated whether all that was still going to be necessary, and decided to talk a bit later as Jamie was being besieged by the media for interviews and quotes. Then the roof fell in.

A matter of hours after the GEC announcement, Kvaerner rejected the deal. To have been taken to what seemed the brink of salvation and then have all hopes dashed was truly gut-wrenching. Kvaerner's public response stated that the GEC offer fell 'very substantially short' of a solution for the Govan yard. It was absolutely clear now that the most significant sticking point was which of the two companies would be responsible for any redundancy costs, should they ensue. GEC had offered £1 million for the yard, stipulating that Kvaerner would be financially responsible for redundancies for the next five years. Kvaerner's response, in essence, was 'No Way!' The shipyard workers' delegation to the Kvaerner headquarters, in London, and thereafter to the House of Commons, was now on. Definitely on!

The next day Jamie and the shop stewards went to Kvaerner and handed the redundancy notices back. The workers at Govan had stood shoulder to shoulder. Not a single one of the letters – which contained details of the individual redundancy payments on offer – had been opened. This was little short of a miracle of solidarity. At Prime Minister's Question Time in the Commons I had tried to get Tony Blair to go on the record by asking him if he knew that the workers were 'looking to the Government to do everything in its power to save these jobs'. Blair offered no guarantees and spoke only of the 'passion and dignity' of the workers.

Then came the stewards' meeting with Scottish Labour MPs, in a committee room in the House of Commons. I was personally dismayed at the low attendance – only about a dozen MPs turned up. Jamie Webster told the meeting that the workers were 'tottering on the brink of despair'. He said that the GEC offer was 'obscene, outrageous and totally unacceptable.' One of the MPs then asked Jamie if he, Jamie, wasn't getting too emotional about the issue of the yard and the jobs. I could see Jamie was near the end of his tether. I discerned the emotion in his voice as he told the MP, 'The day I do not get emotional about an issue like this I'll be a lesser man for it', and I remember thinking that he was near breaking-point. In his book about the struggle, published later, he confessed that he was.

Luckily, we had the meeting with John Reid at the Scottish Office to go to, so, after a few more questions and a summing up, I ushered Jamie out of the room. The meeting with Reid went well, because Reid promised to fight on and tried to convince us that there could still be a deal. There was some discussion about whether the problem of who would pay for redundancy costs was going to scupper the whole project. John Reid said he 'would not leave any stone unturned', although he added that time was running out.

On the Friday of that week, Jamie and the stewards went for another meeting with John Reid at the Scottish Office building in the centre of Glasgow. Donald Dewar, then Scotland's First Minister, arrived along with Reid. What followed was an exchange which might have split the entire campaign, although we managed to avoid that, by the skin of our teeth you might say. I have to lay the blame for creating this potential division with Donald Dewar. Equivocation was a well-established hallmark of Dewar's political approach – 'on the one hand . . . whilst on the other' were his political watchwords. In his opening statement to the stewards, Dewar said there remained some possibilities but then told them that it looked like the game was up – there had been no breakthrough and it now looked as if there wouldn't be one.

Jamie went off at the deep end, criticised the two companies for the way they had 'taken the workers on a nightmare ride, on an emotional rollercoaster'. He then demanded that the Scottish Government should get GEC and Kvaerner to come clean with the truth and 'allow us to get on with the rest of our lives'. Dewar wrongly interpreted this as the white flag of surrender on Jamie's part and, as Jamie records, Dewar then said: 'I fully understand the strains and pressure you and all the workers at Govan have been under. If you feel it's all too much and want to call an end to it, then perhaps it's for the best.'[1]

I found myself reflecting on an exchange there had been with Dewar some months before. We were handing out leaflets outside Govan Cross Underground station, during Gordon Jackson's campaign to get elected to the Scottish Parliament. Dewar had come to Govan to help in the campaign. He said to me: 'The Govan campaign, Mohammad. You know it's never good politics to take a high profile role in a campaign you can't win.' Dewar was gifted intellectually, and will have his place in history for the part he played in the creation of the Scottish Parliament. But he was a lawyer. He wasn't a streetfighter. John Reid was.

On 13 July, four days after the near-disastrous clash between Jamie Webster and Donald Dewar, Reid held marathon 10-hour talks with Kvaerner and GEC at the Scottish Office in London. At the end of the talks he was able to announce that GEC had agreed a deal to buy the Govan yard. Obviously it had involved a lot of political arm-twisting and the promise of government money, but in the end, Reid and Gus MacDonald forced the hands of the two multinationals.

1. Jamie Webster and Russell Walker, *Back from the Brink*, Brown and Ferguson, 2008.

At that time the whole situation was complicated. It was not just about the yard closing or not closing. There were other issues. GEC were involved in merger talks with British Aerospace to create a huge engineering and shipbuilding conglomerate. If things went badly at Govan, maybe there would be weeks, even months, of deliberation at the Monopolies Commission to investigate the merger. Or maybe not. It made sense all round for a deal to be done on Govan, especially since that is what the Government wanted.

On the other hand, if Kvaerner walked away they would become responsible for massive compensation costs for the decontamination of the lands of the shipyard. So it was clear if Kvaerner wanted to avoid that outcome, there had to be a continuation of shipbuilding there. There was a possibility that Clydeport – the port authority for Glasgow and the Clyde – could buy the grounds and lease them back to a new owner to remove the potential contamination burden. And the costs of any redundancies? What would be possible if the government offered some guarantees?

On the latter point, John Reid has offered only partial confirmation without ever giving any details. When the deal was announced he was asked if any public money had been spent on clinching the agreement and replied: 'We have always made it plain that if someone wanted to take over the yard we would be prepared to give financial assistance in return for their investment. That's something that's already on the record. We have to make sure the workforce and management are able to compete in a very competitive world.'[1]

My own recollection is that there was a package of some £12 million guaranteed by the Government for future redundancy costs for the GEC bid, although this was in the expectation that orders would be forthcoming and that therefore there would be no redundancies. Then, in fact, Clydeport bought the lands for £1.00 and leased them back to GEC, which freed Kvaerner of any obligations on the potential costs of contamination. The GEC bid to Kvaerner was increased to just under £2 million. To say what else happened in the exchanges at the Scottish Office in London would be pure conjecture on my part. John Reid has never told me. Perhaps he will one day.

1. Webster and Walker, *op. cit.*

On the evening of 13 July 1999, I first became aware that a deal had been clinched between GEC and Kvaerner when my mobile phone was ringing non-stop with journalists seeking quotes about the campaign and its success. Of course, I knew that there would be a lot of details still to be ironed out, but I felt that it was time for jubilation. First and foremost I made sure that I offered my congratulations to John Reid and Gus Macdonald for the tremendous efforts they had made in securing a successful deal. Then I made it a point to praise the workers. I told the *Herald* that evening: 'Credit must go to the determination of the skilled workforce and the dedicated union team, led by Jamie Webster. They have been immense. They have shown passion, dignity and great faith, when the future looked bleak.'

I felt my strategy was vindicated by the result, irrespective of how close it had been. There had been all those catcalls from Scottish Labour MPs about Jamie Webster being a secret Nationalist and questioning my motives in working so closely with him. Now my point had been proved – the yard had been saved and it was beyond question that it was a Labour government which had saved it. I had long argued with my opponents that if the yard closed, there would be catastrophic repercussions for the Labour Party vote in Scotland. Likewise I argued that if the yard was saved, it would be the Labour Party which would receive the credit. That's exactly what happened.

That Friday was the beginning of the Glasgow Fair holiday fortnight. First thing in the morning I went to the yard and stood with Jamie at the entrance, shaking hands with the workers arriving to go on shift. There was real raw emotion, with a common expression among the workers being 'We bloody well done it'. I told Jamie then that we had won a decisive battle, but there would be more battles to come. I knew that there were massive orders in the pipeline for Type-45 frigates, which I believed would come to the Clyde, but that was probably more than two years away. Until the Type-45s came on stream – assuming that Govan would get its share – the order book for Govan was still dangerously thin. However, that Fair Friday I kept my own counsel and joined in with the jubilation.

By September Jamie and the stewards were back in campaign mode at Labour's annual conference in Bournemouth. I arranged for their delegation to meet once more with a group of Scottish MPs, who were attending the conference. The strategy for the campaign had been decided well before this. BAE Systems – the product of the British Aerospace and GEC merger – had no orders for the Clyde. The work on the promised Type-45 frigates would not start until 2002, at the earliest, so Govan had a gap in orders. But the government had announced a £1 billion contract for six roll-on roll-off ferries. The build part of the contract was worth £300-400 million and the remainder was made up of a ten year repair and maintenance element. The contract for the six ferries became known as the 'Ro-Ro' contract. If Govan secured a decent share of it, our troubles would be over, since it would bridge the gap until the Type-45s came on stream.

As usual, at the conference meeting Jamie pulled no punches. Our fear was that, since the Ro-Ro contract was out to European tender, the UK consortium in the bid, including BAE Systems, could be beaten by competition from Europe or further afield. Jamie told the MPs that if a Labour government allowed what was an MoD contract to go abroad, it would be 'a total disgrace'. He said: 'It won't be forgotten if Labour allows that to happen in the UK.' I remember thinking at the meeting that, whilst his line of argument was practically irrefutable, he wasn't exactly winning friends and influencing people.

Some weeks later, two bombshells dropped to confirm our worst fears. It was towards the end of March 2000. The *Guardian* newspaper had a major article about the Ro-Ro contract which stated that it was likely to go to Germany. It suggested that the German bid was 50% lower than the BAE Systems consortium. Further, there was a 'MoD source' quoted in the *Guardian* article suggesting that Govan did not have the capability to build Ro-Ro ferries. I immediately suspected skulduggery – this was a classic MoD-style leak to prepare the ground for a later disappointing announcement.

My suspicions were confirmed in a phone call from Jamie Webster. He had been at a National Shipbuilding seminar in Manchester on the same day. One of the keynote speakers was Alan Johnson MP, who was then the junior minister at the Department of Trade and Industry, named as the Minster for Competitiveness. Jamie told me that Johnson had referred to the Ro-Ro contract in his speech. He said that Johnson had told people not to focus on competition from Korea but to 'look possibly to Germany.' This was all too much of a coincidence for me.

Any doubts about what was going on were dispelled in the follow-up to the *Guardian* story the next day. An anonymous MoD source was quoted at length claiming that Britain, not just Govan now, no longer had the capacity to build roll-on roll-off (Ro-Ro) ferries. In part of the 'on-the-record' briefing, the source said:

> Yards in the UK haven't built roll-on roll-off ferries for 20 years. It would be potentially high risk for a project manager to use a British yard. We cannot subsidise, it does not make sense to use yards which don't have the capability. This is strictly commercial and completely different from warships where we have a UK-build policy.[1]

Here it was, as clear as day: for Ro-Ro read Europe – all in one paragraph.

The next day being a Wednesday, I decided to try and put Tony Blair on the spot at Question Time in the House of Commons. It was high risk, but by this time I had decided I was prepared to go to the end in the fight, come what may. The early part of Question Time that day was dominated by the debate concerning the British car industry and the decision of BMW to sell the Rover plant at Longbridge, in the Midlands. I thought that augured well for my being called, since the Speaker, Betty Boothroyd, knew of my concerns about another key manufacturing industry, shipbuilding, also being in peril. After the leader of the Tories, then William Hague, had an exchange with the Prime Minister about the government's legislation on Section 28, regarding the rights of gay people, I rose to catch the attention of the Speaker and she called me. The *Hansard* for the day records that I said:

> Is the Prime Minister aware that a Ministry of Defence spokesman has stated that British shipyards are at risk of not receiving the pending roll-on, roll-off ferries order? Does he also

1. *Guardian*, 28 March 2000.

know that, before any decision has been made, a Minister has told a shop steward that the order is likely to go to Germany?

The Prime Minister: I am not aware of that. The Ministry of Defence has not made its decision yet. My Hon. Friend should at least await that decision.[1]

When I put the question the Chamber went absolutely silent. Blair gave me a steely look before replying. Later, one Labour MP said to me that, 'if looks could kill, Mohammad, you'd be a dead man'. It was a defining moment, because I had decided we had nothing to lose. I knew that the fact that I had put Blair in a corner would be frowned upon by the Labour parliamentary hierarchy, but by then I did not care. My reasoning was that if Blair answered 'No decision has been made', then it would be highly unlikely that, in a matter of days or weeks later, the decision could be announced that the ferry contract was going to Germany. Had that been the case, the next question would have been, 'Surely the Prime Minister knew this when he was asked the question at Question Time a matter of days or weeks ago? Has he been misleading the House?' So it gave us precious time.

The corollary was also true – if Blair had admitted the decision had been taken, we would know then that we had to muster every possible trooper to engage in a ferocious battle to save the yard. I think that asking the question finally erased any doubts that Jamie Webster and the shop stewards may have had about my commitment. Sometime before this, Jamie had pointed a finger at me and declared that there would come a time when I would have to decide whether I was a Party man or a man of the people. I think he knew from then on that the question had been asked and I had put the people – the workers at the yard – before Party. Our relationship never wavered an inch after that.

After Question Time, Alan Johnson's office went ballistic and the Minister demanded that I make an apology for my 'outrageous remarks'. I used some shipyard language to let him know what I thought of that. The next day there was massive coverage in the

1. *Hansard*, 29 March 2000.

Scottish newspapers and some of the nationals. The *Herald* was typical of the tone set:

> Ministry rolls right into row over ferry contract
>
> The Ministry of Defence came under heavy fire . . . over a spokesman's comments which appeared to rubbish the UK shipbuilding industry's capacity to handle a £300m ferry contract.
>
> The statement . . . suggested that any decision to award the Royal Navy's proposed 'roll-on roll-off' ferry contract to a British shipyard would be 'high risk' because 'yards in the UK haven't built roll-on roll-off ferries for 20 years . . . Glasgow Govan MP Mohammad Sarwar attacked the MoD spokesman's comments as 'absurd and dangerous' . . . An MoD spokesman said: 'The quote attributed to an MoD spokesman was taken out of context.'[1]

All the media took the same line, and the pasting that the MoD received gave a great boost to our petition campaign. The following weekend, in Govan shopping centre, people were lining up to sign our 'Save our Shipyard' petition. I had persuaded Jamie earlier that a petition with thousands of signatures would demonstrate how high feelings were running in Glasgow about the yard. However, not long after we started to collect signatures, we decided to go well beyond Govan and target Scottish Cabinet Ministers' constituencies, travelling to them at weekends in our hired minibus. We aimed to prove to Blair and the Labour Government that this wasn't just a local Govan issue – it was in fact a Scottish issue and they would pay a Scottish price, in votes, if they ignored it.

Alistair Darling was the Cabinet Secretary of State for Social Security then. One Saturday the 'battle bus' reached the heart of his Edinburgh Central constituency, in Princes Street, in the capital. We had some trepidation about this, as we were unsure how the folk in Edinburgh might react to our 'Glasgow' petition. We need not have worried. As soon as our table was set up a burly worker approached Jamie. He said: 'Am I right? You are Jamie Webster, Govan

1. *Herald*, 30 March 2000.

shipyard, you are Mohammad Sarwar, the Govan MP and the Yard's not closing?' The same sort of positive reaction to the fight greeted us everywhere we went, every weekend. Our destinations included the late Robin Cook's constituency, in Livingston, the Chancellor of the Exchequer, Gordon Brown's constituency, in Kirkcaldy and Cowdenbeath, in Fife, and John Reid's constituency in Motherwell, in Lanarkshire.

The petition was part of our attempts to keep the battle for Govan alive and prominent in the media. We kept it going for about three months: April, May and June – most weekends we packed the 'battle bus' and headed off. If we didn't travel we would set up at our usual pitch in the shopping centre in Govan on Saturday morning. It is not that we had any great illusions that signatures on a petition could change things – but we knew they would eventually convey the impression that all of Scotland was involved.

Towards the end of May 2000 I managed to get an adjournment debate in the House of Commons. Some of the text on my speech is worth quoting, because it summed up all the issues:

I am grateful for the opportunity to debate the future of British shipbuilding. Events in recent weeks have given the debate great relevance, particularly for workers at the Govan shipyard in my constituency. United Kingdom shipbuilding has a proud past and a rich heritage. Britain's empire and wealth were based on our shipyards employing huge workforces. The Clyde yards in particular were pioneers of innovation and shipbuilders of quality. The first iron ships for the British Navy were built in Govan. At one stage, one sixth of the world's shipping was launched from Clydeside berths.

However, the present day has seen an industry in decline for a number of years. It is now readying itself to meet the challenges of the new millennium. Up to 30,000 people are directly employed in shipbuilding, repair and conversion, and an estimated 50,000 are employed by subcontractors, suppliers and support industries. United Kingdom yards now compete strongly for orders, with up to 30 vessels being built annually. Our capacity allows us to build almost as much again . . .

The nature of competition faced by British shipbuilders will shape the future for our shipyards . . . While I recognise that significant work has been done by the European Commission to remove barriers to fair competition across the European Union, it is important for our own industry to remain vigilant and to work closely with the Government when there is perceived unfairness through hidden subsidies on the continent . . .

Last year, South Korea succeeded in replacing Japan as the world leader for incoming orders. The agreed minutes in April of discussions between the European Commission and South Korea offer a real opportunity for fair competition . . . That followed hard negotiations and an ultimatum requiring South Korea to bring its shipbuilding prices into line or face action before the World Trade Organisation . . . it will soon become apparent whether the South Korean Government intend to introduce fair competition or are simply trying to win time for their yards . . .

Defence orders are vital to UK shipbuilding, as can be seen at places such as Scotstoun, which is the biggest shipbuilder in Scotland, working solely on naval vessels . . . [the Govan] yard operates as Britain's biggest merchant shipbuilder and has great flexibility – flexibility which is needed for the modern operations of the Ministry of Defence and which will be of paramount importance in determining future orders for British yards. Last month, the MoD issued invitations to tender for two landing ships logistics. Swan Hunter, Harland and Wolff, Cammell Laird in Birkenhead, Appledore and BAE Systems in Govan are all in the running, with orders expected later this year. Govan's sister yard Scotstoun is involved in designing the new Type-45 destroyer. The first class will be assembled and launched on the Clyde at Yarrows. Thousands of jobs will be safeguarded by that decision, which is part of a multi-billion pound shipbuilding programme.

The Type-45 destroyer . . . and the future aircraft carrier programmes will together create orders with British yards for more than 30 major warships. That is more than was ordered in the whole period since 1979 . . . Orders should be made not only on the best commercial grounds but in the best interests of our shipbuilding industry. The West of Scotland Defence and Aerospace network has looked at the wider economy based around the Govan shipyard. At present about 1,200 people are employed directly by BAE Systems at Govan, with more than 2,000 employed at Scotstoun. Almost 5,000 are employed in and around Glasgow by suppliers and subcontractors to the Govan yard. That is a huge number of jobs reliant on shipbuilding in Govan, and it is not exclusive to Glasgow or even Scotland . . .

Let there be no doubt: the Prime Minister and many other Ministers have assured me on numerous occasions that no decision has been made on this order . . . The message is clear in Scotland – we are fighting for Govan. Our argument has moved on from attempting to secure this order to working effectively as a team to secure the long-term future of shipbuilding on the Clyde. Workers at the yard, through shop stewards led by yard convener Jamie Webster, the trade unions, Members of this House and of the Scottish Parliament are all united in support of Govan shipyard. When my Right Hon. Friend, the Secretary of State for Scotland, brokered the deal that saved Govan last year and saw Kvaerner sell the yard to BAE Systems, it was cause for real celebration in my constituency and across Scotland. The shipyard is the major employer at the heart of Govan, but it is a great symbol of pride across Scotland.

People appreciate that Govan has a justifiable reputation for Clyde-built quality – building ships to last, on budget and on time. Scottish MPs have mounted a positive campaign and made a persuasive argument on the strong merits of the Govan yard. Across Scotland, we have taken our campaign to the streets and asked our constituents to sign a petition in support of Govan. Thousands of people continue to express their full support for Govan.

They believe that Clyde shipbuilding has not only a proud history but great potential for the future and they know how vital this order is for Govan . . . The dedicated and skilled workforce at Govan and their families have suffered greatly through the uncertainty of the past year and a half. I have shared their roller-coaster ride and realise how unbearable the stress can be. They know that the future of shipbuilding depends on flexibility and technology. They deserve the chance to continue proving themselves. This is a vital time for shipbuilding in the UK. Nowhere is that more true than at the Govan shipyard. The Labour Government have worked hard for an end to boom and bust in British shipbuilding. I know that the Minister will continue his good work with colleagues in active and creative support of the industry. I also urge the Government to meet the challenges of securing the future for Govan.[1]

Speeches in the House of Commons can change the course of history, but much of the time, members rise to make points from the floor of the House, as a matter of record; it shows to all those concerned that they have raised, or spoken on this or that issue. Alan Johnson, the Minister for Competitiveness at the Department of Trade, had to reply to my statement. He said that the Government would remain vigilant on the issues of competitiveness and hidden subsidies, and gave little else away. Two weeks later, we had an indication that the campaign was having some effect; Geoff Hoon, the Minister of Defence, announced that the four groups of companies involved in the Ro-Ro bidding all had to re-tender. This was a recognition that our voices were being heard, somewhere in the corridors of power.

It also reflected a growing concern within the shipbuilding industry that the German bid, referred to earlier, was too low to be true; the fact that the German government had, in effect, provided a hidden subsidy to their yards, through a £224 million programme of improvements financed by the German government, had, at last, become an issue.

The repetition of this questioning had, to some extent, breached the wall of constant warnings from civil servants that there was no alternative to the present design of the tender. BAE would have to

1. *Hansard*, 24 May 2000.

sharpen its pencil for its cost calculations, but here was another chance.

The deadline for new bids was 6 July. The day before, Jamie Webster, the shop stewards and I, had presented the petition for saving Govan to the Prime Minister. There was a final total of 80,000 signatures – in more than thirty large Iron Mountain stationery boxes. Around twenty Scottish MPs and their staff helped carry the boxes from my office in the House of Commons, to Downing Street. If the Prime Minster had not known before this that the campaign was an all-Scotland affair, he certainly knew now.

The next day the renewed bids for the Ro-Ro contract were submitted. Nothing was said officially, but there were rumours circulating that the German bid was still ahead of the BAE consortium – by more than £100 million. BAE may have 'sharpened its pencil', but insufficiently to undercut the subsidised German yards. Days later there was an announcement which gave me grave concern about Govan and the Ro-Ro contract.

On 11 July the Minister of Defence, Geoff Hoon, made a special announcement in the House of Commons. He told the House that the Government had decided to bring forward the procurement of a programme of destroyers for the Royal Navy. He said that the total project would involve the building of twelve Type-45 frigates but the building of the first three of the Type-45s would begin in 2001 – two at BAE Systems yard at Scotstoun, on the Clyde, and the other at Vosper Thornycroft, in Southampton. Hoon told the Commons that the first three orders would safeguard 5,500 jobs in British shipbuilding.

I couldn't join in with the general rejoicing. It was great news for Scotstoun, since it meant that, if the first two ships were delivered according to plan, Scotstoun would be in a really advantageous position to secure a further share of the remaining Type-45 orders. Nonetheless, at that moment, I believed that the announcement was part of a softening-up process to mitigate the effect of Govan failing to get the Ro-Ro orders and, as a result, facing closure. It was possible to predict the future Party line there and then: 'It is a great pity that we couldn't save Govan from closure, but we have guaranteed the future of shipbuilding on the Clyde at Scotstoun for decades to come.'

After the Hoon statement I am not sure exactly when I encoun-
tered the Scottish Secretary of State, John Reid, in the House of Commons, but I certainly remember the exchange. He accosted me in
one of the corridors, slating me for never being happy and criticising
what I'd said to the newspapers about the contract not guaranteeing
anything for Govan as negative and unhelpful. I told him that if Blair,
and his government, were responsible for the closure of Govan shipyard they would have achieved something that the Tories, including
Thatcher, had never managed. Reid was enraged at the comparison
between Blair and Thatcher and told me, in no uncertain terms, that
he thought it was ridiculous. I argued with him with my voice raised
also. I told him it was all very well to talk of orders being brought
forward and that Govan would benefit two years from now. I said: 'If
a man has cancer and needs radiotherapy, promising him that in two
years time, would be useless. He'd be dead by then.' We parted. I had
the thought that we had avoided exchanging blows, but only just.

The House was preparing to go into summer recess, but before
that I managed to arrange for a delegation of West of Scotland MPs
to meet with Tony Blair in his House of Commons office. I spoke
about the political repercussions of Govan shipyard failing to get
something from the Ro-Ro contract, which would precipitate its
closure. George Galloway, Maria Fyfe, Ian Davidson and Douglas
Alexander all echoed those sentiments. At this point the number of
signatures on the petition proved useful, because it allowed us to
argue forcefully that there would be electoral consequences, all over
Scotland, if Govan closed. Blair listened and nodded.

An announcement on the Ro-Ro contract was expected before
the recess. It never came. On 26 October the Minister of Defence,
Geoff Hoon, made the long-awaited announcement. He had spoken
to me earlier in the week, saying that Govan would get something in
his announcement, without going into details. Hoon started his address to the House of Commons on the detail of the Ro-Ro contract:

> The strategic defence review . . . established that we should
> secure six Roll on/Roll off ferries to assure a sufficient level
> of strategic sealift. The Kosovo crisis reinforced that require-
> ment. As the House is aware, Ro-Ros are non-warlike vessels.

They will be standard commercial ships, to be used for transporting equipment. They are not expected to enter combat
areas. They are not, therefore, by any conceivable definition,
warlike . . .

Hoon then went on to say that European treaties meant that the
Government had to abide by strict competition rules for the alloca-
tion of major tenders. At this point he therefore concluded:

The winning bid involves the construction of two ships by
Harland and Wolff in Belfast, with the other four to be built
in the Flensburger yard in Germany.[1]

So it seemed that all our efforts had come to nothing. I was devastated. Four out of six of the Ro-Ros had gone to Germany, as we had
expected months before, and Harland and Wolff had the consolation
of winning two. The Harland and Wolff award was a deal done by
Hoon and his Civil Service lawyers so he didn't have to say we had
given the entire contract to German yards. I was crestfallen but also
angry. I had the feeling that the overcautious civil servants might
have chosen to define the contract in another way to make it, in the
main, 'military'.

However there was to be a sweetening of this bitter pill. Hoon
explained that the defence review meant that the MoD had to improve our amphibious shipping assets. These were warships and so
could be built by British yards. There would be contracts for four
ALSLs – as they were termed. The first two were to be designed and
built at the Swan Hunter yard on Tyneside. However due to capacity
constraints there, the other two, subject to the designs completed on
Tyneside, were to be built on the Clyde. Hoon said:

It is expected that the order will secure about 800 jobs at
the Govan yard, together with about 200 jobs off site . . .
I am offering a real lifeline to the BAE yard at Govan, one
that will help to sustain the shipbuilding skills base on the
Clyde until the Type-45 programme comes on stream. I am

1. *Hansard*, 26 October 2000.

confident that the management and the unions there will react enthusiastically.[1]

My disappointment at not securing one of the big orders diminished the next day when I saw the press coverage which hailed the ALSLs order as a tremendous victory. The *Daily Record* of 27 October 2000 was typical:

SAVED: NAVY CONTRACT SECURES FUTURE FOR GOVAN YARD

More than 1000 jobs were saved on the Clyde yesterday after the work-starved BAE Govan shipyard clinched a £150m deal. The contract, for two Navy landing ships, helps plug an 18-month gap in the yard's order book and should secure its future until at least 2004 . . . Work on the landing ships will begin in June next year.[2]

However, doubts remained. The structure of the contract meant that Govan's future was actually in the hands of the managers at Swan Hunter. They had to design the ships, and any steel-cutting at Govan would be six months behind the start of the contract at Swan Hunter. We decided to seek another meeting with Geoff Hoon to try and get some assurances. It didn't go well. When asked about the ALSLs timescales, Hoon told the delegation that steel would be cut at Govan by July 2001. He was high-handed and dismissive. It was clear by this time that he thought that being lobbied by workers desperate to keep their jobs had become tedious. It pains me to say this since he, after all, was a Labour Cabinet Minister.

I was surprised when he lectured the delegation about inefficiency and old working practices, not least because historic underinvestment by the old shipbuilding owners was the root cause of the industry's decline in Britain; his talk of 'old practices' in relation to Govan was also out of key, since the workers at Govan had demonstrated great flexibility in industrial relations and had a reputation for delivering on time, and on budget. Tempers got frayed when

1. *Hansard*, 26 October 2000.
2. *Daily Record*, 27 October 2000.

Jamie made points along these lines. Astonishingly, Hoon then told Jamie in words to the effect that he was fortunate to have 'friends in high places'. He signalled the end of the meeting by telling the delegation: 'Just get your arses back up to the Clyde and get on with it.' In the corridor outside Hoon's office the tension was broken when someone in the delegation declared: 'That Hoon, he's a right slippery character.'

Our visit to Hoon's office had left us in limbo; we were still waiting for Swan Hunter before we could make any progress. The longer the delays at their end, the more the concerns grew on the Clyde. At the same time we were also engaged in lobbying on the Type-45 destroyers' contract and its roll out. By July 2001 there had been no cutting of steel on the ALSLs contract – in fact there were obvious delays during the design stage, after Swan Hunter had subcontracted it to a subsidiary, which as far as I recall was in the Netherlands.

Hoon's announcement on the Type-45s contract was tabled for 10 July 2001. It turned out to be good news. Very good news. Early in 2001 BAE had put forward a bid to the Government to build all of the twelve Type-45 destroyers; the bid offered economies of scale and reduced costs because the work was to be carried out by a single company, irrespective of the fact that it would be developed at different shipyards within the UK. Hoon's statement accepted the deal – for BAE to build the first six of the twelve ships in a contract worth £4.5 billion. Govan and Scotstoun would get the 'lion's share' of those billions. There was also the possibility of securing the further six destroyers, depending on the completion of the first stage.

This contract offered salvation, in the long term, for shipbuilding on the Clyde. But it would not roll out until 2003, so there was still the enduring doubt about the gap in orders for Govan. Hoon had started his statement in the House of Commons at around 4.30 pm. Two hours later, all the hope engendered by it had vanished. BAE announced 1,000 redundancies, which, in effect, meant the closure of Govan.

Here were the facts as I saw them – a British company had been given a contract worth billions of pounds and, on the very day of the award, announced to the nation that it had to make 1,000 workers redundant. I was beside myself with anger. I phoned the Managing

Director at BAE Marine, Simon Kirby, and told him he had sold us down the river. He agreed to a meeting in London in the following week. It turned out to be a pretty ill-tempered affair.

I told the BAE directors that their conduct was unacceptable and unreasonable, and accused them of what amounted to sabotage to strengthen their hand with the unions; of taking the action to announce mass redundancies to frighten the workers into accepting new pay and conditions. I also accused them of duplicity, saying that all the while they were working with me and others to lobby for the Type-45 contract, they must have been planning to make the announcement of 1,000 job losses at Govan, without giving me any warning whatsoever. I complained about the timing of the announcement of the sackings, on the day the Type-45 deal was announced. I also argued that some of the billions coming in the destroyers' contract could be defrayed, in some measure, to avoid redundancies on such a scale.

The meeting ended in acrimony. I felt that the Labour government had gone to enormous lengths to make the original deal, for BAE to take over the Govan yard from the previous owners, Kvaerner, a possibility. Then, on top of that original deal, enormous government contracts had been placed with BAE, guaranteeing them billions of pounds in earnings, and the payback seemed to have taken the form of 1,000 workers being uncompromisingly thrown on the dole. Nonetheless, despite my interpretation of these events, it remained clear that something had to be done about the ALSLs contract, if anything could be saved.

It was July and the summer recess beckoned, so I started lobbying immediately. I went to see John Reid, who was still the Secretary of State for Scotland. He didn't look pleased to see me. In fact, I got the impression that he felt he had done everything possible to save the yard, and could do no more. He told me that there had been fierce lobbying in Cabinet to get the Type-45 contract for BAE, and the landing ships as a stop-gap for Govan, which had now proved so troublesome. Reid said that the ALSL contract had gone to Swan Hunter because their prices were better than BAE; Swan Hunter were behind schedule, but would retain the contract so the only alternative was to get money from somewhere to bring forward the

ALSL contract, or get an additional contract for ALSLs for Govan. I remember Reid looking me in the eye, saying he had done all he could. Then he said, 'Go and see bloody Gordon Brown, your friend the Chancellor who holds all the purse strings.'

When BAE announced the 1,000 redundancies in July, the Scottish Parliament became involved in the struggle for jobs on the Clyde. Wendy Alexander was the Minister for Enterprise in the Scottish Government at that time. She set up the Clyde Shipyards Task Force, which was led by Scottish Enterprise Glasgow. The Task Force produced a comprehensive analysis of the state of shipbuilding on the Clyde, which vindicated all the arguments which I had been putting forward at that time, along with the trades unions.

The Task Force provided powerful arguments about why shipbuilding on the Clyde needed significant Government support, although, in the end, it was politics which saved Govan – politics in the shape of the Labour Chancellor, Gordon Brown. I think it is fair to say that over a period of months I was able to help convince him that Govan had to be rescued. First of all I reminded him of the history of the Clyde yards in the early 1970s. There was the huge struggle to save Upper Clyde Shipbuilding (UCS) led by Jimmy Reid and Jimmy Airlie. Then there was the Chancellor's own admiration of the history of Clydeside, evident in his critically acclaimed biography of Jimmy Maxton, the 'Red Clydeside' MP, written when Gordon Brown was a young rebel himself. Finally, some might conclude that, given this and Brown's own interest in the future of shipbuilding in Scotland, including the Rosyth shipyard in his own Fife constituency, in reality I was 'pushing against an open door'.

Anyway, whether these issues were significant or not, the Chancellor found £120 million from the Treasury to build an additional two landing ships – ALSLs – at Govan. This released Govan from its dependence on the Swan Hunter end of the original deal. The announcement of the building of an additional two 16,000-tonne landing ships at Govan was made late in November 2001. The steel for the ships was cut before the end of that year. Govan's order gap was bridged – the two ALSLs gave Govan work until the Type-45 destroyers came on stream. John Reid's somewhat peremptory advice to pay Gordon Brown a visit had proved invaluable.

I have described this part of the struggle to save Govan at length because the details here – the political lobbying, the Ministry of Defence, the role of the media and the significance of the decisions of Government – were all played out again in the struggle to win the lion's share of the huge aircraft-carrier contract for BAE and the Clyde. Of course, the scale of what was then the £10 billion super aircraft-carrier contract was entirely different, but winning it would mean that the same roller-coaster of events had to be ridden.

Geoff Hoon and the Ministry of Defence were, once again, centre stage and, at one point, seemingly ready to bypass British interests on the grounds of cost. In the end, a political and economic compromise was struck. On 30 January 2003, Geoff Hoon told the House of Commons that a partnership deal was the best way forward. BAE Systems was to be the preferred prime contractor, with responsibility for project and shipbuilding management. Thales UK would assume a major role as the key supplier of the whole ship design.

So it was that the biggest-ever warships to be built in British history – each 60,000 tonnes and 300 metres long – guaranteed the future of the Govan, Scotstoun and Rosyth shipyards. Jamie Webster told the *Scotsman*: 'The Clyde will have the best job security in more than 20 years. We are all very relieved after years of uncertainty, but fortune favours the brave and we've all been bloody brave and determined.'[1]

Later, when the time came and I announced that I was going to retire from the House of Commons, the *Herald* newspaper ran a biographical piece. Its headline was, 'Trailblazer whose proudest role was in saving Clyde shipbuilding'.

I would be happy with that headline today. However, it would be wrong to give the impression that, as an MP, and before that as a city councillor, Govan shipyard and its future was my only concern. In that context, bringing the Glasgow Science Centre to what became known as Pacific Quay, with the add-on development of the Scottish Television (STV)/BBC Scotland media campus on the same site, were matters of consuming importance. These were projects of all-Scotland significance, not just the preoccupation of the politicians and citizens of the city of Glasgow.

1. *Scotsman*, 31 January 2003.

The inspiration for the Glasgow Science Centre complex came from Stuart Gulliver, when he was chief executive of the Glasgow Development Agency. He had studied other cities in Europe which had been subject to the same de-industrialisation of heavy industry as Glasgow, and reasoned that major tourist projects could provide a catalyst for other related economic developments. He argued that the Glasgow Science Centre could provide the catalyst for a cluster of science and technology developments, if it were to be created in one of the city's run-down areas.

That was when the political battles started, since most Glasgow City councillors, including me at the time, were determined to win the project for their own areas. Eventually, it became a battle between the site of the former Glasgow Garden Festival, which was then lying derelict on the south of the river, and a similar site in the East End of the city, north of the river. However, a considerable majority of the city councillors were in favour of the East End project, so it looked as if the Garden Festival site, in my area, was likely to lose out.

The Science Centre project had three related elements: the Tower, rising more than 300 feet above the River Clyde as a national landmark; the Mall, its science exhibition centre, and the iMax 3D cinema. That third element was to be built adjacent to the Mall. The whole project was costed at more than £70 million but the predominant share of the funding was to be provided by the Millennium Commission, which had been set up by the Big Lottery Fund to create major projects across the UK, to herald in the twenty-first century.

The Labour leader of the City Council then, was the pragmatic Bob Gould. He had earlier been the leader of the larger Strathclyde Regional Council, parts of which had amalgamated with the former Glasgow District Council, to create the new unitary authority of Glasgow City Council. His political problem was that even after his election as leader, many of the former Glasgow councillors were plotting his political downfall, since as the former Regional Council leader he was seen as 'not one of them'. Gould wanted to stay above this melee of factionalism and in-fighting. In casting his vote on where the Science Centre should be sited, he didn't want to be seen to favour one group of councillors over another. I gave Bob Gould a way out of this political minefield.

I went to see him in his office and said that it would be best if a battle-royal between councillors in the south of the city and councillors in the east of the city could be avoided. I argued that since a large element of the costs – some £45 million out of a total of £70 million – were to be paid by the Big Lottery Fund's Millennium Commission, it would be reasonable to give the Commission the final say on the respective sites, and so take the decision on the final location of the project. I told him it would be like appointing an independent arbiter.

Somehow he was able to persuade the Labour group of councillors of the value of proceeding in this way to avoid bitter division and finger-pointing. The Commission ruled in favour of the project going south of the river to the Pacific Quay site. When that was announced I had a smile on my face.

Following the creation of the Science Centre on the south-side site, the next stage was to pursue the high technology media 'cluster' by persuading STV and BBC Scotland to relocate from their respective city centre and west end locations to Pacific Quay. Although STV were actually the first to broadcast from Pacific Quay, it was the negotiations with the BBC that proved crucial to making the project happen.

Some of those negotiations have become part of the folklore of Glasgow politics. At that time, BBC Scotland's headquarters was in an old building in Glasgow's trendy West End. It was a stone's throw from the bijou bars and restaurants of Byres Road so beloved of the 'luvvy' set working at the BBC, and Glasgow's prosperous middle classes who lived nearby. The story goes that the BBC 'luvvies' held the City Council, and Scottish Enterprise Glasgow (formerly Glasgow Development Agency) to ransom by demanding special concessions before they moved. Chief among these was the demand that a new £8 million bridge, linking Pacific Quay directly with the West End, had to be built, so that BBC staff living in the West End could avoid traffic gridlock on their way to and from work.

This was only partly true. At this time, the chief executive of BBC Scotland – known as the Controller – was the wily ex-school-teacher John McCormick. He knew the BBC headquarters at Queen Margaret Drive was a crumbling rabbit-warren of a building, and that it would soon be a necessity to relocate to a much more modern, integrated media campus elsewhere. Pacific Quay offered BBC Scotland that opportunity; but it wasn't BBC Scotland and McCormick who wrote the ransom note about the bridge, it was the chiefs from London, who after a visit north first demanded its construction. Thereafter, McCormick and Co had to obey the 'party line' – 'No Bridge, no BBC move to Pacific Quay.'

After exhaustive negotiations between City Council officials, Scottish Enterprise Glasgow, and the BBC, a deal was struck for the building of the bridge. Each party had agreed the design and their share of the costs. All that remained was the granting of planning permission from the City Council. Then the Lord Provost of the City, Councillor Alex Mosson, declared: 'Over my dead body.'

The problem was that the bridge, and surrounding feeder roads, ran through the heart of the area represented by the Lord Provost on the City Council. He was arguing that the bridge would mean his constituents would have to put up with a huge increase in car traffic, as a result of the BBC not wanting its journalists to be inconvenienced by what could become a forty-minute journey to work. In April 2000, with battle lines drawn, Councillor Mosson told the *Sunday Herald* newspaper: 'If it [the bridge] is detrimental to people's lives, that's got to bullet it. As a local council we are committed to creating jobs and we are trying to regenerate the whole of the Clydeside to the best of its advantage, but not at the risk of alienating people it may cause problems with.'

In the same article the *Sunday Herald* concluded:

Doubts now hang over the £8m bridge which forms the central plank of the redevelopment [of Pacific Quay]. Without the bridge the BBC's long mooted move from Queen Margaret Drive will not go ahead. Without the BBC, the media village looks like a non-starter.[1]

This stalemate loomed in the heart of my Glasgow Govan constituency. As the local MP, the redevelopment of the derelict Pacific Quay had been a cherished hope of mine for years, as a key element in the economic renaissance of that part of the centre of the city. It

1. *Sunday Herald*, 20 April 2000.

now looked as if those plans were about to become broken dreams. One way or another the Lord Provost had to be persuaded to a compromise. The discussions with Alex Mosson were extremely ill-tempered. I tried to get Alex to look at the bigger picture. I reminded him that his intransigence had led the local radio station, Radio Clyde, to leave its Glasgow base for another location in another local council area, in Clydebank. For whatever parochial reason, Councillor Mosson and his cohorts had blocked the sale of the Glasgow site, and the result was that Clyde moved out of the city.

Alex Mosson was clearly furious at this suggestion. I then argued that if the building of the bridge was blocked the BBC might decide to move its headquarters to Edinburgh. He more or less said, 'So what?' Frankly, our relations have never been the same since. One of Alex's big arguments was that his local community council was opposed to the bridge and he had to support them. The irony was that a local community council in my area, on the other side of the River, was also opposed but my argument with them was that I supported the bridge for the good of Glasgow as a whole. The same sort of thing happened with another local community council in another area who were demanding, before the 1997 Election, that I give a commitment to oppose the bridge. I refused to do so for the same reasons I had stated before.

The Alex Mosson saga meant we had to find a political way out of the impasse if his staunch opposition was to be altered. It was time to visit the Machiavellian leader of the City Council once more. To say there was no love lost between Bob Gould and Alex Mosson would be a gross understatement. In the elections for the leadership the Gould camp had outmanoeuvred the Mosson camp and, as I have said, there had been bitter political acrimony between the two camps from that time on. So now Bob Gould was open to any suggestions that might result in his 'comrade', Alex Mosson, getting a political bloody nose.

I told Bob Gould that it was a political and economic certainty that if there was no bridge, there would be no BBC on the south side of the river, and the whole Pacific Quay project would be put in jeopardy. We decided that the Lord Provost's concerns would have to be addressed. It was agreed that Gould would suggest to Mosson, and other councillors who were opposed to the bridge, that before the bridge project was given a go-ahead there would have to be a proper traffic study done to identify possible impacts. That would allow Mosson to save face by publicly demanding a traffic survey. After this, the leader of the City Council, Gould, would agree to his demands and inform Scottish Enterprise Glasgow that they had to produce a Traffic Impact Survey, before any final decision on granting planning permission for the bridge could be made; although we knew what the outcome of the survey would be.

The plan came together. Scottish Enterprise Glasgow produced a traffic survey which made specific recommendations about traffic flows to ensure that the traffic on the bridge did not produce local gridlock – these restrictions exist to this day. That cleared the way for planning permission for the bridge. The bridge was built, on time and on budget. BBC Scotland declared at the time – 18th September 2006 – that the 'Squinty Bridge', or the Clyde Arc to give it its proper name, was for the first time open to vehicles. It was nicknamed the 'Squinty Bridge' because it was the only bridge on the Clyde that ran at an angle to the river. All the other bridges run perpendicular to the course of the river. 'Squinty' is a Scottish word meaning 'not straight'. The Bridge eventually cost nearly £20 million, but it secured the BBC's move to Pacific Quay and they, in turn, became the cornerstone of the creation of the media campus.

If you look at that area of the Clyde today there can only be one conclusion – an astonishing transformation has taken place. There is the Science Centre, the iMax cinema and the Tower complex. Adjacent is the media village with the BBC and STV buildings, and not far from there the Springfield Quay entertainment complex with bars, restaurants and cinemas. All this where, not too long ago, was only a no man's land of weeds and dereliction. Of course there needs to be a balance sheet drawn, because the Science Centre complex has suffered difficult times, although it is now emerging from them.

Opposite Pacific Quay there have been other signs of economic regeneration on the banks of the Clyde; the construction of major hotels, the SECC entertainment complex, and further west, the Glasgow Harbour housing development. The new twenty-first-century arena, The Hydro, is now complete next to the SECC complex, and has become one of the UK's premier concert venues. So, although there have been tribulations along the way for the redevelopment of both banks of the Clyde, a miracle in bricks and mortar is proof of its success.

In my time as an MP in Glasgow there has been another miracle – the transformation of Glasgow's social housing with the creation of the Glasgow Housing Association and the revolution in the quality of housing stock that it has brought about. When I arrived in Glasgow from Pakistan in the late 1970s, I remember being astonished at the state of the housing which was endured by ordinary working-class people. I use the word 'endured' advisedly, because for huge numbers of families in the city their housing conditions were indeed a trial of endurance. At that time Glasgow had the highest proportion of lo-cal council housing anywhere in Britain. In some constituencies, like Provan in the east of the city, for example, the percentage of those living in council housing reached 93%.

By the late 1970s, these huge local council housing estates (or schemes as they were known in Glasgow) on the outskirts of the city, which had been built after World War Two as 'Homes Fit for He-roes', had become forgotten acres of decline. The fabric of the hous-ing there reflected the continuing crises of unemployment and social deprivation that were engulfing them. The comedian and actor, Billy Connolly, famously said that Glasgow's housing estates had become 'deserts wi' windaes'. Deserts with windows, that says it all.

In this context there are many examples that could be quoted in evidence of the poor quality of housing. One with which I had direct involvement concerned the scandal of damp housing in the highrise complexes which were built in the Gorbals area of the city in the early 1960s. A matter of a few years after their construction, the Gor-bals multi-storey flats had become towers of dampness, which made the lives of those who inhabited them a total misery. The role of the Housing Department in this controversy became symbolic of its in-competence and, in my view, its deliberate duplicity. The Department spent years denying the existence of the dampness problem, rather than taking action to do something about it.

That fact affected my view of the Housing Department forever. I had been in these flats myself and had seen people's clothes in their bedrooms covered in mould, and then had to listen to a housing official tell me it was caused by the tenants not opening their windows to let in fresh air. The resulting 'condensation' was thereby the cause of the dampness. Later, that argument was turned on its head, when it was explained by officials that the dampness was being caused by tenants leaving their windows open too long during the day, which caused the penetration of moisture from the atmosphere, hence their 'cure-all' explanation for the reeking dampness – 'condensation'. Of course the real reasons for the dampness were fundamental flaws in the planning, design and construction of the flats. In the end, history proved that the only effective remedy for that was demolition of almost all of the blocks concerned.

Scandals such as the dampness in the Gorbals high flats meant that much of the blame for the degeneration of the city's council housing was laid at the door of the City's bureaucratic, uncaring Housing Department, with its legions of officers, very few of whom lived on the estates they administered. However, there is much more to the decline of Glasgow's public housing than that. Put simply the main cause was a mountain of housing debt – which in recent times reached the heights of a billion pounds. The interest charges alone on Glasgow's borrowing meant that for every pound tenants paid the housing authority in rent, 75p or more went on servicing the housing debt. That is to say, on paying the interest charges, not even paying off the permanent Everest of debt. This crippling financial burden meant that there were always inadequate funds for maintaining the housing stock, far less improving it.

The first steps in fulfilling the promise of a new Glasgow were taken by Frank McAveety when he was the leader of the City Council. He was first to raise the problem of the billion-pound debt of the city and how that would plague the city's housing provision for an eternity. A new plan was needed, he said, to wipe out the debt. Wendy Alexander MSP, who was the Minister of Communities after the first elections to the devolved Scottish Parliament in 1999, took up the cause. Within a year of the election she presented a new plan for Glasgow's housing. Over a period of years the proposal was to pay off the accumulated housing debt by the injection of massive government funding, which, in turn, would free up millions for new investment in the housing stock. But the offer came with conditions – there had to be a transfer of all of Glasgow's housing stock – around 90,000 houses and flats – to a new Glasgow Housing Association (GHA). In other words, the City Council Housing Department would be no more.

I was totally convinced of the positive value of the housing stock transfer, not least because the best quality of social housing in the city, at that time, was provided by the housing associations in different parts of the city. All of these were funded by Central Government, not Local Government. Not everyone saw it my way, and there was soon a well-organised protest movement against the stock transfer. Suddenly it seemed that, in the eyes of opponents of the transfer, the City Council Housing Department had become the last bastion of socialism in the city, so had to be defended; the protestors wanted the housing debt paid off, but were against the transfer of the housing stock which they claimed was privatisation by another name.

The coalition of opposition had its say in the voice of Scotland's largest trades union, UNISON. They stated their opposition to the transfer 'because of the potential threat to the 4,000 existing employees and staff in the housing and repairs services of the Council'. I was flabbergasted when I read that – this was the greatest social change to be proposed in the post-war history of Glasgow, being opposed by a union which supposedly espoused the ideals of a better life for all. For UNISON, a 'potential threat' to the jobs of their 4,000 members in the Housing Department was enough to embargo the hopes of hundreds of thousands of Glaswegians desperately in need of better housing. It seemed they could go hang as far as the union bosses were concerned.

From that point on, I spent time and energy arguing the case for the creation of a Glasgow Housing Association (GHA). I went to tenants' meetings across my constituency, explaining why the transfer should be supported, and also argued with councillors on the City Council who were opposed to it. The original proposal was for the Scottish Government to pay Glasgow's £50 million annual interest charges. That would create new money for new investment. However, there were continual questions about whether those sums had been done correctly when the original proposal had been put together by the civil servants in Wendy Alexander's office. Then, in September 2001, the Chancellor, Gordon Brown, announced that the total housing debt of £1 billion would be paid off by the Treasury. The pay-off package announced by the Chancellor involved a number of local councils, although Glasgow was the biggest and was to get the biggest debt repayment.

But despite this bonanza being on offer, there was still a climate of uncertainty among Glasgow's tenants. It remains my view that the real reason for the continuing doubts over the stock transfer were the prevarications and waverings of the Labour City Council leadership on the issue. Of course it was right that the Council Leader at that time, Councillor Charlie Gordon, should raise questions and demand answers about what was being proposed. However this was never done on the basis of him demonstrating that he and the Labour Council were giving unequivocal support for the GHA transfer in general. Rather it seemed to be more about voicing continual doubts about the entire project. But to stop the waverers, in my view, you have to stop wavering yourself.

In April 2000, when the first announcement of the proposals was made, Charlie hailed them as 'a once in a generation opportunity that offered the best hope for Glasgow's housing.' A year and half later, in September 2001, after yet another report from his own Council officials which was critical of the plans, Councillor Gordon was declaring that he could not recommend the proposals to the City's tenants 'if key questions on the "fundability" of the Glasgow Housing Association's plans are not answered'.

In January 2002, after delay upon delay, the date of the ballot for the cancellation of the debt and the stock transfer to the Glasgow Housing Association was announced for April. Finally on 5 April, 78,000 Glasgow tenants voted by a 3 to 2 margin in favour of transferring the city's council stock to a new landlord, the Glasgow Housing Association.

That cleared the way for cancellation of the City's £1 billion housing debt and the promise of a near £6 billion budget to be spent over 30 years, on a new housing deal for Glasgow. Delivery on that new deal has been comprehensive. Of course much remains to be done, but large swathes of Glasgow's housing schemes have been transformed for an overwhelming majority of those who live there. As for UNISON, not one of their members lost their job – under employment law they were all transferred to the GHA. I have never been more disappointed than I was in this case at the total lack of vision and myopic self-interest displayed by a trade union. Incidentally there has never been a word uttered publicly by the leaders of UNISON admitting that they got it wrong. Once again, the doomsayers were confounded in bricks and mortar.

The saving of Govan shipyard, the development of Pacific Quay, the cancellation of Glasgow's housing debt and the creation of the GHA were all big campaigns in my time as an MP in Glasgow. My last great campaign before I bowed out of the House of Commons, was the helping to bring the killers of Kriss Donald to justice. That terrible story has already been covered in the opening chapter.

In June 2007 I wrote to all the Labour Party members in my constituency informing them of my decision not to stand for election the next time round. I told them:

> After three terms in the Commons I feel that the time is right for me to move on to new challenges. I hope to commit myself further to charitable interests in international development, continuing my work in promoting multiculturalism and community relations across Glasgow and enjoying family life especially with my young grandchildren.

From time to time I watch the cut and thrust of politics in the House of Commons and miss the glory of it all. But I do believe the time was right for me to move on. I am enormously proud that my son, Anas, followed in my footsteps as the MP for Glasgow Central. He was defeated in the 2015 General Election when the SNP took all but one of the seats held by Labour across Scotland in what was, in my view, an unstoppable political 'tsunami'. My belief is that he has already shown great ability and commitment in politics. My hope is that it will not be long before he is back.

After the 2010 General Election, the then Party Leader, Gordon Brown, dropped me a note thanking me for my contribution to the Party. He said: 'Your loyalty to our Labour values through the most difficult of times is something I will never forget, and of which you can be enormously proud. Labour owe you a debt of gratitude we can never fully repay.' Similarly Harriet Harman, then Deputy Leader, wrote: 'You will be missed but you have forged a path and blazed a trail which others will follow.'

I was pleased that both had taken the time to express these sentiments.

Three months before the dissolving of the Parliament in advance of the General Election, there was a parliamentary reception to mark my work in the House of Commons. Around 50 MPs and members of the House of Lords came to pay their tributes to my work in the House. I was touched by their praise of my contribution down the years. However it was an approach by the group of my fellow Muslim MPs and House of Lords members which almost brought tears to my eyes. I cannot single anyone out, because one way and another they all expressed the same sentiments. One captured this for the group: 'You know, Sarwar, you are like a father to us. You opened the gate.'

It may be that I have blazed a trail, it may be that I have remained loyal to the estimable values of the Labour Party, but I also owe a debt of gratitude. It is to the people of Glasgow. I am proud to have been given the opportunity to serve them.

The 9/11 Wars 10

'The reality is that Britain is being asked to embark on a war
without agreement in any of the international bodies of which
we are a leading partner – not NATO, not the European Union and, now, not the Security Council.'

Robin Cook MP, Leader of the House of Commons,
resignation speech, 17 March 2003.

On Tuesday 11 September 2011, Perveen and I were on our way to
Lossiemouth, in the north of Scotland, to spend a week there. Parliament was in recess. The phone rang. It was my son Anas. He said,
'America has been attacked.' It flashed through my mind, 'Who can
attack America? Russia?' Then he explained.

We thought of going back to Glasgow immediately, but we were
half an hour from Lossiemouth, so we continued our journey and
stayed there overnight. The enormity of what had happened, and
who was likely to be responsible, perplexed me terribly as I watched,
again and again, those planes hitting the Twin Towers in New York.

The next morning we rushed back to Glasgow. I organised for
the leaders of the Muslim community to convene a media conference
at the Central Mosque in Glasgow. We agreed that we had to send
out immediately the message that this was an atrocity, an abomination. We condemned the attacks, the true horror of which was now
known. If indeed this was an al-Qaeda operation, which was not, by
any means, certain at that point, and if Muslim fanatics were responsible, they might say that they had acted in the name of Islam. We
rejected that notion completely, and demanded that those responsible
had to be brought to justice. The media conference was subdued by
the enormity of the events.

Parliament was recalled early, on Friday 14 September. I had spent
the preceding days trying to work out what to say in my speech. I
knew I had to condemn the attacks as forcibly as I could. I also knew

I had to defend the Muslim community in Britain. Right from the start I believed this meant war; that the Bush administration would seek terrible revenge and retribution, no matter what.

Prime Minister, Tony Blair rose to speak. It was 9.30 in the morning. The Chamber was packed to standing room only. I closed my eyes as he was speaking, some of his words passing me by as though this were all a dream. A nightmare. I heard him say the Muslim community should not and could not be blamed in any way for this atrocity and it should not be allowed to divide communities across Britain. The other party leaders followed, and then one MP after another piled anguish upon anguish; and in some cases there was anger and talk of the need for retribution.

For two hours I rose to speak but wasn't called. At one point I felt a trickle of sweat rolling off the back of my neck down my back. *Hansard* shows that the veteran Father of the House, Tam Dalyell, was the first to break the unity of condemnation, with a qualification. He said, with incredible prescience, that unless what was happening in Palestine and elsewhere in the Middle East was not addressed, this would happen again. He implored the Foreign Secretary, 'For God's sake, look at 10 years of bombing Iraq and sanctions.'[1]

When I was called to speak, I first sympathised with the American people and the other nations which lost their people in the tragic and inhuman act of terrorism. I said:

> It is hard to comprehend or to come to terms with the tragic and staggering death toll that has been inflicted upon the American people and those of other nations. Our hearts and our thoughts are with all those who have lost friends and family. People of all nationalities and faiths have perished in this meaningless atrocity.
>
> I speak on behalf of my constituents, and undoubtedly on behalf of the Muslim community in this country and beyond, when I say that this barbaric and inhumane terrorist atrocity must be condemned unreservedly. We would solidly support all legitimate efforts to bring the perpetrators to justice. Whoever the culprits turn out to be, it is critical that we send a

1. *Hansard*, 14 September 2001.

clear message that they cannot possibly claim to represent the true interests of any religious or ethnic group.

I continued:

In the recent past we have seen how hysteria can be whipped up at times of tragedy and the corrosive effect that that has on society. It is for that reason that I support the Prime Minister in his clear message about the danger of stereotyping communities, particularly the Muslim community. With those words, my Right Hon. Friend has given comfort to people in this country and across the world. It is critical that, in giving support to any action, we do so observing the principles of justice and within the framework of international law. We must naturally give our support to our American allies, but we must counsel against unilateral action. We must avoid action that could result in the deaths of thousands of other innocent civilians, thus perpetuating the cycle of violence.

We cannot afford to isolate any of our allies in finding solutions, and in particular, if there is evidence that Osama bin Laden is responsible, our allies who recognise the Taliban government – namely, Saudi Arabia, Pakistan and the United Arab Emirates – will be crucial to influencing the situation.

I closed by calling on the Government not to adopt a knee-jerk reaction, but to question why this atrocity had occurred:

It is a difficult time, but I believe that it is the right time to examine more deeply our role and responsibilities in the world. We must attempt to understand why some extremists feel driven to the abhorrent madness that we have witnessed in New York and Washington. There can be no justification for this vulgar terrorist atrocity, but we cannot be blind to the plight of oppressed people who look to Europe and the USA for support.

As a former colonial power we have a special responsibility. We should use our influence with the Americans and other allies to redouble our efforts in search of a just solution to the outstanding issues in the Middle East and other parts of the world. This brutal terrorist attack is profoundly contrary to the doctrine of Islam and has been strongly condemned by Muslim states, Muslim clerics and individual Muslims throughout the world. I can only reiterate that condemnation and, on behalf of all my constituents, express my hope that the international community can achieve justice for the innocent victims and their grieving families.[1]

When I sat down I felt I had done my duty. Looking back on this now I feel that this speech has stood the test of time. In the Members Lobby when the morning session closed there was a lot of support, pats on the back and 'Well said, Mohammad'. I recall one Tory backbencher upbraided me. He demanded to know what 3,000 dead in New York had to do with the reference to the Palestinians. He said he thought I should consider it time to think of the victims.

On the following Monday, Tony Blair called leaders of the Muslim community in Britain to a meeting at 10 Downing Street. Blair was very calm and reassuring. He said he would do everything in his power to make sure that the 9/11 events would not split communities across Britain – that in the event of any serious backlash the forces of law and order would be mobilised to defend the Muslim community. I was there with Khalid Mahmood – we were the two MPs from the House of Commons from a Muslim background as well as Lord Ahmed and Baroness Uddin from the Lords. I said that this one terrible incident should not be allowed to tarnish the reputation of all the Muslims in Britain. I emphasised, 'There may be claims that this has been done in the name of Islam, but it has nothing to do with Islam.'

The fear of a backlash against the community was tangible in the meeting. As I recall at some point Blair said that many innocents had perished in that attack and that we had to show the Americans that we stood 'shoulder to shoulder' with them. 'We have to show solidarity with the American people,' he said.

1. *Hansard*, 14 September 2001.

The backlash wasn't long in coming, although there was some consolation in that it only took the form of isolated attacks on unfortunate individuals caught in the wrong place at the wrong time by racist thugs, and thankfully there was no organised mass violence anywhere. There were some incidents in Glasgow but quietly the word went out in the Asian community that it was better to be indoors at night.

There was no discrimination in the assaults which took place: the Sikhs were getting assaulted as well as the Muslims, because of their skin colour. There were moments of what might be termed 'gallows humour' because of this. One day one of the leaders of the Sikh community in Glasgow stormed into my offices. He was outraged. 'You guys, you guys caused all the trouble and now we are paying the price,' he spluttered.

'What do you mean by "you guys"?' I retorted. 'It wasn't us.'

He demanded that I should make some sort of statement about the Sikhs. I couldn't help laughing. I said to him, 'What do you want me to say to the morons who might be attacking people – "By the way, for the record, if you want to attack someone because of 9/11, don't attack the people in turbans because they are Sikhs, not Muslims." I'm afraid we are in this together, brother.'

In these early days word reached me from Pakistan that people close to Mullah Omar, the leader of the Taliban in Afghanistan, wanted to have an 'unofficial' line of communication for information that might be useful to open up a dialogue with the British government, beyond official channels. I went to see Robin Cook, one of my closest friends in Parliament, who was the Foreign Secretary in those days. I told him I was prepared to go to Kabul or some other agreed location in the Pakistan borderlands to see if there were any genuine possibilities for a last-ditch face-saving compromise. 'A very brave offer Mohammad,' he said, 'but the die is cast, I am afraid. We are only awaiting the UN.'

We now know that there was an alternative to what was called 'shock and awe' on the poorest country in the world. It seemed to me that the vision of the Twin Towers had blinded the Western world to reason. Consider this – the American government somehow persuaded the rest of the non-Muslim world that the answer to the Taliban's refusal to give up Osama bin Laden was to bomb an entire country. For those who may not recall what the Americans were thinking about back then, let me remind you – the issue was the hunt for Osama Bin Laden. That was the reason for the massive US-led aerial bombardment of the most economically and technologically backward nation-state on the planet. They would use bunker-buster bombs, daisy cutter bombs, cluster bombs and depleted uranium shells; the West was determined to deploy a new lexicon of death and mutilation against defenceless communities to avenge the 9/11 attack.

Of course I was totally opposed to this strategy, and had sharp exchanges in the corridors of the House of Commons. Time and again I used Northern Ireland as an example. The IRA bombed and maimed thousands of innocents in Northern Ireland *and* on the British mainland, in the name of their cause of a United Ireland; blood and slaughter on a scale unknown in recent history. 'Did the Brits decide that the only way to search out the terrorists responsible was to bomb Belfast and even Dublin to smithereens?' I asked frequently of those in favour of attacking Afghanistan.

Bush had his way – someone had to be shown to pay the price for 9/11 and it was the Afghans; ironically they were ruled by the Taliban who were the Frankenstein monsters born of the arming of the mujahedin in the war against the Soviet occupation. The bombing started on 7 October 2001. This was 28 days after 9/11. The so-called diplomacy to avoid this contingency was a sham of gigantic proportions. There was no House of Commons vote – this failure was justified by the Government by the breadth of support in the UN, Europe and international community.

The House of Commons had a major debate the next day. By this time my strategy was to continue arguing that the course taken was folly and would have worldwide repercussions, even although I recognised that the voices of opposition had totally failed to prevent this modern-day Armageddon. I also attempted to make a roll call on Palestine, Israel, and the double-standards of American foreign policy. This time there was no nervousness or trepidation when I was called to speak, because my words were fuelled by anger – one of the opening phrases was a verbal dagger echoing back to Blair's 'tough on crime, tough on the causes of crime'. I began by saying:

I am grateful for the opportunity to discuss the crisis today. Many of my constituents serve in our armed forces. I pray for their safety and for their families at this time.

Let me make it absolutely clear that the war is not between the west and Islam or between Christianity and Islam. Muslim communities across the UK and Muslim leaders around the world all condemned the terrorist attacks last month. We are all united in our fight against terrorism and want to remove its threat everywhere.

Yesterday, I visited Annandale Street mosque in Edinburgh, the scene of a recent fire attack. I gave the message that the Prime Minister has expressed solidarity and support with Britain's Muslims and condemned acts of hatred against them. That view is shared by all political parties and leaders in Scotland and Britain.

People advocating violence and religious hatred do not represent anyone, whether they are extremist groups or Muslim individuals. The vast majority will not support such people. They will not succeed. I was encouraged in Edinburgh by the presence of more than 100 members of the Edinburgh Inter-Faith Community to show their solidarity and support for the city's Muslims. The vast majority of people know that Islam is a religion of peace, understanding and tolerance.

We should be hard on terrorism, but also hard on the underlying causes of terrorism. The Prime Minister outlined his vision of the world in his conference speech, where he emphasised the peaceful resolution of conflicts and the eradication of poverty. For that vision to become reality, we need to address long-standing issues in Palestine and the dispute between India and Pakistan. We need to re-examine our policy of sanctions against Iraq. The Iraqi people have suffered, while Saddam Hussein has been strengthened.

I then argued that what would follow from the war would be an increase in terrorism and the destabilisation of the Middle East:

We must remain united against terrorism. Terrorists and those who support and harbour them must all be brought to justice. An international court should deal with charges against individuals and states accused of terrorism. We must also give serious consideration to the repercussions of military action against Afghanistan. The whole region is facing severe destabilisation. We face the most miserable refugee crisis in history. Seven million people face starvation in Afghanistan, and aid must reach them.

It is not disrespectful to question America's international policy. If the United States treated everyone equally, it would rule the world not by military might, but by winning hearts and minds. An even-handed, neutral approach in areas of conflict would, in time, replace hostility with genuine affection and respect for the USA. The potential exists to make that change.

Then I demanded that lessons must be learned from what had happened in Afghanistan in the past:

Lessons must be learned from our previous involvement in Afghanistan. We supported the mujahedin against Soviet aggression and armed groups against the invaders. One million lost their lives in the struggle against Russia. The war blighted millions of lives in Afghanistan, caused total ruination of the modest economic infrastructure and devastation of its towns and cities. The country had been bombed back to the Stone Age by the Russians during their 12-year onslaught. With the withdrawal of the Russian forces, the power struggle among different warring groups in Afghanistan degenerated into total chaos.

When the Soviets left, the West also walked away. What has happened in Afghanistan during the past 12 years is the result of the West and the USA turning their backs on both Afghanistan and Pakistan after the destruction of communism. Had we adopted an objective policy based on the long-term interests of the region and helped Afghans to rebuild their devastated country, the Taliban would never have come to power in Afghanistan. An economically viable and developing Afghanistan would never have been a safe haven for terrorists or extremists of any denomination.

I urge the Government to reach out to moderate, progressive and liberal forces in Afghanistan and Pakistan. Not only should we seek allies among ruling leaders, but it would be of great benefit to build a bond of trust with ordinary people. I very much welcome the Prime Minister's assurance that we will not walk away this time when the military action is over.

Then finally I raised the scope of the potential refugee issue:

We must also do more to avert the mounting refugee crisis. The huge number of people fleeing Afghanistan will increase rapidly. During the Soviet occupation, the response in humanitarian aid was initially inadequate; when the Russians withdrew, that response became one of disinterest, as civil war raged in Afghanistan. Neighbouring countries have struggled to cope with the millions displaced by conflict. We expect and demand better support from our Government and allies for the millions of people who face hunger and live in terrible conditions.

The abject poverty facing the refugees represents a huge burden on countries such as Pakistan, where there are currently 2 million to 4 million Afghan refugees. That is underlined by the decline in living standards and widespread poverty among Pakistan's citizens. General Musharraf has taken a bold step in siding with the United States. Measures must be taken to show the people of Pakistan that that decision is in their interests. Recent moves to lift sanctions and extend payments are a start, but on their own, they are nothing.

The crippling burden of debt must be lifted from Pakistan. Debt should not simply be rescheduled; it should be cut. That is the only way forward. Reduced debt would allow real progress to be made in alleviating poverty for millions of people, and it could help deliver basic education and develop decent health care for the poorest people in Pakistan.

Without real benefits, support for America will lead to dark days, not only for President Musharraf and his Government, but for all the people of Pakistan and Afghanistan. Support for terrorism will be strengthened where we fail to lift people out of poverty, deprivation and injustice, whether in Afghanistan or elsewhere. That is the real fight that we face. [1]

By now I felt that the epithet that 'truth is the first casualty of war' was being writ large. Scarcely a word of this speech appeared in the written press the next day, and there certainly was no queue of TV journalists waiting for a sound-bite. The doors to truth were being slammed shut. After the speech a number of MPs approached to tell me that what I was saying was absolutely right.

Two weeks into the war the Chief Whip, Hilary Armstrong, summoned Khalid Mahmood MP, Lord Ahmed, Baroness Uddin, Lord Adam and me – the Labour Party Muslims in the Houses of Parliament – to a meeting in the Chief Whip's office. A statement for the five of us to sign had been drawn up. She told us Tony Blair had asked her to ask us if we would sign the statement. As I remember it, the first paragraph took up the Palestine/Israel issue, noting that it remained unresolved and that the Government must use its support for the war in Afghanistan to press for a political solution to the Palestine question. The second paragraph noted that, in these circumstances, we all supported going to war in Afghanistan.

I was sitting there gazing at Hilary Armstrong in incredulity. We politely said we would need some time to discuss the matter among ourselves and would come back to her. We didn't sign the statement. However it was still issued by Downing Street that evening as though we had. One journalist who challenged the Downing Street media corps told me some time later that, when he asked about what had happened, he was told there had been a 'misunderstanding'.

When I reflect on this now I might have realised at the time that this represented 'a cloud, no bigger than a man's hand' – a faint harbinger of the hurricane of 'misunderstandings', 'misinformation', and more, that was to follow. Looking back now on my experience in the House of Commons, I would argue that the 'fog of war' which

1. *Hansard*, 8 October 2001.

surrounded British participation in the Afghan war has been one of the most pervasive and impenetrable in British history.

For more than ten years we have been told by British generals that 'progress is being made but challenges remain'. That is army-speak for 'the war in Afghanistan is doomed to failure'. For years we have been treated to breathless reports by embedded TV journalists, from the front-line, about the struggle to overcome the Afghan insurgency.

The British Army was defeated by the Taliban in Helmand, and the major element of its original operations there had to be taken over by the US Army. The original aim of the British involvement in Afghanistan was the elimination of al-Qaeda. That raison d'être was achieved years ago. Successive governments altered the terms of engagement, and the sole purpose of British troops remaining became to support the war aims of the American government, frantically hanging on to their combat coat-tails.

There can be different interpretations. But the subsequent inquiries, parliamentary debates and Government reports supported my viewpoint. In 2009, the House of Commons Foreign Affairs Committee warned the British Government about this – about the implications of what ended in 'mission creep'. The Foreign Affairs Committee Report further concluded that the Helmand deployment was on the verge of degenerating into a fiasco:

> We conclude that the UK deployment to Helmand was undermined by unrealistic planning at senior levels, poor coordination between Whitehall departments and crucially, a failure to provide the military with clear direction. We further conclude that as the situation currently stands, the 'comprehensive approach' is faltering, largely because the security situation is preventing any strengthening of governance and Afghan capacity.[1]

The Foreign Affairs Committee has served the nation well concerning Afghanistan. Its most trenchant criticism of the Afghan war was contained in its Report on Afghanistan and Pakistan published

1. House of Commons Foreign Affairs Committee Report, 21 July 2009, para 236.

two years after its previous one, quoted above. The 97 pages of the follow-up report are a staggering indictment of the war in Afghanistan, and the role of the British and American forces. I speak here of the generals, of course, not the 'poor bloody infantry'.

The conclusion of the report stated:

That some of the language used by the military, in particular, risks raising expectations beyond a level that can be sustained…It is useful to remember that Helmand accounts for only 3.5% of the population of Afghanistan and those living in areas under the control of UK armed forces make up only 1% of the population.[1]

The Report, on its last page, demanded that when 'British combat operations' have ceased, there should be a 'full and comprehensive public inquiry into the Government's policy in Afghanistan'. I could not agree more. The diplomatic correspondence and conclusions drawn by the British ambassador of the time – Sherard Cowper-Coles – were no different. It remains puzzling to me – after more than ten years of the war in Afghanistan – that this devastating cross-party analysis of the war was mostly ignored by the British media; it was published in the House of Commons but to little effect. One wonders if this indicates that the accusations of 'a conspiracy of silence' on Afghanistan have real substance.

In my view the plans for Afghanistan after the withdrawal of NATO forces amount to little more than handing over an ongoing war to the Afghan government and the Afghan National Security Force (ANSF). What is likely to happen is that the future stalemate that will ensue between the Taliban and the ANSF will only be maintained as long as the American Congress is prepared to foot the $6–7 billion annual bill that supporting the ANSF entails. The 30,000-strong American 'troop surge' of 2010–11 was supposed to clear the ground of the Taliban to make the task of the ANSF much easier. It didn't work.

Any military stalemate can only be prolonged as long as billions of dollars continue to flow from the US to the Afghan forces. If this

1. House of Commons Foreign Affairs Committee Report, 2 March 2011, para 92.

support is reduced as America, once out of Afghanistan, considers other spending priorities, it will be a matter of time before the reduced ANSF forces will be defeated by the Taliban. The patience of the Taliban may prove to be greater than that of the American Congress. Then another civil war, reminiscent of the post-Soviet conflagration, will beckon. All the pledges to create an Afghanistan that was 'no longer a haven for international terrorism' will be found to be irredeemable.

Despite the recent successful installation of a new government in Kabul headed by President Ashraf Ghani and the signing of the stalled 'Basic Security Agreement between Afghanistan and America', the situation remains unstable. Though the crystal ball is opaque, the forewarnings are clear. Unless efforts are made to engage all stakeholders, especially the Taliban, peace will remain elusive. Talking to the Taliban in Afghanistan is not an option – it is an imperative. The sooner the world realises this, the better it will be for global peace and development.

Of course it was not only in Afghanistan that Britain blundered. The entire proceedings of the House of Commons debate, 'Iraq and Weapons of Mass Destruction' testifies to the folly of the war in Iraq. In September 2002, Tony Blair in his infamous speech told the nation that Saddam's 'weapons of mass destruction programme is active, detailed and growing. The policy of containment is not working. The weapons of mass destruction programme is not shut down; it is up and running now.'[1]

In closing, the Prime Minister said that he acknowledged that there was international resentment at the state of the Middle East peace process, and that a new international conference was needed to address that, 'based on the twin principles of a secure Israel and a viable Palestinian state.' As I sat there in the House, a matter of yards away from him, two thoughts were in my mind. I didn't believe a word of the statement on Iraq's WMDs, not least because the UN inspectors were still saying they wanted to go back to make further investigations. Secondly, we were going to war in Iraq.

It turned out that millions disagreed with that. And they would prove it a matter of months later. On 15 February 2003, Britain saw

1. *Hansard*, 26 September 2002.

its biggest-ever demonstration when – under the banner of the 'Stop the War' coalition – more than million people marched in London to oppose the war. In Hyde Park, the Reverend Jesse Jackson was a keynote speaker. George Galloway was at his brilliant oratorical best that day. He took the crowd by storm. When I spoke I raised the astonishing bravery of the police and, particularly, the firefighters on 9/11. 'And when the bravest of the brave were climbing the stairs of the Twin Towers to save lives, where was Bush? Bush the Brave was hiding in his bunker!' There were roars of approval.

The Stop the War demo made for no changes of mind in the corridors of power in Washington and London. Earlier in February, Bush's Defence Secretary, Colin Powell, had addressed the UN Security Council. Powell told the Assembly that there was 'no doubt' that Iraq possessed and was ready to use biological and chemical WMDs, and was actively engaged in acquiring nuclear weapons.

Scarcely a year after Powell's February speech, David Kay, who was charged by the Bush administration with running the Iraq Survey Group (ISG) to find the evidence of WMDs confessed: 'We were almost all wrong'. A later ISG report said, 'with high confidence', there were no WMDs in Iraq.

After Powell's February 2003 speech at the Security Council, there was another major debate in the British Parliament. It concerned a proposed amendment to an earlier Government Paper which had laid out the case for intervention. The amendment was essentially framed to say that the case for going to war had not yet been made and that Saddam should be given one more chance to comply with inspections. The anti-war supporters' numbers in the Commons were considerable, but far from enough. In my speech that day I began by pointing out vehemently that opposition to the war did not mean support for the regime of Saddam Hussein:

> It is important to re-emphasise that those of us who are opposed to war in this House and across our nation are not friends of Saddam Hussein. We were against him when he invaded Iran, we opposed him when he invaded Kuwait and we spoke out against him when he used chemical weapons against his own people. Unfortunately, the UK and US Governments

supported and armed him in the 1980s. I am surprised that no apology was forthcoming from Conservative Front Benchers for supporting Saddam Hussein when he used chemical weapons against his own people. The American Administration is extremely well informed about Iraq's weaponry. As the *Scotsman* pointed out last Friday, Donald Rumsfeld probably still has the receipts. Like many opponents of military action, I am proud to say that we have been friends of the Iraqi people over two decades of Saddam's rule and we remain their friends today. We are concerned about the tens of thousands of lives at risk through an attack on Iraq. That is the real moral issue that we must all face.

Then I continued on the question of support for the War:

The overwhelming majority of people in Britain support us in sharing that sceptical view. In my constituency, my party membership is unanimously opposed to war, including the former Member of Parliament for Govan and Cabinet Minister Bruce Millan. Among the general public, people from all walks of life are openly talking about opposition to war, including Govan's most famous son, Sir Alex Ferguson. Given that we have seen more than 70,000 people gather in Glasgow alongside one million in London to demonstrate their opposition to war, I must ask my Right Hon. and Hon. Friends on the Front Bench if they are listening to the people of Scotland and of Britain. I have not found anyone outside this House – no one among the real people whom we seek to represent – who is in favour of war. People here and around the world are clearly against war. There is no groundswell of support for military action.

The 52 African governments expressed their opposition at their recent summit. If Al Gore had been elected President by the Supreme Court Judges instead of George W. Bush, we would have an American administration opposed to war. Our own policy on Iraq demonstrates that the Government are not at the heart of Europe, but in the heart of President George Bush.

I went on to speak about our isolation in Europe, and the previous political dalliance with Saddam:

> The policies of our key European allies, led by President Chirac and Chancellor Schroeder, are more in line with British opinion than my Right Hon. Friend the Prime Minister. The French President expressed that clearly when he said, there is no reason 'to change our logic, which is the logic of peace, and switch to a logic of war'. I do not doubt my Right Hon. Friend the Prime Minister's good intentions but I disagree profoundly with his support for President Bush. I am suspicious of the genuine motive for the American position. Saddam Hussein is as great a monster today as he was 20 years ago. The only difference is that he was our monster then.

War was inevitable by this time, but I was incensed by the way that, in the likely absence of a second UN resolution, America was blatantly offering bribes to potential allies to send some troops so that they might camouflage the American and British isolation. I added:

> Iraq has the largest oil reserves in the world today. The American administration is brimming with oil interests. Almost every key member, from President Bush downwards, has been heavily involved in the oil industry. The United States should not try to buy support in the United Nations Security Council. The 15 nations should be given enough objective evidence to reach a fair and independent assessment of the situation in Iraq.
>
> The international coalition is being built with bribery and by bullying smaller nations such as Chile and Cameroon. That starkly contrasts with the joining of forces to repel Iraq's invasion of Kuwait. The business press always gives the bottom line on what is really happening. Yesterday, the *Financial Times* reported that America was preparing to pay a high price for support in its bargaining with Turkey. The *Financial Times* stated that 'this time America's allies are waiting to be

bought off', and that the cost would be dear in 'hard cash' and 'IOUs'.

It is sad to see America's loyal ally, Turkey, 'haggling furiously'. From a first US offer of $2 billion to $3 billion and an initial Turkish demand for $92 billion, it appears that a settlement of $16 billion has been reached. Is that any way to pull a stable international coalition together? Dr. Mahathir bin Mohamad, the Prime Minister of Malaysia, puts matters more starkly. He believes that it is no longer a war against terrorism, it is in fact 'a war to dominate the world'.

I recently spoke to Americans who opposed military action. They made it clear that their biggest problem is not President Bush but my Right Hon. Friend the Prime Minister. If he did not support United States policy, any backing for war would collapse across the Atlantic. Those who argue that President Bush would go to war alone, without our Prime Minister's support, are wrong. President Bush needs Prime Minister Blair to sell the war in the United States. That is shown in the efforts to prove a tenuous link between al-Qaeda and Saddam, based on the presence of an al-Qaeda group in northern Iraq. It is disappointing that the fair-minded Colin Powell could present that to the United Nations as evidence.

We all know that al-Qaeda terrorists operate in Britain, the United States and many other nations. Clearly, that does not mean that our Government or any other support al-Qaeda. The claim has no credibility. Saddam and Osama bin Laden are implacable opponents. They oppose each other as much as President Bush opposes them both. We should not look for a spurious link to terrorism as an excuse for war against Iraq.

The UN weapons inspectors are in Iraq for a reason. The international community sent Dr Blix and the skilled inspectors to do a job. They should be allowed the time that they need to complete it. I end with a quote from the leader comment in the *Guardian* today: To go to war now would be to act without the freely given consent of the vast majority of nations; without the support of key allies; without a legally unambiguous mandate; without just cause, and against the wishes of the people of the west and the Muslim world. I shall vote for the amendment.[1]

Bush and Blair in these days used to refer to the 'coalition' that they were trying to establish as a 'coalition of the willing'. After this speech I used to joke that it was really the 'coalition of the shilling'. The delaying amendment was beaten by 393 to 199, a 2–1 majority for war.

There was one event in the House of Commons that stood head and shoulders above all the other debates about going to war in Iraq; Robin Cook's resignation from the Cabinet. It towered above everything else that was said. It will go down in the annals of the history of the British Parliament. Every single word of it was a hammer blow against those in favour of the war. Hansard records that there was applause when Robin sat down. In truth it should record a standing ovation, because that is what actually happened. It was a remarkable, momentous moment. The BBC's Andrew Marr described it as 'without doubt one of the most effective, brilliant resignation speeches in modern British politics'.

One sentence in the speech summed up Cook's opposition:

The reality is that Britain is being asked to embark on a war without agreement in any of the international bodies of which we are a leading partner—not NATO, not the European Union and, now, not the Security Council.

His closing remarks were typical of his unflinching performance:

From the start of the present crisis, I have insisted, as Leader of the House, on the right of this place to vote on whether Britain should go to war. It has been a favourite theme of commentators that this House no longer occupies a central role in British politics. Nothing could better demonstrate that they are wrong than for this House to stop the commitment of troops in a war that has neither international agreement nor domestic support. I intend to join those tomorrow night

1. *Hansard*, 26 February 2003.

who will vote against military action now. It is for that reason, and for that reason alone, and with a heavy heart, that I resign from the Government.[1]

The days leading to the Tuesday 18th of March vote on Iraq – the day after Cook's resignation – were among the worst in my time in the British Parliament. By the day of the vote, things had reached fever pitch as Labour Whips roamed the House of Commons corridors looking for target MPs to browbeat. The atmosphere was poisonous as the Whips delivered the Party line that 'if you are not with us you are against us', frequently toe to toe and inches from the faces of the MPs they were accosting. I don't recall whether it was on the 18th, or earlier, that I was approached by Jim Murphy MP, then one of the Whips. He asked me which way I was going to vote. I told him, against the war. He said, 'So you've lost all ambition to hold an important position in any Labour Government?' I told him that I had never had that ambition in the first place. I was livid.

Late in the afternoon I met Khalid Mahmood MP somewhere in the corridors. He was ashen-faced. He said he'd just been accosted by John Reid, who had a reputation in the Commons of being far from a shrinking violet, to say the least, as he had demonstrated in the battle for the shipyards in Glasgow. At this time Reid was in Tony Blair's Cabinet as Minister without Portfolio – otherwise termed by us backbenchers as Minister for Enforcement. Khalid said that John Reid had told him he must vote for the Government because this was no longer a vote about Iraq, it was effectively 'a vote of confidence in the Tony Blair government" Those who did not do their duty would be remembered, he'd told Khalid.

I could see then that Khalid was wavering. I told him: 'Look, when that Division bell rings at the end of the debate, the Lobby is going to be crowded with the Whips and the Reids staring you down. You'll never make it. You'll crack and go into the "Yes" lobby. If you don't want a stain on your record for ever, get into your car and drive home to Birmingham.' I knew he would regret it if he ended up voting for the war. I literally bundled him out of the Commons. He went to Birmingham.

1. *Hansard*, 17 March 2003.

The debate was a pretty roughhouse affair, with Tony Blair being asked to 'give way' time and again. He never really got into his stride, but it has to be said that he delivered a very combative performance. The vote on the Opposition's amendment to the Government motion on going to war was lost by 396 votes to 217. The main motion for war was then carried 412 to 149 – a crushing majority. The Foreign Secretary, Jack Straw, summed up for the Government in the debate. Towards the end of it, Alex Salmond of the SNP managed to intervene to ask the Foreign Secretary what this was going to cost. Salmond ventured a figure of $100 billion – 'if it is a quick war'.

Jack Straw said in reply:

The honourable gentleman speaks with great confidence about the costs of reconstruction. I do not have his confidence in his figures. I say to him that Iraq is an astonishingly wealthy country. The oil is important to this extent: it has the second-largest oil reserves in the Middle East. One of the other agreements clearly reached in the Azores, which must also be endorsed by a United Nations Security Council resolution, which we shall propose, is that every single cent and penny of those oil revenues are not plundered by Saddam Hussein and his friends, but used for the benefit of the Iraqi people. I am quite clear that, when that happens, the costs of reconstruction to the rest of the world will be remarkably insignificant.[1]

Straw's conceptions were a carbon copy of what was being served up on the other side of the Atlantic. When Larry Lindsay, President Bush's economic advisor and head of the National Economic Council, suggested the costs of war might reach $200 billion his estimate was dismissed as 'baloney' by Defence Secretary Donald Rumsfeld. Rumsfeld estimated the costs in the range of $50 to $60 billion.[2] His deputy, Paul Wolfowitz, suggested that post-war reconstruction could pay for itself through increased oil revenues.

By 2008 the American academics Joe Stiglitz and Linda Bilmes

1. *Hansard*, 18 March 2003.
2. Joseph Stiglitz and Linda Bilmes, *The Three Trillion Dollar War: The True Cost of the Iraq Conflict*, Penguin Books, 2008.

had determined that the 'running costs' of the war – operating costs for the US Government alone – were projected to exceed $12.5 billion *per month*. The early estimates of the Bush and Blair administrations proved to be disastrously wrong.

The achievements of Tony Blair's premiership cannot be gainsaid. Not least his leading Labour to power in three successive General Elections. For that achievement his stature as a Labour leader will be acknowledged in history. At many moments of crisis his command of the situation was remarkable – as he would prove in subsequent events in the UK. Despite this, at the time of going to war in Iraq, the enmity towards Blair felt by those opposed to it, was actually greater than that felt towards Bush. Bush was recognised as a mediocrity, an accident of history; it was widely acknowledged that the real power behind his throne were the 'neo-cons' led by the dastardly Dick Cheney, the Vice President. There was a tangible feeling then, among the opponents of war, that it should have been Blair cautioning Bush about what needed to be done. Rather than Bush marching Blair 'shoulder to shoulder' into this folly.

Those, like me, who opposed both wars, were right and the Hawks were wrong. All the strategists of the British and American armies were taken by surprise. In a matter of weeks, if not days, the occupied Iraqis were throwing bombs, not roses. Then the unity of the original Iraqi Intifada gave way to an internecine sectarian war, in which thousands upon thousands of Iraqis perished. Bush's glorious 'global democratic revolution' drowned in its own blood.

I have written this book to put on record the struggles of my life, but also, as a politician, to give my opinion on some of the great controversies of our times. So I want to consider, briefly, the costs and the price of the 9/11 wars. On the costs there is one work that is without peer – *The Three Trillion Dollar War – The True Cost of the Iraq Conflict*, by Joseph Stiglitz and Linda Bilmes. They have carried out a forensic investigation of the operational costs of the war in Iraq; the permanent medical and social security costs for injured veterans; payment to the families of soldiers who died in the conflict; the macro-economic costs, like the hike in world oil prices caused by the conflict. They conclude that the bill for the Iraq war is at least three million, million dollars.

They consider this is a conservative estimate:

Under the circumstances, a $3 trillion figure for the total cost strikes us as judicious, and in all likelihood, errs on the low side. Needless to say, this number represents the cost only to the United States. It does not reflect the enormous cost to the rest of the world or to Iraq.[1]

The authors argue that for a fraction of one percent of these costs a Marshall Plan for Iraq could have been delivered which could have spent *three times more* per Iraqi than what was spent on each European in the original Marshall Plan post World War Two. They use similar calculations to reach the staggering conclusion that if the costs of Iraq and Afghanistan are added together, then a 'realistic-moderate' estimate of the total cost to the USA budget is $4.995 trillion.

If anything, when the statistics are broken down they become even more revealing. One of the UN Millennium goals for 2015 is the eradication of illiteracy. That is costing $8 billion a year at present and the target elimination of illiteracy won't be met. $8 billion a year represents what two weeks of the wars in Iraq and Afghanistan cost, according to the Stiglitz and Bilmes calculations.

When it comes to the price that has been paid in lives in Afghanistan and Iraq, the toll is terrible. The most reliable statistics for the deaths of British troops comes to 625 – 446[2] in Afghanistan (to October 2013), and 179 in Iraq[3] (to February 2009). American losses are 6,243 – 1,835 in Afghanistan[4] and 4,408 in Iraq[5] (both to end May 2011). The most authoritative recent report on civilian deaths in Iraq was published in October 2013, by the PLOS Medicine Foundation. Following a detailed research study inside Iraq, PLOS Medicine concluded that the death toll of Iraqi civilians as a result of the war was around half a million. The PLOS report noted that:

1. Stiglitz and Bilmes, *op. cit.*
2. Guardian Datablog, 'British deaths in Afghanistan'.
3. BBC News Online, 'British military deaths in Iraq'.
4. Guardian Datablog, 'British dead and wounded in Afghanistan month by month'/ 'US casualties in Afghanistan and Iraq'.
5. Guardian Datablog, *ibid.*

The authors estimate the total excess Iraqi deaths attributable to the war, through mid-2011, to be about 405,000. The researchers also estimated that an additional 56,000 deaths were not counted due to migration. Including this number, their final estimate is that approximately half a million people died in Iraq as a result of the war and subsequent occupation from March 2003 to June 2011.[1]

These figures do not take account of the deaths in Iraq attributable to the years of sanctions. If that toll is taken into account, in these circumstances a total for both wars reaching two million dead is not an unreasonable estimate.

The real facts of the 9/11 wars are irrefutable. There were no WMDs. Saddam's regime did not train or arm al-Qaeda. Iraq has not become a 'watershed event for the democratic revolution in the Middle East'; on the contrary, terrorism has grown exponentially across the globe. The world is not a safer place. History has already issued these judgements.

1. 'Mortality in Iraq Associated with the 2003-2011 War and Occupation', PLOS Medicine, 13 October 2013.

Israel and Kashmir – the Fight for Just Causes 11

'It is time for our Government to make clear to the Israeli Government that their conduct and policies are unacceptable, and to impose a total arms ban on Israel. It is time for peace, but real peace, not the solution by conquest which is the Israelis' real goal but which it is impossible for them to achieve. They are not simply war criminals; they are fools.'

Gerald Kaufman MP, *Hansard*, 15 January 2008.

The historical injustice represented by the 1948 war to create Israel, on Palestinian lands, and the blood-soaked decades that have followed, are a touchstone for any Muslim, anywhere in the world, who has a scintilla of interest in politics. My own support for the Palestinian cause stretches back to my early 20s, when I was demonstrating as a college student at the time of the 1967 war. Later, in 1969 when Leila Khaled famously hijacked a US aircraft bound for Athens and diverted it to Damascus, she became one of my heroes.

My own views about the resolution of conflict have shifted from youthful radicalism to a greater understanding of the unavoidable necessity of political negotiation. Nonetheless, the young Leila Khaled still has a place in my heart, because she was the first to force the Palestinian question onto the world's political agenda. It was Leila Khaled who put the Palestinian question into newspaper headlines across the world. It is interesting to reflect that at that time, world public opinion was very much on the side of Israel. That has changed decisively now. The killing machine that is the Israeli state has made that certain. The most recent history of the struggle for Palestinian rights has confirmed that. The slaughter caused by Israel's 2014 war in Gaza made Netanyahu and his government into war criminals in the minds of millions, including me. My burning sense of injustice regarding the history of the Palestinian struggle is as intense now as it was a long time ago, in the days of my youthful protests.

I first met the late Yasser Arafat, the leader of the PLO, at the end of the 1980s, when he was in exile in Tunis. I travelled to Tunisia with George Galloway, then an MP in Glasgow, Alex Mosson, who was an elected member of Glasgow City Council, and the late Bill Speirs, of the Scottish Trades Union Congress. We were all involved in Glasgow in the charity, Medical Aid for Palestine. The heroes' welcome we thought we might get at the airport in Tunis never happened. George, Alex and Bill had no problem with Immigration, but I was refused entry and detained for questioning. I could not believe it – here was I, one of their Muslim brothers, and the Tunisian authorities had waved the others through Entry and blocked me. I couldn't speak Arabic and the officials didn't speak English – or only enough to tell me to sit on the benches beside Immigration Control.

Three hours passed. I was beginning to think that my cherished dream of meeting Chairman Yasser Arafat was doomed and that I was going back to the UK on the next available flight. Then a planeload of new arrivals filled the hall. I went up and down the queue asking if anyone spoke English. I got lucky. One man, a Palestinian, helped me plead my case. He explained that I was on a charity 'mercy mission' to help Palestinian refugees. The immigration officials relented and stamped my passport.

My three comrades had given up waiting for me and had long departed for the hotel. I had the name of the hotel written on a scrap of paper. The problem was that the taxi driver thought he knew where it was, but when we arrived at our first destination he was proved to be wrong. I am not sure if this is a common hope of the lost traveller, but I think there is a tendency to believe, in such circumstances, that after the taxi driver takes advice from the staff at the first hotel, the next stop will be the right one. It wasn't. Nor was the next one. Here I was, ready to give blood for the rights of the Palestinian people to a homeland, on a tour of Tunis in the dark, unable to find my hotel. When I eventually reached the right one, the total experience of my arrival in Tunis had stressed me out completely. Meanwhile the comrades had retired to their respective beds many hours ago.

In the morning nobody in the hotel could tell us where the PLO headquarters was in the city. After a series of hasty phone calls, George managed to speak to somebody who told us to wait at the hotel and a PLO official would come there to see us 'immediately'. 'If he can find the hotel, Inshallah,' I thought. The PLO official arrived the next morning. He told us that Chairman Arafat knew of our visit but, due to security issues, no advance arrangements could be made for our meeting. He instructed us to wait at the hotel and said that in due course a car would arrive to pick us up when the meeting with Arafat could go ahead. I can't remember but I think we waited two or three days – almost unable to move from the hotel lest we missed the call. When it came, it was two in the morning and I was asleep in bed. I scrambled out of my pyjamas in minutes.

We met Yasser Arafat in a large villa in a residential area of Tunis. He was dressed in his army uniform and trademark black and white keffiyeh. He welcomed us like long-lost brothers, By then it was nearly three in the morning. The main points on the agenda concerned how to develop the Medical Aid for Palestine (MAP) campaign, as well as the PLO solidarity campaign in local councils in Scotland.

After these issues were considered in some detail, I raised some questions about a recent visit Arafat had made to India. He had been quoted in the media there as supporting India's claim to the disputed territories of Kashmir. I told him that this had lost us a lot of ground for the Palestinian cause in Pakistan, and within the Pakistani community in the UK. Arafat told me he was surprised that people would accept what was written in the Indian newspapers about Kashmir as reliable. He said that Zulfikar Ali Bhutto was a brother, and when Bhutto became the Prime Minister of Pakistan he was the leader of the Muslim world, not just Pakistan. 'How could I make life difficult for my "niece" [Benazir Bhutto, who was PM of Pakistan then] by taking the side of the Indians? It is preposterous,' he exclaimed. I was actually pleased with the Chairman's reply. It resolved any lingering doubts I had about the issue. To be honest, at that point I could scarcely believe that I had just spent an hour in the company of the great man.

About a year or so after our first visit to see Yasser Arafat, Alex Mosson and I accompanied George Galloway on a second trip. George was then vice-chairman of the Parliamentary Labour Party's Foreign Affairs Committee and had been sent by the Committee to report on the first Palestinian Intifada. There is a saying in politics that an 'ounce of experience is worth a ton of theory'. Well, the ounce of experience of my first visit to the Occupied Territories of the West Bank and Gaza was worth all the discussions and meetings on Palestine I had ever attended, all the TV news documentaries I had watched, and all the newspaper articles and books I had read. It burned the rights of the Palestinians into my political consciousness forever.

Israel was not an open door in those days, so for the purposes of the visit our story was that we were on a business trip to visit an Edinburgh tobacco company's factory in the West Bank. The history of the Tunis trip repeated itself at Immigration Control at Tel Aviv airport – George and Alex sailed through and I was detained for questioning. After initial exchanges with immigration officials – I was a businessman going to see a tobacco factory – some pretty serious-looking guys in black suits arrived. The interrogation was all about my links with Palestinians – as a Muslim did I support their cause, had I given them money, would I be meeting Palestinians when I was here, where was I staying, even how many times did I pray during the day. I held to my tobacco factory story, and after another two hours' grilling they relented. At least this time I knew I was to take a taxi to the imposing Colonial Hotel in East Jerusalem.

At this time the flames of the intifada were still burning, if perhaps not as intensely as the inferno of its early days. Nonetheless there were clashes between the Palestinian youth and the Israeli Defence Force (IDF) every day. We visited the West Bank towns of Jericho and Ramallah and Nablus in the north. The IDF had turned the whole of the West Bank into a prison camp. There were soldiers and checkpoints everywhere. Only Israeli settlers with long black beards, toting machine-guns in their pick-up trucks, seemed to have automatic rights of passage.

I think we were in a meeting in Ramallah when our hosts learned that sometime that morning, a dozen young Palestinian stone-throwers had been shot in a clash with the IDF. Our hosts insisted we should accompany them to the local hospital to see the realities of what was happening. In the ward we visited there were half a dozen boys suffering from tear gas inhalation with rubber bullet wounds. I asked one of the victims how he was. His reply has stayed with me: 'The Jews are doing to us what Hitler did to them, but we will not surrender the way they did. We will not give up. When I recover I am going back to the stones until we are free.'

Later in the visit we went to Gaza – the strip of teeming human misery that abuts Egypt and Israel. On the way there we passed a Jewish settlement with armed guards at its entrance. In anger, George rolled down the window and remonstrated with them. A few miles down the road at a temporary checkpoint, set up by a detachment of the IDF, our car was waved down. The soldiers were rude and abusive and demanded to see our passports. The leader asked us why we had been shouting at the people at the settlement we had just passed. George said it was only he who had done the remonstrating. He told them he was a British MP. Then he said ironically that surely in 'democratic Israel' he was allowed to make his feelings on political issues known. 'No stones were thrown. No-one was hurt,' he said. The officer replied, 'We are tired of British MPs coming here.' In a flash George said that he was surprised at this wearying of the British visitors. 'After all,' he said, 'you are only here in Israel because it was the British who gave you the land, even though it belonged to someone else.' The officer concerned left us to make a phone call to his superiors. Something to change his mind about us must have been said on the phone. After making the call he came back, handed the passports back to George, and, with a dismissive throw of his left hand waved us through the checkpoint.

A decade later – in a House of Commons debate about the Israeli bombing of Gaza, George Galloway laid the blame for the historic horrors inflicted on the Palestinians at the door of the British. He said:

> It started in this building, when Arthur Balfour, on behalf of one people, promised a second people the land that belonged to a third people. We are the authors of this tragedy.[1]

In an instant my mind went back to our confrontation on the road to Gaza, all those years before.

During those days of the first Intifada, if I had been asked would there ever be peace between the Palestinians and the Israelis, I would have replied that the time for lullabies was over. Following our

1. *Hansard*, 15 January 2009.

'Intifada visit' I could see no prospect of peace whatsoever. Then, some five years later, out of the blue came the Oslo Accords, and the prospect of Israel signing up to a two-state solution, involving the creation of a Palestinian entity. You couldn't really call the first offer a Palestinian 'state', because it was based on discontinuous parts of the West Bank and Gaza. In February 1994, this 1993 'Declaration of Principles' was followed by the signing of a more detailed agreement creating what became known as the Palestinian National Authority. I, like many others, felt it favoured Israel at the expense of the Palestinians. Nonetheless, it was seen by most of us sympathetic to the Palestinian cause as the start of a journey which was being undertaken more in hope than expectation.

The negotiations survived more slaughter. On 25 February 1994 an American-born settler, Baruch Goldstein, of the extreme right Israeli Kach Party, opened fire with his Israeli Defence Force assault rifle at the Tomb of the Patriarchs/Ibrahimi Mosque in the city of Hebron, on the West Bank. Twenty-nine Muslim worshippers were killed, including five twelve-year-old boys, before Goldstein was shot by Israeli soldiers. More than a hundred worshippers were wounded. In the Palestinian street protests which followed in the next four weeks, another seventy-six Palestinians were killed.[1]

Some months later, in the new spirit of the time, I led a delegation of around fifty prominent Muslim businessmen and community leaders from the UK to the West Bank and Gaza. We met Yasser Arafat in his Palestinian National Authority headquarters in Gaza. He told our delegation that he now believed that there could be peace with Israel, although he still felt that the Israeli side was only involved 'reluctantly' in doing a deal. He said he believed that Rabin was shaking hands on peace with his right hand whilst at the same time using his left hand to give the go-ahead for a huge expansion of Israeli settlements on Palestinian territory.[2]

On the West Bank the delegation visited the Al Aqsa mosque in Jerusalem – one of Islam's holiest sites – and also made a pilgrimage

1. Greg Philo and Mike Berry, *More Bad News for Israel*, Pluto Press, 2011.
2. Between 1992 and 1995 when Rabin was the Prime Minister of Israel the settler population in the Occupied Palestinian Territories (OPT) rose from 74,000 to 136,000 (see Philo and Berry, op. cit).

to the Ibrahimi mosque, in Hebron, to pay respects to the martyrs of Goldstein's terrorist attack. In researching for this book I came across the statement that Prime Minister Rabin made to the Israeli Knesset at the time of the Goldstein massacre, condemning those who were part of the extremist right-wing within the settler movement:

> You are not part of the community of Israel . . . You are not part of the national democratic camp which we all belong to in this House, and many of the people despise you. You are not partners in the Zionist enterprise. You are a foreign implant. You are an errant weed. Sensible Judaism spits you out. You placed yourself outside the wall of Jewish law . . . We say to this horrible man and those like him: you are a shame on Zionism and an embarrassment to Judaism.[1]

In content and tone this compares to the rejection of the extremists of fundamentalist Islam who have perpetrated terrorist outrages that I myself have made on countless occasions. However it is also seems fair to make the point here that after the Goldstein attack, there was no Western media chorus proclaiming that violence was an inherent part of the religion of Judaism, in like manner to the accusations laid against Islam after murderous Islamic fundamentalist attacks.

On the West Bank visit I met the mother of the first suicide bomber who carried out a bombing inside Israel. Twenty-one-year-old Amar Amarna, blew up an Israeli bus in the central bus station, at Hadera, in northern Israel. That happened in April 1994. Months later his mother was still inconsolable. She told me that she had three sons – one killed in the 1989 Intifada, one serving a long prison sentence for fighting in it, and now a third son who had become a suicide bomber. She told me that on the day of the bombing her son's last words to her were to say 'For whatever I do today I will be accountable to Allah on the day of judgement'.

I need to make it clear that I agree with Amnesty International's assessment on suicide bombing, that indiscriminate attacks on civil-

---

1. Yitzhak Rabin, speech to the Knesset reported in the *New York Times*, 1 March 1994.

ians are indefensible, whatever the circumstances or provocation.[1] That is a humanitarian consideration. In purely political terms I have opposed such attacks in Israel, principally because they have alienated a huge swathe of moderate opinion inside the country that supported a two-state solution. The right-wing Likud and Netanyahu and his cohorts have used Palestinian suicide bombings as justification for their own terrorist attacks in their invasions of Lebanon, the West Bank and Gaza, and also for their construction of 'the Wall' dividing up the Occupied Territories, which is a clear breach of international law.

In February 2004 the House of Commons International Development Committee published its report on 'Development in the Occupied Palestinian Territories'. Although that was more than a decade ago, all the observations made then still stand now. So it can be said that the Report's findings were far-sighted, even if they did not predict just how bad the situation confronting the Palestinians would become in the years to follow. The Report noted:

> Between September 2000 and June 2003, 747 Israelis died in the renewed hostilities which comprised the second Palestinian intifada and Israel's military re-occupation of the Palestinian territories. Although the conflict has involved losses on both sides, the Palestinians have suffered most. In the period mentioned above, 2,494 Palestinians are estimated to have been killed.[2]

These figures were revised to October 2003 when the total deaths had risen to 824 Israelis and 3,379 Palestinians. These were the early years of the second intifada. In the following years the proportions were to change with the increased ferocity of the Israeli onslaught. Between 2006 and 2012, almost 3,000 Palestinians were killed by Israel, against 47 Israelis killed by Palestinian attacks. That's 60 eyes for an eye.[3]

1. Amnesty International Annual Report 2000, 'Israel and the Occupied Territories'.
2. IDCR, 2004, *op. cit.* p.15.
3. Adam Shatz, *London Review of Books*, 6 December 2012.

One of the conclusions in the final pages of the IDCR, from 2004, could be rewritten with even greater emphasis today:

> The fact is that Palestinians in Gaza and the West Bank have no state, neither *de jure*, nor *de facto*; no citizenship; no rights; no remedies, and no one from the international community taking the responsibility to seek to ensure that an occupied people in these circumstances are treated as humanely as possible.[4]

The last set-piece debate in the House of Commons in which I took part concerned the Israeli invasion of Gaza, in December 2008. The blanket bombing of Gaza started on 27 December 2008. On 18 January 2009, when the ceasefire came into effect, three Israeli citizens and 10 Israeli soldiers were dead. The Palestinian Centre for Human Rights estimated that 1,415 Palestinians were dead – including 1,185 civilians, and 230 combatants.[5]

The House of Commons debate on this despicable slaughter took place on 15 January 2009. The House of Commons benches were packed that day. At three in the afternoon when my friend Gerald Kaufman MP rose to speak, a hush fell on the Chamber. His words deserve to be recorded here:

> I was brought up as an orthodox Jew and a Zionist . . . I first went to Israel in 1961 and I have been there since more times than I can count. I had family in Israel and have friends in Israel . . . On Sky News a few days ago, the spokeswoman for the Israeli army, Major Leibovich, was asked about the Israeli killing of, at that time, 800 Palestinians – the total is now 1,000. She replied instantly that '500 of them were militants.' That was the reply of a Nazi. I suppose that the Jews fighting for their lives in the Warsaw ghetto could have been dismissed as militants.
>
> The Israeli Foreign Minister Tzipi Livni asserts that her Government will have no dealings with Hamas, because they are terrorists. Tzipi Livni's father was Eitan Livni, chief

4. IDCR, 2004, *op. cit.* p. 76.
5. Philo and Berry, *op. cit.* pp.142-3.

operations officer of the terrorist Irgun Zvai Leumi, who organised the blowing-up of the King David Hotel in Jerusalem, in which 91 victims were killed, including 4 Jews.

Israel was born out of Jewish terrorism. Jewish terrorists hanged two British sergeants and booby-trapped their corpses. Irgun, together with the terrorist Stern gang, massacred 254 Palestinians in 1948 in the village of Deir Yassin. Today, the current Israeli Government indicate that they would be willing, in circumstances acceptable to them, to negotiate with the Palestinian President Abbas of Fatah. It is too late for that. They could have negotiated with Fatah's previous leader, Yasser Arafat, who was a friend of mine. Instead, they besieged him in a bunker in Ramallah, where I visited him. Because of the failings of Fatah since Arafat's death, Hamas won the Palestinian election in 2006. Hamas is a deeply nasty organisation, but it was democratically elected, and it is the only game in town. The boycotting of Hamas, including by our Government, has been a culpable error, from which dreadful consequences have followed. The great Israeli Foreign Minister Abba Eban, with whom I campaigned for peace on many platforms, said: 'You make peace by talking to your enemies.'

However many Palestinians the Israelis murder in Gaza, they cannot solve this existential problem by military means. Whenever and however the fighting ends, there will still be 1.5 million Palestinians in Gaza and 2.5 million more on the West Bank. They are treated like dirt by the Israelis, with hundreds of road blocks and with the ghastly denizens of the illegal Jewish settlements harassing them as well. The time will come, not so long from now, when they will outnumber the Jewish population in Israel.

It is time for our Government to make clear to the Israeli Government that their conduct and policies are unacceptable, and to impose a total arms ban on Israel. It is time for peace, but real peace, not the solution by conquest which is the Israelis' real goal but which it is impossible for them to achieve. They are not simply war criminals; they are fools.[1]

1. *Hansard*, 15 January 2008.

This was a remarkable speech for a man like Kaufman with his family ties to the British Jewish Community and to Israel. The tension in the Chamber was palpable, the atmosphere electric, when he resumed his place. Even although it took me two hours after Gerald had spoken to catch the Speaker's eye, I was still seething at the hypocrisy, injustice and wanton murder in Gaza. I said:

The sustained acts of brutal aggression to which the inhabitants of Gaza are being subjected at the hands of the Israeli Government must be condemned utterly, without qualification. Such acts of aggression are not just disproportionate; they are outrageously disproportionate . . . the Israeli military has given a terrifying display of its military might, killing more than 1,000 people, including 300 children. Does the Israeli Government truly believe that those innocent young children were terrorists firing rockets? The Israeli Government are also responsible for injuring more than 4,000 people, destroying thousands of homes and reducing countless buildings to their foundations. In doing so, not only have they broken established rules of international law, but they have brought shame on humanity and the entire world.

The brutal scenes that we have witnessed on our television screens and read about in our newspapers have horrified the vast majority of the British public, including in my constituency, who support the Palestinian cause and feel strongly that we have so far failed the Palestinians in the current crisis. I pay tribute to the tens of thousands of people who have peacefully marched and demonstrated throughout the UK to show their solidarity with the people of Gaza at this terrible time and to demand an end to the bloody violence.

The call for peace has come from members of all faith communities. I would like in particular to thank the group Jews for Justice for Palestinians for its recent statement in *The Times*, which was signed by more than 500 Israeli academics, artists and writers, calling for an immediate end to the slaughter in Gaza. They have asked for an end to the blockade, the opening of dialogue with Hamas, without which there can be no durable peace, an investigation into war crimes that may have been committed by any party to the conflict and the suspension of the EU-Israel association agreement until Israel fulfils the basic human rights conditions on which it is predicated. I congratulate Jews for Justice for Palestinians on issuing that statement.

It is important to stress that the actions of the Israeli Government should not reflect negatively on Britain's Jewish community . . . The atrocities being committed by the Israeli Government will do nothing to achieve peace and stability in the region. They will only cause more hatred and suffering, further damage and delay any possible peace process and make the world a more dangerous place, giving a propaganda victory to terrorist groups, which will use them to mobilise more support and radicalise young people around the world. The humanitarian situation in Gaza is now desperately dire as several aid agencies have reported that Gaza's population of 1.5 million is in urgent need of food, shelter, fuel and basic medical aid.

It is important to clarify a couple of myths put forward by the Israeli Government. This conflict did not begin 19 days ago with the firing of Hamas rockets into Israel. It began 60 years ago with the illegal occupation of Palestinian territories. The ceasefire in Gaza was not broken 19 days ago by the firing of Hamas rockets into Israel. It was broken 10 days into an agreement previously made by Israel to end the inhumane siege of Gaza. The Israeli Government have, throughout the current crisis, used their military might to cause the relentless destruction of infrastructure and they have inflicted misery on innocent Palestinian people. In their excessive use of military force, they have shown little, if any, restraint while wreaking utter carnage in Gaza. It is time that we began to hold them to account. After 60 years of waiting for peace and justice – 60 failed years – we owe it to the people of Palestine to find a lasting solution to this conflict.[1]

1. *Hansard*, 15 January 2009.

I received many letters, emails and messages of congratulation about my forceful attack on the butchery of the Israeli government. At the time I considered it to be among the best speeches I made in the House. Events caused me to reconsider that, because the new slaughter of the Palestinians in Gaza in July and August of 2014 made me wish that the demands I had raised in 2009 had gone so much further.

In the speech I have quoted above I demanded that the Israeli Government should be 'held to account' for their actions but stopped short of declaring that they should be indicted as war criminals. Perhaps, even then, I harboured some forlorn hope of some sort of negotiated peace after a ceasefire. No longer. There is no doubt in my mind that the results of the Israeli Operation Protective Edge of 2014, by any objective consideration, constitute war crimes by the Israeli Government.[1] I would have said so from the floor of the House of Commons if I had remained a British MP. I would have demanded that the UN Security Council should do something to redeem its tarnished status in the eyes of the world by using its rights to refer the Israeli Government to the International Criminal Court in the Hague for war crimes. And if not them, then the European Union should have taken such action.

In my opinion the disproportionality of reaction in the Israeli bombings of 2014 and the extent of the breaches of the Geneva Convention that they constitute, justify such indictments. There can be no further grounds for equivocation. It is my firm belief that Benjamin Netanyahu, the Israeli Prime Minister, his Government ministers and his Generals, are war criminals. There are no other words for it. And some standing UN inquiry can go nowhere near providing justice for those subjected to the Israeli state's wanton operations which bombed Gaza back to the Stone Age. Netanyahu and his government and his generals will never remove the stench of the blood of innocents from their hands.

1989 was the first full year of the first Palestinian intifada. The Kashmiri intifada started in the same year and was a revolt which

1. According to UN figures quoted by BBC News, in the conflict 2,104 Palestinians died, and 73 Israelis, including 6 civilians; 10,200 Palestinians were seriously injured and 475,000 made homeless (BBC News Online, 26 August 2014).

raised the same demands as its Israeli counterpart – the right to self-determination of an oppressed people. India responded to the uprising using the same methods as the Israelis – abductions, beatings, torture and extra-judicial murder. Gang rape was added to the Indian arsenal of oppression, as was the occupation of Indian-held Kashmir by an initial force of 100,000 Indian troops. But if the world knew about the Palestinian revolt, Kashmir essentially became the forgotten intifada, allowing the Indian state to operate, using Emergency Powers, with utter, brutal impunity.

In Chapter 2 I have outlined already how Mountbatten and Nehru conspired to perpetrate the greatest fraud of Partition on the people of Kashmir. Under the agreement on Partition, Muslim majority states were to accede to Pakistan and Hindu/Sikh majorities to India. Kashmir was overwhelmingly Muslim. The princely state was 77% Muslim and Kashmir itself 92% Muslim. The eventual invasion of the state by the Indian army violated all the agreements reached prior to Partition. In effect Kashmir was colonised by the newly independent Indian state, led by Nehru. The Indian army troops were led by British generals who were under the direction of Mountbatten.

Since that time successive Indian governments have justified their occupation of Kashmir on the grounds of a scrap of paper allegedly signed by the ruler of Kashmir, acceding Kashmir to India. A scrap of paper since exposed as a forgery. V.P. Menon, a high-level civil servant in the British administration of the Subcontinent, produced the forgery in the shape of a letter he had obtained from the Maharajah declaring the accession. Late in October 1947 Menon had allegedly travelled to Srinagar in Kashmir to get the document signed. Menon in fact never left Delhi and the Maharajah never signed a document of accession.

At the time of the seizure of Kashmir, a plebiscite to test the will of the people of Kashmir on accession to India or Pakistan was promised. That never happened and numerous UN resolutions to this effect have been abandoned. By the late 1980s the new generation of young Kashmiris who had grown up under the brutal Indian occupation reached the point of no return. In unison they rose against their oppressors. Two years into the struggle, through my contacts in Indian-held Kashmir, I knew the dreadful truth of what the oppression of that occupation meant in the toll of lives and in torture and tyranny.

The leaders in the Pakistani community in Glasgow were desperate to play a part in breaking down the continuing wall of silence about the murderous Indian assault on human rights in Kashmir. At that time Bob Wylie, who would become my tireless partner in the writing of my autobiography, was running his own freelance journalism agency, Features Independent, which specialised in producing foreign feature material for newspapers in the UK and Europe. When approached about Kashmir and told we had contacts who would work with him in Srinagar – the capital of Indian-held Kashmir – he agreed to go. He secured a commission from the *Guardian* newspaper for an article for its G2 review section.

Kashmir was then a closed area for foreign journalists. There was a total ban under the new draconian powers introduced by the Indian Government – the Armed Forces (Jammu and Kashmir) Special Powers Act, 1990. So how could we get Wylie in to do the story, and then get him out in one piece to tell it? It was arranged through our contacts to make him 'a carpet wallah'. In the Subcontinent that's what they call someone in the business of buying and selling carpets. This was considered a plausible ploy because Kashmir was still renowned for its carpet industry, especially its high value silk carpets, despite the troubles there.

Mohammad Bashir, from the Pakistani community in Glasgow, went to Islamabad with Wylie to help make all the necessary arrangements. A Kashmiri family who still own a high-class emporium in Islamabad, specialising in carpets and fine goods from all over the Middle East and South Asia, including carpets and goods from Kashmir, were the key. The oldest son of the business spent two weeks training Wylie to become a carpet buyer. This involved the grading of cotton, wool and silk carpets – their quality, price, how to select possible purchases, and how to conclude a deal.

Wylie left Islamabad with business cards, notepaper and envelopes embossed in the name of the 'renowned' Kilgour-Wylie Associates Ltd – Consultants to the British Carpet Manufacturers Association. For the first days he toured the carpet factories in Srinagar, seemingly inspecting their wares for possible imports to the UK. Once this cover was established he had a certain freedom of movement in Srinagar and other parts of Kashmir which allowed him to get the story.

The *Guardian* published his report in the weekend edition of 3-4 August 1991:

> It was early evening on May 8 in the Khanyar district of Sri-nagar, the capital city of Kashmir. A large funeral procession was approaching the green and white portals of the Pir Dista-gir shrine. At its head were the coffins of two new 'martyrs' of the secessionist struggle to free Kashmir from Indian rule . .. a crowd of about 5,000 mourners filled the square in front of the shrine . . . Abdul Kinnoo, the 52-year-old superinten-dent of the graveyard at Pir Distagir was there. He says the CRPF (Central Reserve Police Force) commander fired a shot in the air and then 'the special constables just opened up with their machine guns. Everyone tried to run. They were run-ning down alleyways screaming.' Kinnoo says 25 people were killed and more than a hundred injured.
>
> Another eye-witness Ghulam Dar says 'There were . . . women's burquas scattered in the street beside the bodies. Blood and burquas everywhere.' Abdul Majid, the first ambu-lance driver on the scene was shot in the chest.

The *Guardian* story detailed other atrocities including shootings and the gang rape of women by Indian security forces at the village of Pazipora.[1] It lies in the north of Kashmir, near the Line of Control that separates Indian-held Kashmir from Azad Kashmir in Pakistan. The investigation by the Jammu and Kashmir Basic Rights Commit-tee, headed by Bahauddin Farooqi, a former chief justice of Jammu and Kashmir state found:

> 25 people had been killed, 10 to 15 women raped, and mil-lions of rupees of damage done to houses and shops.

The *Guardian* also noted that Farooqi had collected evidence of human rights abuses in a 385-page report which had been submitted

1. On 10 August 1990.

to the High Court in Srinagar, indicting the Indian Government and its army and police officers. Farooqi told Wylie:

> We have dealt with only the tip of the iceberg; it is difficult to imagine the scale of what is going on. There are more than 4,000 petitions of habeas corpus pending at Srinagar High Court alone . . . I know of no convictions of any member of the security forces for any of these violations.[1]

The publication of the report created a furore in Britain. The Indian High Commissioner to the UK wrote to all the broadsheet newspapers in the UK – notably, the London *Times*, which gave his complaints wide coverage. The High Commissioner claimed that the report was a fake, a fabrication and said that it was unlikely that Wylie could ever have reported from Srinagar and other parts of Kashmir. That kept the story going. Copies of Wylie's stamped passport and bills in his name from Srinagar were sent to the *Times* but my recollection is that our rebuttals were not published. In any case it was more important for all those involved in the production of the *Guardian* article that it was covered in newspapers all over Pakistan. At that time we considered it as an important break-through.

The success of the *Guardian* article was reflected in the interest it provoked on the issue of Kashmir, within the Labour Party in the UK. It started a process where Asian members of the Party, particularly from London, Bradford and Glasgow, became determined to put the Kashmir issue on to Labour's political agenda. That culminated in a motion on Kashmir, calling for the implementation of UN resolutions, being considered by the 1995 Labour Party conference. It was passed overwhelmingly – despite more protests from the then Indian High Commissioner that Kashmir was 'no business of the British Labour Party'. That meant that resolving the Kashmir issue became part of Labour's international policies. I was enormously proud when the Kashmir resolution was passed. In fact if my memory serves me correctly, a reference to Kashmir was made in the Party's manifesto for the 1997 election campaign. Another breakthrough.

1. *Guardian*, 3-4 August 1991.

Time has passed and some things have changed. The events of 9/11 constituted an enormous setback for the struggles in Palestine and Kashmir because, in the short term, they had the effect of raising questions about the struggles of Muslims everywhere; it was as if 'freedom fighters' became 'terrorists' overnight in the eyes of the world's media.[1] However that temporary political difficulty has not altered the rights of the Kashmiris to self-determination, nor diminished the reality of the cataclysmic abuse of human rights by Indian state forces there.

In the 1991 *Guardian* article there is reference to the Jammu and Kashmir Basic Rights Committee's 385-page indictment of human rights abuses in Kashmir. In Srinagar, on 6 December 2012, the International Peoples' Tribunal on Human Rights and Justice in Indian-Administered Kashmir (IPTK), published its 354-page report on continuing human rights abuses. The latter could have been written at the same time as the former, given the almost identical nature of its accusations. Significantly, however, for the first time, the later report on human rights atrocities in Indian-held Kashmir has been documented with specific accusations naming those who allegedly perpetrated them:

> The institutional culture of moral, political, and juridicial impunity has resulted in enforced and involuntary disappearance of an estimated 8,000 persons (as of November 2012) besides more than 70,000 deaths, and disclosures of more than 6,000 unknown, unmarked and mass graves. The last 22 years have also seen regular extra-judicial killings, punctuated by massacres . . . Among the alleged perpetrators are 2 Major Generals and 3 Brigadiers of the Indian Army, besides 9 Colonels, 3 Lieutenant Colonels, 78 Majors, and 25 Captains. Add to this 37 senior officials of the Federal Paramilitary forces, a recently retired Director General of the Jammu and Kashmir Police as well as a Serving Inspector General.[2]

1. It is a matter of public record that Netanyahu used 9/11 to gain concessions on settlement building with the Bush Administration.
2. International Peoples' Tribunal on Human Rights and Justice in Indian Administered Kashmir (IPTK)/Association of Parents and Disappeared Persons (APDP), 'Alleged Perpetrators – Stories of Impunity in Jammu and Kashmir', 6 December 2012.

The IPTK report is only the most recent to charge the Indian state with the stream of atrocities perpetrated by its military. In September 2006, Human Rights Watch published 'Everyone Lives in Fear – Patterns of Impunity in Jammu Kashmir'. In Chapter 4 there is an analysis of how the 1990 Indian Special Powers Act virtually guarantees all Indian security forces exemption from legal prosecution; this Act has been the foundation on which their reign of terror has been built:

> Particular attention is given in this report to the problem of impunity from prosecution, whereby those responsible for abuses rarely get investigated, let alone tried and convicted. [1]

The report notes further that Human Rights Watch, despite several requests made to the Indian Government

> has received no details of any cases in which members of the Indian security forces have been prosecuted and convicted for serious human rights violations.[2]

As far as I can determine, the Human Rights Watch Report overlooked an important qualification. The Kashmiri freedom struggle was originally led by the JKLF – the Jammu and Kashmir Liberation Front. However the scale of the onslaught perpetrated by Indian forces led to the secular JKLF, and its attempts to build a mass movement against Indian occupation, losing that ground to the armed militant jihadists. Their rise in influence was a product of the reaction to the scale of Indian brutality and the mistaken idea that somehow the might of the Indian army could be defeated by taking up the individual armed struggle.

It seems that at present support for the mujahedin groups, Lashkar-e-Taiba, Hizbul Mujahideen, and Harkatul Mujahideen in Kashmir is waning. The new mood in Indian-held Kashmir is less supportive of the insurgency and more in favour of civil liberties and human rights. That may or may not endure. There have been recent

1. Human Rights Watch, 'Everyone Lives in Fear – Patterns of Impunity in Jammu Kashmir', Vol. 18, No. 11, September 2006, p.2.
2. Human Rights Watch, *op. cit.*, p. 6.

reports on the BBC on the resurgence of the Kashmir tourist industry, with hundreds of thousands of new visitors arriving there. However no-one should entertain any illusion that if the rights of Kashmiris are not recognised there will be a volcanic return to struggle; it is permanently bubbling under the surface, and as events have shown it can erupt at any time.

Some years ago I had the opportunity to meet with the former Prime Minister of India, Mahmohan Singh. We met at his offices in New Delhi. The meeting was arranged for thirty minutes, but we had a discussion for about an hour. During this time the vexed issue of Kashmir came up. We exchanged views and at the end of that I said to the Prime Minister, 'Let's think that India and Pakistan are part of one big family – if the elder brother shows affection to the young brother then the younger brother will show more respect; if India, as the big brother, became more friendly then surely the younger brother, Pakistan, would return the gesture.' I felt that, in this matter, it was India that should really be taking the initiative.

The importance of confidence-building measures being introduced to promote further dialogue should be acknowledged. I believe that India, as a member of the United Nations Human Rights Council (UNHRC), should issue a standing invitation to the relevant United Nations human rights rapporteurs, or working groups, to go to Jammu and Kashmir to investigate the human rights situation. It follows that the UNHRC could appoint a special rapporteur to publish regular reports on the situation in Jammu and Kashmir and Azad Kashmir, with the guaranteed co-operation of the governments of India and Pakistan. I consider this to be a reasonable starting point, if India is serious in intent, because the available evidence establishes India as the main transgressor in the violation of human rights in Kashmir.

The present immunity from prosecution of members of the Indian armed forces in Kashmir is the single most important factor in all the human rights abuses that have been perpetrated by Indian forces over the last decades. That needs to change and the relevant laws – or sections of them – particularly the Armed Forces (Jammu and Kashmir) Special Powers Act 1990, should be repealed. Pakistan would then support the process of conciliation wholeheartedly.

This is a step-by-step process. Ultimately neither India nor Pakistan can have a genuine peace in Kashmir without the Kashmiris being allowed to exercise their right to self-determination. In politics it is necessary to judge between what is necessary and what is possible. All these initiatives may be necessary to create a road map for peace in Kashmir. History may prove that they are not possible. What cannot be disputed is that there is a huge peace dividend to be gained for all. As long ago as 2002 I spoke on that issue in the House of Commons:

> I am grateful for the opportunity to debate peace in south Asia. This is a timely debate, as events across the region have moved rapidly in recent days. Peace and stability go hand in hand, but where there is no peace, bold leadership is required . . . Jane's latest estimates place Indian defence spending at almost $14 billion a year, and Pakistan's at $3.3 bn. With a standing army of well over 1 million in India and one of around 600,000 in Pakistan, this confrontational madness must end for the sake of the security of the whole region . . .

> For more than five decades, Kashmir has experienced persistent conflict. Since partition, India and Pakistan have fought three wars over this disputed land. Bilateral talks between India and Pakistan have taken place, but they were not successful . . . There are gross violations of human rights in occupied Kashmir and we have a responsibility as Members of Parliament to do whatever we can to end such violations in occupied territories . . .

> Our Prime Minister should also use his special relationship with President Bush and the USA. There must be a change in priorities for the United States as the world superpower. Instead of making sabre-rattling threats against Iraq, Iran, Syria and North Korea, it must focus clearly and concentrate on outstanding issues such as Kashmir and Palestine. That will bring greater peace and stability not only for the people of those disputed regions, but for us all, and build trust among Muslims that the West is even-handed.

> That will not happen while the US continues to threaten

other nations in the ongoing war against terrorism. The people of Kashmir deserve a just and peaceful settlement, and the leaders of Pakistan and India must show commitment to achieve it, bringing peace and stability to the region and enhance the quality of life of the poor people of those two great countries.[1]

I was once asked by a close friend about my continued support for the Kashmiris and Palestinians and their right to self-determination. He inquired, with a hint of irony, as to whether I was an adherent of St Jude, popularly identified as the Patron Saint of Lost Causes. I told him that I didn't consider the causes I supported on the basis of whether they were 'winnable' or not. I supported them because I thought them just and right. I lived through tumultuous times as a British Member of Parliament. On many of the great debates I supported parliamentary motions for causes that were lost. I supported them because they were right.

1. *Hansard*, 26 February 2002.

7/7 and Reflections on Terrorism 12

'While nothing is easier than to denounce the evil-doer, nothing is more difficult than to understand him.'

> Dostoyevsky, *The Possessed.*

'For America, Britain and the Western powers, the rise of ISIS and the Caliphate is the ultimate disaster. Whatever they intended by their invasion of Iraq in 2003 and their efforts to get rid of Assad in Syria in 2011, it was not to see the creation of a jihadi state spanning northern Iraq and Syria run by a movement a hundred times bigger and much better organised than the al-Qaeda of Osama bin Laden.'

> Patrick Cockburn, *London Review of Books,*
> 21 August 2014.

It was twenty minutes past seven on the morning of 7 July 2005. Four British men – three from a Pakistani background, the other from a Jamaican background – met at Luton train station and boarded the next train to Kings Cross station. CCTV footage recorded them saying their goodbyes outside Boots the Chemist, on the Kings Cross station concourse, at twenty-four minutes past eight. At ten to nine, three of the four detonated their bombs, simultaneously, on different parts of the London Underground. 39 people were dead and more than 600 were injured, many of them seriously. Just under an hour later the fourth in the group let off his bomb on a bus in central London. Now 52 people were dead and 750 were injured. 9/11 and suicide bombing had reached London. What began as just another Thursday morning in central London had been transformed forever.

The ringleader, Mohammad Sidique Khan, was 30. His bomb went off on the Circle Line, just after the train had left Edgware Road Tube station. His fellow bomber closest in age, Shehzad Tanweer, was 22. He detonated his bomb on the Circle Line also – between Liverpool

Street and Aldgate stations. Germain Lindsay, whose mother was Jamaican, set his off on the Piccadilly Line between Kings Cross and Russell Square. He was 19. The youngest of the group Hasib Hussein, was only 18. His bomb failed to detonate first time, due to a faulty battery. He fixed it and blew up a London bus in Tavistock Square.

Two of the four, at one time or another, had been noticed by British Intelligence but were not considered a serious threat: 'Prior to the 7 July attacks, the Security Service had come across Sidique Khan and Shehzad Tanweer on the peripheries of other surveillance and investigative operations . . . As there were more pressing priorities at the time, including the need to disrupt known plans to attack the UK, it was decided not to investigate them further or seek to identify them.'[1]

Since 9/11 British Intelligence had largely concentrated its efforts on identifying the possibilities of foreign militants arriving in the UK and, with the help of local collaborators, creating terrorist missions here. The 7/7 bombings were not the product of foreign militants coming here to commit terrorist outrages but rather the opposite – British militants going abroad to seek training, and then returning home to go 'local' in their attacks. It's known that Khan and Shehzad went to Pakistan between November 2004 and February 2005; their original intention seems to have been to seek training there, to fight in Afghanistan. Their al-Qaeda contacts convinced them they would better serve 'jihad' by training to take action in the UK. 'Home-grown' terrorism, not seen since the end of the decades-long IRA campaign in 1994, had arrived and the security services in the UK were not prepared for it.

The bombings took place on the last day of the G8 Summit, which was held in Gleneagles, in Scotland. I had travelled home from the House of Commons to attend a commemorative dinner in Glasgow. I cannot express the cold fear I felt when I heard the news. 9/11 had been been disastrous for the standing of Islam in the UK, irrespective of what we knew to be the truth. The assumption made, almost immediately, was that the London attacks had been carried out by Islamist extremists.

1. House of Commons Intelligence and Security Committee 'Report on the London Terrorist Attacks on 7 July 2005', May 2006, para 55.

As soon as I heard about the attacks my worst fear was that they would also turn out to be the work of *British* Islamist fanatics. On the Sunday following the Thursday attacks the first indications of that came from the Intelligence establishment. On BBC news, the former Commissioner of the Metropolitan Police, Lord Stevens, said he believed those responsible 'were almost certainly born or based in Britain,' and would not 'fit the caricature of an al-Qaeda fanatic from some backward village in Algeria or Afghanistan'.[1]

I got a phone call not long after that news bulletin from Shahid Malik. At the May 2005 Election he'd become the new MP for Dewsbury, in Yorkshire. With Sadiq Khan, elected for Tooting in London, that brought the number of MPs in the House who were Muslims to four. Shahid and I were close colleagues from the outset. We just got on well together. He told me on the phone that there were more than just rumours that the bombers were British. He'd been told, from a reliable source, that some of the police investigations were being carried out in Leeds, a matter of miles from his Dewsbury constituency. I was dismayed, because I knew what the implications of that were. The fact that Tony Blair had called a meeting of the MPs and members of the House of Lords who were Muslims for the following Monday more or less confirmed our worst fears.

The Downing Street meeting was eerily similar to the one that had followed the 9/11 events. Blair gave assurances that he would make it clear that although there were definite suspicions that Islamic extremists were involved, he would take the same line as before that this had nothing to do with 'moderate Islam, the true Islam'. He said the police were following lines of inquiry about them being British – documents had been found at one of the Underground sites – but the fact that the bombers were British was still not definitely confirmed. We told him we would condemn the outrages in the strongest language possible. Everyone was concerned not about *whether* there would be a backlash but exactly *what* form it would take and *when*.

It is interesting to reflect that, even at this time, we did not know for certain that the bombings were the work of suicide bombers. In the Monday debate in the House of Commons Tony Blair said that

1. Lord Stevens quoted on BBC News, 10 July 2005.

the bombings were *likely* to be the product of Islamic terrorism but still spoke of bringing those responsible to justice:

> It seems probable that the attack was carried out by Islamist extremist terrorists . . . I cannot give details, for obvious reasons, of the police investigation now under way. I can say that it is among the most vigorous and intensive this country has ever seen. We will pursue those responsible – not just the perpetrators but the planners of this outrage – wherever they are, and we will not rest until they are identified and, as far as is humanly possible, brought to justice.[1]

I managed to intervene in the debate along the lines agreed in the morning meeting:

> Does the Prime Minister agree that last week's attacks on our great city of London were an attack on people of all faiths and communities? We stand united against the perpetrators of those evil, barbaric acts of terrorism. Can he assure me that the Government recognise that the overwhelming majority of the Muslims who live in this country are tolerant, law-abiding citizens who respect other religions and do not support terrorism? Can he assure me that the Government will do everything they can to prevent any backlash against Muslims?

> The Prime Minister: I can certainly assure my hon. Friend of that, and the whole House will agree with his sentiments, which come particularly strongly from him as . . . the first Muslim MP in the House. I know that he speaks for the whole Muslim community, apart from a very small number of extremists, in this country.[2]

By that time the world's media had descended on London. St Stephen's Green – the park opposite the House of Commons where camera crews can have a background shot of the House behind those

1. *Hansard*, 11 July 2005.
2. *Hansard*, 11 July 2005.

being interviewed – had become a giant recording studio. There was a huge contingent of crews from America and all over Europe; I did two interviews with stations from New Zealand that day. Shahid and I spent hours on the Green. We had decided on three lines. We condemn these outrages, no effort should be spared to bring the guilty to justice; it may be claimed that this was done in the name of Islam but, on the contrary, it has nothing to do with true Islam; the bombings must not be allowed to split communities across the UK. The media interest would be huge and unabated throughout the following weeks.

Due to the effectiveness of the British police operations after the 7/7 events, we did not have long to wait for our worst fears to be confirmed. On Tuesday 12 July, West Yorkshire Police raided six houses in Leeds – one in Alexandra Road was confirmed shortly afterwards as the site of the terrorists' bomb factory. Shahid Malik phoned: 'They are all British, three of them from Leeds. The fourth is from Aylesbury, but lived in Huddersfield, and is directly connected to the others. It's going to be confirmed that they were suicide bombers. I've been told all that, off the record.'

If the battle to defend Islam post 9/11 – 'Not in Our Name' – had been enormously difficult, what we were now confronting was immeasurably greater. These terrorists were 'home-grown' they were not from Riyadh, Saudi Arabia. They were from Beeston, a district of Leeds. And they were suicide bombers. It emerged later that, ten days before he went on his killing spree, Shehzad Tanweer was playing cricket with his mates in the local park, in Beeston. The bus bomber, Hasib Hussein, played for Holbeck Hornets, the local football team.

Shahid and I agreed, there and then, that we had to mount a more extensive campaign than the one after 9/11. Along with the MPs Khalid Mahmood and Sadiq Khan, we decided that we should go on a tour of major cities and towns in the UK with large Asian populations, to set the record straight on our total rejection of Islamist terrorism and all that it represented. This could be arranged through local Labour Parties, or community associations, or the local mosques, as long as we got the message out as soon as possible. We hammered home the idea that the terrorists, irrespective of what might be their claims, were plain criminals and had no right to claim that they were acting in the name of Islam.

This campaign was not easy. Within our community the wounds of Afghanistan and Iraq will never heal. Despite the political promises made, nothing had been done about Israel and Palestine or Kashmir. There would be accusations that millions of Muslims had perished because of Bush and Blair, that there was a backlash against Muslims everywhere, and here we were trumpeting Tony Blair's words. I said to Shahid that we needed to appeal for calm. 'Try that in Leeds to-night,' he said.

My recollection is that we started the tour in Dewsbury, in Sha-hid's constituency. There was an advantage in all of us speaking – each supported the other. There were meetings in Leeds, Hudders-field, Manchester, Bradford, London and Brighton. They were among the first, and others followed, including a meeting in Glasgow. Con-sistent themes emerged – there was overwhelming condemnation of the attacks; there was anger about Palestine and Kashmir; a minority claimed the bombings were the work of the CIA or British Intelli-gence – the bombers were 'patsies' – to ensure the onslaught against Islam was maintained. We dismissed the latter opinions as being 'in denial'.

However, probably the most common theme was 'linkage' – con-demnation of the bombers was linked to the foreign policies of the British and US governments. Here's how the argument was present-ed – the bombers were extremists, but they saw themselves as tak-ing revenge for Afghanistan, Iraq and other outrages perpetrated by the West against the Muslim World. We dealt with that by rejecting any idea that somehow any linkage justified terrorist actions, whilst acknowledging that there was undeniable linkage between foreign policy and revenge-inspired terrorism.

This chapter is entitled '7/7 and Reflections on Terrorism'. I was the first Muslim to be elected to the British Parliament. During my thirteen years there, global terrorism became one of the greatest per-ils of our times. As a consequence I have long felt it was my duty to offer some analysis about this from my previous experience as a Brit-ish MP and, in that context, I will comment in some detail about the events in the UK. Nonetheless I feel that much of what I have to say on these matters has general relevance which is not restricted simply to the horrors of terrorist outrages in Britain.

For the record, all my political life, I have been an opponent of individual terrorism whether committed in the name of Allah, or any other religious or political inspiration. No cause can justify the slaughter of non-combatants; no cause can justify the butchery of innocents. These are moral objections. There are political considerations also – individual terrorism rarely achieves its aims. Al-Qaeda's objectives of an Islamic Caliphate from Iran to Morocco were not advanced a jot by 9/11 and what followed. Of which more later.

On 1 September 2005, Al Jazeera broadcast a videotaped statement from the leader of the 7/7 bombers, Mohammad Sidique Khan:

> I, and thousands like me are forsaking everything for what we believe . . . Until we feel security you will be our targets and until you stop the bombing, gassing, imprisonment and torture of my people we will not stop this fight. We are at war and I am a soldier. Now you too will taste the reality of this situation.[1]

On 6 July 2006, a similar videotaped statement by Shehzad Tanweer was broadcast by Al Jazeera:

> What you have witnessed now is only the beginning of a string of attacks that will continue and become stronger until you pull your forces out of Afghanistan and Iraq. And until you stop your financial and military support to America and Israel.

Tanweer insisted that the non-Muslims of Britain deserved such attacks because they voted for a government which 'continues to oppress our mothers, children, brothers and sisters in Palestine, Afghanistan, Iraq and Chechnya'.[2] Linkage.

Bilal Abdullah's parents were Iraqi-born doctors. Their son was born in prosperous Aylesbury, in Buckinghamshire. He too became a doctor, latterly working as a diabetes specialist in the Royal Alexandra

1. Al Jazeera, 1 September 2005.
2. *The Times*, 6 July 2006.

Hospital in Paisley, in the west of Scotland. Abdullah isn't saving lives now. He is serving life imprisonment for his part – along with others – in the 2007 attempt to drive a Cherokee Jeep, loaded with explosives, into the heart of Glasgow Airport and blow it up. At his trial – in Woolwich Crown Court where Abdullah was also found guilty of an earlier bomb plot in Central London – he told the court that his motive was revenge for the destruction of Iraq, and a protest against the UN sanctions which were responsible for the deaths of countless Iraqi children. He said:

> Without Blair, Bush couldn't have invaded Iraq . . . Everyone was saying you are a terrorist, you are arrested under the Terrorism Act . . . That is my case in a nutshell. I am told I am a terrorist. But is your government not a terrorist, is your army not a terrorist?' [1]

In December 2013, at the Old Bailey in London, Michael Adebolajo, 28, and Michael Adebowale, 22, were found guilty of the murder of British Gunner Lee Rigby in Woolwich in London. Adebolajo and Adebowale, were British, from a Nigerian background. Both were raised as Christians by their parents, but were Muslim converts. On a May afternoon in Woolwich, in suburban south-east London, Adebolajo and Adebowale lay in wait, in a dark blue Vauxhall car. They were a few hundred yards away from the British Army's Royal Artillery Barracks. Lee Rigby was wearing a 'Help for Heroes' T-shirt. The two rammed him with their car. Then they hacked Rigby to death with knives and a butcher's cleaver. Their trial heard later that Adebolajo had tried to behead Rigby.

On the morning after this horrible slaughter, the Mayor of London, Boris Johnson, performed the role of 'foreign policy denier' in the comments he offered the media. He said it was wrong 'to try to draw any link between this murder and British foreign policy'. This simply does not accord with the statements Adebolajo made minutes after the slaughter. He asked a woman passerby to record them on her iPhone. His hands covered in blood, and holding a meat cleaver still dripping with blood, Adebolajo declared:

1. BBC News Online, 16 December 2008.

The only reason we have killed this man today is because Muslims are dying daily by British soldiers and this British soldier is one, he is an eye for an eye and a tooth for a tooth. By Allah, we swear by the Almighty, that we will never stop fighting you until you leave us alone . . . when you drop a bomb do you think it hits one person? Rather, your bombs wipe out a whole family. This is the reality . . . Tell them to bring our troops back so we can all live in peace. Leave our lands and you can live in peace. That's all I have to say. Allah's peace and blessing be upon you. Asalam Aleikum.[1]

These examples are sufficient to establish the case. I should point out that studies of the Quran made by religious scholars find all of these statements profoundly wrong in their interpretation of Islam. There is nothing in the Quran that justifies such slaughter. Likewise there is nothing that justifies the practised refusal of political leaders in the UK to join the dots between wars abroad and terror at home. Any reference to the terrorist outrages perpetrated in America would show the same sort of linkages being offered by the perpetrators, and the identical refusal of American political leaders, and commentators, to join up the same dots.

During my time as an MP I began to draw certain conclusions about terrorism. I realised, in due course, that there seem to be consistent elements in Islamist terror in Britain which may also apply elsewhere. Almost always there is evidence of a radical cleric, or radical groups within a mosque; 'hate speeches' on the internet or on video seem to have an influence; terrorist training being undertaken abroad is a usual feature; and almost always the terrorists do no act alone but have some sort of support network.

In my time in the British Parliament I always believed that the British Government's response to the vicious proselytising of extremist Islamist clerics was insufficiently robust. At the time of the 7/7 bombings I said so in an interview with Fox News, arguing that, where the evidence existed, if these people were found promoting hatred, violence and terrorism, they should be dealt with using the

1. The *Sun*, www.thesun.co.uk/videonews, 24 May 2013; BBC News Reports, 19 December 2013.

full force of the law, and where it was legally justified they should be expelled from the country. 'Look, if they don't like it here, they can go,' I said. The interviewer put me on the spot and asked me to 'name names'. I think he was surprised when I told him that we could start with Abu Hamza and and Omar Bakri Mohammad.[1]

Bakri, along with another hate preacher, Anjem Choudary, were founder members of the militant group al-Muhajiroun. It has become clear that the Woolwich murderer, Adebolajo, was radicalised by the now-banned al-Muhajiroun. In fact Bakri claims to have converted him to Islam. Haras Rafiq of Cenri, the counter-extremism research group, said: 'if Woolwich was these guys going up to 100 mph, al Muhajiroun got them to 80.'[2]

What I argued then was that radical clerics who preach violent ji-had should feel the full weight of the law being applied against them to ban or at least restrict their activities. At that point I was far from being convinced that such a hardline approach was being taken by the police and intelligence services in Britain. In fact I told Tony Blair, on a number of occasions, that a much more ruthless approach to these hate preachers was needed, especially in London, where it was my view that they were allowed to say and do much as they liked. I should say here that I am not suggesting that there is a simple legal course of action which can resolve these issues. Prevention is much better than cure. So I demanded then that education campaigns re-garding the futility of 'jihadism' should be developed further, and have a much greater outreach. I also said that every leader of every mosque in the UK had a duty to speak out in this manner. It followed that I believed that the British media, especially the tabloid press, had to recognise its responsibilities. In this regard I thought that there was a real necessity for their approach to be forcefully challenged, given that, in essence, it amounted to little more than a veiled politi-cal assault on the values of the entire Muslim community in the UK.

It is possible to argue that the al-Muhajiroun group, which in-fluenced Adebolajo and Adebowale, was a typical support network of the kind that seems to be common to the actions of Islamist ter-rorists. Three of the four 7/7 bombers were associated with the same

1. Two notorious extremist Islamic clerics who lived in the UK at the time.
2. The *Observer*, 26 May 2013.

youth club – the Hamara Youth Access Point. All the Glasgow Airport bombers had reported links with a particular Islamic sect. The additional point is that they all acted in consort with others. Not alone.

Reports also suggest that, at one time or another, extremist internet chat rooms and videos had influenced the members of all three groups. As an MP I took a tough line on 'hate speech' videos and such incitement on the internet; I argued that where this could be deemed to be beyond the law, the videos should be banned and those responsible made to face the legal consequences of their actions.

The undertaking of jihadist training abroad for terrorist missions at home, was the last common feature in most British Islamist terror. It's almost certain that three out of the four 7/7 bombers had training abroad; it is fact that, in 2010, Michael Adebolajo was arrested in Kenya when on his way to Somalia to seek jihadi training with al-Shabaab, the al-Qaeda-linked group. The ring-leader of the failed 21 July 2005 bombers, Muktar Ibrahim, went to Sudan in 2003, and is thought to have been in Pakistan for training at the same time as Khan and Tanweer, the 7/7 bombers. If terrorists want to go abroad to learn to kill and maim at home, then the tariffs of justice for being caught so doing should be more severe than they are at present.

Which brings me to the issue of where the terrorists get their training and how something can be done about it. Pakistan comes in for frequent criticism in this regard, and I believe there is a need for a sense of proportion. The Federally Administered Tribal Areas of North West Pakistan (FATA), and the far reaches of Khyber Pakhtunkhwa province – both in north-west Pakistan – are often perceived to be safe havens for terrorist training and terrorist camps. However, false impressions can be created about this. Consider these comments from one of Pakistan's national newspapers, *The News*, from early December 2013. It concerns speculation about where, in Pakistan, the newly appointed leader of the Pakistan Taliban (TTP), Mullah Fazlullah, may have been hiding out:

> The fugitive ameer of the Tehrik-e-Taliban Pakistan has decided to use Dir district of Khyber Pakhtunkhwa province as the headquarters of his terrorist outfit instead of North Wa-

ziristan which has been declared insecure by his aides due to the growing intensity of the CIA-run drone attacks.[1]

The main political conclusion generally drawn by Pakistan's international critics from such commentary is that 'Pakistan must do better in the war on terror'; as if it were only a matter of sending a small army platoon, in jeeps, to the district of Khyber Pakhtunkhwa province, and the arrest of the fugitive leader would follow. In this regard some comparisons may be useful.

A succession of British governments fought the terror campaign of the IRA in Northern Ireland for almost 30 years; during that time the biggest political miscalculation made by the British government was the introduction of internment – imprisonment without trial. Catholic neighbourhoods, all over the towns and cities of Northern Ireland, were subjected to dawn raids and people arrested and thrown in jail with no charges, no trial and often for lengthy periods of time. The move drove thousands of young Catholics into the arms of the IRA. Yet even with such draconian legal measures at their disposal, the British failed to subjugate the organisation's leadership and, in the end, had to seek a political solution to 'the Troubles' in a negotiated settlement.

If we add some geographical considerations to these observations, then the possibility of Pakistan 'doing better in the war on terror' can perhaps begin to be seen with a greater sense of proportion. The area of Northern Ireland is approximately 14,000 square kilometres, much of it urban landscapes. The combined area of the FATA and Khyber Pakhtunkhwa province in north-west Pakistan happens to come to a round figure of almost 100,000 square kilometres – much of it mountain fastnesses. Things are often not quite what they seem to be, when seen through the eyes of Western commentators, delivering conventional wisdoms from afar. However that is not to say that more should not have been done in anti-terrorist operations in those areas before now.

In that context let us consider what the former US Secretary of State, Robert McNamara, regarded as 'the blood price' – in his case, he was referring to the willingness of the British to join their American allies in the Vietnam war, and take casualties in their tens

1. *The News*, 6 December 2013.

of thousands, as proof of their commitment to the US/UK 'special relationship'.[1] In those times, to his eternal credit Harold Wilson, the British Prime Minister, told McNamara the answer to his 'blood price' question was 'No'. However, were the same question to be repeated by the American media commentators about Pakistan and the 'war on terror', they would have to conclude that Pakistan has paid the 'blood price' of commitment tens of thousands of times over. In fact, after the dead of Afghanistan and Iraq are counted, it is Pakistan that is next in line in the scales of 'blood price' sacrifice.

In an article written in the *New York Review of Books*, ten years after 9/11, the Pakistani writer, Mohsin Hamid, put it this way:

> The past decade has been devastating for Pakistan. The country's annual death toll from terrorist attacks rose from 164 in 2003 to 3,318 in 2009, a level exceeding the number of Americans killed on September 11. Some 35,000 Pakistanis, including 3,500 members of security forces, have died in terror and counter-terror violence. Millions more have been displaced by fighting.
>
> Similarly, until a few years ago, there had never been a suicide bombing in Lahore. Now one occurs every three or four months. The Pakistani government puts direct and indirect economic losses from terrorism over the last ten years at $68 billion.[2]

The figures quoted here by Hamid mean that, on average, in the ten years after 9/11, Pakistan experienced the equivalent of the 9/11 attacks in deaths from terrorism, counter-terrorism and sectarian violence every year of that decade. According to Pakistani figures, the death toll by 2013 had reached 50,000.[3] So before Western journalists and critics of Pakistan demand more sacrifice, perhaps they should count the 'blood price' which has already been paid.

1. Robin Cook, *The Point of Departure*, Simon & Schuster, 2003.
2. Mohsin Hamid, 'Why they always get Pakistan wrong', *New York Review of Books*, 29 September 2011.
3. Army Intelligence reports submitted to the Supreme Court of Pakistan on 26 March 2013.

Today in the global media it is now commonplace for commentary about terrorist events to automatically link the idea of terrorist outrages with Islam. It is perhaps worthy to note that this was not always the case. Far from it. In other times, it was 'the Irish', as a whole, who faced those pointed fingers. That started as far back as the mid-nineteenth century.

In 1867 three members of the Fenian Brotherhood – the Irish organisation then campaigning to get the British colonialists out of Ireland – blew a hole in the wall of London's Clerkenwell Prison, in an attempt to free some of their comrades held there. The 500 pounds of gunpowder they used also wreaked devastation in the neighbouring slums – six people there died, including a child of seven and a 67-year-old grandmother. Only one MP spoke out against the public and media hysteria, William Gladstone, who, a year later would become Britain's Prime Minister. He said it was necessary to look behind the violence to find out why Irishmen felt driven to violence against England. He drew the conclusion that it was religious oppression and the Crown's occupation of Ireland that drove this form of Irish nihilism. That political conviction stayed with Gladstone all his political life, as his several attempts to promote Irish Home Rule bills in the British Parliament confirm. In 1973, during what would become the longest terror campaign in British history, the historical descendants of the Fenian Brotherhood, the IRA, struck on the British mainland. They planted a bomb at the Old Bailey in London. That started a new twentieth-century wave of finger-pointing about 'the Irish' and 'terrorism'.

Clerkenwell illustrates that terrorism in Britain has long predated Woolwich, the Glasgow airport bombers, 7/7 and 9/11. In sections of the Western media, particularly in the USA, there now is a tendency to overlook history and suggest that 'Islam' and 9/11 was where it all started. In fact terrorism has been with us since the start of time. In the first century AD, the Zealots ran a terror campaign against the Roman occupation of Palestine; their targets were Romans, and anyone who could be defined as collaborators of Rome; their favoured tactic was stabbing to death those so identified in public places, so as to increase the terrifying effect of their deeds.

I have drawn on the examples of Clerkenwell and the Zealots

from the same academic source – Louise Richardson's *What Terrorists Want*, first published in 2006. Richardson argues cogently that if the world's great powers want to combat terrorism, it is necessary to understand it beyond the rhetoric of 'good' combating 'evil'. She identifies the motives of terrorists by what she terms the three 'R's – 'Revenge', 'Renown' and 'Reaction.' She considers the crucial element of revenge in all terrorism as follows:

> The most powerful theme in any conversation with terrorists past or present, leader or follower, religious or secular, left wing or right wing, male or female, young or old, is revenge. It is not the objective severity of the grievance, any more than it is the objective severity of poverty that drives terrorists, but a desire for revenge is ubiquitous among them.[1]

Islamist terror has to be considered in the same light. The point here is that Richardson is offering an academic analysis of terrorism which makes the link between terrorism and revenge for perceived injustice; or to put it another way, according to her analysis, those who persistently deny any link between international foreign policy and terrorism are wrong.

Legions of terrorists have demonstrated the validity of Richardson's second 'R' – Renown. It is highly unusual for the perpetrators of such killings to hang around at the spot where they committed their foul acts. It seems the Woolwich attackers did precisely that to allow themselves to make some sort of statement for their cause, as Adebolajo duly did. That's 'Renown', which confirms that, contrary to the usual description of 'mindless violence', most terrorists have deliberate aims behind their desperate deeds. Recognising the crucial political importance of the 'propaganda of the deed' was central to Osama bin Laden's strategies; in fact you could say that the 9/11 events were a political testimony to that.

Richardson's third 'R' is 'Reaction'. Terrorists seek to provoke reaction to their deeds. They see the strength of the reaction by democratic governments as a reflection of their own power – what they are capable of provoking their enemies to do. They also hold the

1. Richardson, *What Terrorists Want*, p.113.

philosophical view that if there is draconian action taken following their operations, that, in the long run, will expose the hypocrisy of their enemies and become a further impetus for new recruits to join the struggle. There's no dispute now that the Afghanistan and Iraq wars produced an unprecedented explosion in Islamist terrorism. It wasn't 9/11 that changed the world as George W. Bush would have it; it was America's reaction to it that changed the world.

The wars in Afghanistan and Iraq, as I have already noted, were based on the disastrous misconception held by most of the intelligence strategists of the American state that there is a military solution for terrorism, which is the so-called 'war on terror'. In more recent times, confirmation that these theories still hold sway is the evolution of drone warfare. When Obama announced in his 2008 election campaign that there would be 'No more Guantanamos', it was difficult to imagine then that not only would there be no closure of the notorious detention centre, but that he would continue Bush's 'war on terror' by signing off the world's greatest drone kill-list. The available estimates, from organisations like the Bureau of Investigative Journalism at the City University, London, suggest that between 2004 and 2012 some 2,500 to 3,500 people have died in drone attacks in Pakistan. As a result, they estimate that some 900 civilians and some 200 children have been killed in these attacks.

According to a Pew Group opinion poll, drone warfare has resulted in 74% of Pakistanis considering the USA as an enemy. Drone warfare, as the latest attempt to conquer terrorism by military means, allows the political 'war on terrorism' to be postponed at best, or at worst dismissed as no longer necessary. The author Ahmed Rashid wrote in the *Financial Times* that:

> The real tragedy of the war against terrorism, which Mr Obama has merely redefined, and which will continue, is that he has yet to spell out a strategy, a series of steps, to counter and combat the causes of burgeoning militancy in the Islamic world, and increasingly among a small minority of Muslims in Europe.[1]

1. *Financial Times*, 31 April 2013.

The drone programme 'has taken on a life of its own where tactics are driving strategy, rather than the other way round.'[1]

What I am considering here is the drone warfare carried out now for years by the American military, and its British collaborators, on Pakistani territory. I am certain that this breaches international law – including the sovereignty of Pakistan and the laws of engagement enshrined in the Geneva Convention, and the basic right to human life. In that context we have to ask the question, why a huge number of the American public would be in favour of such extra-judicial operations. That, in turn leads me to another question which is why a majority of non-Muslim opinion across the globe seems to be now convinced that 'Islam = Terror'?

There is a paradox in this, because I believe that Islam is the most tolerant and respectful religion in the world. Islam is a religion of peace for all. It places maximum emphasis on preserving human life and abhors killing, equating any assassination of an individual with an attack on all of humanity. Alas, Islam's message of peace is being drowned out by the voices of violence. It is time to recognise that; time to recognise that many in the world see the massacre of innocents by suicide bombers, sectarian killings between Shia and Sunni, and merciless terrorist attacks, all as testimony to their growing belief that violence is inherent in Islam. We don't need to look any further than Malala Yousafzai.

On 9 October 2012, Malala and fifteen of her classmates were packed into a school bus taking them to the Khushal Girls High School, in Mingora, in the north-west of Pakistan. Two armed men stopped the bus, demanded that Malala identify herself and then shot her in the head. Two of her classmates were also wounded in the attack. Shortly after the shooting, the Pakistan Taliban (Tehreek-e-Taliban Pakistan or TTP) announced that they had tried to kill Malala because she had become 'a pro-Western symbol of infidels and obscenity'.

The shooting sparked outrage across Pakistan, and later across the world, when the desperate details became known. The then army chief, General Ashfaq Kayani, visited Malala the day after the shooting. He described it as 'a heinous act of terrorism', declaring that

1. A. K. Cronin, 'Why Drones Fail', *Foreign Affairs*, July/August 2013.

the twisted ideology of those involved had 'No respect for the golden words of the Prophet that "the one who is not kind to children is not amongst us".' Thankfully, Malala's story has turned out to be one of courage and recovery rather than a terrible tragedy. I am among those in Pakistan who are enormously proud of what she has achieved – including being a Nobel Peace Prize winner – and what she represents in the struggle against terrorism and the obscurantist merciless leaders of terror in our midst.

The revulsion felt across Pakistan about Malala's shooting produced a new unity in the country and, with it, a new hope. We did not know then that more desperate deeds would confound that unity, and that hope, in the truly terrible events of 16 December, 2014, at the Army Public School in Peshawar, in north-west Pakistan. The final death toll has been established as 152, including 133 schoolchildren. After the attack I visited the local hospital in Peshawar where many of the survivors were being treated. It was horrific to hear their stories of how this slaughter of the innocents was carried out by the Pakistan Taliban. Frankly, it brought tears to my eyes.

As I have already explained, 'Revenge' is the major motive for most terrorist attacks. And indeed the Pakistan Taliban announced that the Army School outrage was perpetrated in revenge against the 2014 Pakistan Army operations in North Waziristan. But 133 children murdered at their school desks represents the murder of humanity itself. It is an affront to the civilisation of mankind, barbarism is its real name. In my view, the killing is a blasphemy against true Islam.

The killings of 16 December must become a watershed in the battle of the people of Pakistan against the terrorists in their midst. We must face up to the fact that the myth of 'good Taliban' and 'bad Taliban' has to be dispelled, once and for all. Thankfully, the All Party Conference held in Pakistan after the Peshawar events agreed on this stance. All terrorism is terrorism. I agree with the commonly stated proverb that you cannot keep snakes in your back garden and expect them only to bite your neighbours.

The mass of the people of Pakistan would support the cry of 'Enough!'. We must not let this moment in history slip from our grasp. The embodiment of the will of the people was demonstrated by the heroism of the teachers at the Army school in Peshawar – many of whom literally perished laying down their lives to try to save their beloved pupils. It is now known that the head teacher of the school, Tahira Qazi, escorted a group of pupils out of the school to the safety of the grounds beyond it, only to return to the school to try to save other children still in peril. For that she paid with her own life.

I remain utterly and completely convinced that there is no lasting solution in a so-called 'war on terror' if it is based only on military action. I remain in favour of negotiating peace when the time is right and the terrorists agree to give up violence. That has to be combined with a 'hearts and minds' campaign by the entire political leadership of Pakistan. It is not possible to shoot an idea out of existence. If there has to be a military challenge to terrorism, there has to be an ideological one also. We should start with education. There should be a mass education programme to build the state education sector across the country, so as to educate our children to challenge the extremism pervading the country's school system. It is an historic failure of successive Pakistani governments to develop a uniform quality state education system, which should be plural and inclusive, and a failure which has brought us to the cusp of extremism which haunts the country. Such failures cannot be tolerated any longer. Education must be transformed.

But that can only be a part of a wholesale revolution in Pakistan which challenges the status quo. Too much Pakistani blood has been spilled and too many Pakistanis have been going to bed hungry for too long. That revolution should include a political leadership which speaks out against the terrorism, in its every form, which haunts Pakistan. In that spirit I will close these reflections on terrorism with reference to the emergence of the medieval militants of ISIS (the Islamic State of Iraq and Syria), or the so-called Islamic State.

ISIS has its antecedents in the Iraq war. It was the sectarian war that followed the invasion of Iraq by America and the UK that was responsible for the creation of al-Qaeda there. AQI (al-Qaeda in Iraq) was led by the bloodthirsty brigand Abu Musab al Zarqawi, who built the organisation on a reign of terror and sectarian war. In 2006 Zarqawi was assassinated in a drone strike by US forces. After 2010 the current leader, Abu Bakr al Baghdadi, united a number of disparate jihadi outfits in Iraq and when these joined Syrian detachments, ISIS, with its pledge of creating an Islamic Caliphate under Sharia law across the whole of the Middle East, was born. When we ask the question 'How did this happen?' we might want to know who funded Baghdadi and his militants. However we might also point the finger of accusation at the West's historic political blunders as having a large share in the sum of culpability.

If the war in Iraq was the foster parents of ISIS it can also be said that the impetus for its growth, from a fledgling terrorist outfit to an army of tens of thousands, was also a product of the doomed policies of American imperialism. After the invasion of Iraq and victory over Saddam, American policy in Iraq delivered the disbanding of the entire upper and middle ranks of the Iraqi army. 'De-Baathistification' was carried out on the grounds that the US strategists thought these ranks were historically bound to the Saddam regime, and could never be relied upon to break those ties. I have had reliable intelligence reports given to me that suggested that significant elements of those dismissed Baathist officers are now directly linked with ISIS and, in effect, form a crucial element of what might be called its military backbone. It is now a matter of public record that al Baghdadi's two deputies served as generals in Saddam's army – Abu Ali Anbari controls ISIS operations in Syria, and Abu Muslim al Turkmani controls ISIS operations in Iraq.[1]

The *Financial Times* has estimated that the US has provided the regime in Iraq with at least $25 billion worth of military hardware. $25 billion can pay for a mountain of tanks, rocket launchers and guns.[2] When ISIS's June offensive moved to take the key cities of northern Iraq, including the key strategic town of Mosul in northern Iraq, the demoralised soldiers of the Iraqi army literally ran away when confronted with the enemy. Some 6,000 ISIS combatants allegedly put to

1. A. K. Cronin, 'ISIS is not a Terrorist Group', *Foreign Affairs*, March/April 2015.
2. This included 140 Abrams tanks at $860 million, 36 fighter jets at $6.5 billion, as well as additional billions on a huge stockpile of weapons, armoured vehicles, fleets of Humvees and a vast quantity of ammunition. *Financial Times*, 2 October 2014.

flight tens of thousands of Iraqi soldiers, whose generals were the first to lead the retreat. As a result, part of the mountain of military hardware donated to the Iraqi forces fell into ISIS's hands. The victories to follow and territory captured bequeathed more and more weaponry to the rapidly expanding 'Caliphate' of ISIS. In mid-2014 the siege of the Syrian town of Kobane, on the Turkish border, was perpetrated by ISIS using American armoured vehicles, tanks and weapons that were the plunder of war. I think that it would be difficult to find a more ironical outcome for America's arming of the Iraqi military – ISIS winning battles firing American bullets from American guns and moving American armoury to the front in American trucks and transporters.

It is difficult, at the time of writing, to estimate what territory ISIS holds now and how many troops it has. There are a variety of estimates. It has captured around a third of the territory of Iraq and a quarter or more of Syria.[1] Patrick Cockburn, the well-respected journalist who writes on the Middle East, estimated in August 2014 that ISIS-held territory was greater, in area, than the United Kingdom, and under its thrall were more than 6 million people – more than the population of Scotland or Ireland.[2] Most estimates of the numbers of ISIS fighters are estimated consistently at around 20 to 30,000 troops.

Given this, there can be no underestimation of the dangers that the emergence of ISIS represents. They have ideas – the restoration of the ideals of a Caliphate under Sharia law. They have organisation – testified by their troop numbers, territories and towns held. And they have money. In the middle of 2014, ISIS plundered the equivalent of millions of dollars from banks in towns it took in its runaway expansion. But significantly, beyond that, it now has constant revenue from oil sales from the dozen or so oilfields under its control. According to most reports I have read, that amounts to an income of at least $1 million a day – and this is without doubt a conservative estimate. Where once the Afghan Taliban depended on the trade in heroin for sustaining its empire, so the new Taliban, ISIS, needs oil money.

By August 2014 there was considerable speculation about the possibility of ISIS taking Baghdad. It was predicted there would be

1. *Financial Times*, 6 January 2015.
2. Patrick Cockburn, 'ISIS consolidates', *London Review of Books*, 21 August 2014.

an uprising of ISIS cells in the Sunni areas of the capital to join forces with ISIS troops marching on the city. After all, at that time ISIS had taken and held the city of Falluja, a mere hour and half's drive west of Baghdad. But instead, ISIS moved to take the border town of Kobane, to build a front between there and its capital, Raqqa, probably for a march on the major Syrian town of Aleppo. At the time, the American Secretary of State John Kerry implied in his statements that it was not really a question of '*if*' ISIS would take Kobane but '*when*'. But the conquest was never delivered.

I believe that there will be significant military defeats for ISIS to come. But I also think that, in time, new factors will emerge to prevent ISIS fulfilling its Caliphate predictions. ISIS, although remaining a huge danger for a considerable time to come, will meet the same fate as all similar fundamentalist terrorisms. They will lose the people who temporarily offered them succour and support. Modern history suggests that jihadis are able to take power, but not capable of holding on to it. The history of the Taliban in Afghanistan demonstrates this. In the fullness of time the same analysis will apply to ISIS. Firstly, the power of ISIS in the areas it holds is sustained by the sword, wielded with merciless brutality. Sooner or later this means that the Sunni Muslim populations who may have supported ISIS victories when they occurred, will come to oppose them due to the rivers of blood ISIS spills to sustain its rule.

The second factor which will eventually become more significant in the demise of ISIS is economic. The 'Caliphate' will not deliver 'bread, peace and jobs', and in time, ISIS will be confronted with revolt. The picture of the leaders of ISIS as a corps of selfless holy warriors will be destroyed by emerging reality. Eventually they will be smitten by the sword of economic crisis. I think that those commentators who have predicted the coming of the ISIS Caliphate will be proved wrong. I make these remarks now whilst recognising that, given the extent of current ISIS operations there is every possibility that at some stage an ISIS-linked outfit of some description will appear in Pakistan. These predictions of the eventual demise of ISIS should not, however, be seen as any underestimation of the threat that they pose. ISIS is a more dangerous foe in its current form than al-Qaeda could ever have been. Without any shadow of doubt ISIS represents the post al-Qaeda jihadist threat. There will be horror in plenty to come at their hands.

I have argued that Islamist terror has not just dropped from the sky as a political thunderbolt. It is a response – albeit a horrible and totally misguided response – to perceived grievances. Chief among these is the recognition of the duplicity of the foreign policy of the United States and its allies – a duplicity that has meant there has been an historical failure to deal with the demands for justice for the oppressed Muslim peoples across the world. When the war in Iraq was perpetrated, there was a promise that no effort would be spared in resolving the Palestinian/Israeli conflict in the Middle East. The failure to address that, and other Muslim causes like Kashmir, remains a factor promoting terrorist revenge.

It is right that in the twenty-first century we should aspire to the growth of genuine democracy in the Muslim world. But this ideal can only be enjoined when the rights of the oppressed are recognised and fulfilled by delivering justice as a response to the great Muslim causes of today. A democratic Muslim world, and with it an end to wars and terrorism, can only arrive together with the West deciding to abandon the blunders of its present political imperatives.

Charity Begins at Home – Rajana and Chichawatni 13

'The local people tell me that this is a piece of heaven in Punjab.'

Professor Altaf Rathore, Medical Director,
Rajana Hospital, Toba Tek Singh, August 2011.

I was brought up in the village of Saleempur. We had a small land-holding which gave us a certain security in life. However the one thing which set us apart from the rest in the village was my father living and working in Britain. The money he sent back to Pakistan every month meant that, although we were not well-off by any stretch of the imagination, we had a little bit more than most.

In these circumstances my mother became a benefactor for the poor of the village. First she looked after the tenant farmers and their families who were working for us. She always made sure that if they were in trouble there would be a helping hand. It would not be in huge amounts of rupees, as we did not have that, but if you have nothing 100 rupees – then worth £5.00 – can be a lifesaver.

Then there were those in the village among the poorest – widows who may have had young families, or orphans, living in poverty, after losing their parents – who if they came to our door with an outstretched hand, could be guaranteed that my mother would find something to put in it. We always gave generously to the poor at the Eid celebrations following Ramadan as well. As I grew up, you might say that *Zakat*, or giving to charity and the poor, was a way of life for us in Pakistan.

That tradition stayed with me when I first came to the UK. As I have already explained, I was ekeing out a fairly meagre existence on around £30 a week, in Glasgow; even then, during the month of Ramadan and the Eid festivals I made sure I had saved enough to send money home to the village for charity. It was always this way with me – a certain percentage of my income was given to the poor.

Now, that being an accepted principle, you can see that as my family income began to grow, and as my businesses became more and more successful, so the amount of money I was capable of giving to charity grew in the same proportion. Eventually the amount of money I had to give was much more than the sums needed for charity in the village. So it was then that I started to donate to major charities in Pakistan such as Imran Khan's cancer hospital, the Al Shifa Trust, the Sahara Trust eye hospital in Sialkot, the Edhi Trust and many others. Then a further transformation began to take place when, beyond my own giving, I began to help these charities in Pakistan by raising money for them in Britain.

That is how the process developed – I was able to generate donations of a considerable amount of money from my own businesses, but I also then became quite adept at going to the Pakistani community in the UK and asking key individuals to match the sort of donations I was making myself. So it was that I reached a stage where this combination of circumstances led me to create my own charity.

It began when I met a friend of mine, Mian Kamal ud Din, when I was visiting my home area in Pakistan. I think this was in late 2000, and at that time he was the deputy commissioner for the district of Toba Tek Singh – that's the second highest position in the local government structure in any district of Pakistan. He told me that during his career he had worked in ten different district areas in Punjab, and it was his opinion that Toba Tek Singh was the poorest.

He told me a story about a young student from the local area. In his exams the boy had achieved the highest marks of all students at his grade in Punjab. Mian and some others from the local government offices went to see the family to offer their congratulations and present them with a small commemoration letter for the boy's achievement. It turned out that the boy came from a poor family. His father had a small business selling vegetables from a stall on one of the main roads into Toba Tek Singh. Contrary to Mian's expectations, the father had no aspirations of further education for his son. He told Mian, 'When my son leaves school we will buy a second stall for vegetables and he will work for me. I cannot afford the fees to send the boy to college.' So Mian returned from the boy's house and arranged with a few friends from the business community to pay the boy's college fees and related costs. In our discussion he used this example to argue the case of how a small amount of money raised through charity could completely transform lives.

Mian said that the greatest need in the area was for proper hospital services, as the local health services were chronically poor. The nearest hospitals to Toba Tek Singh were more than fifty miles away, in Faisalabad, or nearer a hundred miles away, in Multan. We decided we were going to build a hospital somewhere in the Toba Tek Singh area. At first we had thought of a smaller dispensary unit with two or three doctors providing free medicines, but after some further deliberation we decided against that and went for the much bigger project. The first task was to find a suitable plot of land on which to erect the building.

The best plot of land was found in Rajana and, as that was central to the whole local area, we started negotiations with the owners to buy it. They wanted three million rupees, which at that time would have been around £25,000. So, in Scotland, I called a meeting of my friends and acquaintances who originally hailed from the Toba Tek Singh area, and explained about the project. There was not a great number of people there, however we raised around £40,000 in that one evening. So I founded my charity the Pakistan International Foundation – which would later become Ucare Foundation – and the project to build the Rajana Foundation Hospital was established. The real work had started.

It was not plain sailing, because for every person who was prepared to support the project by giving money, there were a hundred who argued that it would never happen. They said that it would be impossible to build such a hospital in a backward, rural area in Punjab; that any major building project in Pakistan was likely to descend into a nightmare of chaos. Further, they dismissed the idea, saying that even if by some chance the building project were completed, it would be doomed to failure since it would prove impossible to attract skilled surgeons and doctors to work in this locality. 'You are telling us that you will attract surgeons and gynaecologists to Rajana, in the middle of Punjab, where there is nothing, no proper schools for their children, no proper shops, no recreation facilities – there's nothing, nothing except never-ending poverty,' the sceptics moaned.

My argument was that if we could provide good wages and good accommodation, then we would get doctors to come. So, in 2001, we bought the land for the agreed terms. Five years later, the gleaming new Rajana Foundation Hospital was opened.

However to get to that point, major challenges confronted us. Not the least of these was the money that had to be raised. In the end I think the building project cost nearly £500,000. I raised the money mainly through approaching wealthy Pakistanis in the UK; I have found over the years that if you have a good cause and you are asking people to support it by giving money, they can become remarkably generous. I would go to potential donors and say, 'I am only asking you for your money. You don't need to do anything else. I will take responsibility for what else has to be done, all I need is your money.' Then I'd put my hand out, so to speak, and they often responded in thousands of pounds. So a couple of years of this kind of hard sell raised the initial funds.

Of course, the original sceptics who doubted that the project could be completed had a point; it is difficult in Pakistan to get major building projects completed to specification, and on schedule. Put it this way – for the contractor there is always the temptation to put less cement and more sand in the mixture and this, on a grand scale, can be a recipe for disaster. We overcame these difficulties by persuading my brother-in-law, Riaz Ullah, to become the project manager for the Pakistan Foundation Hospital in Rajana. He spent day and night on the project until the hospital was completed. I cannot give him enough praise for his heroic efforts over such a sustained period.

With the hospital completed, we had to find the doctors and all the other highly skilled medical personnel needed. In a way this would become the most difficult task of all. When we started to search for staff they didn't come. And, eventually, when they did come, it became a process of giving them everything they asked for.

They wanted good salaries; they got good salaries. They wanted doctors' residences; they got doctors' residences. They wanted nurses' residences; they got nurses' residences. They wanted a mosque in the hospital grounds; they got one. They wanted a dedicated imam; they got a dedicated imam. These negotiations were tough. It was almost as if in every contract there were personal conditions that had to be met before an agreement could be struck. In the end they came; they came to Rajana. So it was that in February 2006, Pervez Elehi, the Chief Minister of Punjab, cut the ribbon on the new Rajana Foundation Hospital. This was some five years after that very first meeting with Mia Kamal ud Din.

We had serious problems in the months which followed the official opening of Rajana's doors. 'Mr Sarwar, this is a hospital without patients,' Professor Altaf Rathore, Rajana's medical director, told me when I was on a visit. He was right. The reception area with its spacious halls and adjoining rooms were like a ghost ship drifting in the fog. Only the occasional sound of footfalls on the marble floors or the scraping of a chair being moved broke the eerie silence.

This was clearly not the expectation we had of the locals' response when the whole project had been conceived. So we had to establish an inquiry to find out what was going on. The results were surprising. The surveys we carried out in the surrounding villages all reached the same conclusions. Local people knew about the hospital, but they thought that such a large, gleaming building could not possibly be for the likes of them. They thought it had been built by the MP, Mohammad Sarwar, to treat rich folks in Pakistan and also those visiting from Europe.

These impressions were also being given an additional weight by a campaign being run by the private doctors in the area. Quite simply, they saw the arrival of Rajana as a direct threat to their livelihoods – patients would go to the hospital for free treatment rather than go to them for treatment that they would have to pay for. So the local private doctors were only too keen to perpetrate the myth that Rajana was really only for the rich – they told everyone the treatment fees were colossal. You can imagine how I felt – five years of all-consuming effort to get this hospital up and running, and now the desperate poor in my own home area were driving past the gates of Rajana in their donkey carts or rust-rattling trucks, thinking: 'Nice hospital, beautiful building, but not for the likes of us'.

We decided we would use word of mouth reports from the few patients we were treating, backed up by a small-scale publicity campaign. We had established the hospital to be free for the poor, including their drug treatments, but those who could afford to pay would pay half the costs of seeing a private doctor or going to a private hospital. We had also established that Rajana would provide a high-quality gynaecological service, as a major core element in our hospital's contribution to local health care. This was because childbirth complications and mortality rates in the area were horrendous, since local specialist pre-natal and ante-natal care was practically non-existent; at that time the only access to such services involved travel to hospitals a day's return journey away. So we decided to target, and prioritise, pregnant women in the surrounding villages.

For a period our doctors and administrators literally got in their cars and went to knock on doors and invite families who were expecting the arrival of a baby to come to our hospital. When they came and their babies were born, we did not charge them but in return asked them to tell their families about their treatment. Previously we had quite a substantial leaflet campaign to publicise the coming of the hospital, but we underestimated the scale of illiteracy in rural Pakistan, because clearly the word had not got through to those who needed to know most. So now we relied almost exclusively on this word of mouth campaign. In time that had its desired effect.

Of course, looking back, there was no need for the mild panic sweeping through the leadership of Rajana. In 2005 we had 11 babies born at Rajana. In 2006 there was a leap in that figure to 561. By 2010, however, we had established the hospital as a trusted provider of gynaecological care, and 1,785 babies were born in Rajana. That 2010 figure remains a high point, but the number of babies born has stabilised at around 1,600 each year.

In July 2011, the Kashif family had their triplets delivered in Rajana. In some ways their story is typical. Nargis Kashif had fertility treatment at Rajana and fell pregnant with triplets. Her progress was monitored and the pregnancy seemed to be going normally. Then complications developed, and Nargis became an emergency admission and had to give birth through an emergency Caesarean operation.

All three babies were fine, and in time the mother made a complete recovery. It is true to say that had Rajana Foundation Hospital not been built, the results for the Kashif family could have been very, very different. Mohammad Kashif told me the hospital was a gift from Allah, and that he didn't have the words to convey the gratitude he felt towards the hospital and its staff. I heard of the Kashif family story when visiting the hospital not long after the babies were born – two girls and a boy, laid out side by side in their small cots in the nursery. It's when you see such things that all the efforts made to get the project delivered, all the tribulations, fade into insignificance.

There are no empty corridors in Rajana nowadays. In fact they are teeming with the anxious and afflicted of the district, desperately seeking help and reassurance for a whole range of conditions and illnesses. In 2005 the number of out-patients coming to Rajana that year reached only 1,300. The latest outpatient total is just over 68,000. All the myths we had to hear about the hospital in its beginnings have been shattered.

My charity work in Pakistan has made me more aware of the fact that those who are well off in the UK take so much for granted. There is a truly national health service, and for the most part people are not haunted by the need to find money to pay for drugs and medicines which may keep them alive. Not so in rural Pakistan. There, in the countryside areas of Toba Tek Singh, people are haunted by the spectre of diseases like tuberculosis and hepatitis.

Two years ago, Mohammad Sharif, who comes from one of the villages near Rajana, was in that situation – stricken with tuberculosis but too poor to pay. Rajana's free tuberculosis programme saved his life. When he eventually reached the doors of the hospital, the 70-year-old could not have weighed much more than eight stone or 60 kilos, and had an immediately identifiable rasping cough. His nine months drugs prescription and monthly monitoring in our TB clinic cured him. When I last saw him he had put on nearly two stones and was back working in the fields.

His story is only one of three hundred or so tuberculosis patients who have been successfully treated by the programme, in the last two years in the clinic run by Dr Mian Zeeshan – one of Rajana's brightest and most dedicated young doctors. But let me return to the fact that the well-off in Scotland take much for granted. The drugs for Mohammad Sharif's life-saving treatment cost the Rajana Hospital about 15,000 rupees. In our money that's about £100. We would never think of holding back on paying £100 in a life and death situation. Yet the stark reality for Mohammad Sharif is that if it was not for the Rajana Foundation Hospital he would be dead.

It costs around £25,000 each year to run Rajana's TB programme, or three million rupees in Pakistani money. The analyser for blood testing in the laboratory in the hospital, is currently in need of renewal. This will cost maybe double the money required for the TB programme. These constant capital and revenue costs are clear evidence that we cannot always just rely on the generosity of others to keep Rajana going.

The reason we have to think on these lines is that it seems there is one certainty in charity work – one commitment leads to another. It was the summer of 2007 when an old friend of mine turned up at Rajana. It was Rai Hassan Nawaz, who was then the mayor of Sahiwal, one of the major towns in the area. What he told me was surprising. He said that large numbers of people from his own city, and the neighbouring town of Chichawatni, were going from their home areas and travelling fifty miles to get to Rajana for hospital treatment. He told me that he had begun a project to build a hospital in one of the poorest areas of Chichawatni, and it was about three quarters finished. He promised he would sign over the title deeds to Ucare for the substantial property where the partly completed hospital stood. But there was one condition – Ucare – my own Foundation – would take over the project to complete the construction and then run the new hospital.

This presented me with a massive dilemma. At that stage the Rajana project was under control and beginning to expand in a big way, so I didn't want to undertake huge new obligations which might jeopardise the great steps forward that were being made there. On top of this, I had not long since completed making a major investment in time, money and effort to support a huge project in Azad Kashmir, for the victims of the terrible earthquake of 2005.

So there was not a lot of money in the charity coffers to take on the Chichawatni project immediately. In addition, given that half a million pounds had been raised for the earthquake victims, where was I going to get more funds for this if we decided to go ahead? Especially as I have always had the view that you cannot go back to the same people time and again asking for more and more donations.

The Ucare board of management was now split. The main arguments against making a commitment were that we had enough responsibilities meantime, and wasn't it the case that taking on Chichawatni might, in the end, result in damaging Rajana if we could not raise enough funds to develop both. It was also said that when I retired from politics, the assumptions that I was making about the flow of funds to the charity might be over-optimistic, as I might not be able to raise as much money when I was not an MP.

On the other hand my own experience had always been to take calculated risks to expand my business when opportunities presented themselves; I argued that I might still have been running a couple of shops in Maryhill and Pollokshields in Glasgow instead of creating a warehouse empire worth hundreds of millions, if I had not been prepared to take calculated risks. I also had a hunch that since Chichawatni was new territory for Ucare, there would be money to be got from people there who had never been asked to make commitments to any project in their own area, before now.

Frankly, I was also attracted to the idea of taking on the challenge of Chichawatni because it would mean that Ucare would not just have projects that would be identified only with my home area in Punjab. In the end we came down on the side of taking the gamble, and signed up for the development of the Rai Hassan Nawaz Foundation Hospital in Chichawatni.

Of course, following on from the development of Rajana, we now had the experience to proceed reasonably confidently with the Chichawatni development. The town and its hinterland probably encompass about two million people, so at least we had few fears of not being able to build a patient base when the construction work was completed. The money was raised – including sizeable donations raised in the local area – the construction was completed, and then came the final task of recruiting the staff.

I had not expected that this would prove as onerous a task for Chichawatni as it had been for Rajana, since there were more facilities in the town to attract people and it was not as isolated as Rajana. However, I had not taken account of a relatively new variable in these matters – the Gulf. Doctors from Pakistan were now on the radar of major medical facilities in the Gulf States who were able to offer quadrupled salaries and all sorts of other benefits in the blink of an eye.

The knock-on effect of this was that, as the best doctors based in Pakistan's main cities like Karachi, Lahore and Rawalpindi left for Dubai and Abu Dhabi and the like, their posts were being filled by others not as high up the medical pecking-order in Pakistan. That meant that when you reached the end of this particular 'production line', we still struggled to get doctors for the Foundation Hospital in Chichawatni. I might note here that, in our first years, after we had finally organised the staff complement for Chichawatni, one of our biggest crises there was precipitated by the departure for the Middle East of Chichawatni's medical director. In one blow we lost the medical director of the hospital and his wife, who was also our head of gynaecological services. We managed to recruit replacements for them, but it was not easy to fill two such high-profile posts.

The Rai Hassan Nawaz Foundation Hospital at Chichawatni was officially opened in January 2009. The new medical director at the hospital, Dr Amir Bashir, says blithely that he reckons our treatments since then may have saved 100,000 lives. Now, any day of the week if you go to Chichawatni's reception hall, you will be immediately impressed by the sheer numbers of patients waiting for the doctors at the different clinics there. The costs to complete and set up the Chichawatni project were probably in the region of 60 million rupees, which isn't far from half a million pounds in our money. The latest figures show that in an average year we are treating 65,000 out-patients at Chichawatni, and delivering almost 750 babies in the hospital. A precious advance for the lives of local people.

If you had told me in 2000 that some ten years later, not only would there be one hospital but two, and significantly more than 150,000 patients using them, I would have said that maybe you should be seeing a doctor! The thought of raising the best part of two million pounds, when all these new ventures were being contemplated, would have been beyond my wildest dreams.

So from what were two vacant lots some fifteen years ago, Ucare Foundation now has two state-of-the-art hospitals which, according to the latest figures, together are treating 180,000 patients of all types a year. Not bad.

The Rajana and Chichawatni projects taught me a lot which has stood me in good stead with other ventures. Among the most important things I learned is that, if you have commitment, determination and dedication then, somehow or other, there will be someone who comes forward to help you. This has convinced me that, within reason, it is necessary always to be prepared to take risks. It is rare to achieve great things without being bold.

Another thing learned from business that was underlined in the hospital experience was the importance of monitoring. In business, on a weekly basis, you have to check sales against costs, income against expenditure, margins, product lines and their popularity, and the possibilities of theft and fraud, among other things. I introduced that mode of operation to the work of the hospitals, combined with quarterly visits by me to the projects in Pakistan. Attention to details is crucial to success in such enterprises.

So is the shopfloor. I have learned almost as much about both hospitals by talking regularly with the gardeners, the street sweepers and the cleaners, on my hospital visits, as I have from all the hours-long meetings with the management staff, notwithstanding their great dedication. That led me to make ward visits on my own to talk to the patients. I feel we've made a lot of improvements in the way things are done because I went to bedsides and said: 'Hello I'm the Chairman of the Hospital Board, how are you? Are you being treated well?'

There's now a pleasing permanence about both hospital projects. I believe they stand in bricks and mortar as testimony to my own commitment to help the poor and give something back to the part of Pakistan where I was brought up and educated. The success of the hospitals evokes another great tribute. It is to the dedicated staff of doctors, nurses, and ancillary staff who work there. Without their inspiring, dedicated commitment we could never have achieved what we have. To every one of them I owe an enormous debt of gratitude.

The other two great challenges that the Ucare Foundation has faced, in a way were much more testing. They were less about a grand long term mission to provide medical care to save lives and more about confronting tears, blood, and death – the aftermath of the 2005 Earthquake and the 2010 Floods.

Earthquakes and Floods 14

'Mohammad Yaqub says when it happened, he saw the mountain coming down in one rolling wave. At the crest of it, there were houses – hundreds of them – being swept away to the sound of screams and wailing.'
Daily Record, 30 September 2006.

'Mohammad Hanif remembers that it was about one o'clock in the morning when he was awakened by the loudspeaker from the local mosque . . . at first he thought it was the first Call to Prayer of the day. But . . . the imam wasn't chanting his usual message about the greatness of God. Instead he was desperately demanding that everyone in the village should make a run for it. The floods were coming.'
Daily Record, 11 August 2011.

The worst earthquake in the history of Pakistan took place on 8 October 2005. It struck at precisely eight minutes to nine on a Saturday morning. Its epicentre was in the far north of Pakistan, around the town of Muzaffarabad, in the mountainous Azad Kashmir province, and around the town of Mansehra, in Khyber Pakhtunkhwa province.

I became aware of the tragedy when the first reports were posted on the BBC's Online service. The headlines were: 'Hundreds die in South Asia quake. Pakistan says more than a thousand people may have died in a powerful earthquake that also hit India and Afghanistan.'

Of course, in time, history told a different tale. India had some destruction in Kashmir on the Indian side of the Line of Control, the line dividing Azad Kashmir in Pakistan and Occupied Kashmir on the Indian side. By comparison, Afghanistan was almost unaffected.

However, the magnitude and extent of the devastation in Pakistan was almost unimaginable. About two weeks after the day of the disaster I remember being flown over the earthquake area in a helicopter, put at my disposal by the good offices of the then prime minister, Shaukat Aziz. I sat in the helicopter with tears in my eyes, totally shocked by the magnitude of the devastation and the plight of the millions whose lives had been ruined. This had been a tsunami of the mountains, and its power took more than 70,000 lives, literally destroying almost everything in its path, over an area which was the size of Switzerland.

The first Early Recovery Plan produced by the government's Earthquake Reconstruction and Rehabilitation Authority (ERRA) had all the headline numbers of the earthquake's toll. It stated that the number of deaths had reached 73,338, with another 69,400 seriously injured and more than 3.3 million people left homeless.

A later ERRA report gave further clarification of the scale of the disaster. The death-toll stayed the same, but the numbers suffering serious injury reached 128,000; 600,000 houses were destroyed, 5,000 schools, and 2,400 km of roads made impassable.

The people of Scotland did not look the other way when confronted with the challenge created by these events. As soon as I heard what had happened I was on the phone to my team at the Ucare Foundation and my friends at the Islamic Centre – the charity run by Glasgow Central Mosque. We had an emergency meeting that Saturday night in the Mosque, and immediately agreed on a plan of action, including a mass fundraising campaign based on the mosques in Glasgow and across central Scotland.

I was also in touch with the Reverend Neil Galbraith and Mohammad Tufail Shaheen of Glasgow the Caring City charity, to ask for their help and, in turn, World Emergency Relief (WER), an organisation with which the Caring City had a partnership. In a matter of weeks our efforts with the Caring City and WER meant we had filled two cargo planes with tents and blankets, cooking materials, medicines, clothing of all types, and wellington boots and shoes, in their hundreds. Most of the goods were sourced through the Caring City. WER organised the transport, while Ucare and the Central Mosque guaranteed the funds to pay for that.

When news of the earthquake broke, Qaiser Khan left his home in Glasgow to go to Pakistan to help in the search for his extended family members, who were caught up in the horror. Qaiser originally comes from the Azad Kashmir area. He was born and raised there. He left with his family when he was thirteen years old to come to the UK. He reached Pakistan scarcely more than a day after the earthquake, and managed to get to Muzaffarabad by hitching a lift in an army convoy. He then joined the teams working in the mountains of rubble, in the university area in the town. He was actually looking for his niece Sara, who was studying at the university. Four agonising days later, Qaiser was working with the team that pulled her dead body from the rubble. Out of the hundred and ten girls who lived in Sara's university halls of residence, only ten survived. They were the ones who had classes to go to that morning, so they left the halls of residence early; like Sara, those who didn't have classes to attend that morning and were still in the halls of residence when the earthquake struck, perished.

The Glasgow link to the earthquake zone was strengthened on the ground by the arrival of Ghulam Rabbani, Mohammad Sharif, Mohammad Saleem and Shamim Ahmad, all from the Islamic Centre in the city; working with the Ucare Foundation they created what they called the Glasgow Team. Led by the tireless Ghulam Rabbani, they worked miracles. In one call home they told us of the desperate need for assistance with the collapse of the phone system – all the normal phone infrastructure had been destroyed. So it was that some days after the earthquake I was in touch with a friend, Adnan Jamil, one of British Telecom's senior officers, to ask him if BT could help. Adnan and the Scottish Regional head of BT at that time, Paul Faulkner, and I had a dinner at the House of Commons that week. They were both extremely sympathetic and confident about a deal.

In a couple of days Paul came back to me and told me BT would provide, and set up, four satellites for free, which would create 200 separate lines. The only condition would be a guarantee for the security of their engineers. They wanted to send two of their security people to Pakistan to check out the situation. In due course, they went to Islamabad and I arranged for them to meet with the city's police chiefs. The BT people came home satisfied that there would be police or army protection guaranteed for their engineers, and gave the project the go-ahead. There were smiles all round, but also a recognition that our problems on this project were just beginning.

By the time I got to Pakistan, the BT engineers were already in Islamabad. Jamil was their team leader. When I met him I could tell by the look on his face that there were problems – all the telecommunications equipment had failed to get Customs clearance. Everything was impounded at the airport, waiting for clearance. I spoke with the Chief of Customs and the Minister responsible and told them that all these goods had been donated for relief work for the earthquake. We managed to get the matter resolved there and then. There were always benefits to being Britain's first Muslim MP when the bureaucracy of government in Pakistan decided to say 'No'.

However it appeared to be one step forward, two steps back – it transpired that there were problems with the Army and the new head of the the Earthquake Reconstruction and Rehabilitation Authority. Myself and the two MPs, Sadiq Khan and Khalid Mahmood, who were with me on the first fact-finding mission, went to see the retired General who had been put in charge of ERRA. Surprisingly he struck an attitude, no matter what issue we raised, of what seemed to be, 'The answer is No. What is the question?' I put it to him that we had come to Pakistan to help, with considerable resources made possible from the British government and money we had raised by our own efforts. I was disappointed with his attitude and told him we had not travelled to Pakistan to listen to sermons from him or anyone else. Then he became a bit more polite: 'Perhaps we need lessons in diplomacy,' was his reply. So we left the meeting still rather downcast, but equally resolved to find a way round the obstacle that the General seemed to present, rather than trying to go through him by way of a direct challenge to his authority.

By pure chance, the answer came with a call from the Prime Minister's office. On our arrival, Sadiq, Khalid and I had called to let his office know that we were in Islamabad and now here was the offer of a meeting to discuss British aid for the victims of the earthquake. When we went to his office the next morning, Shaukat Aziz welcomed us like long-lost brothers. He asked immediately if we could do anything to help with Pakistan's desperate need for helicopters to go the earthquake zone. He said that one of the greatest logistical problems about getting aid to the people who needed it, was how to do that when, in the worst affected areas, many roads and bridges had been destroyed. Not only that, he then asked if the British could help with the immediate costs of fuel for helicopters. We pledged to raise this with the British government ministers on our return.

When we raised the problems we were having with the BT satellites he assured us that he would make the necessary arrangements to allow their installation. I recalled that the same man had made promises during the Kriss Donald campaign which he hadn't delivered on, but this time he was as good as his word. Adnan Jamil and his team of engineers got army escorts to Muzaffarabad a day or two later, and the telephone system became a major resource for communications across the earthquake zone; not just for the local people and aid agencies, but also key army personnel as well.

When we returned to London, Sadiq, Khalid and I went first of all to see Hilary Benn who, at that time, was Secretary of State for International Development. He pledged that if we could secure British helicopters to work in Pakistan, as part of the general British relief efforts, he would ensure that he would find the necessary funds for the costs of running the helicopters there. Enter John Reid, at that time, the Minister of Defence, whom I knew exceedingly well. He could not have been more helpful. Once we had outlined the situation he was on the phone displaying his Scottish tenacity and asking someone or other in the chain of command about the possibility of Chinook helicopters, from somewhere, being deployed for relief work in the Pakistan earthquake. And that was how British Army pilots and crew, and four Chinook helicopters, played a vital role in the early weeks after the disaster; hundreds of people stranded in isolated areas were rescued by them and taken to relief centres; tons of emergency supplies were delivered to where they were needed, breaking through the previously near insurmountable obstacle of impassable roads.

The Ucare Foundation and the Central Mosque had raised £600,000 in donations, in what was yet another tremendous effort; this was more evidence to support my opinion that those who can't do themselves will often give enormously generously for others to act on their behalf. We decided to build temporary villages in a number of areas where the need for shelter, as winter advanced, was, by now, truly desperate. We had plans for houses and schools; we had negotiated prices with suppliers of the flat steel sheeting and corrugated tin needed for temporary dwellings; but the question was, where to start. Then, once a location had been identified, the next issue was how we could overcome the logistical challenges of getting the materials to the location and then completing construction.

You could say that the answer to these questions came in the shape of one man, Brigadier Nadeem Sadiq, of the Pakistan Army, who was heavily involved in relief work in the Bagh district, about one hundred miles or four to five hours drive from Islamabad. Bagh, in Azad Kashmir, had been designated by the earthquake authority as one of the four field hubs – along with Batagram, Mansehra and Muzaffarabad – for the organisation of relief. The Glasgow Team had made contact with Nadeem Sadiq at some point in their work, and accordingly the Sarbuland village project was established.

The Team was able to offer assistance for the construction of the dwellings and, more importantly, funding to purchase the materials. Brigadier Sadiq had the personal authority, and the will, to see the village constructed; he also commanded the soldiers to provide additional labour for that. You might say a plan came together when the Glasgow Team's path crossed with the Brigadier's.

Bagh was not the area worst hit by the earthquake – it had some 6,000 displaced persons due to the earthquake compared to 135,000 in Mansehra and 110,000 in Muzaffarabad – but it was the easiest to reach from Islamabad. The Sarbuland village project was to become a model for what would be done later in Mansehra. It provided temporary accommodation, schools and a health centre for some of those in Bagh district who had lost everything, and were equally desperate as any other earthquake victims. The project was led by the ERRA, co-ordinated by the Pakistan Army on the ground, with teams from Glasgow's Central Mosque and the Turkish Red Crescent working on the construction of all the units; funding was provided by Oxfam and the money raised in Scotland.

By the end of the Sarbuland project there were around 200 houses built, plus a primary school, a medical clinic and a training centre. Brigadier Sadiq proved to be an indefatigable organiser for getting materials delivered and providing troops to help speed the construction. However, at the site on a daily basis, Shahid Shigri was a man-mountain of inspiration, always dressed in an all-black *shalwar kameez*. He was a retired Air Commodore from the Pakistan Air Force, and dawn to dusk he seemed to have a limitless supply of energy. He didn't only bark out orders urging people on, he also got his own hands dirty. Shigri was one of the few working on the construction who could hoist a corrugated roofing sheet above his head and walk with it unaided, and held high, to the next house ready for roofing.

In fact it was Shigri's enthusiasm that took us to the next stage of the earthquake project. We had a meeting in a kebab restaurant in Islamabad. He asked me how much was left in our funds, and when I told him he exclaimed: 'Good. I spoke with Brigadier Sadiq last week. He is going to set us up with contacts in Mansehra and we can build another village the exact same as Sarbuland over there. We know how to do it, so let's just do it.'

Of course it wasn't that simple. There was much more negotiation involved than Shigri's 'just let's do it!' although it was this type of enthusiasm and directness that fired us up to make a difference. I am proud to mark his enormous contribution in the post-earthquake work in this book, as he died tragically in an accident on the motorway between Islamabad and Lahore some time ago. God rest his soul.

In the discussion in the kebab restaurant, Shigri argued that we could use the design of the school at Sarbuland to create a school-building programme across the earthquake zone. I told them that our funds might not stretch to all that although we would give what we could, depending on what was left if the Mansehra village project came off. The Glasgow Team, along with Shigri, convinced the Pakistan Army, a local Pakistani NGO, and one of the biggest charities in America, USAID, to get together with them and, along with some of the money raised in Glasgow, they completed 25 schools for more than 5,000 pupils all over Azad Kashmir. It would be later, during the flood relief project, that I would realise the true significance of this type of partnership.

The school-building model was also good enough to serve as a template for a hospital ward, and so the National Rural Support Programme (NRSP), along with Unicef, funded, and helped to organise, the building of local clinics in villages which had lost whatever medical facilities they had. New wards were also added to the main health service hospitals in Bagh City and Muzaffarabad. The 'Healing Hands' report goes into great detail about the projects that were undertaken, which is incontestable proof that, working in partnership with others, a pound raised in Scotland can go a long, long way in Pakistan. So can £600,000 for that matter.

About a year after the earthquake, BBC Scotland sent their reporter, Bob Wylie, to Pakistan to make a report on how money raised in Scotland had helped rebuild lives shattered by the earthquake. The films and radio reports were vivid and brought the scale of the tragedy to life, as well as evidence of new hope. So did an article Bob wrote for the *Daily Record* which was published in a two-page spread on 30 September 2006:

> Mohammad Yaqub says when it happened, he saw the mountain coming down in one rolling wave. At the crest of it, there were houses – hundreds of them – being swept away to the sound of screams and wailing. They ran, babes in arms, dragging the older ones by their shirts to get down, down off the hillside, away from this tsunami of the mountains. The Yaqubs are eight in all – Mr and Mrs and six kids. They all survived.
>
> He's a government official and once was well off, with a big house in Muzaffarabad – the biggest town hit by the Pakistani Kashmir earthquake. Now they all live in two tents in a relief camp, one year after the disaster.
>
> The Yaqubs live in Essas camp on the mountainside above the city. It gives you a shake when you see it for the first time. In the city below there's evidence of life getting back to normal. The horns honk in the morning rush hour. Young girls walk in lines going to school and policemen blow their whistles at traffic checkpoints.
>
> Up the hillside, round the last corner, suddenly there's an armada of green and blue and white in front of you. Not sails but tent sheets marked with UN and charity logos. They shimmer in the sun above a sea of brown dust. 'When we had

our house, we had everything,' Yaqub says. 'Now we have nothing, nothing but a fear of the winter coming.'

Today, a year on from the earthquake in October 2005, there are more than 30,000 souls along with the Yaqubs still living in tents in relief camps in Muzaffarabad. Double that number are under canvas, in cities like Mansehra and Balakot. Tents are pitched all over the place among the twisted ruins where once their living-rooms stood.

Beside one stairway – reaching now for the stars – there's a pair of plastic sandals outside what once might have been a front door. On a nearby wall a jacket still hangs on a set of lurching wooden coat pegs.

A team of volunteers from Glasgow's Central Mosque worked day and night to help build temporary homes for the dispossessed. One of the villages is in Sarbuland, near the town of Bagh. There, money from Scotland has taken survivors beyond tents and fear of the winter.

From a distance, Sarbuland village looks like it's made of Lego. Up close in the schoolroom made of steel sheeting topped with a concave roof, the kids are learning English for 'Owl', 'Crow', 'Eagle' and 'Quail'. Most of them have blue tracksuit tops with a saltire breast badge. 'A gift from Scotland' it says below the badge . . .

Towards the end of my journey, I met the prime minister of Azad Kashmir, Sardar Attiq Khan. He told me: 'It is quite remarkable but the Scottish charities were among the first here after the earthquake. Of course we owe a debt of gratitude to them, but please tell Scotland we still need help. So much still needs to be done.'

One year on from the tragedy, the UN Special Representative in Pakistan, Jan Vandemoortele, spoke to the media about the progress made in Pakistan. By that time the relief phase had been completed and the construction phase was fully developed. Vandermoortele made the point that there were still more than 100,000 people living in emergency camps, most of them in tents, which was undeniably unsatisfactory. However, he said that a year after the quake, 350,000 of the 600,000 houses destroyed in the disaster had been rebuilt, which he described as 'pretty good going'. Tellingly, he then offered the opinion that the organisation of Pakistan's response to the earthquake had been more effective than the relief work completed in the countries affected by the South Asian tsunami of December 2004, and the USA's response to Hurricane Katrina since it struck in August 2005.

At the time this assessment was supported by the head of Concern, Dorothy Blane, one of the biggest charities then working in Pakistan. She told the media if the work done in Muzaffarabad was benchmarked against what had been done in New Orleans, then the work in Pakistan would get a higher mark out of ten than the relief efforts in New Orleans. Her views would, in part, be borne out later in group legal actions taken against the USA's Federal Emergency Management Agency, and the New Orleans Police Department, which were sued by victims for their failure to respond effectively to the crisis.

The work done after the earthquake was new territory for Ucare, but we all learned much which would stand us in good stead when the floods came to Pakistan in late July 2010. One of the most practical lessons concerned land ownership. We learned that we needed to be exact about land titles before building anywhere. In the earthquake zone we took it for granted that if we had permission to build from a local council that was sufficient. But later, in one or two areas, we have had legal disputes over who owns the land, and whether compensation is due. In the flood areas, before a brick was laid, we made sure that the agencies that we were working with had established who held the land titles, and so we've had no legal challenges at all after building almost 700 houses. Being more particular about legal issues has paid dividends.

But probably the most important lesson was an understanding of the value of working with others in partnership. We had started in Scotland with that understanding so Ucare worked with the Glasgow Central Mosque and we then had links to all the mosques in Scotland – that's how we were able to raise such substantial amounts of money. That also allowed us to have a division of labour in our efforts, or what I like to call a combination of talents.

We had our point of contact with the Glasgow Team led by Ghulam Rabbani out in Pakistan, which was absolutely essential for accurate information on where money raised in Scotland might be spent in Pakistan; my own efforts were mainly devoted to raising money, as I had the contacts across Scotland and the UK for that; others could actually concentrate on collecting donations in kind, where people couldn't give money but were prepared to offer things. For example, it seemed that Hanif Raja, from Glasgow Central Mosque, must have filled two planeloads with the amount of donations in clothes, shoes, medicines, blankets and all manner of other goods he collected on his own.

We took that understanding of working in partnership to Pakistan when the floods came. As a result we've had highly significant partnerships with the National Rural Support Programme in the provinces of Azad Kashmir, Khyber Pakhtunkhwa and other areas. We've worked with the Pakistan Army and the Pakistan Rangers. We also learned that you have to make links with the administrative bureaucracy at a local level, otherwise officials can become an obstacle. It all works from the bottom up, not the top down. Of course, it is important to have the blessing of top politicians, but it's more important to get the local government administration onside when you want to get something done.

When the floods came we had an organisational structure in central Scotland that was capable of responding. A matter of weeks after the floods, we had raised more than half a million pounds and we had a vital local contact in a major flood area, in the form of Saleem Iqbal. In the early 1980s he had left Pakistan for Scotland, and had spent the best part of fifteen years in Glasgow. Ten years later he returned to his native city of Multan and was running a restaurant chain there which had made him the uncrowned Curry King in Multan, and in the neighbouring city of Bahawalpur. Saleem gave Ucare and the Glasgow Central Mosque charity what might be called an indispensable link for delivering relief aid to the poor of the 2010 floods.

Saleem was actually in Glasgow when news of the floods reached us. He immediately returned to Multan to see what needed to be done. There he made a decisive link with Major General Nadir Zeb, the local army commander there. Together they made a plan to reach the most severely stricken villages with emergency relief. In Glasgow, Saleem's link was to the charity run by the Central Mosque. So while his Glasgow friends were raising money, Saleem was in Pakistan making plans about how it could be spent. By late August 2010, about a month after the floods devastated Pakistan, Ucare and and the Central Mosque had raised an astonishing £750,000 in cash and cheque donations, as well as medical supplies worth millions more.

So in the last week of August I was in the army headquarters in Multan, along with Saleem, and Ghulam Rabbani from the Central Mosque, to make final arrangements for the distribution of emergency aid packs. Ghausabad, an isolated village in the Dera Ghazi Khan district, had been identified as in desperate need, along with one or two others in the surrounding district. For the previous five days and nights the men from the Mosque, along with Saleem, had put together the aid packages, and now there were a dozen lorries filled to the brim with them, ready for delivery. We had kept our side of the bargain; we had raised the money and put the packages together, and now Major General Zeb and his soldiers were about to keep theirs – a military operation to distribute the emergency relief packages to the villagers of Ghausabad. It was to be the first and then others would follow.

The relief packages became known as the 'Glasgow Gift'. And here's what was in them, all put together with some thought, precision and remorseless bargaining with local suppliers to get the best prices:

1 Red plastic bucket with lid;
1 Large cooking pot;
1 Small cooking pot;
1 Frying pan;
6 Cups;
6 Plates;
6 Plastic glasses;
6 Spoons;
6 Knives;

1 Ladle;
1 Serving plate;
1 Bottle of cooking oil;
10 Kilos of flour;
1 Bag of rice;
1 Bag of lentils;
1 Bar of washing soap;
1 Bar of face soap;
1 Bundle of cloth for making shirt and trouser suits;
1 2-litre bottle of water;
1 First aid and medicine pack;
1 Heavy-duty white woven plastic sack;
Salt/Pepper/Sugar/Spices and Garlic.

During our discussions with Major General Zeb, he put what had happened in the floods in context. He told me, as only an army man could, that the mathematics of the floods were truly astonishing. He said that in normal monsoons the rate of flow of water in the entire area usually reached 300,000 cubic metres per second. In 1958 – the year of the last major flood – the rate reached 700,000 cubic metres per second. This time, in the whole of the Dera Ghazi Khan district, the water flows reached more than a million cubic metres per second. A flood that swept all before it. In the entire district this meant that from a total population of nine million people, one third were displaced by the floods. One month on he was still dealing with 100,000 homeless families. 'It's grim, grim and desperate,' the Major General told me.

The next day we all set out from Multan for Ghausabad, in a convoy of army jeeps. About three hours later, after a bone-crunching journey on broken and flooded roads, we reached the village. What confronted us was a scene of biblical proportions. The Army had set up its aid distribution point at the edge of the village. Stretching away from it, in every direction, in orderly queues, were hundreds and hundreds of villagers. One by one they shuffled forward, showed their identification cards to the soldiers at the checkpoint, and collected their goods. This went on all day in the broiling 45°C heat. The men from the Mosque – Ghulam Rabbani, Mohammad Sharif,

Shamim Ahmad, and Mohammad Saleem – stood shoulder to shoulder with the soldiers to assist with the giving out of the parcels. They were all soaked in sweat after ten minutes, and after an hour they had to retreat from the heat into the cool of an air-conditioned tent set up by the army. I have to confess that I only lasted about twenty minutes in the heat.

At the end of the day more than 4,000 families from Ghausabad had received parcels; thousands more were given out by the Army from the lorries packed with parcels which had gone to other places. According to what one Army commander later told Saleem, in total, more than 10,000 packages were distributed. That included the 4,000 packages given out in Ghausabad, and what was distributed elsewhere in three or four other villages like it.

As on so many occasions when I was involved in big events in Pakistan, Bob Wylie was following my footsteps. In Ghausabad he was working on a radio documentary for BBC Scotland, and a news feature for the Scottish *Sun*. Here's what he wrote for the *Sun* – which was published on 13 September 2010 – about that momentous day:

The Feeding of the 4,000 – the Glasgow Gift in the Punjab

Shamim Ahmad is sweating. Big style. No wonder, because this is deep in the Punjab in Pakistan, and it's 45 degrees. That's 120 degrees Fahrenheit in old money. He's part of a team of four from the Central Mosque in Glasgow delivering aid to flood victims.

He's the one charged with humping 10kg bags of flour into red plastic buckets to get them ready for handing out. Hot work. The Glasgow boys have got to a part of the Punjab that other relief agencies haven't reached. They're in Ghausabad, an isolated village three hours drive from the major city of Multan, slap bang in the middle of Pakistan.

The parcels of hope they're about to give out have been paid for by money raised in Glasgow's Central Mosque. £150,000 to be exact. When the ex-Labour MP, Mohammad Sarwar and I, get there thousands of villagers are standing in line, waiting. They spider out in lines in two or three directions from the makeshift distribution centre.

Mr Sarwar and Mr Ahmad make a ceremonial presentation of a bag of flour to the first man in the hunger queue. Although he's no youngster he almost skips away to collect the rest of the gear making up these gifts from Glasgow. It's all in a white plastic sack. When he lifts it you hear the metal plates inside clanking around.

The clanking will echo around the village until late in the day. By then four thousand will have been checked in and checked out by soldiers from the Pakistani army. They are organising the show to make sure everything proceeds in good order. And it does.

A couple of hours into this and I have to pinch myself. This is the deepest Punjab. This is thousands of flood victims. And this is thank you Glasgow. Mind you it has been made possible by a Punjabi curry king, Saleem Iqbal. He was brought up in the Punjab but moved to Glasgow in the 1980s to marry. His wife comes from the city. They raised their family there.

But in 1995 Mr Iqbal came back to Multan. He's now built a chain of restaurants there, and in another city near Multan. He's a burly mover and shaker in these parts who makes things happen. That's exactly what he's done with the people from the Glasgow Central Mosque.

When the floods hit, Mr Iqbal was actually on holiday in Glasgow, at his home in Pollokshields. He rushed back to Multan. There he spoke to Major General Nadir Zeb who was running relief operations in the Multan area. They identified Ghausabad village as one in the most desperate because it had been obliterated by the deluge. But its remoteness meant it hadn't had much help.

Saleem Iqbal phoned his friends from the Mosque in Glasgow. The pay-off came today in Ghausabad. 'We brought twelve lorries of aid here. We haven't slept for four nights getting the packages put together,' he tells me in the blistering sun.

Lieutenant Colonel Majid Manzoor is in charge of the operation in Ghausabad. He says, 'Bob, the Glasgow packages are the best that's ever been delivered to flood victims here. I tell you, the best, no doubt about it.' Talib Hussein agrees. Since the floods hit Ghausabad he's been living in a tent on the levee above the river Indus. There are twelve of them sharing the tent. 'This is a lifeline from Glasgow for my family,' he tells me.

So far so good. After the whole operation on emergency relief was completed, we had given out around 10,000 packages and spent more than £100,000 from the money raised in Glasgow. That still left us with more than £600,000 to spend. We had pledged in meetings in Glasgow that, after the emergency relief operation was finished, we would move to a second stage of building houses in four or five regions in the country, for those who had lost everything in the floods.

So it was that in early September 2010 I found myself in the Pearl Continental Hotel in Lahore with Shah Jamal, who was then the Consul General in Glasgow for the government of Pakistan. Later he moved on to become the Ambassador of Pakistan in Baghdad. We were both sitting in my room wondering what we were going to do to get the £600,000 project to build houses for the desperate in Pakistan started. We knew what we wanted to do, but didn't know how we could do it. As I have said before, often when impasse threatened in this or that charity venture, someone or something turned up.

When I established the hospital projects in the Punjab I always stayed at the Pearl Continental in Lahore. Firstly, the manager there, Irshad Anjum, is a very good friend who is a great supporter of the Ucare Foundation; among many other things they give us discounted rates to stay in the hotel. Secondly, the movers and shakers of the government of Punjab, and of the Army, are often at this or that function in the Pearl Continental, known locally as the PC. So it is often possible, by chance, to engage with people there who can help to get things done.

That day in September Shah Jamal and I had spent until midmorning trying to speak to a number of people by telephone, to see if they could help. We decided to get room service to deliver some coffee, but then changed our minds. Jamal said: 'We've been in the room all morning, let's go down to the ground-floor café and take coffee there for a change of scene.' With the benefit of hindsight it's possible to say that the future of our flood relief programme turned on this simple twist of fate. When we reached the café in the foyer who should be sitting there, in another group of people, but the head of the TV Channel 42, based in Lahore. Mohsin Naqvi has been a friend of mine for many years. In fact, he addresses me in Punjabi, by the familiar, yet endearing, *chacha*, meaning 'uncle'. 'Ah, *chacha*,' he exclaimed, '*Assalam o Aleikum*, what brings you to Lahore?'

I explained that we were there to start a second stage of our charity work for flood victims by building houses for those most seriously affected, and that we did not really know where to start, beyond an understanding that the rural areas in this part of Punjab had been devastated. Naqvi told me that, some days before, as part of their reports on the floods, Channel 42 had filmed in a village near the town of Muzaffargarh: 'The story was about a division of the Pakistan Rangers collecting money from their own men and building nine houses for flood victims with the proceeds, somewhere in that district.'

'How can we get in touch with those people?' I pressed him. He asked me for my room number and said he would phone me in the morning, and with that he hurried away to another meeting. The next morning, around nine o'clock, the phone rang in my hotel room. It was Naqvi. True to form, he said that he'd been in touch with General Mohammad Yaqub, director general of the army unit the Pakistan Rangers, who was in charge of the relief operations for a large part of the southern Punjab. He told me he'd made an appointment for me to go to Yaqub's office, at the headquarters in Lahore, at noon precisely.

I made sure I arrived on the dot for the meeting with the General. These protocols can sometimes be very difficult because you don't know what is expected of you, and how to be quite direct in the discussion without appearing to be demanding. I decided to put my cards on the table, so to speak. I told him I had around £600,000, or 80 million rupees in his money, to spend on building houses for flood victims. He raised an eyebrow. 'A lot of money,' he said, nodding.

I said that, of course, I wanted to spend a large amount of that money to help victims in my native Punjab, but that it was necessary to ensure there were houses built in other areas – in Azad Kashmir and Khyber Pakhtunkhwa in the northern areas, and in Sindh in the south. 'We have built nine houses in a village west of the town of Muzaffargarh,' he explained, 'so why don't you come there with me tomorrow and have a look, and, if you like the houses we can make a plan.'

Early the next morning we went by helicopter to Muzaffargarh. The General had an engagement there to check progress in the flood relief work, in any case. The new houses built by the Rangers were substantial by the standards of Pakistan, with two rooms and an adjoining verandah in between. I told General Yaqub I liked the design. He told me that the nine houses the Rangers had built cost about 150,000 rupees per house. I calculated that with a bit of negotiation here and there and given the numbers we were planning to build, there would be enough money to make a pledge for some 700 houses. That meant we would make a big effort in Punjab and then maybe build around 400 houses in the other provinces – 100 houses in each province.

I know that this might not sound like a great achievement – after all, 700 houses would only give new shelter to that number of families or maybe around five or six thousand people, including relations and children. That number does not seem much when compared to the figures of nine or ten million people made homeless by the floods. That is one way of looking at it. I prefer to say that money collected in Scotland proved to be a salvation for some of the most desperate people stricken by the floods. I don't think that a single family who were given a new house through our efforts would say that they thought what we were doing was insignificant when compared to the general scale of need.

So the next question after General Yaqub showed me the houses, and we discussed costs, was where would we build the relief houses with the money raised in Scotland. Yaqub put me in the hands of Brigadier Abid Saleem, one of his most trusted, reliable adjutants. I had been so affected by the scale of the devastation that I immediately agreed with the Brigadier that, instead of returning to Lahore with the General, I would stay with the Brigadier to determine how and where our money could be spent. The following day he drove me all over the worst flood-hit areas of the southern Punjab.

It remains a fact in Pakistan that the poorest of the poor live in mud houses. So it was relatively easy to identify those in most desperate need, because their mud houses were swept away by the floods and all that remained to be seen in their villages was families living in tents among the rubble of what had once been their homes. That was the sight which confronted me when Brigadier Saleem took me to a village called Garibabad, about two hours away from the town of Muzaffargarh, by army jeep. There were tents everywhere among the detritus of ruined houses.

In a matter of minutes we were besieged by dozens of local people who immediately began to lament about the desperateness of their plight. They were enraged that the Brigadier and I were the first 'dignitaries' to have taken the time to go to the village since the floods struck. No government officials and no local MPs had gone to see what needed to be done. There was no clean water for the village and no medical supplies to help deal with the injured.

I told them immediately that I would do everything in my power to have that remedied in 24 hours. The villagers gave me that sort of look which betrays doubt – 'We've had promises from your type before,' their eyes seemed to say. Money can make things happen, so by spending some of our funds on supplies, the next day the villagers had a tented medical centre and a large bottled water station. With the help of the Brigadier, and the money from Ucare, we managed to arrange that through the director of Rescue 1122, the local emergency services in Muzaffargarh.

After the residents' meeting, Brigadier Saleem then took me to a meeting with the local Pakistan Rangers commander responsible for relief in the Garibabad area, Colonel Ejaz Najaf. He would prove to be totally committed to the task of getting things done for the flood victims. Lt Colonel Mohsin Essan was Colonel Najaf's right-hand man on the ground. In the meeting he said that if we would provide the money for the materials, the Rangers would build 20 houses, renovate and develop the village's damaged primary school, and two mosques, in four weeks. Given the devastation in the village, this seemed to me, at the time, to be bordering on what can only be called the miraculous. Lt Colonel Essan suggested that we could come back after four weeks and see what had been done; then sign up for three hundred houses to be built in the area if all that had been done was satisfactory.

We shook hands on the deal. A matter of days later, after all this had been reported back to our volunteer team in Multan, we all decided to spend the celebration feast day of Eid in Garibabad. The team from the Central Mosque and I put our own money together to provide food for the celebration for all the villagers, gifts for the children and clothing gifts for the women of the village. In actual money terms it did not cost all that much; as I have explained already, one pound can go a long way in Pakistan among the poorest of the poor. Nonetheless, at the ceremony for Eid in part of the primary school which wasn't too badly damaged, as the food and gifts were given out, the affection for us shining in the eyes of the villagers was touching.

Four weeks later, almost to the day, it was 44°C in Garibabad when the Chief Minister of the Punjab province, Shahbaz Sharif arrived. He's the brother of the present Prime Minister Nawaz Sharif. We had been acquainted since the time of his foreign exile after the military coup against his brother's government, led by General Musharraf. Along with members of Ucare and the Glasgow Central Mosque, Shahbaz presented the keys for the twenty new houses that the Rangers had built for flood victims.

Almost a year later, Bob Wylie told the Hanif family's story in an article in the *Daily Record*, when we returned to Garibabad to celebrate the completion of 200 houses there, and 100 houses in two neighbouring areas. Mohammad Hanif, and his wife, from Garibabad, have eight children. Here's their story from the *Daily Record* of 11 August 2011:

Mohammad Hanif remembers that it was about one o'clock in the morning when he was awakened by the loudspeaker from the local mosque. He'd been sleeping, so at first he thought it was the first Call to Prayer of the day. But it was the 30th of July last year and the imam wasn't chanting his usual message about the greatness of God. Instead he was desperately demanding that everyone in the village should make a run for it. The floods were coming.

There are eight members of the Hanif family – the young-est then being two-year-old Alina. Mohammad Hanif swept his baby daughter into his arms and after he counted heads, everyone fled the coming torrents.

They made for the neighbouring village which stood on higher ground than their own. The Hanifs spent the night un-der the shelter of its petrol station along with many others from their village.

The Hanifs' village is called Garibabad. It's deep in the Punjab, about an hour and a half's drive from the teeming city of Multan. On the way from Multan to Garibabad you cross a bridge which spans the junction of three of Pakistan's great rivers – the Jhellum, the Chenab and the Ravi.

That reality, combined with a monsoon that was twenty times greater than normal, determined that the wall of water which engulfed this part of the Punjab reached twenty-seven feet high. It swept all before it – including most of the houses in Garibabad.

Mohammad Hanif learned of the catastrophe the next morning when he was still camped in the petrol station. His mobile rang. It was a villager who lived on a hill above Gari-babad. 'Everything is gone, including your house,' the caller told him. Mohammed Hanif is a strong man. He works in a garage greasing the fuel tankers from the huge lorry depot which is a stone's throw from his village. But the stress of his own personal disaster broke him.

Only days after his family moved in with relatives in the area he had a heart attack. He was rushed to hospital in Multan. He didn't know it then but salvation was coming from Glasgow – five thousand miles away. Enter Mohammad Sarwar and his charity, the Ucare Foundation, and the men from the city's Central Mosque. In a matter of weeks after the catastrophe they raised nearly three quarters of a million pounds for Pakistan's flood victims.

Mohammad Sarwar and Ghulam Rabbani, who heads the Mosque's charity committee, went to Pakistan to make a plan about how to spend the money raised in Scotland. On that visit they met a commander of the Pakistan Rangers – a section of the Pakistan army.

The deal was struck that one of the major priorities would be to build new homes for flood victims in Garibabad. The reconstruction of the primary school and the rebuilding of the mosques that had broadcast the flood warning, was included. The Rangers would organise the construction and the Scots would provide the funds to make it happen.

The Hanif family got the keys to heir new home early last October. At the start of this week I went to the house to meet Mr Hanif. Delighted somehow doesn't really capture his present demeanour. He told me: 'This house is a gift from Allah. And a gift from Scotland.'

Everyone in our party was overwhelmed by what the Pakistan Rangers had achieved in such a short time. In addition to the houses they had also refurbished the primary school, extended it with three new classrooms, and rebuilt and refurbished the village's two mosques. There was no doubt in my mind that agreeing on a working partnership with the Rangers was the way to get houses built for families who were in dire straits. It also carried with it the advantage of not having to pay for labour as the Rangers provided that for nothing. Finally, the Rangers' system involved building the new house on the exact site of the family's old one, thus avoiding any dispute about who owned the land where the new houses were being erected.

By August 2011, the transformation in Garibabad was amazing. Like the Hanifs, another two hundred families had new brick-built, two-room houses – all with a logo stencilled on the side of them, 'Constructed by the Pakistan Rangers. Donated by Glasgow Central Mosque and Ucare Foundation UK.' Another hundred homes, just like those in Garibabad, had been built in two neighbouring villages. This fulfilled the promise I had made to Brigadier Abid Saleem that we would find the money in Scotland to guarantee four hundred new houses in his part of Punjab.

When we returned to Garibabad to see what had been achieved, Ghulam Rabbani from the Central Mosque and myself were treated as guests of honour at a ceremony in the primary school. Most of the village seemed to have turned out. When all the delightful protocols were over – there were speeches, and songs and poems from the schoolchildren – I went to meet Mohammad Hanif at his house.

Those who still cast doubt on the effectiveness of our efforts to raise money in Scotland to help the needy in Pakistan haven't met Mohammad Hanif. They haven't seen him smile when he shows you his living room with the ceiling fan. They haven't heard his laugh when he pumps fresh water from his new well right outside the house. They also haven't met the Sabir Din family.

They live, all eight of them, in the village of Akbarabad, just outside the town of Charsadda, at the other end of Pakistan from Garibabad, right up against the border with Afghanistan, about 500 miles away. Akbarabad was almost totally wiped out when the floods hit the north of the country. Almost 500 houses in the village were destroyed – the Din family lost everything. Now 55-year-old Sabir Din and his family have a new brick-built house with two rooms and a brick-built toilet in the yard. When I visited Mr Din he told me that this was the first inside toilet the family had ever had. Standing on the verandah he pointed to the house and said: 'No words can express my gratitude to the people of Glasgow and Scotland.'

There is one image that sticks in my mind about Akbarabad. When I first visited the area early in September 2010, after the floods, most of the dispossessed of Akbarabad were living in a tented village set up by the UN, on what had once been the grazing lands for the village animals. There were about 400 tents with 3 to 4,000 dispossessed people living in them.

When I arrived a year later all the tents were gone. Our work had been a success. In total, Ucare and the Central Mosque built about 100 new houses in Akbarabad and the surrounding area, and in the village we also contributed to the building of a new pharmacy and a new mosque. Again, all of this was made possible by creating an enduring partnership between Ucare, the Central Mosque and agencies in Pakistan. In the case of the work done in the Charsadda area, and similar work carried out in the province of Azad Kashmir, our partnership was with Pakistan's rural poverty programme, the National Rural Support Programme (NRSP).

Attique Rehman, who works with the NRSP in Azad Kashmir, was our link for all of this – again on the now established basis of the NRSP and others completing the construction of houses and buildings, which was funded by Ucare and other Scottish money. The work that the NRSP completed in the north of Pakistan, along with the efforts made by Ucare and the Central Mosque in the Punjab and Sindh provinces, delivered just over 700 houses for flood victims, as was pledged at the start of our operations. Given the huge logistical problems which had been confronting us, this was no mean achievement. However along with the construction of the houses it is worth noting the importance of the relief work done with schools.

Two examples should be enough. In Garibabad and in Charsadda, the money raised in Scotland helped to pay for the renovation and redevelopment of a primary school in each area. Damaged classrooms were repaired and three new classrooms added to the each school, along with new equipment and uniforms for the pupils. In one year, the numbers of pupils attending the school in Garibabad rose from 70 to almost 450, more than six times; they doubled in Charsadda from 350 to almost 700.

In a way this development was as significant as building hundreds of houses. About a third of Pakistan's population live below the UN-defined poverty line and the average income – although this hides the huge disparities between the rich and the poor – is around $2,500 a year. According to the UN, only half the population over 15 years can read and write – the figures broken down for males who can read and write come to 63% and to 36% for females. For the rural poor the only way out of this abyss is education. That's why the increases in the pupil numbers in Garibabad and Charsadda, quoted above, are so significant. They demonstrate, yet again, the huge effect that relatively small amounts of money raised in Scotland can have in Pakistan.

There is an epilogue to be added to this part of my story. It is to say that throughout the history of Pakistan the intervention of the armed forces of the country into its politics – notably the Zia ul Haq dictatorship – has tarnished their reputation, especially internationally. To assert that military police dictatorship has damaged the historical development of Pakistan is a justifiable accusation. However it needs qualification. There have been times in our history when the armed forces have been the saviour of our nation. It is without doubt that two of those historical occasions were during the time of the 2005 earthquake and the floods of 2010.

The Governor of Punjab 15

'LAHORE: Chaudhry Mohammad Sarwar – a British citizen who is tipped to be appointed as the Governor of Punjab – arrived from the United Kingdom here on Saturday. A senior PML-N leader told *Dawn* that Mr Sarwar would meet Prime Minister Nawaz Sharif on Sunday and the party might nominate him as Punjab Governor.'

Dawn newspaper, 21 July 2013.

'Former Glasgow Govan MP Mohammad Sarwar has been installed as Governor of Punjab, the largest state in Pakistan. In his first speech in the post he highlighted the importance of education, promising to ensure school provision for more children.'

BBC Online News, 5 August 2013.

I officially retired as an MP when the General Election was held in May 2010. However, long before that date I had started to think about when I would leave the House of Commons. After years of building my Cash and Carry business and then 13 years in Parliament, when work seemed to be 24 hours a day, seven days a week, the idea of taking life a bit easier and spending more time at home with my family – especially with my grandchildren – was very attractive. I was tired to the point of near exhaustion.

Then there was the political factor. I wanted my successor to be chosen democratically by the Labour Party members in the constituency. It wasn't that I wanted to anoint my successor, but instead that I wanted to ensure that the local Party had the right to do so. There was one major issue on the political horizon which could have interrupted that process if I delayed announcing my standing down. If Gordon Brown, the then Prime Minister, decided to call a snap General Election, that could result in the National Executive Committee of the Labour Party deciding to impose local candidates, because a snap election would not allow adequate time for the normal selection procedures to be undertaken. Given that, I decided to announce standing down early to avoid that possibility and allow the local Party to choose its candidate. The additional advantage in doing that was also that whoever was selected would have time to campaign in the local area to introduce himself or herself to the electorate. After all our local struggles I didn't want the possibility of a freak result where a candidate imposed by London might become unpopular and Labour could lose the seat.

When I was taking that decision I knew in my heart that I could not face the possibility of another five punishing years as a Labour MP, probably on the Opposition back benches. Also I thought that this would be a suitable time to stand aside for a new, younger generation, which might well involve my son Anas, who was keen to stand as a candidate, although there was no guarantee that he would be successful. The local Party would decide that. In the end all these factors influenced my decision that the time was right to move on to other things. As it turned out Anas was successful in his bid to become the Labour candidate for Glasgow Central when the selection process took place. There were other strong candidates in the field, but the way he argued his case at the numerous Party meetings that took place, saw him through. In May 2010, after a superb campaign, Anas was elected as the Labour MP for Glasgow Central, increasing the Labour majority by 2,000 votes to 10,551.

After the May 2010 elections I had a couple of months of taking it easier every day, playing with my grandchildren and not rushing for flights to London. Then, in that July, the unprecedented floods hit Pakistan. It was the experience of organising relief for flood victims there that made me begin to think, for the first time, about what I could achieve for the people of Pakistan if I had the opportunity to work there more permanently. With my charity work it would be possible to help tens of thousands of people; if I wanted to go beyond that and help hundreds of thousands then the only way to do so would be to work closely with the Government of Pakistan. Otherwise, I realised my influence would be restricted within the boundaries of my charity, the Ucare Foundation.

So how did it come about that I became the Governor of Punjab, in what would the first crucial phase of my return to Pakistan, and my direct involvement in politics there? A major factor was my decision to quit British politics. That opened up the opportunity for me to get much more directly involved with my charity work in Pakistan, which, in turn, made me reflect on the possibilities of working with the Government of Pakistan to make real change on a large scale.

As I have already noted earlier, I was involved directly with Nawaz Sharif in October 1999 when he was deposed as Prime Minister, in the military coup led by General Musharraf. I met him when he was under house arrest to make sure he was being treated properly. In the end both Nawaz and Shahbaz Sharif were given long jail sentences, after a rigged trial; then, in 2000, they were allowed to go into exile in Saudi Arabia. That was much better than spending years behind bars, but this meant both were banned from active Pakistani politics, in any form, during their exile. Then one day the phone rang. It was Shahbaz Sharif – could I help him get a visitor's visa to come to the UK for urgent medical treatment?

I took up his case, starting with representations to the relevant civil servants in the Home Office. It was a dialogue with the deaf. I went to see the Home Secretary, Jack Straw. He told me that there were problems, because the authorities in Pakistan were insisting that the Sharifs had strong connections with the Taliban. I scoffed at the idea, but my protests made no difference – we were caught in a Civil Service Immigration Department limbo.

By luck, in 2004 and 2005, the Secretary of State for Citizenship, Immigration and Nationality at the Home Office was Des Browne, a Scottish Labour MP. I knew him well, and soon wore out the carpet on the stairs leading to his office to make the case for Shahbaz Sharif to get a visitor's visa on health grounds. Within a month or so of my representations, Des Browne became convinced of the merits of granting Shahbaz a visitor's visa for six months so he could come to the UK to get treatment for his health problems. When that visa expired, his treatment was still ongoing, so he was granted an additional two-year stay.

Nawaz Sharif's case proved more complex. The Taliban question was raised again and again in his case, with even more gusto. By this time, Charles Clarke was the Home Secretary in the British Government. He seemed convinced that granting a visa to Nawaz might be interpreted as taking sides in the affairs of another government, and could provoke adverse reactions, not least from the government in Pakistan. One afternoon we had a frank exchange in the Members lobby. 'How can you treat a man who has been a Prime Minister twice in such a way? And let me tell you, in the not too distant future, he is going to be the Prime Minister of Pakistan for a third time!' I said.

There were also health grounds in Nawaz's case, because his son was seriously ill in London. Nawaz clearly wanted to be with his son at such a time. Clarke told me that Nawaz Sharif's files were on his desk, and he promised me that he would make the decision that evening and let me know. He phoned me later to say that he had instructed the Home Office to issue a six-month visitor's visa for Nawaz Sharif.

When Nawaz Sharif arrived in London, both brothers met me in my offices at Portcullis House, beside the Houses of Parliament. They were effusive in their praise of what I had done on their behalf, to the point where I became somewhat embarrassed at their expressions of gratitude. Nawaz said: 'Chaudry Sarwar, we will never forget what you have done for us.' I told them that their position in politics in Pakistan made each of them a special case, but said that in reality I had not done anything different for them than what I would have done for a constituent of mine faced with similar problems – the processes were always the same, go to the civll servants and when they do nothing, try and get to the Minister concerned! Of course I didn't know then that I had started on a path of acquaintance with the Sharifs that would lead to my being appointed as Governor of Punjab.

In Punjab, at the time of the 2010 floods, our charity effort was concentrated in a number of villages outside the city of Multan. In one village, Garibabad, as I have described, we built more than 200 houses for villagers who had lost everything in the floods. Shahbaz Sharif had travelled to Garibabad to present the keys to the families who were given the first houses built by the Pakistan Rangers on behalf of our charity. He commended us for our organisational efforts, and the way in which we had combined with the Pakistan Rangers. He said that meant our effort was not some sort of imposition from well-off 'outsiders', but rather a genuine collaboration with official local organisations in Pakistan, and thus all the more praiseworthy for that.

So, stage by stage, my relations with the Sharifs were growing. Then, about a year or so before the General Election of 2013, they asked me to begin analysing the PML-N prospects in Punjab; in particular looking at the selection of Party candidates to stand in that election. The lure of becoming involved again in active politics was irresistible. So in the six months before the May 2013 vote, I spent a huge amount of my time in Pakistan organising for the PML-N, in my home area in Toba Tek Singh district, in Vehari district, and in Faisalabad, one of the Punjab's great cities.

At this time I genuinely felt that the PML-N represented the most progressive political forces in Pakistan, capable of making the changes necessary so that the country could confront its enduring economic crisis and other major challenges. Then, in the political scheme of things, I saw the PML-N as the party of business wedded to the idea that the development of Pakistan's economy was crucial to the country's future. In addition the PML-N was most popular in Punjab, where all my family ties still existed. All this meant I was totally comfortable with my new allegiance to the PML-N.

So, to my part in the campaign to secure an election victory for the party. The election arithmetic was not that complicated. There are 272 'first past the post' seats in the National Assembly – so the magic figure for a parliamentary majority is 137. In the 2008 election, the PPP won enough seats to set up a coalition with a parliamentary majority; this was largely as a consequence of their political exploitation of Benazir's assassination, shortly before the election. In that election the PML-N was the second largest party. So the task was to increase its numbers to get to the majority figure, or as near to that as possible to realise a PML-N coalition.

The seats in the PLM-N's Punjab power base were vital for that. Our strategy did not involve assessing every potential candidate, as there were many senior political figures who were obvious candidates in the seats they already held. Rather, for both the National

Assembly and the Punjab Provincial Assembly, we concentrated on 'swing seats' that were currently held by the PPP but which we estimated could fall to the PML-N. We looked at the candidates' political history, the strength of their local support, their known abilities, and their family networks. Recommendations were then made to the PML-N's Parliamentary Board for final decisions. The National Assembly candidates were more significant, because the Party had already established a huge base in the Punjab Provincial Assembly, where, in 2008, Shahbaz Sharif had been elected as Chief Minister. I was predicting that the Party could reach a total of around 110 National Assembly seats, which would guarantee it would be able to build a coalition for government.

Early in April I had to depart from the fray to take a break to attend my nephew's wedding in Glasgow. The flight home from Lahore to Manchester was at ten in the morning, Friday 5 April. I was staying overnight with friends in Lahore on the Thursday evening. Perveen, who had been on a family holiday in Pakistan, was still in Faisalabad, so we had arranged to meet at the airport before the flight. I think it was about four in the morning when I woke with tremendous chest pains. I had no idea where they had come from but I knew they were more severe than anything I had ever experienced. I woke up and went for a walk in the garden of the house to get some fresh air. One of the staff there gave me painkillers to try to ease the pain; when I left for the airport I was still in considerable discomfort.

I met Perveen at the airport. She knew immediately that something was wrong and insisted I should see one of the on-call doctors at the airport before taking the flight. He checked my blood pressure and pulse and both were OK. Now in Pakistan, for whatever reason, there is a common conception that if you are having a heart attack you will have pain in your left shoulder – there should really be a health warning against that. The doctor asked if I had pain in my left shoulder and I said that I hadn't. He told me that it wasn't a heart attack and gave me more painkillers. I was a little relieved by the diagnosis and we boarded the flight.

During the flight the pain intensified. I asked one of the stewards for more painkillers. All that was available was high-dose Disprin so I took a few of them. That may have saved my life. When we arrived in Manchester I was keen to drive home and get checked there. By this time my son Athif was on the phone insisting that I should go to the hospital in Manchester to get another check-up before travelling. Then my son-in-law Shahzad, who is a GP, phoned to repeat that I should go to the hospital. He made arrangements for me to go to Accident and Emergency at the University Hospital in Manchester.

At the hospital I was admitted for a check-up including blood tests. By now some family friends in Manchester, including the Pakistan Consul General, had arrived to see me. I was feeling a lot better and wanted to leave, but the doctors insisted that I had to stay to get the results of the blood tests before that was possible. It was about six in the evening when the results became available. The doctor asked for a private word which immediately set the alarm bells ringing. He told me that the tests showed I had had a major heart attack. I asked if he could run the tests again for a second check and he told me that it was beyond doubt that I had had a heart attack, and its severity, combined with the fact that I had sustained the attack for eighteen hours without proper treatment, meant that my heart would probably have suffered serious damage. After preparations to get me ready, an operation would be necessary, he told me.

When I woke on the Saturday morning, Anas, and my son-in-law, Shahzad, were there at the hospital. They were both very concerned about my health, but in a way relieved that I was now getting proper care. They both ventured the opinion that if I had insisted on making the journey to Glasgow the day before, I would never have made it alive. The care and attention I received from the hospital staff was beyond first class. The NHS in the UK, despite the brickbats it receives in the media, is an organisation without peer anywhere else in the world. The doctors told me that my operation would probably be the following Monday or Tuesday. On Sunday morning Anas and Shahzad told me that Perveen didn't want to disturb me when I was sleeping and had left to return home. They said she wanted to be in Glasgow for the start of the wedding celebrations and that, after a month on holiday in Pakistan, she was really keen to see our grandchildren. Given the perilous state of my health I thought that was pretty strange, but l let it pass. It transpired that her journey home had been made a necessity because, in the early hours of the morning, my dear father had passed away. He had been admitted to hospital the previous week with pneumonia and it had overcome him.

On the Sunday afternoon my long-term friend, Lord Ahmed, visited me in hospital and let the cat out of the bag by expressing his condolences for my father. As soon as he said that, I knew the terrible truth even though he tried to backtrack when he realised I didn't know. When I confronted Anas and Shahzad about this, they told me that the doctors had advised that it was best if I avoided any shock at the news and that in any case I couldn't travel to Glasgow in my condition anyway. So they decided not to tell me. They also thought that if I had found out I would have insisted there and then that I must go home. I was distraught and overcome with my helplessness. I would miss my own father's funeral.

Two days later I had heart surgery and a stent was put in one of the arteries leading to my heart. I cannot express enough thanks to the doctors and nurses who helped to save my life, or to the air steward who gave me the pills which just might have been critical for my survival. After the operation the consultant who carried out the surgery wished me well and told me I was lucky to be alive. I had to have a lengthy recuperation, which meant I could not travel to Pakistan for the election on 11 May. After my operation, Nawaz and Shahbaz Sharif phoned me at the hospital in Manchester to express their sadness at my father's passing and saying that they were seriously concerned about my health. They both insisted that I should have a full convalescence and not give a second thought to politics meantime.

My disappointment at not being in Pakistan for the election was mitigated by the election results. In the National Assembly Elections, the PML-N won around 120 seats. This was almost double what they had held in 2008, bordering on a landslide victory. Following the election, Nawaz Sharif approached a number of the Members of the National Assembly who had been elected as Independents. Nineteen of them agreed to join the PML-N, which consolidated a convincing majority in the National Assembly. The PPP was reduced to around 40 members. Imran Khan's PTI won 35 seats, but the political 'tsunami' he had predicted did not happen at the polls.

During the campaign I was impressed by the PTI and had misgivings that Imran might be able to deliver. Nonetheless I had confidence that the PML-N machine for delivering the vote was much better organised than the relatively inexperienced PTI. The PML-N, led by Shahbaz Sharif, won its greatest ever majority in the Punjab Provincial Assembly, taking 214 out of some 300 seats; that ensured Shahbaz Sharif's subsequent re-election as the Chief Minister of Punjab.

The Prime Minister's oath ceremony was held in President House, in Islamabad, on 5 June 2013. Shahbaz Sharif's ceremony was the next day at Governor House in Lahore. At that time a good friend of mine – Ahmed Mahmood – was the Governor of Punjab. I called to tell him I was coming to Lahore for the Shahbaz Sharif ceremony, and said I would l like to see him. It was a fortuitous phone call. Ahmed told me there was a huge attendance expected. He said that the cars would be lined up for miles up the Mall Road waiting to get in for the oath proceedings. He invited me to stay at Governor House overnight before the ceremony.

When I arrived I could not believe the grandeur of Governor House and the beauty of its setting. My room was on the ground floor of the building, looking out over the rolling lawns and gardens in front. At one point Shahbaz Sharif called and said he was coming to see me at Governor House. Ahmed Mahood, myself and Shahbaz met in the rather imposing Ivory Room. Shahbaz said there had been discussions with his brother, and they wanted me to consider appointment as the Pakistan High Commissioner in London. I can't say I was totally surprised, because there had been a hint or two in previous discussions, but nonetheless when the official offer was made I was delighted.

In London I called on Baroness Warzi, who was then the chairperson of the Conservative Party, to take her view of how my possible appointment as the High Commissioner would be viewed. She said that she would support my appointment, but urged caution. She said that I had retired with a huge reputation from the House of Commons, and a return to such a posting might have complications – not least because my son, Anas, was in the House of Commons and the High Commissioner's role might compromise his career, one way or another. On my return to Glasgow I told everyone about the offer of the appointment. Perveen was the first to react. 'What wonderful news,' she said, 'that's recognition for all the tremendous work you've done in the campaign. And it's the best of both worlds – in government, but in London! So we don't have to leave the whole family behind. I was sure they would have wanted you to take something in Pakistan.'

Anas supported the idea, but both my other sons, Athif and Asim, were opposed – mainly because they felt that if I was going back into politics in Pakistan, then a post in the actual government of Pakistan would be much better. We had time to deliberate, since the actual appointment would not be officially made for some time, but the more I thought about it, the more the prospects appeared as a new challenge which I would relish. Then once more I had to return to Pakistan – this time to be present at an official lunch for the British Prime Minister, David Cameron, when he was visiting Pakistan at the end of June. Nawaz Sharif invited me to attend the function.

The lunch for Cameron was held in the rather grandiose halls of the Prime Minister's Office in Islamabad. At the end of it I was in the group which escorted the British Prime Minister to his car. Nawaz Sharif was walking in front with Cameron, both deep in conversation. At one point, the British Prime Minister seemed to become a bit agitated, and the goodbyes at the car were somewhat perfunctory.

I was second-guessing on the final exchanges with Cameron, but decided to speak my mind. I told the Pakistani Prime Minister that I had a hunch there may be problems with my appointment as Pakistan High Commissioner in London. I said that I had heard there had been questions raised, in high level British government circles, about my suitability for appointment, because of my strong ties with the Labour Party in the UK. I told the Prime Minister that I knew for a fact that David Cameron was not comfortable, since he believed that the High Commissioner's post was always seen as a 'non-political' appointment.

The Prime Minister agreed, and then said it would be better to offer me a more substantial post in the Government of Pakistan anyway. He said: 'You know the Britishers still think it's the days of the Raj when they can order us to do their bidding. Well, they may be able to block you as the High Commissioner in the UK, but Cameron can't stop me appointing you as the Governor of Punjab!'

'The Governor of Punjab?' I repeated.

345

'Yes, the Governor of Punjab,' Nawaz said.

Both Chaudhry Nisar, the Minister of the Interior, and Shah-baz Sharif, who had attended the lunch, said immediately that they thought it was a marvellous idea. I accepted the offer on the spot. The Prime Minister was smiling, in fact everyone was smiling. There was some back-slapping as we all shook hands. 'You'll have to give up your British citizenship, you have to be a Pakistani national to be a member of the government. No dual nationalities. You'll need to see to that,' was the PM's parting shot. That was it.

People may find it strange that such a big decision was reached in this way. That's sometimes the way it is with power politics – right, let's do this, bang, decision made. When I flew back to the UK I went straight to my barrister's office and instructed him to begin the legal process of renouncing my British citizenship. He was surprised, but persuaded of the scale of the opportunity for me. Would the family be of the same mind, was the next big question.

It is fair, to say the least, that Perveen was shocked, and her first reaction was to persuade me to refuse the offer. I told her I wanted to go back into Pakistani politics to do something for my people, to give something back. I also confessed that I had some nagging doubts about whether I had left 'big game' politics in the UK too early. I knew that she thought my international reputation should have been exploited more when I was at the top of British politics. Athif, Asim and Anas were really enthusiastic about the prospects and said so.

The next day Perveen relented. She told me that I deserved to face one more big challenge in politics. She said that the writings in the Quran suggested that sometimes your destiny has to be accepted. She considered this development to have become my destiny. There was one caveat. If she missed the grandchildren, I had to guarantee that I would send her on a flight to the UK as soon as she asked. I agreed, of course.

Firstly I had to complete the renouncing of my British citizenship; it wasn't easy to do that. I had fought hard to gain dual national-ity; also all my children, Athif, Anas, Asim, my sons, and Faiza, my daughter, were born in Britain and had British passports. And my grandchildren would have British passports when they came of age also. So here I was making a declaration which meant I would need to apply for a visa from the UK High Commission in Pakistan, if I wanted to go back to Glasgow to see my dear children and grandchildren. But life is full of hard choices. The rules for becoming a member of the Pakistan government dictated it had to be done, and so it was done, although there were complications. I had to give up my British citizenship before actually securing nomination for the appointment as Governor. So I was giving up my British nationality without any guarantee that I would become Governor. Before I could be nominated I had to be a Pakistani national only; I had to walk across a kind of political No Man's Land. I chose to take the risk, and that is exactly what it turned out to be.

On Saturday 20 July 2013, Perveen and I arrived at Lahore airport to be met by what they would call nowadays, 'A Perfect Storm'. Since the General Election, in May, there had been fierce speculation in the media in Pakistan about who might be nominated by the Prime Minister for Governor of Punjab. For example, early in June 2013 the national newspaper *The Nation* declared:

> Sources say that former Punjab Governor Sardar Zulfiqar Ali Khosa, Senator Jaffar Iqbal and former bureaucrat Saeed Mehdi are the likely contenders for the governorship but there may be a dark horse as well. They say that the party wants to appoint the next governor from south Punjab where it has Sardar Zulfiqar Ali Khan Khosa and Jaffar Iqbal as strong candidates. Sources say that former bureaucrat and principal secretary to the Prime Minister (1997-99) Saeed Mehdi may be the second choice of the Party leaders.

There's reference here to 'a dark horse' but there was not even a whisper that I might be a candidate. My name had never been mentioned anywhere in the media. So when the political rumour mill did pick up the possibility of my nomination, you can imagine the effect that had in newsrooms across the country. When that possibility was confirmed, albeit by unofficial off-the-record briefings, combined with my arrival in Lahore, a media frenzy developed overnight.

When Perveen and I arrived at Lahore airport, there was a huge crowd of reporters, with cameras, microphones and tape recorders at the ready. If any of Lahore's top journalists were missing they must have been on holiday. My recollection is that one of the media pack yelled, 'Mr Sarwar, are you here to become the new Viceroy – you know, like a Britisher who comes from Britain to rule over the Pakistanis?' Then I'm sure another yelled, 'If there are 100 million people in the Punjab, how come we have to go to the UK to find a Governor?' It was the 'Perfect Storm' right enough; these questions were entirely legitimate, but at that time I could not answer them. There had been no official declaration of the nomination by the Prime Minister, so I couldn't comment. I had to make do with what I hoped was plausible semi-denial that final decisions had not been taken in these matters at this stage, and that 'I would be honoured to play whatever role I could in the government of Pakistan', whilst emphasising that I had not been made any official offers whatsoever. The political limbo allowed those who considered themselves as possible nominees for the appointment to create a storm of accusation in the media. They pointed fingers in the sure knowledge that it was difficult for me to answer the questions.

Perveen and I had booked into my favourite hotel in Lahore, the Pearl Continental (PC), which is on Mall Road, about ten minutes' walk away from Governor House. Some days later an enterprising newspaper photographer snapped Perveen and I sitting in the hotel lobby. The newspaper ran the photograph above a caption which read:'Waiting for the keys of Governor House?' We retreated to another hotel, further away from Governor House. The media storm was raging. On the day of our arrival there had been a leak to sections of the media which had originally promoted the storm. On 21 July the *Dawn* newspaper had a front-page splash. It noted: 'A senior PML-N leader told *Dawn* that Mr Sarwar would meet Prime Minister Nawaz Sharif on Sunday and the Party might nominate him as Punjab Governor.'

On the same day, Pakistan's *Express Tribune*, part of the International New York Times group, probably had the most detailed report: 'Coveted posts: Shahbaz backs ex-British MP as Punjab Governor.' Notably the article had a quote separately in bold, highlighted from the main article, from an Independent MP who told the newspaper:

The Punjab cabinet has very few ministers from the South and the appointment of a Viceroy would create a sense of alienation in the area.[1]

I noted, with interest, that the term 'Viceroy' had not even been put in quotes. The other issue raised time and again questioned the appointment of 'an outsider' as Governor, when there were 110 million Punjabis who could potentially fill the post. Another theme which emerged in a growing number of commentaries was that somehow David Cameron, the British Prime Minister, had been pushing for my nomination as Governor when he had visited Pakistan, at the end of June. In the febrile atmosphere of the controversy over my nomination, the wholly coincidental timing of Cameron's visit and my possible nomination was seized upon by sections of the media. The logic was simple: Brit Prime Minister visits Pakistan. Britisher to be nominated as Punjab Governor – surely no coincidence.

The more time passed without word of an official nomination, the greater the media storm raged. After ten days of the frenzy the political situation was becoming perilous, even to the point where I was beginning to think that the sheer weight of criticism might lead the Prime Minister to change his mind – could the political price of supporting my nomination become too great? I decided I had to 'take the bull by the horns' and flew to Islamabad to put all these concerns to the Prime Minister. Nawaz Sharif assured me that later that day he had arranged to send a summary to the President, Asif Zardari, advising him to appoint me as Governor of Punjab. He told me that it would be approved the next day. He was as good as his word. The next day, Wednesday 31 July, the President approved the appointment. It was announced to the media that evening.

Enter Anas Sarwar. Anas, who as I have said, for a time followed in my footsteps to the British Parliament as MP for my former Glasgow constituency, had joined me in Lahore to help with media coverage of my appointment as Governor. Instead he was confronted with what he called 'a fight to the finish for my political survival in Pakistan'. He is much more of the modern Facebook/Twitter/ iPad world than I will ever be. He is what they call nowadays 'media savvy'. He

1. *Express Tribune*, 21 July 2013.

knows how modern media works and the power of 'the message'. He argued that we had lost a huge amount of ground to my opponents because I could not argue my case until the Prime Minister's recommendation to appoint me as the Governor had been made public. So we had to have a plan to come out all guns blazing, with a media counter-offensive, when the announcement was finally made. We decided on three central messages for the campaign: I was returning as a son of Pakistan not to take but to give / It would be an honour to serve my country and my experience in business, politics and charity work meant I was well qualified for the post / I was no longer a British citizen. I had given that up to serve Pakistan.

The time had come. We had decided to mount the campaign in the TV studios to regain ground from all the commentary against me in the newspapers; I gave the first major interview to one of the biggest TV news stations in Pakistan. I agreed to a recorded interview with one of their news presenters that morning, and it ran all day on their news bulletins. Of course at that point I felt a little nervous, but another factor soon became clear which boosted my confidence. The interview was being conducted in my mother tongue, Punjabi; no matter how much I have grown accustomed to speaking with the British media in English, arguing and making my points in Punjabi and Urdu was like losing an intellectual ball and chain. I had been freed – I knew exactly what to say, how to say it, and when to say it. I smiled my way through the interview.

My recollections of the media interviews are a bit hazy, because of the number that were conducted in our media blitz. At one point the presenter said something along the lines of: 'You say you are here to give to Pakistan, but you haven't given much for the last thirty-odd years when you have been living in the UK, have you?' I started modestly saying that it was a fair question although he was overlooking all my years in the British House of Commons when I had spoken up for, and, time after time, defended Pakistan. Then I spoke about the two hospitals my charity had developed in Rajana, in district Toba Tek Singh and in the city of Chichawatni – together serving more than 180,000 patients a year; that hundreds of thousands of pounds had been raised for the thousands of families devastated by the 2005 earthquake, in Azad Kashmir. Finally I told him about the

700 houses built all over Pakistan for the flood victims by my charity working with the Pakistan Rangers.

That interview set the tone for the others as I went from one TV station in Lahore to the next, beating the same drum. While I was on this detail, the team back at Faletti's hotel had organised a media conference for late in the afternoon. When I got back there after the rounds of a dozen TV studios the pack were out in force again – more TV, radio and newspapers. The first questions then were about my appointment. I explained why I was qualified to do the job. Others followed on the previous lines about being a new 'Viceroy', and why did the Punjab have to go to the UK to find a Governor. I just hammered out the same messages – here to serve, here to give, international experience, politics, business, charity work, and 'I have surrendered my British nationality to serve the people of Pakistan.'

It worked. The TV stations had run my interviews all day. The next morning's newspaper coverage was front page all the way. 'Here to serve, to give, not to take' had hit the mark. It was a turning point. After three days of battle we believed that we had argued our case and convinced a big section of the 'commentariat' that there was, in fact, a justification for my appointment as Governor. I recall that on one of the Saturday evening TV talk shows, they conducted a live poll – should Mohammad Sarwar have been appointed Governor of Punjab. Of 100 people polled, 92 said Yes!

The swearing-in ceremony as Governor, at Governor House in Lahore, was on the following Monday, 5 August, at 8.30 in the morning. That prompted the next policy debate among my advisors about what should be said in the swearing-in speech and the state address thereafter. We were clear that although the Governor's position was traditionally ceremonial, with some official Government responsibilities, that I should announce a departure from that. In the discussions that had been held after my acceptance of the appointment, it had been agreed that my political experience should be harnessed by the Government to allow me to develop a role in education and in the affairs of overseas Pakistanis, which would go beyond the traditional Governor remit.

To that purpose, before the oath ceremony I had already taken important steps. I had conducted briefings with the head of the British government's Department for International Development (DfID), regarding a campaign to get young children in Punjab, who should have been in primary school but were not, into education. The DfID response to the idea of getting something done in Pakistan was extremely positive. In addition I had been in contact with the former British Prime Minister, Gordon Brown, due to his role as UN Special Envoy for Global Education. In July 2012, the UN Secretary-General, Ban Ki-moon, appointed Gordon Brown to help galvanise support for the Global Education First Initiative, which aims to achieve the goal of safe, quality education for every girl and boy by the end of 2015. That is the deadline of the UN's Millennium Development Goals. Of course I have known Gordon for many years through our years together in the British Parliament, and he was enormously enthusiastic about my proposals for children in the Punjab and other regions in Pakistan. Not only that, he had serious money to spend on the right kind of project. The sums in question were in hundreds of millions of US dollars.

Looking back on this now, I am really pleased we made the education pledge part of the swearing in ceremony; that made it clear that I was not only going to use the office of Governor for ceremonial pomp; that I was determined to make a difference.

At 8.30 am on 5 August a volley of ceremonial trumpets announced the beginning of the swearing-in ceremony in the Grand Hall. Chief Minister Shahbaz Sharif was on my right and the Chief Justice of Punjab, Atta Mohammad Bandail, on my left, as we entered. We stepped up on the stage in the hall in the same order. First I had to repeat the oath after the Chief Justice in which I promised 'to show allegiance to Pakistan' and to protect its constitution. After all the struggles to get to this point, the official part of the swearing-in was probably over in ten minutes. Then it was time for my acceptance speech. For the record here's what I said:

> In this holy month of Ramadan, I am grateful to Almighty Allah who has blessed me to take the oath as the constitutional head of the Islamic Republic of Pakistan's largest province, the Punjab. I also want to thank the people of Pakistan, especially

the people of Punjab, who have wholeheartedly supported my appointment as Governor.

Of course this is not my first oath of swearing-in. By the grace of Almighty Allah, I am the first Muslim and Pakistani who in the thousand-year history of the British Parliament, took the oath as a British MP on the Quran. That was the first time this happened in history. That Quran is still there and will remain there with the Grace of God.

I am highly honoured that the Prime Minister of Pakistan, Mian Nawaz Sharif, has decided that I have the necessary abilities to take up such an important post in Pakistan. I am delighted to serve with him and the Chief Minister of Punjab, Mian Shahbaz Sharif, in the coming years; their quest to promote the national interest of Pakistan including the security, stability and prosperity of our nation is now my quest also ...

Today Pakistan is surrounded by many difficulties – poverty, unemployment, education and health issues all present great challenges. Terrorism and human rights violations stalk the land. Also there are the real problems of everyday life for countless millions in the difficulties of load shedding and electricity delivery. But we need to find solutions to these problems and have to fight to make things better, rather than simply lament our difficulties. I believe we Pakistanis will win this fight. We will struggle together and it will be a privilege to be part of that fight to make a better Pakistan. From today, let me say the Governor House is not the Governor's, it is a house of the people, for the people, of Punjab.

Allah has given me every blessing in this world. I have taken this appointment not to gain something personally from it, but to give something back to the people of Pakistan. To eliminate poverty, I believe we need to transform Pakistan's educational system. The Punjab government is already taking on this great challenge and now I intend to join that struggle for change, with them.

It is my aim to develop a better image for Pakistan across the world. But that is not just about the country's reputation but improving that so we can attract the foreign investment

353

we desperately need. By using my expertise and my experience, I hope and believe we can bring more investors to Pakistan. That will mean more jobs for the people of Pakistan, improve the economy and guarantee the future.

I can assure all the leaders of all political parties that as the Governor I will preserve the constitution I am charged with and I will seek that we all work together for the benefit of all the people. This includes the vision of Quaid-e-Azam Mohammad Ali Jinnah's that the minorities in Pakistan have to have their rights protected and guaranteed . . .

Finally I have to pay respect to my father who was a small farmer in the village. It is by his struggles and those of my mother that I am here today. My early education was sitting on the floor in school under a tree. I walked miles every day to get to school. It was the urgings of my parents that I should learn and become educated that has put me in the position I am in today. By the grace of Allah today I am honoured with this position. My wish is to provide opportunities in Pakistan for every child, rich or poor, from the countryside or city, man or woman. I give this pledge to you today. Long live Pakistan!

The acceptance speech marked the end of the swearing-in, but there was still the state address and then a media conference to follow. In the state address speech I made the pledge to make the development of education central to the struggle against poverty. I told the gathering that some seven million children in Pakistan who were of primary school age didn't go to school. I pledged to reduce their number by a million each year while I was Governor of Punjab. I said:

Education is the only route out of poverty. I'll spare no effort to make sure an extra million kids who don't go to school now will be enrolled for primary school every year when I am Governor. Education has always been a passion of mine, so I'm going to campaign to give children in the Punjab a better chance for a better life.

There was a certain unity in the coverage both in Pakistan and in the UK. The English edition of *Dawn* headlined the educational pledge. The Scottish *Daily Record*, which had given positive coverage to my becoming Governor, declared: Sarwar pledge to fight poverty – 'I'll campaign to get kids in the Punjab a chance for a better life.'[1] I am pleased to say that although my circumstances in the politics of Pakistan have changed irrevocably, both these speeches and the pledges made in them have stood the test of time. Everything I said then about what needed to be done remains true of today.

Governor House was built in the middle of the nineteenth century when the powers of the British Raj were probably at their greatest across the Subcontinent. Its white colonnaded mansion house sits in 80 acres of immaculate lawns and woodlands. These were the days when the British built big to remind those subject to their rule – lest they should forget – just who was the power in the land. I remember when all the business of the ceremony and media interviews was over, we posed for family photographs. Then suddenly I was alone in the Grand Hall. Upstairs, behind the first storey balustrades, there are black and white portraits on the walls of every Governor there's ever been. I had just joined their number. My constituency in Glasgow had had around 80,000 people living there. In my new role as Governor I would be responsible for 110 million. A new chapter in my life was beginning. A new challenge beckoned. At that very moment the enormity of it all struck me.

In my acceptance speech I had pledged to do everything in my power to bring more foreign investors to Pakistan to create jobs and prosperity for the people. It was only a matter of weeks later when that pledge was put to the test. Early in September 2013, to be precise. At that time, Gohar Ijaz, the group leader of the All Pakistan Textile Mills Association (APTMA) led a sizeable delegation of his top committee members to meet me at Governor House. This was the third time Ijaz had come to see me, about the same thing – Pakistan's 'favoured nation status' deal for trade with the European Union, which was known as GSP+. Ijaz was alarmed. He told me that the Pakistan Government departments involved in the European project did not realise the real situation; he believed Pakistan

1. *Daily Record*, 6 August 2013.

attaining GSP+ status in Europe was in jeopardy. The alarm bells were ringing. Loudly.

Before going any further, it is probably useful to explain the European Union's Generalised System of Preferences (GSP) which offers favourable trading concessions to developing countries which are exporting to the European Union. GSP can be defined as follows: GSP allows developing countries' exporters to pay lower duties on their exports to the EU. This gives them vital access to EU markets and a competitive advantage, so providing impetus for economic growth, development and poverty alleviation for developing countries.

The EU also operates an enhanced system of duty concessions known as 'GSP+'. It offers what can be defined as: full removal of tariffs on essentially the same product categories as those covered by the GSP. This is granted to those developing countries which ratify and implement international conventions relating to human rights, labour rights, environment and good governance.

So GSP offers reduced import duties and GSP+ offers their complete removal for an agreed period of time, provided certain conditions are observed by the applicant countries. For the purposes of the GSP+, in the 2013 round of applications, Pakistan had been 'bundled' in a group of 10 – Pakistan, Armenia, Bolivia, Cape Verde, Costa Rica, Ecuador, Georgia, Mongolia, Paraguay and Peru.

The process of application has three stages. The European Commission – the EU administration – assesses the applications and then defines the 'bundle' of applicants for GSP+ status which it deems as eligible to be included in the GSP+ arrangements. This approval is known as the Delegated Act, in EU terms, but for the purposes of our comments we will refer to this as the 'Commission Recommendations'. In the second stage the Commission Recommendations go before the appropriate European Parliament Committee which, in this case, is the International Trade Committee, known as INTA. INTA considers the Commission Recommendations and then puts its stamp of approval or its rejection to a full session of the European Parliament's 766 Members of the European Parliament (MEPs). That then becomes the third stage of the approval process.

Pakistan had been approved within the Commission Recommendations. The 'bundle' of applications was now being considered by

INTA – the International Trade Committee. When the Pakistan Textile Mills people visited me at Governor House, that was where their fears lay. They believed that INTA was going to block our application and that Pakistan's officials did not realise the seriousness of the situation. In part, I think this was also because the Government officials did not fully understand the decision-making mechanisms of the European parliament. I have found this a consistent characteristic of many Government officials in Pakistan – people who *think* they know something when they don't.

David Martin is a Scottish Labour Member of the European Parliament. He has been a close friend of mine for decades. He was first elected to the European Parliament in 1984, and so is one of its longest-serving members. In three separate sessions of the Parliament he has been elected Vice President, and is widely recognised as one of its experts on trade. I knew that he sat on the INTA committee. The final INTA vote on the GSP+ proposals was due on 5 November. I was going back to Glasgow at the end of September, on holiday, so I set up a meeting with David at his Edinburgh office, early in October, to seek his advice. The news was grim. Totally grim. David told me: 'I don't want to upset you, but the situation is extremely difficult for Pakistan. Bleak in fact.'

There were 31 MEPs on the INTA committee. David told me that, at that time, there were only four or five who would support Pakistan's case; worse, there was no sign of any campaign on our behalf. Then the hammer-blow came. Seven of the INTA members had already signed a motion to reject the Commission Recommendations for GSP+ status. They included the chair of the INTA committee, Vital Moreira, from Portugal, who actually moved the motion in favour of rejecting the Commission Recommendations. David said we were confronting two distinct strands of opposition – one group that was opposed to the deal because of the 'bundling' of ten countries together, and another group of MEPs, who were of the same view, but also wanted specifically to exclude Pakistan because of its human rights record.

The full European Parliament does not vote by national delegation, but instead according to political groupings – of which there are seven in the Parliament. The five largest of these are the European

People's Party group (EPP), basically Christian Democrats, with 275 MEPs supporting it; the Socialists and Democrats (S+D) are next with 195 MEPs; then the Liberal Democrat group with 85 MEPs, the Greens with 58 MEPs and the European Conservatives and Reformists (ECR) with 56 MEPs. David did the maths. On the INTA committee, of the seven who had signed the INTA opposition motion, three were from the EPP, two from the S+D, one Green and one from GUE, the hard Left group. That meant there was potentially a pretty comprehensive spread of the Parliament's political groups ranged against us. I had put Pakistan's case to David – we had managed a democratic transfer from one elected government to another for the first time in Pakistan's history; we had suffered terribly from the war on terror, with official figures counting 50,000 Pakistanis dead as a result; we were making progress on human rights with government ratification of the 27 international conventions stipulated in the GSP+ rules; we wanted 'trade' not 'aid'. He agreed wholeheartedly with my point of view.

The British lobby to secure GSP+ for Pakistan took place between 1 and 10 October 2013. David insisted that the first plan had to be to reverse the rejection vote on INTA. Incidentally that was based on rejecting the 'bundle' of countries put forward by the Commission in favour of 'one by one' recommendations being made, country by country. David and I agreed a plan. I should go to London to try and meet as many of the British MEPs as I could and persuade them of the validity of our case, in the hope that they would then influence others in the Parliament. On my way to London, I stopped off in Manchester to see Sajjad Karim, MEP. That would prove to be one of the most crucial moves in the whole campaign.

Sajjad was a Conservative Party MEP, which meant he was part of the influential EPP group in the European Parliament. Two other factors were extremely important for our cause. Sajjad had been an MEP since 2004. Between then and 2008 he had been a member of the INTA committee; he knew how it operated and also had good contacts with some of those still on INTA. Now we had David on the committee and Sajjad with contacts within it, and beyond. In addition, Sajjad was the chair of the 'Friends of Pakistan' grouping in the Parliament, which included members of the major political groups inside the Parliament. We now had an 'A Team' assembled – David, Sajjad and me – which was capable of reaching parts of the European Parliament that no-one else could.

In London, Yasmeen Qureshi MP and Khaled Mahmood MP had organised a reception for MPs and MEPs which was well attended. I met the Shadow Foreign Secretary, Douglas Alexander MP, Gordon Brown and Glenis Wilmott MEP, the leader of the British MEPs' delegation to Europe; she was a Labour Party MEP. I also spoke to a number of MEPs from other political parties represented in Europe. By now we had another line of argument. During the period of the Musharraf government, Pakistan had GSP+ status. That was rescinded due to a trade dispute. So I started to argue that the EU had been seemingly able to overlook human rights concerns when a military dictator was in power, but was now taking a hard line when we had achieved the first democratic transfer of power – government to government – in Pakistan's history.

In Scotland Alex Salmond, the then First Minister, was very supportive, and so were the MEPs from the Scottish National Party who were in Europe. The First Minister was extremely helpful. He joked that his assistance to me as Governor of Punjab was always guaranteed, especially since my new post meant I could not be in Glasgow organising against his Party in election times – especially during the September 2014 Referendum on Scottish independence!

The stakes in the bid for Pakistan were high. All the sectors of the country's manufacturing that were covered in the GSP+ products lists would benefit from that status, but there was one sector which would benefit more than any other – textiles. That is why my discussions on the bid started with Gohar Ijaz of APTMA. Their calculations were startling. The APTMA delegation had told me that textiles – knitwear, home textiles, woven garments, towel, yarn, grey fibre and dyed fibre etc – accounted for $13 billion out of the Pakistan's total exports to the EU of $25 billion. That's 52%. Their estimates were that the advantages of GSP+ status could increase exports in the first year by at least $1 billion. They were confident that in five years it was possible to double exports to $26 billion, if the textile industry was given priority for electricity and gas supply. That meant we were playing for hundreds of thousands of new jobs, as well as a hefty contribution to Pakistan's balance of payments problems.

When I returned from London, the messages from the relevant government departments in Pakistan were disquieting. My impression was that the seriousness of the situation was still not understood. I was told that 'people at the top strategic level are alert to the situation and acting accordingly'. Then further, that concerns about GSP+ had been 'taken care of'. I should have realised at that time that such complacency was a warning that my future as Governor was going to involve a gigantic collision with the self-serving bureaucracy of government.

My gut feeling was that I had to arrange a meeting to see the Prime Minister as soon as possible. I spoke to the Prime Minister's Chief of Staff, who told me that the Prime Minister was going to be in Lahore soon for the Eid celebrations, and would come to Governor House to wish me Eid Mubarak and to congratulate me on becoming Governor. 15 October was set for the meeting. When the Prime Minister arrived, I managed to explain the problems, and the potential, in our GSP+ application. He was immediately deeply concerned. He asked me to go to Strasbourg to develop a lobbying campaign on behalf of Pakistan. This matched the representations that were being made by David Martin and Sajjad Karim at the same time.

The first European lobby to secure GSP+ followed between 21 and 24 October. So to Strasbourg towards the end of October. The Pakistani Ambassador to Belgium, Munawar Bhatti, joined David, Sajjad and me in the 'A Team'. He would prove to be a formidable organiser. He worked with David and Sajjad to target all 31 members of the INTA committee, as well as other influential members, and set up meetings for me.

On 22 October we hosted a reception at an Asian restaurant in Strasbourg's city centre. We had worked flat out. We had managed to have face-to-face discussions with 22 MEPs – around a dozen of whom were members of the INTA committee. In general, their main issues concerned human rights, but I felt that our explanations that the Pakistan government had ratified all 27 parts of the international conventions was getting an echo. The other big hits in the discussions were 'trade' not 'aid', which played well, as did the Musharraf conundrum

– the EU had supported Pakistan in times of dictatorship, so surely it would give the new democratic government a chance.

Daniel Caspary MEP, is a German Christian Democrat member of the INTA committee. He was one of the seven who had signed the INTA motion to oppose the original Commission Recommendations for GSP+ membership. In the discussion with him I felt we had shifted him from opposition to 'undecided'. Before I returned to Pakistan, we made an assessment of where we stood. Of the 31 votes on the INTA committee, we had five or six fairly firm possible votes in our favour, although four of them were British MEPs; 12 totally against us, and, most significantly, there were now 13 'undecideds'.

On 28 October, I phoned Munawar Bhatti to ask him about the current position. With one week to go before the vote, he told me that there had been no identifiable shift in our favour, and it seemed we could still only rely on six votes. I pleaded with Munawar to keep going. We should never give up. David and Sajjad agreed we should not stop until the INTA votes had been cast. In the week before the 5th of November INTA committee, I made as many personal phone calls to MEPs as I could manage, following up with letters to the INTA Committee members. Obviously our aim was to convince the 'undecideds' to come over to our side.

Then there was an indication of a possible breakthrough. The day before the vote, Daniel Caspary MEP withdrew his signature of support from the INTA motion. We were praying that this was a sign that the wind was blowing in our favour at last.

The bell tolled on the afternoon of 5 November. We knew the vote was on a knife-edge. The INTA motion to block the Commission Recommendations – which meant Pakistan's membership of GSP+ being blocked – was lost by 15 votes to 13. The vote on the Commission Recommendations to be sent to the plenary session of the full Parliament was then carried by 16 votes to 12. David Martin was the first to phone. 'Brother, we have won,' he said. Then Daniel Caspery emailed to say, 'We have removed the first obstacle, so let's work together to win in the final vote.' We had delivered a political miracle. I could hardly believe it.

There was now just over a month to secure a vote for the Commission Recommendations when they were put to the full parliament on 12 December. David was confident that they would be carried, because of the way the voting system works in the Parliament; it is highly unusual for a powerful Committee's vote in favour of a particular motion to be rejected by the full parliament.

Then, as if it had all been planned, Malala Yousafzai stepped into the fray on our side like a fresh division of fearless soldiers. The Malala lobby in favour of GSP+ for Pakistan emerged between 19 and 23 November. On 20 November 2013 Malala was presented with the prestigious Sakharov Prize by the European Parliament. The annual award honours 'exceptional individuals who combat intolerance, fanaticism and oppression'. I was in the visitor's gallery of the Chamber of the European Parliament when the President of the European Parliament, Martin Schultz, presented the award. He described Malala as 'a global icon'.

Some weeks before the award was to be made, I spoke to Munawar Bhatti, Pakistan's ambassador to Belgium. I asked him to help me get a visitor's ticket so that I could attend the Sakharov award for Malala. He told me that he had made applications for the Speaker of the National Assembly and other dignitaries from Pakistan and his requests had been turned down. 'All the gold in the bank vaults in Switzerland couldn't buy you a ticket, Sarwar Sahib,' he told me.

Undaunted, I decided to phone Britain's former prime minister, Gordon Brown, who has become an international guardian for Malala and her family. He put me directly in touch with Ziuaddin Yousafzai, Malala's father. I told him it would be a great privilege to be there when Malala lifted the Prize. I explained that I would be in Strasbourg at the time of the presentation, because I was leading a delegation lobbying MEPs about a very important trade deal between Pakistan and the European Union that was in the offing. He said that he would try his best to get me a ticket. Ziuaddin Yousafzei and Malala wrote to the Sakharov Committee to make urgent representations on my behalf. The letter asked for a special dispensation: I was the first Muslim to be elected to the British Parliament; I was now the Governor of Punjab, Pakistan's biggest Province, and was actively supporting her education campaign there, and was considered as a family friend. Their wishes were granted.

It turned out that on the great day of the award I was the only person in the gallery who had travelled from Pakistan. Days before, when her father phoned me to tell me there was a ticket waiting for me in Strasbourg, I was delighted. I pushed the boat out and invited Malala and her father to address a 'Friends of Pakistan' reception that was organised for the evening of the award. He said he and Malala would speak to the organisers to see what could be done. I made the request because those working on the campaign with me had emphasised that if Malala attended the reception, it would give a huge boost to our standing among European MEPs and, as a result, assist our lobbying on the GSP+ trade deal.

I met Malala and her father the night before the award ceremony. We were staying in the same hotel – the Hilton in Strasbourg. I told her how proud we were of her struggle to recover from her terrible ordeal a year before, and her determination to speak out for the rights of all children in the world to a proper education. Malala is totally enchanting; she's an endearing combination of one who can appear as quite a seasoned political campaigner, yet one who is also fond of giggling a lot. It was quite moving for me when she said she loved Pakistan, and the people of Pakistan, and would return there one day. She wanted to finish her studies in the UK before that. At that meeting in the Hilton, it was agreed that Malala would address the Friends of Pakistan meeting on the evening of the award. I was elated. That is the only way you could describe my feelings.

There was a hush in the entire Chamber of the Parliament when Malala rose to speak. To my surprise she said she was pleased to see the Governor of Punjab, Mohammad Sarwar, in the visitor's gallery. I was really gratified. In her address Malala said that she was hopeful the European Parliament would look beyond Europe to the countries of great suffering where people were still deprived of their basic rights, had their freedom of thought suppressed, and their freedom of speech enchained. She continued: 'Many children have no food to eat, no water to drink and are starving for education. It is alarming that 57 million children are deprived of education . . . this must shake our conscience . . . children in countries such as Pakistan do not want an iPhone, a PlayStation or chocolates, they just want a book and a pen.' She also made a passionate plea that the European and international community should support Pakistan in promoting education, trade and the creation of jobs. I was proud of her but also recognised, there and then, that her words constituted an undeniable request for those in the Parliament who intended to vote against Pakistan on the GSP+ deal to think again.

The Friends of Pakistan reception proved to be an enormous success. I don't recall the numbers precisely, but there must have been 50 or 60 MEPs at the gathering. Malala reiterated some of the remarks she had made in her speech at the award, but made specific mention of the importance of the GSP+ trade deal. At the end of the proceedings it seemed as if every MEP there wanted a photo with Malala for posterity. She posed happily for pictures – among them countless 'selfies'. What a day. What a night.

After the Malala meeting we continued the programme of meeting MEPs we had not spoken to until then. Relentlessly. We were greatly encouraged by the fact that two MEPs – Ana Gomes, from Portugal, and Michael Gahler, from Germany – seemed now to be firmly in favour of the Commission Recommendations. They had originally been in favour of the moves to block them. We interpreted their support as the beginning of a decisive shift in our favour, because we recognised they were both influential in the political affairs of the Parliament. Our meetings with almost 40 MEPs during the visit seemed to be bearing fruit.

At the end of November, however, the political sky darkened yet again. News reached us that the Greens and the far left group, GUE, despite the defeat of the INTA blocking motion at the committee, had tabled almost the same motion for the plenary session of the Parliament. David Martin and Sajjad Karim were confident that we would have enough votes – the fact that Pakistan was in a 'bundle' with ten other countries was advantageous – but both suggested I should return to Strasbourg for one last push on the two days before the vote on 12 December. Munawar Bhatti argued vehemently that even at this stage we could not take anything for granted. The 'A' team was back in business.

My old friend Shahid Malik, the former Labour MP, had arrived in Lahore at the beginning of December. He was on his way to Qatar for business, but stopped off to say hello for a day or two. Shahid immediately threw himself into the discussions about GSP+. I discussed the general strategy for the remainder of the campaign with him, and asked him what he thought of sending a personal letter, stating the case for GSP+ for Pakistan, to every MEP, to reach them a day or two before the vote. He agreed that it was a personal touch well worth the effort. The main issues we covered were governed by the line of argument we had been using in the run up to the INTA vote, but we embellished them with slightly more detail. Shahid and I worked together to produce the email letter.

The final countdown of our lobbying took place from 10 to 14 December. On the Monday I was travelling to Strasbourg, my office sent out the email to every MEP – all 766 of them. We had taken the trouble to address each of them by their first name. I say this only to give an indication of the attention to detail that was paid. My office team, the Secretary to the Governor, Tariq Pasha, and my assistants Khadija Tulkhubra and Sumiya Siddiqui, had worked tirelessly to help us get to this stage. They worked all day Saturday and Sunday, before the vote, to organise the despatch of the emails. For good measure, Sumiya sent out a duplicate email on the Wednesday, just in case any of the first missives had been overlooked.

On the first lobby of the European Parliament we had held the reception of MEPs at an Asian restaurant in Brussels, owned by a friend of mine, Chaudry Naseer. Naseer promised to fix a meeting with Elmar Brok MEP, one of the leaders of the EPP group; he said he knew Brok because the MEP was a frequent diner at his restaurant. I had forgotten about that. But on 10 December Naseer phoned me to say he had arranged a meeting for me with Brok that morning. Brok is hugely influential in the Parliament, as he chairs its Foreign Affairs Committee.

Until this point we had assumed that the votes of the EPP group – the biggest in the Parliament with a block of 275 votes – were going our way. I began our conversation by thanking Brok for the meeting and telling him we were indebted to the EPP Group for their support. He pulled me up short by telling me that the EPP Group decision on GSP+ hadn't been taken. The vote was due at a meeting that evening. After I presented our case to him, to my delight he signalled he would support the Commission Recommendations, although he said he still had some reservations, and that convincing the EPP group to do the same would not be easy. His support would prove to be crucial – he's a German Christian Democrat, which is the largest party in the EPP block.

Then Ioan Pascu MEP came into the battle. He is one of the leaders of the Romanian delegation. I was introduced to him through Bob Wylie. Pascu is a great friend of Bob and his family; Bob and he have known each other since the days of the Romanian Revolution in 1989. Pascu was Romania's Minister of Defence between 2000 and 2004 and is acknowledged as the driving force behind Romania's admission to NATO, which in turn opened the gates for admission to the EU. He is the kind of man whose reputation goes before him, and that includes in the corridors of power in Strasbourg.

Pascu is Vice President of the Parliament's influential Foreign Affairs Committee[1] but, almost equally important, from our point of view, he is a charming man and seems to know everyone in the Parliament. He had set up a meeting for me, later in the morning of the 10th, after I had met Elmar Brok, with Jose Salafranca MEP. Salafranca is also in the EPP group, from the Spanish delegation. Both Brok and Salafranca spoke in Pakistan's favour at the EPP meeting that evening. In my opinion their intervention was decisive in the Group agreeing to support the Commission Recommendations at the plenary session on the 12th.

When I met with Ioan Pascu on 11 December, the day before the vote, he told me he thought that things were going well. He put me in touch with the four foreign policy co-ordinators of the main political groups in the Parliament. The Romanians have a favoured phrase when something turns out to be unexpectedly of good fortune – it's deemed 'a gift from God'. Ioan Pascu certainly delivered one such 'gift' for us.

At the end of our meeting, Pascu told me that we might have a lot to thank Facebook for. When I was on my way from Pakistan to Strasbourg, and unreachable, Pascu was desperate to firm up the details of the meetings he was setting up. He was in Committee, and Wylie's number was in his other mobile phone in his office. He texted

1. Late in 2014 Pascu was elected as the Vice-President of the European Parliament, which bears out just how influential he was in helping secure the vote on GSP+.

his daughter, Teodora, to tell Wylie's daughter, Kathryn, to ask her father to get in touch immediately with Pascu; the hour for decisions was approaching, urgently. The girls are Facebook friends. Teodora got Kathryn and she got her father; he reached Ioan Pascu and the arrangements for my meetings were finalised. With one of his wide grins, after he told me the story, Pascu said 'If you win the vote you might say that my Teodora, and Bob's Kathryn, have played their part in making a bit of history for Pakistan!'

We had lobbied day and night for the first two days and continued pressing for support all morning on the day of the vote. Nirj Deva, now an MEP, was formerly a British MP, so we knew each other well from our days together in the Commons. I had met him at a dinner the night before. He brought a dozen MEPs to meet me in one of the Parliament's coffee bars, hours before the vote itself. It finally took place in the Parliament's Chamber at just after twelve noon, on 12 December. I was in the Gallery. When the MEPs pressed their electronic voting buttons, the Greens' blocking motion was beaten by 409 votes to 182. The substantive motion, in favour of the Commission Recommendations, was then carried by a similar margin. We had done it. From 1 January 2014, Pakistan – along with an additional nine other countries – would have GSP+ status for their exports to the EU!

In the end there had been a united team effort. The Pakistan Government ministries, our ambassadors, the Friends of Pakistan, and many, many more, had gone the extra mile to make it possible. Mind you, it would be difficult to convince me that this could have happened without the 'A Team' – David Martin, Sajjad Karim, Munawar Bhatti and me. However I need to make an additional point. During the European Parliament campaign I must have met more than 100 European MEPs face to face. I could never have achieved that without the help of dozens of my personal friends. I remain hugely indebted to them.

It may be that I have gone into too much detail on this GSP+ part of my story. I have done so with a purpose. I believe that it was important to put on record what can be achieved in politics when there is a clarity of aim and a unity of purpose. Unfortunately, although I did not realise it at the time, the GSP+ struggle would come to represent what I might call my days of hope as Governor. These were to give way to what might be called my days of disappointment, and disillusion, which arrived remarkably early.

In my time as Governor of Punjab I argued consistently for a new way of governing Pakistan. For real democracy with transparency and accountability, and for an end to the seemingly never-ending poverty that afflicts the vast majority of the ordinary people of Pakistan. But the more I pleaded for good governance and a culture of accountability, transparency and the elimination of financial corruption as the only means to entrench genuine democracy in our country, the more I was viewed in Government circles as an 'outsider'. I was told in no uncertain terms that the raising of such demands indicated that I didn't understand the reality of the power politics of Pakistan. So it was not long into my time as Governor before it became apparent to me that the elite in politics, business and bureaucracy in Pakistan were working for promotion of their own interests and not those of the people as a whole. The elite now stand as a barrier to the creation of a more equal, more just, more prosperous Pakistan. The 'haves' in the country are determined to cling on to their privileges to thwart the right to social justice of the 'have-nots'.

Some might ask, didn't I know this before leaving the UK to accept the Governor appointment? Of course I understood those realities, but in the process of my accepting the post of Governor, there were promises made which convinced me that genuine change was possible and that as Governor I could play a part in that. However events eventually convinced me that I could do more for the 95% of the people whose lives are ruled by the 5%, who have power and wealth, by pursuing political change outside the walls of Governor House than by holding title within them.

For most of the second half of 2014, the Government of Pakistan was beset by street protests led by Imran Khan's political party, PTI (Pakistan Tehreek e Insaf) and PAT (Pakistan Swami Tehreek) the movement headed by the Islamic cleric, Tahirul Qadri. The protests called for an end to corruption among Pakistan's politicians, and demanded the resignation of the Prime Minister who stood accused of massive electoral fraud in the 2013 general election which brought him into power.

The protest movement began in June with small PTI and PAT rallies in Islamabad and Lahore, but at their height, in August and September, the protests embraced huge demonstrations in the capital, which numbered well beyond 100,000. Early in June there were clashes between PAT supporters and the police in Lahore. Eight protesters died and from that moment on there was a momentum in the protests that ensured they grew and grew. The Prime Minister appointed me to lead a negotiating team on behalf of the Government, after two previous attempts to find a way out of the growing impasse had failed. I was able to offer some immediate concessions, among them an inquiry into the election in certain areas where there were allegations of vote-rigging. But the protest leaders would not drop the demand for the PM's resignation.

The first real flashpoint, after the deaths of the protestors early in June, emerged when Tahirul Qadri came from his home in Canada to lead the protests in Pakistan. When his flight was diverted from Islamabad to Lahore he promised not to leave the plane until the army came to give him a safe escort to meet with the Prime Minister to make his demands for a 'democratic revolution' known. I went to the airport and boarded the plane to negotiate with Qadri. After some hours and the promise of further high-level negotiations he was prepared to be escorted to his home in Lahore.

At that time I felt as if I had managed to defuse a political time-bomb. But from the way Qadri spoke and his attitude in the plane, I sensed that it was indeed only a matter of time before the bomb exploded. That happened in August, when there were mass protests in Islamabad which resulted in a huge occupation of the grounds of the Parliament. By then the time for negotiations had gone, despite previous concessions from the Prime Minister about an official inquiry into the election process and into the protest clashes where protestors had died. The politics of Pakistan were on a tightrope in those days. There was even talk then of the army intervening to restore peace and stability by taking the reins of power.

At the end of October, Qadri withdrew his forces from the occupation. Had he negotiated in a meaningful way when the opportunity was presented, he could have achieved much more than a wholesale retreat whilst promising more protests to come. His hour had come and passed. Imran Khan withdrew his forces of protest, as a mark of respect, when the December massacre in the school in Peshawar occurred. In those days I said in one newspaper interview that had I not been a member of the Government, I might have been one of the protesters. I said that because I believed that their protests were not simply about the election results. Their movement actually reflected a much greater concern among their ranks, about the corruption, injustice and inequality which pervades Pakistani society.

Maybe one day I will account in detail for all the broken promises that convinced me to resign as Governor. For the moment I can say that I had UN pledges for a massive revolution in education that reached towards funding of a billion pounds, that were ignored by those in Government with the power to do something; from the outset as Governor I argued for a new local government in Pakistan, but the local government elections were postponed indefinitely; I was central to creating a new commission to look at the peril of overseas Pakistanis having their land in Pakistan seized by the land mafia or Qabza; a commission was created but filled with lackeys who will do nothing; I have run my own campaign for Clean Water in Pakistan while the Government campaign has literally run into the sand. I could go on – the energy crisis endures year after year – but these broken promises, combined with a sense of hopelessness, are what brought me to my resignation speech as Governor on 25 January 2015.

I delivered it in Urdu, although my team had also prepared an English version. Even the Urdu version suffered from misquoting, so for the record, here is the English text. To avoid repetition from what I have already outlined in other parts of this book, I will take up the speech at the point of my explaining my resignation as Governor:

> That brings me to where I stand now as the Governor of Punjab. All the experience of my charity work convinced me that whilst charity work can make a difference to the lives of thousands, if I wanted to affect millions I needed to become directly involved in politics and the Government of Pakistan. When that opportunity beckoned after the 2013 elections I took it with both hands. Prime Minister Mian Muhammad Nawaz Sharif honoured me with appointment

as the Governor of Punjab. I am also thankful, in this regard, to Chief Minister Mian Muhammad Shahbaz Sharif, and Pakistan's Interior Minister, Chaudhry Nisar Ali Khan.

I did not accept the post of Governor with a blindfold on but knew that the Governorship would present obstacles as well as opportunities. My dream and ambition was to work for the deprived and poverty-stricken people of Pakistan, to attain justice for the overseas Pakistanis and to build a society where justice, education, employment and development prevail over the horrors of never-ending poverty. I made definite plans to those ends which were agreed when I accepted the Governor's post.

Alas, I have to say that from where I stand today there is little or no sign of such change in Pakistan. On the contrary it seems to me that things don't get better for the poor, they get worse. It is with deep sorrow and regret that I say that cruelty and injustice is mounting in Pakistan; the problems of the poor are increasing day by day and complex national issues like the energy crisis remain permanently unresolved. Landgrabbers and their gangster counterparts are an enduring blight on life in rural Pakistan; justice is weak, cases of rape and acid-throwing are not declining but increasing and children being kidnapped and murdered is not an infrequent occurrence. Meanwhile those responsible – the rapists, the acid-throwers and murderers apparently are allowed to escape justice, while the bereaved families of the victims knock endlessly on the doors of justice without ever seeing them opened to deal with their protests.

Reluctantly I have, as a result, come to the conclusion that I can serve the people of Pakistan more effectively outside the walls of Governor House than continuing to fight with one hand tied behind my back as a result of all the protocols and obligations of being Governor. Thereby I have taken the difficult decision to resign as Governor. I want to witness a democracy in Pakistan where a common man's son or daughter can get the same opportunities and rights as the elite in this country. I will live and die in Pakistan. My belief that the struggle for the rights of workers, labourers, famers and the poor is better fought outside Governor House has actually been strengthened by the very experience of being Governor.

It should be the mission of all Pakistanis to fulfil the dreams of Quaid e Azam Mohammad Ali Jinnah and the Poet of the East, Allama Iqbal. I will fight for a Pakistan where the resources are not just confined to a few hands, which is free from unemployment, poverty and illiteracy, where the rule of law prevails, where the state system protects the weak against the powerful, where tyrants have the fear of the writ of the state and where every man's rights, the poor as well as the rich, are protected. I am sad to say that throughout Punjab the Qabza Mafia and its vicious, unchallenged, land-grabbing has become a huge business, and that unfortunately the muscles of this Mafia seem to be stronger than the authorities of the Governor. It is a great cause of concern that the 23 million children who are currently working as domestic workers in the houses of landlords and industrialists, are out of school instead of being educated. Consider this disgrace – it is a fact that 68 years after the foundation of Pakistan, three-quarters of its people do not have daily access to clean drinking water. Illness from waterborne disease in Pakistan is at epidemic levels. The religious and political minorities in our midst are haunted by day to day fear of what is to become of them next.

In my 18 months as Governor my own performance is open for all to review. I have spared no effort to fight for my people – be it the matter of convincing the European Union for the attainment of GSP+ status for Pakistan; be it the provision of clean drinking water to a host of schools and institutions across Punjab; be it re-introducing the paramountcy of educational merit in institutes like Aitchison's or be it raising my voice in criticism of Pakistan's redundant foreign policy. I can now openly state that President Barack Obama's recent visit to India, without visiting Pakistan, is a diplomatic catastrophe for the Government of Pakistan and the people of this land. Pakistan has lost more than 50,000 lives in the so-called war on terror, so far. Even today, our Army and our nation are fighting this war. In such circumstances, Obama's failure to visit Pakistan is an astonishing omission. Our Government is culpable in this issue as much as the Obama administration.

I have always raised my voice for the truth and what is right. I believe that justice delayed is justice denied. In this respect my actions as Governor, in a small way, demonstrated my commitment to the poor and my fight against injustice. I have been the first Governor in the history of Pakistan to open the doors of Governor House to the people of Pakistan – to the underprivileged, to the poor, to the orphans, to those suffering physical and mental disablement, to the minorities of Pakistan whose religious beliefs were celebrated in many ceremonies on the spacious acres of Governor House.

Today I would like to thank all the staff of Governor House who have made such things possible. They have delivered their duties with dedication, efficiency and enthusiasm during my stay here. I owe them a debt of gratitude and leaving them has been one of the great sorrows of my life . . . I have always believed that all public offices, including the office of the Governor of Punjab, are only the means by which to serve the people. It follows that if I am not able to serve my people, my nation, my land in my capacity as a Governor, there is no point in hanging on to the post just for the sake of it. I have tried my level best to use each and every day of my official capacity for the betterment of my people but now, I feel with total conviction, that the time has come for me to relinquish my official responsibilities so that I can fight for a better, more equal, more just, more peaceful and secure Pakistan. I shall do everything in my power now to continue that fight and make these aims a reality. Pakistan Zindabad!

In coming to these conclusions I was faced with two stark realities. Either I could give up the struggle and return to the UK beaten but unbowed, or find fresh forces to join to continue the fight. I will not abandon the people of Pakistan, I will not accept that nothing can change and so have decided to accept a senior position in the leadership of the party of Imran Khan. His crusade represents the only force for real change in Pakistan, and I aim to use all my experience and knowledge to make the PTI an even more potent force for that than it is now. I am convinced that what I have learned about the importance of structure and organisation in the politics of the British Labour Party can grow in a new and more powerful way on the soil of Pakistan. As the chief organiser of the PTI in Punjab, my aim is to make that possibility a reality.

Of course there will be cynics who say that my sojourn as Governor of Punjab has proved to be a huge misadventure. I disagree. Time is never wasted in politics. I would not have the understanding of what needs to be done now in Pakistan without the experience of working as Governor. At the last General Election Imran Khan predicted a political 'tsunami' was on its way in Pakistan which would change things utterly in favour of the poor of our country. The powers that be in Pakistan should understand the 'tsunami' has been delayed. Not postponed indefinitely. Nothing can stand against the power of an idea whose time has come.

Bibliography

Books

Ali, Tariq, *The Clash of Fundamentalisms* (Verso, 2002).

Ali, Tariq, *The Duel: Pakistan on the Flight Path of American Power* (Simon & Schuster, 2008).

Bennett Jones, Owen, *Pakistan: Eye of the Storm* (Yale University Press, 3rd edition, 2009).

Bhutto, Benazir, *Reconciliation: Islam, Democracy and the West* (Simon & Schuster, 2008).

Bhutto, Fatima, *Songs of Blood and Sword* (Jonathan Cape, 2010).

Braithwaite, Rodric, *Afgantsy: The Russians in Afghanistan* (Profile Books, 2011).

Burke, Jason, *The 9/11 Wars* (Penguin, 2011).

Chandler, David, *From Kosovo to Kabul* (Pluto Press, 2002).

Cole, Juan, *Engaging the Muslim World* (St Martin's Press, 2009).

Cowper-Coles, Sherard, *Cables from Kabul: The Inside Story of the West's Afghanistan Campaign* (Harper Press, 2011).

Collins, Larry and Lapierre, Dominique, *Freedom at Midnight* (Harper Collins, 2nd revised edition, 1997).

Cook, Robin, *The Point of Departure* (Simon & Schuster, 2003).

Dalrymple, William, *Return of a King* (Bloomsbury 2013).

Fisk, Robert, *The Great War for Civilisation* (Harper Collins, 2006).

Galloway, George, *I'm Not the Only One* (Penguin, 2005).

Galloway, George, and Wylie, Bob, *Downfall* (Futura, 1991).

Granta, 'Pakistan', Issue 112, 2010.

Hamid, Mohsin, *Discontent and Its Civilisations* (Penguin Books, 2014).

Hanif, Mohammed, *A Case of Exploding Mangoes* (Vintage Books, 2009).

Horne, Alistair, *A Savage War of Peace* (Macmillan, 1977).

Jenkins, Roy, *Churchill* (Macmillan, 2001).

Kampfner, John, *Blair's Wars* (Free Press, 2004).

Khan, Yasmin, *The Great Partition: The Making of India and Pakistan* (Yale University Press, 2008).

Lieven, Anatol, *Pakistan: A Hard Country* (Penguin, 2011).

Manto, Saadat Hasan, *Mottled Dawn* (Penguin India 2000).

Milne, Seumas, *The Revenge of History* (Verso, 2012).

Montefiore, Simon Sebag, *Jerusalem, The Biography* (Phoenix, 2011).

Powell, Jonathan, *Talking to Terrorists: How to End Armed Conflicts* (Bodley Head, 2014).

Peston, Robert, *Who Runs Britain?* (Hodder and Stoughton, 2008).

Rashid, Ahmed, *Taliban* (Yale University Press, 2000).

Richardson, Louise, *What Terrorists Want* (John Murray, 2006).

Sanaullah, Mian, *Indonesia-Pakistan – Signs of Trusted Friendship* (Ghulam Ali and Sons, 2014).

Steele, Jonathan, *Defeat: Why They Lost Iraq* (I.B. Tauris, 2009).

Steele, Jonathan, *Ghosts of Afghanistan: The Haunted Battleground* (Portobello Books, 2011).

Stiglitz, Joseph and Bilmes, Linda, *The Three Trillion Dollar War: The True Cost of the Iraq Conflict* (Allen Lane, 2008).

Webster, Jamie and Walker, Russell, *Back from the Brink* (Brown and Ferguson, 2008).

Reports

House of Commons Foreign Affairs Committee, 'The UK's foreign policy approach to Afghanistan and Pakistan', Volume 1, March 2011.

House of Commons Foreign Affairs Committee, 'British foreign policy and the "Arab Spring"', July 2012.

House of Commons Defence Committee, 'Securing the future of Afghanistan', April 2013.

House of Commons International Development Committee, 'Pakistan', April 2013.

Newspaper References

Glasgow Herald (Scotland).

Scotsman and *Scotland on Sunday* (Scotland).

Financial Times (UK).

Guardian (UK).

Independent (UK).

Dawn (Pakistan).

The News (Pakistan).
Express Tribune (Pakistan).

Periodicals

London Review of Books.
Foreign Affairs.
Economist.
Newsweek Pakistan.

Index

Maxwell Road warehouse 85-96,
99
  fire at 91-95, 99
May, Theresa 195
Medical Aid for Palestine 256, 257
Mehdi, Saeed 347
Menon, V.P. 268
Menzies, Duncan 181-183, 188
Metropolitan Police 192, 193
Miliband, Ed 129
Militant newspaper 110
Militant Tendency 109, 116
Millan, Bruce 175, 246
Millennium Commission 175, 221,
222
Ministry of Defence 210, 212-215
  order for Type 45 frigates 213,
215
Mohamad, Dr Mahathir bin 248
Mohammad, Omar Bakri 286
Mohammad, Ruksana (niece of
MS) 66
Mohammad, Sameena (niece of
MS) 66
Mohammad, Yar 100
Mohammed, Zahid 2, 3, 5, 12, 19,
22
Monopolies Commission 203
Moreira, Vital 357
Mosson, Alex 223-225, 256-258
Mountbatten, Lord 34-36, 268
mujahedin 237, 239, 273
Multan 35, 144, 302, 321-324,
330, 331, 339
Murdoch, Rupert 166, 191, 192
Musharraf, Pervez 12-17, 20, 21,
108, 240, 241, 330, 338, 359,
360
Muslim League – *see* All-India
Muslim League *and* Pakistan
Muslim League
Muslim MPs 24, 163, 196, 235,
279

Mustaq, Faisal ('Becks') 2, 11,
25-29
  arrested in Pakistan 27
  convicted of Kriss Donald murder 28, 29
  fleeing to Pakistan 11
Muzaffarabad 311, 313, 315, 316,
318-320
Muzaffargarh 327-329

Najaf, Col Ejaz 329
Naqvi, Mohsin 327
Naseer, Chaudry 365
National Irrigation Department
61-65
National Rural Support Programme
317, 321, 333, 334
Naurin, Uzma 153
Nawaz, Rai Hassan 307-309
Nehru, Jawaharlal 31, 33, 268
Netanyahu, Benjamin 255, 262,
267, 272
New York Review of Books 289
News, The (Pakistani newspaper)
287
News International 190, 191, 193
News of the World 116, 140, 144,
151, 163, 166-171, 173, 179,
184-187, 189-193
Newsnight Scotland 16
9/11 attacks on USA 107, 232-240,
245, 272, 278
Nisar, Chaudhry 346
Nobel Peace Prize 294
North American Space Agency
(NASA) 195
North Atlantic Treaty Organisation
(NATO) 243, 249, 366
North Waziristan 294
North-West Frontier Province (later
Khyber Pakhtunkhwa) 32

Obama, Barack 292, 372, 373